RUSSIAN
HISTORICAL GRAMMAR

LONDON EAST EUROPEAN SERIES

(LANGUAGE AND LITERATURE)

Under the auspices of the Department of Language and Literature
School of Slavonic and East European Studies
University of London

GROUP I. DESCRIPTIVE GRAMMARS

Handbook of Old Church Slavonic, Parts I and II
I. *Old Church Slavonic Grammar*, by G. NANDRIŞ
II. *Text and Glossary*, by R. AUTY

GROUP II. HISTORICAL GRAMMARS

W. K. MATTHEWS. *Russian Historical Grammar*
S. E. MANN. *Czech Historical Grammar*

GROUP III. READINGS IN LITERATURE

J. PIETRKIEWICZ. *Polish Prose and Verse*
E. D. TAPPE. *Rumanian Prose and Verse*
V. PINTO. *Bulgarian Prose and Verse*
G. F. CUSHING. *Hungarian Prose and Verse*
VERA JAVAREK. *Serbo-Croatian Prose and Verse*

RUSSIAN HISTORICAL GRAMMAR

W. K. MATTHEWS

LATE PROFESSOR OF RUSSIAN LANGUAGE
AND LITERATURE IN THE
UNIVERSITY OF LONDON

UNIVERSITY OF LONDON
THE ATHLONE PRESS

Published by
THE ATHLONE PRESS
UNIVERSITY OF LONDON
at 2 Gower Street London WC 1
Distributed by Constable & Co Ltd
12 *Orange Street London* WC 2

Canada
University of Toronto Press
Toronto 5

U.S.A.
Oxford University Press
Toronto

First impression, 1960
Reprinted with corrections, 1967

FIRST PRINTED IN GREAT BRITAIN
AT THE UNIVERSITY PRESS, OXFORD
REPRINTED BY PHOTO-LITHO BY
THE ALDEN PRESS, OXFORD

EDITORIAL NOTE

THIS book was still in the early stages of printing when Professor W. K. Matthews died of a sudden heart attack on 3 May 1958. He had just received the first of the galley proofs and had started to read and correct them. But he had not had time to go through much more than a quarter of the whole when he died, and some of his corrections were clearly provisional.

As Director of the School of Slavonic and East European Studies and as a colleague and friend of Professor Matthews, I had watched the progress of the book with great interest. I knew how much effort and learning had gone into the writing of it and how much store Professor Matthews set by it, and when he died I considered myself in duty bound to see it through the press on his behalf. Professor B. O. Unbegaun, Professor of Comparative Slavonic Philology in the University of Oxford, very kindly agreed to share the task with me, and we have together read the successive proofs and corrected such oversights, ambiguities, inconsistencies, and misprints as came to our notice. We have also compiled a fuller table of contents than that in the manuscript. But we have not regarded ourselves in any sense as editors and have accordingly made as few changes as possible in the text as Professor Matthews left it.

Our thanks are due to Professor F. Norman, Professor of German in the University of London and Chairman of the Council of the School of Slavonic and East European Studies, for reading through the final page proofs, and to Mr. V. Swoboda, Lecturer in Russian and Ukrainian at the School, for compiling the general index and the index of Russian words.

G. H. BOLSOVER

School of Slavonic and East European Studies

PREFACE

THIS book is addressed in the first instance to such readers as are studying the history of Russian; for 'historical grammar' to be historical must also be the history of the language. Accordingly the diachronic point of view has been consciously adopted and maintained throughout, except inevitably in Chapter VI which attempts to envisage Russian as a static system at the turn of the eleventh century. Such an arbitrarily chosen 'moment of time', in effect the 'crystallization of a century', is the obvious starting-point for a review of subsequent linguistic developments within a framework which has been tested and sanctioned by tradition.

The material which makes up the text of the book is arranged for convenience of reference in three coherent parts, of which the last is essentially a supplement to the preceding two. Part I provides the requisite orientation for readers who may be new to linguistics, and its first two chapters should be useful to students of both Russian and the other Slavonic languages. The remainder of Part I is intended specifically for those studying Russian and constitutes, as it were, the prolegomena to Part II. This is entirely concerned with the evolution of the Russian phonological and grammatical system in its conventionally accepted domains and categories. Part III contains a series of appendixes, of which the first illustrates the evolutionary process with excerpts from the historical records of the language covering a space of nine centuries. My selection of excerpts was in part dictated by the need of avoiding mention of authors and specimens cited at the end of my book *The Structure and Development of Russian* (Cambridge, 1953), so as to eliminate overlapping and coincidence. Unlike the passages in the earlier book, which had English versions *en regard*, these have been sparingly annotated. Appendix II follows the vicissitudes of the study of Russian historical grammar from its synchronic beginnings, and Appendix III is a classified bibliography with brief notes on most of the items contained in it. As will be seen, the purpose of

Part III is to assist the reader in various ways, after he has memorized Parts I and II and outgrown tuition, to enter the field of independent personal endeavour, which is the rational goal of all serious scholarship.

The reconstructions of comparative Slavonic linguistics are a necessary background for an understanding of Old Russian, which is here shown as emerging from the conjectured Common Slavonic, itself conceived as a dialect of the even more hypothetical Indo-European. Although it makes its deductions from generalizations, the comparative-historical method of linguistic analysis is in point of fact scientific, because it relies for these on historically authenticated, if heterogeneous, facts, and the picture which it traces of the unverifiable unrecorded past is nevertheless not too distorted a silhouette of the verifiable recorded past, a sort of reconstructed 'pluperfect' to an extant 'perfect'. And so, while we do not carry our linguistic credo to the point of lending substance to the shadow of our reconstructed forms and equate, say, the patent unreality of Common Slavonic *golva* 'head' with the historical reality of both Old Church Slavonic *glava* and Old Russian *golova*, we can reasonably postulate the former as the abstracted prefiguration of the two latter.

The Old Russian illustrations in the text of the book have been variously modified: they occur 'normalized' in Part I, conventionally simplified in spelling in Part II, and are given their original form, if not their Palaeocyrillic typeface, in Part III. All this has been deliberately done for propaedeutic reasons. Furthermore, Old Church Slavonic is distinguished from Old Russian by being represented in its original Cyrillic form within the limits of Neocyrillic (cf. OCS начѧти 'to begin' with OR начяти); Indo-European forms are distinguished by the conventional asterisk (e.g. *$kmtóm$ 'hundred'); phonetic transcriptions in the alphabet of the International Phonetic Association (IPA) occur now and then in bold-face type; tables of transliteration will be found in Chapter IV (the 'International' being used here to transliterate Russian Cyrillic); and diagrams have been occasionally resorted to as visual aids to comprehension.

Parrhasius of Ephesus justly records in an epigram that per-
fection escapes human hands (ἀμώμητον δ' οὐδὲν ἐγένετο βροτοῖς),
and I would therefore draw the reader's attention here to the
words which Ioan the copyist of the 'Svjatoslav Miscellany' of
1076 wrote in his colophon: идеже криво братиѥ исправивъше
чьтѣте. The English version of this will be found on pp. 133–4.

W. K. MATTHEWS

School of Slavonic and East European Studies
1957

CONTENTS

PART III. Appendixes

LIST OF ABBREVIATIONS AND PHONETIC SYMBOLS

abs.	absolute	fem.	feminine
acc.	accusative	fn.	footnote
act.	active	fol.	folio
Af. Nik.	Afanasij Nikitin	fut.	future
AL	Archivum Linguisticum	G.	German
Alb.	Albanian	Gc	Germanic
aor.	aorist	gen.	genitive
Apoff.	*Apoffegmata*	Gk	Greek
app.	appendix	Goth.	Gothic
Arif.	*Arifmetika*	gram.	gramota
Arm.	Armenian	gramm.	grammatika
Att.	Attic	Hitt.	Hittite
Av.	Avestan	Hom.	Homeric
Avv.	Avvakum (Petrovič)	ibid.	ibidem
B.	Bulgarian	id.	idem
Balt.	Baltic	IE	Indo-European
c.	*circa*	IH	Indo-Hittite
cent.	century	Ilar.	Ilarion
cf.	confer	imp.	imperative
chap.	chapter	impf.	imperfect
comp.	comparative	impfv.	imperfective
ComGc	Common Germanic	ind.	indicative
ComS	Common Slavonic	indef.	indefinite
CS	Church Slavonic	instr.	instrumental
Čud.	Čudovskij, &c.	IPA	International Phonetic
Cz.	Czech		Association
D.	Dutch	Ipat.	Ipat'jevskij spisok
Dan.	Daniil (Zatočnik)	Ital.	Italian
dat.	dative	iter.	iterative
def.	definite	jev.	jevangelije
dial.	dialect	Jur.	Jur'jevskij, &c.
dog.	dogovornaja (gramota)	Kal.	Kalita, kn. Ivan
Dom.	Domostroj	Kir.	Kiril
Don.	Donat(us)	Kir. Tur.	Kirill Turovskij
du.	dual	Klim.	Kliment Novgorodec
duch.	duchovnaja (gramota)	kn.	knjaz'
dur.	durative	knig.	kniga
Dvin.	Dvinskij, &c.	Kol.	Kolomenskij, &c.
E.	English	korm.	kormčaja
e.g.	exempli gratia	Kot.	Kotošichin, Grigorij
Est.	Estonian	kur.	kuranty
F.	French	L.	Latin

ABBREVIATIONS AND PHONETIC SYMBOLS xiii

Len.	Leningrad	par.	paremejnik
Latv.	Latvian	part.	participle
Laur.	Laurentian	pass.	passive
Lavr.	Lavrent'jevskij spisok	Per.	Perejaslavskij, &c.
Leks. trej.	*Leksikon trejazyčnyj*	Peres.	Peresvetov, Ivan
let.	letopis'	perf.	perfect
LG	Low German	pers.	person
lit.	literary	pfv.	perfective
Lith.	Lithuanian	PIE	Proto-Indo-European
loc.	locative	pl.	plural
M.	Moscow	(p)p.	page(s)
Mac.	Macedonian	pres.	present
masc.	masculine	prol.	prolog
med.	medieval	psalt.	psaltyr'
MHG	Middle High German	Pskov.	Pskovskij, &c.
Mil.	Miljatin, &c.	pt	part
Min.	Mineja	*Put.*	*Putešestvije iz Peterburga v*
mod.	modern		*Moskvu*
Mol.	*Molenije Daniila Zatočnika*	q.v.	quod vide
Mos.	Moskovskij, &c.	R.	Russian
Mst.	(gramota) Mstislava Volo-	Rjaz.	Rjazanskij, &c.
	dimiroviča	Ros.	Rossijskij, &c.
neut.	neuter	Run.	Runic
Nif.	Nifont	s.a.	sine anno
Nik. Čern.	Nikon Černorizec	Sav.	Savva
nom.	nominative	sc.	scilicet
Nov.	Novgorodskij, &c.	SCr.	Serbo-Croatian
Nov. ber.	Novgorodskaja berestjanaja	seq.	sequentes, sequentia
	gramota	*SEER*	*The Slavonic and East Euro-*
N.Z.	Novyj Zavet		*pean Review*
obs.	observation	sg.	singular
OCS	Old Church Slavonic	*Skaz. B.G.*	*Skazanije o Borise i Glebe*
OE	Old English	Skt	Sanskrit
OHG	Old High German	Slav.	Slavonic
OIr.	Old Irish	Slov.	Slovene
ON	Old Norse	Smol.	Smolenskij, &c.
OPr.	Old Prussian	Sp.	Spanish
op. cit.	opus citatum	stich.	stichirar'
opt.	optative	sud.	sudnaja (gramota)
OR	Old Russian	Sum.	Sumarokov, Aleksandr
OS	Old Saxon	Svjat.	(Sbornik) Svjatoslava (Ja-
Osc.	Oscan		roslaviča)
Ost.	Ostromirov, &c.	Tmut.	Tmutorokan'skaja nadpis'
OSw.	Old Swedish	Toch.	Tocharian
P.	Polish	*Učen.*	*Učenije i chitrost' ratnogo*
pal.	paleja		*strojenija pechotnych ljudej*
pand.	pandekty	*Ulož.*	*Uloženije Alekseja Michaj-*
Pant.	Pantelejmonov, &c.		*loviča*

Umb.	Umbrian	W.	Welsh
Ukr.	Ukrainian	WR	White Russian
Var.	Varla(a)m	ŽMNP	Žurnal Ministerstva narod-
voc.	vocative		nogo prosveščenija

PHONETIC SYMBOLS

Characters

ą (Lith.), now only oral a (IPA a:)
æ (IPA) as in 'man'
ʌ (IPA) as in 'but'
c as in 'wits'
č as in 'choose' (IPA tʃ)
ɣ (IPA) as in Sp. 'luego'
ð (Av.) as in 'this' (IPA ð)
ę (ComS) as in P. 'język'
ě (ComS) as in E. 'man'
ė (Lith.) long e (IPA e:)
ə (schwa) as in 'again' (IPA ə)
ǵ (Mac.) as in Cz. 'děd' (IPA ɟ)
ĝ (IE) as in R. 'gips' (IPA ɡʲ)
θ (Av.) as in 'thin' (IPA θ)
ḥ (Skt) as in 'hot' (IPA h)
ḫ (Hitt.) an indefinite 'laryngeal'
ï see ь
i̯ asyllabic i as in 'soil'
ɩ (IPA) as in 'sit'
ï (IPA) as in R. 'byk'
ķ (Mac.) as in Cz. 'tělo' (IPA c)
k̂ (IE) as in R. 'kit' (IPA k,)
ļ as in E. 'temple'
m̥ as in E. 'prism'
ñ as in F. 'vigne' (IPA ɲ)
ņ as in E. 'open'
ŋ (IPA) as in 'song'
ǫ (ComS) as in P. 'gałąź'
ø (Danish) as in 'Bøige' (IPA ø)
r̥ (Skt) as in Cz. 'krk'
ś (Skt) very approx. as in 'she' (IPA ɕ)
ṣ (Skt) cacuminal s (IPA ʂ)

š as in F. 'chou' (IPA ʃ)
ʃʲ (IPA) as in Moscow R. ščʲi
ь (OCS) as in 'sit' (IPA ɩ)
ʼь (OCS) as in 'put' (IPA ω)
ŭ see ʼь
u̯ asyllabic u as in 'out'
ω (IPA) as in 'full'
χ as in Scots 'loch' (IPA x)
y (Lith.) long i (IPA i:)
ž as in 'leisure' (IPA ʒ)
ʒ,ʒ̧ (IPA) as in Moscow R. 'ujezžat"

Diacritics

˘ (over vowels) brevity mark
^ (IE over k, g) mark of palatal quality
‾ (over vowels) length mark (macron)
ʹ Skt and R. (over vowels) stress-mark
ʹ (R. after consonants) palatalization mark ('soft sign')
ʹ (SCr.) long rising tone
ʹ (Lith.) long falling tone
ˋ (Gk) short falling tone
ˋ (SCr.) short rising tone
ˋ (Lith.) short falling tone
ˮ (SCr.) short falling tone
~ (Gk) see ^ below
~ (Lith. over vowels and sonants) long rising tone
^ (Gk) long falling tone
^ (SCr.) long falling tone
* (IE before letter or form) reconstructed item

PART I

I

INTRODUCTION

I

1. Since the publication of Ferdinand de Saussure's *Cours de linguistique générale* by his pupils in 1916, it has been fashionable in the West to contrast speech (*parole*) with language (*langue*). The contrast is analytical and to that extent artificial, and its validity has been seriously impugned;[1] but it serves a practical purpose and may be legitimately adopted as a working hypothesis, if not necessarily as a principle of linguistics. It will be apparent after a little thought that speech and language presuppose each other, that the latter is abstracted from the former, and that speech uses language as its 'terms of reference'. Speech operates through language, and language systematizes speech. In the study of language, its actualization in speech is most obvious where the investigator is confronted with new facts 'in the field'. This inevitably leads to particular emphasis on the phonetic or articulatory-acoustic side of language. Where, on the other hand, investigation is confined to the analysis of written records, the investigator is also confined by the tradition of linguistic science.

2. The linguistic tradition in Europe is both ancient and recent. Language study goes back to the pre-Christian Greek philosophers, especially to Plato, Aristotle, and the Stoics,[2] who not only involved themselves in metaphysical debate on the origin

---

[1] A. S. Čikobava, 'K voprosu ob istorizme v jazykoznanii v svete trudov I. V. Stalina' (*Protiv vul'garizacii i izvraščenija marksizma v jazykoznanii*, ii, Moscow, 1952, pp. 15–19).

[2] J. E. Sandys, *History of Classical Scholarship*, i, Cambridge, 1921, pp. 88–102, 146–66.

of language but—what is more to our purpose—evolved a grammatical terminology. This was systematized and enlarged by the Alexandrian grammarian Aristarchus and his pupils in the second century B.C. Dionysius Thrax, a pupil of Aristarchus, first summarized Greek as a 'grammatical art' (γραμματικὴ τέχνη), and some centuries later the codification of the grammatical data of the language culminated in the work of Apollonius Dyscolus and his son Herodian.[1] It was from these authors that Roman grammarians, from Varro in the second century B.C. to Donatus and Priscian in the fourth and sixth centuries A.D. respectively,[2] learnt their grammatical system and terminology and adapted both to Latin, thus making them the common heritage of post-Classical linguistic scholarship.

3. The Classical conception of grammar was pre-eminently static and descriptive;[3] and as throughout the Middle Ages Donatus and Priscian, whose work illustrates this conception, were held in high esteem, their authority was multiplied by copyist and compiler. The focus of attention was Latin, the language of West European culture and of Western Christianity. With the revival of Greek during the Renaissance, however, came the opportunity to compare these languages, and the Reformation and Counter-reformation stimulated a liberal interest in the neglected European vernaculars.

4. In 1599 J. J. Scaliger made the first attempt to group the languages of Europe[4] into eleven *matrices*, each of them with many dialects (*propagines*). The four major *matrices* are designated by their word for 'God' as the *Deus-*, *Θεός-*, *Godt-*, and *Boge-* languages, or Latin, Greek, Germanic, and Slavonic respec-

---

[1] *Dionysii Thracis Ars grammatica*, ed. G. Uhlig, Leipzig, 1883; *Apollonii Dyscoli quae supersunt (I–III)*, ed. R. Schneider and G. Uhlig, Leipzig, 1878–1910; *Herodiani Technici reliquiae*, ed. A. Lentz, Leipzig, 1867–71.

[2] *M. Terenti Varronis De lingua latina quae supersunt*, ed. G. Goetz and F. Schoell, Leipzig, 1910.

[3] H. Pedersen, *Sprogvidenskaben i det nittende Aarhundrede. Metoder og Resultater.* Copenhagen, 1924, p. 1.

[4] 'Diatriba de Europaeorum linguis' (*I. I. Scaligeri opuscula varia*, Paris, 1610, pp. 119–22). This first appeared in P. Merula's *Cosmographiae generalis libri tres*, Leyden, 1605, as 'Europaeorum linguae'. A still earlier work was the small encyclopaedic compilation of the Swiss scholar Conrad Gesner which appeared in 1555 under the title *Mithridates. De differentiis linguarum . . . observationes*. Gesner too was aware of the *matrices* and *propagines*, but his classification was less systematic.

tively.[1] The seven minor *matrices* are Albanian (*lingua epirotica*), Tartar, Hungarian, Finnish (with Lappish), Irish, Welsh (with Breton), and Basque. But Scaliger expressly says of all these that they are not interrelated (*nullo inter se cognationis vinculo coniunctae*).

5. In the period between the sixteenth and eighteenth centuries much was written on individual languages from the historical point of view.[2] The notion of a protoglossa existed,[3] and Hebrew was taken *a priori* to be the source of all extant languages. It required the acumen of a Leibniz[4] to disprove this theory and deliver linguistic scholarship from its bondage.

6. The eighteenth and early nineteenth centuries witnessed the appearance of the polyglot collections of P. S. Pallas,[5] Lorenzo Hervás,[6] and J. C. Adelung,[7] which, as V. Thomsen[8] says, represent the culmination of the older linguistics, which catalogued rather than discriminated and separated what it should have joined (e.g. Rumanian from Romance, Albanian from Indo-European, and Hungarian from Finno-Ugrian). The difference between the aims and methods of the old and the new linguistics may be seen from a comparison of, say, Adelung's *Mithridates* with F. Müller's *Grundriss der Sprachwissenschaft* (Vienna, 1878–88), the next large work of this kind.

7. Between 1817, when J. S. Vater completed Adelung's *Mithridates*, and 1878, when Müller's first volume appeared, a new and fruitful method had been introduced into linguistics and had passed through all its phases of development except the latest. The new method, adumbrated by such comparative studies as

---

[1] 'Sunto igitur quatuor haec verba, *Deus, Θεός, Godt, Boge*, notae quatuor maiorum Matricum, Latinae, Graecae, Teutonicae, Sclauonicae.' Of the *Boge*-languages Scaliger says: 'Haec Matrix siue lingua Boge in multas propagines diffusa est, Rutenicam, Polonicam, Boemicam, Illyricam, Dalmaticam, Windicam et alias.'

[2] *O. Ferrarii Origines linguae italicae*, Patavii, 1676.

[3] E. Guichard, *L'harmonie étymologique des langues*, Paris, 1606.

[4] *Miscellanea berolinensia*, Berlin, 1710.

[5] *Linguarum totius orbis vocabularia comparativa*, 1786–7.

[6] *Catalogo delle lingue conosciute e notizia della loro affinità e diversità*, 1784; *Catálogo de las lenguas de las naciones conocidas, i–vi*, Madrid, 1800–4.

[7] *Mithridates oder allgemeine Sprachenkunde*, Berlin, 1806–17 (completed by J. S. Vater). The title is taken from Gesner's sixteenth-century work but his alphabetic arrangement of the material is not followed. See p. 2, n. 4.

[8] *Sprogvidenskabens historie, en kortfattet fremstilling af dens hovedpunkter*, Copenhagen, 1902; 2nd ed. 1919.

S. Gyarmathi's *Affinitas linguae hungaricae cum linguis fennicae originis grammatice demonstrata* (Göttingen, 1799), was the outcome of the Western discovery of Sanskrit and of the works of Indian grammarians, who had described their language in detail in the course of a scrupulous study of religious texts. As Greek grammar was concatenated with philosophy, Indian grammar was concatenated with religion. But in neither case was formal investigation precluded, and in both cases a grammatical terminology had been evolved. The Greeks had advanced the conceptions of the parts of speech and of sentence structure, and the Indians emphasized the conceptions of a phonological system and of roots. The alliance of Classical and Indian grammar in Europe, after William Jones's discovery of the European affinities of Sanskrit in 1786,[1] produced the first comparative grammar of Indo-European[2] languages between 1833 and 1852. This was Franz Bopp's monumental *Vergleichende Grammatik des Sanskrit, Send, Griechischen, Lateinischen, Litauischen, Altslavischen, Gothischen und Deutschen*, which came out in its third and final edition in 1868–71 under the editorship of A. Kuhn. The third edition introduced Armenian, which J. H. Petermann[3] had shown to be an independent branch of Indo-European, but Celtic, which Jones had recognized as Indo-European, had to wait till the appearance of Schleicher's *Compendium* (1861) for belated admission.

8. Bopp's grammar had been preceded by the pioneer publications of Rasmus Rask[4] and Jacob Grimm,[5] who emphasized the historical side of language and simultaneously applied the method of comparative study. At this time too the russianized German A. Ch. Vostokov (Osteneck) used much the same method in his treatment of Old Church Slavonic.[6] Bopp himself was interested in the genetic aspect of language and investigated it with the new technique. This, so far as he was concerned, exploited the Indian method of root-extraction and

---

[1] *Asiatick Researches*, i, Calcutta, 1788, p. 422.

[2] The term 'Indo-European' was first used by Thomas Young (see *Quarterly Review*, no. 19, London, 1813, p. 255).

[3] *Grammatica linguae armenicae*, Berlin, 1837.

[4] *Undersøgelse om det gamle nordiske eller islandske Sprogs Oprindelse*, Copenhagen, 1818.

[5] *Deutsche Grammatik*, 2nd ed., Göttingen, 1822.

[6] *Rassuždenije o slavjanskom jazyke*, St. Petersburg, 1820.

entailed emphasis on morphology; but Bopp had also observed phonetic changes and even referred to them as 'physical laws', although he did not proceed to formulate 'sound laws' as the enthusiasm of his successors was to do in the 1870's. Like Rask and Grimm, he was letter-conscious.

9. A collateral phase of later moment in the development of Indo-European linguistics is represented by Georg Curtius's findings in Greek etymology.[1] But the interest in comparative-historical study was not confined at this time to the Indo-Iranian, Germanic, and Classical languages only; it rapidly extended its field by taking in Romance, Celtic, Slavonic, and Baltic.[2] And here we come to the second important grammar of Indo-European, viz. August Schleicher's *Compendium der vergleichenden Grammatik der indogermanischen Sprachen* (Weimar, 1861; 4th ed. 1876), which, more even than Bopp's, illustrates the impingement of the natural sciences on linguistics. Schleicher's biological conception of language introduces the notions of 'evolution' and 'decay' peculiar to living organisms, and permits him to postulate such 'organic' language-groups as the 'isolative', 'agglutinative', and 'flexional'. His botanic studies and terminology enable him to exhibit the history of Indo-European in the form of a genealogical tree (*Stammbaum*). Unlike Bopp, Schleicher divides his assembled material into comparatively short paragraphs like those of a scientific treatise or, to use Delbrück's simile, 'of a code of law',[3] and devotes one half of his book to phonetics. Like Bopp's, his 'phonetic laws' admit of exceptions; there is, moreover, constant reference to the Indo-European protoglossa (*Ursprache*); and Schleicher exercises a gift for reconstruction to produce imagined or 'starred' forms (e.g. *agras*[4] 'field' < Skt *ájraḥ* + Gk *ἀγρός* + L. *ager* + Goth. *akrs*) and even a short text in 'Indo-European', which looks suspiciously like a 'normalized' Sanskrit. His belief in the phonetic antiquity of this language leads him to reconstruct the Indo-European form of, say, 'father' as *patā(r)* in contrast to the

---

[1] *Grundzüge der griechischen Etymologie*, i–ii, Leipzig, 1858–62; 5th ed. 1879.

[2] F. C. Diez, *Grammatik der romanischen Sprachen*, i–iii, Bonn, 1836–42; J. K. Zeuss, *Grammatica celtica*, i–ii, Leipzig, 1853; 2nd ed. 1868–71; F. Miklosich, *Vergleichende Grammatik der slavischen Sprachen*, i–iv, Vienna, 1852–75; A. Schleicher, *Handbuch der litauischen Sprache*, Prague, 1856–7.

[3] B. Delbrück, *Einleitung in das Sprachstudium*, Leipzig, 1880, p. 65.

[4] Now reconstructed as *aǵros*.

modern reconstruction of the same word as *pǝtē(r), which has a manifestly Greek appearance (cf. πατήρ).

10. The peak in the development of comparative-historical linguistics was reached in the middle of the 1870's with the researches and theories of August Leskien, Berthold Delbrück, Hermann Osthoff, Karl Brugmann, and Hermann Paul. This group of scholars is loosely and incorrectly—though conveniently —called the Neogrammarian School (*Junggrammatiker*), and its authority is usually associated with the formulation of rigid 'phonetic laws' (*Lautgesetze*), with the largest grammar of Indo-European which has so far been compiled,[1] and with the intrusion of psychology into linguistics.[2] The Neogrammarians emphasized the rigour of 'phonetic laws' and explained away apparent exceptions to them as the outcome of the wide operation of analogy. They continued to give precedence to phonetics and morphology, but Delbrück had already annexed the field of syntax and made the first detailed study of it (see n. 1). The historical and psychological bias of Neogrammarian linguistics, however, appears in its theory, which was enunciated by Paul.[3] To Paul and his colleagues, as to Grimm before them, language is conceived as having a history, not an organic evolution, and linguistics becomes from now onwards a historical and social, not a biological science. This is the latest expression of the interest in the genetic aspect of language. And the gravitation of linguistics into the psychological orbit is best seen in the work of Wilhelm Wundt,[4] who was primarily a psychologist, though it is found also in Paul. Linguistic study then was still pursued 'inclusively' or in conjunction with the discoveries of other disciplines, as it had been in earlier times, and its empirical comparative method was elaborated under the influence of the natural sciences.

11. The modern statement of the findings of the comparative-historical school is still largely the history of German scholarship, though very considerable and important contributions have also been made by scholars of other European countries, and by

---

[1] K. Brugmann, *Grundriss der vergleichenden Grammatik der indogermanischen Sprachen*, i–ii, Strassburg, 1886–92; 2nd ed. 1897–1916. Vols. iii–v of the *Grundriss* cover syntax and were written by B. Delbrück (Strassburg, 1893–1900).

[2] H. Paul, *Prinzipien der Sprachgeschichte*, Halle, 1880; 5th ed. 1920; W. Wundt, *Die Sprache*, Leipzig, 1900.

[3] Op. cit.   [4] *Die Sprache*, Leipzig, 1900.

America no less than by Europe. The latest large-scale comparative grammar of Indo-European is Hermann Hirt's *Indogermanische Grammatik*, i–vii (Halle, 1927–37), which, though it draws on later developments in the Indo-European field, does not entirely supersede Brugmann's as a reference work, as this had superseded the grammars of Schleicher and Bopp. Brugmann's *Grundriss* too is the source of a series of 'introductions' to Indo-European such as those of A. Meillet, J. Schrijnen, and J. Baudiš.[1] Here again the latest published work to date is Hirt's *Die Hauptprobleme der indogermanischen Sprachwissenschaft* (ed. H. Arntz, Halle, 1939), which presents an epitome of his *Indogermanische Grammatik* as Brugmann's *Kurze vergleichende Grammatik der indogermanischen Sprachen* (Strassburg, 1904) presents a more massive epitome of his monumental treatise. But this is by no means a terminus in the development of the study of Indo-European. Newly discovered languages such as Tocharian and Hittite, both of them known in more than one distinct form, were familiar to Hirt, but were not incorporated in his work. The continued investigation of both languages in relation to 'traditional' Indo-European will provide material for the next *Grundriss*, which may either accept or reject E. H. Sturtevant's Indo-Hittite hypothesis[2] (§ 30).

II

12. So far we have followed only the main line in the development of Indo-European linguistics, noting the expansion of material and the consolidation of doctrine, and have not considered the assaults on the validity of the comparative-historical method on which this doctrine is founded. The origin of these assaults must be sought in the late nineteenth century, although none of them became vigorous for a number of years. The most serious of them came from de Saussure or rather from the results of the publication of his posthumous *Cours* in 1916. De Saussure's linguistics was influenced by developments in sociology as Paul's was by developments in historical studies. The psychological

---

[1] A. Meillet, *Introduction à l'étude comparative des langues indo-européennes*, Paris, 7th ed. 1934; J. Schrijnen, *Inleiding tot de studie der vergelijkende indogermaansche taalwetenschap*, Leiden, 1917; J. Baudiš, *Struktura jazyků indoevropských*, Prague, 1932.
[2] *An Introduction to Linguistic Science*, New Haven, 1947, pp. 162–3.

element appears in the works of both. De Saussure's decisive discrimination between speech and language, which we have already referred to (§ 1), led him to adopt a differentiation of approach. Language could be studied statically or 'synchronically' on the one hand and historically or 'diachronically' on the other. The pretentious terminology, a weakness with innovators,[1] drew an unnecessarily sharp distinction between the descriptive and the historical. De Saussure had remarked the predominance of history in the investigations of the Neogrammarian School, from which he himself had emerged, and in radical opposition to the orthodox emphasis, he urged the claims of the neglected 'synchronic' grammar, which had been cultivated by Classical philology and insistently advocated by Curtius (§ 9). The influence of de Saussure on modern linguistics has been extraordinarily strong. Linguistic fashions like Nikolaj Trubetzkoy's 'phonology',[2] Danish 'structuralism' in the specific form of Louis Hjelmslev's 'glossematics',[3] and even the modern American school, which looks back to Leonard Bloomfield[4] rather than to Edward Sapir,[5] owe their more salient characteristics to the de Saussure 'heresy'. From de Saussure, moreover, we derive our present conviction that language is an autonomous field of study. Yet de Saussure and his followers have not been able to resist the distorting influence of other disciplines. Linguistics in the West today is still variously bound to experiment in phonetics and acoustics, to logic, mathematical symbolism, and statistics, if no longer as obviously to psychology, sociology, anthropology, and philosophical fashions. One may also recall here the now discredited Marrism[6] and the prevalent Leninist Marxism in Eastern Europe, where linguistics has been bedevilled by following other 'strange gods'.

13. Another assault on Indo-European linguistics, this time against the infallibility of 'phonetic laws', which had been proclaimed by the Neogrammarians as an article of faith, came

---

[1] See J. Baudouin de Courtenay, *Versuch einer Theorie phonetischer Alternationen*, Strassburg, 1895, p. 6.
[2] *Grundzüge der Phonologie*, Prague, 1939.
[3] *Omkring Sprogteoriens Grundlæggelse*, Copenhagen, 1943.
[4] *Language*, New York, 1933; 2nd ed. 1935.
[5] *Language: an Introduction to the Study of Speech*, New York, 1921.
[6] W. K. Matthews, 'The Japhetic Theory' (*The Slavonic and East European Review*, xxvii. 68, London, 1948, pp. 172–92).

from Jules Gilliéron,[1] the linguistic geographer, whose domain had been opened up by Georg Wenker[2] in the 1880's and whose influence was felt most in the Romance-speaking world and represented, as Dauzat[3] says, a French national reaction to German hegemony in linguistics after the Franco-Prussian war. Gilliéron's isoglosses, like those of his followers outside France, enriched linguistic research with new materials on dialectal hybridization. The fresh vistas disclosed by linguistic geography were followed by a further expansion of linguistic horizons, for which phonology, glossematics, and the new science of semantics[4] were chiefly responsible.

14. Trubetzkoy's interest in the phonological aspect of language went back to the Pole, Jan Baudouin de Courtenay,[5] who enunciated an early theory of the phoneme, and he imbibed his concept of 'oppositions' from de Saussure himself. His butt at the outset was Indo-European linguistics as understood by the Russian scholars A. I. Sobolevskij and A. A. Šachmatov. He confronted orthodox phonetics with his own phonology; and his new 'discipline' has won great popularity since 1926, when its 'manifesto' was published at the International Congress of Linguistics at The Hague. Since then 'dialectal' variants of phonology have appeared not only in Western Europe and the United States (here as 'phonemics') but in the U.S.S.R., where, after its beginnings had been stifled by the Marrists, it has been partly rehabilitated, though still not generally accepted.

15. Phonology too has not been without its influence on 'structuralism' as this has taken shape on both sides of the North Atlantic. Glossematics, the Danish variety, is obsessed with theories deriving in part from 'logical positivism'[6] and has so far subordinated its analyses to them.[7] In the United States also the deleterious effects of linguistic theorizing by persons who are not specialists in the 'auxiliary' disciplines is apparent in linguistic

[1] *Atlas linguistique de la France*, Paris, 1902–12.
[2] See *Der Sprachatlas des deutschen Reichs*, Marburg, 1895. The first part of the atlas appeared in 1881. The work was continued by F. Wrede under the title of *Deutscher Sprachatlas* in 1926 ff.
[3] *La Géographie linguistique*, Paris, 1943.
[4] S. Ullmann, *Principles of Semantics*, Glasgow, 1951.
[5] *Versuch einer Theorie phonetischer Alternationen*, Strassburg, 1895.
[6] R. Carnap, *Der logische Aufbau der Welt*, Berlin-Schlachtensee, 1928.
[7] K. Togeby, *Structure immanente de la langue française*, Copenhagen, 1951.

periodicals and monographs.[1] The 'synchronic' focus is the only one recognized by prevailing fashion in Western linguistics; and where description of already described or not yet described languages is attempted, the linguistic facts are subordinated to a preconceived schematicism.[2]

16. Unlike phonology and glossematics, to which form is all-important, semantics concentrates on meaning and change of meaning. As meaning is associated here with objects (referends) in the widest sense of the term, the relation between culture and language becomes evident and their divorce impossible.

17. Here at length we come to realize the 'intermediate' position of linguistics as a discipline. It is obviously connected with other disciplines centred in man and has been repeatedly 'annexed' by them. In the course of its long history linguistics has been intimately associated with philosophy and religion, with history and sociology, with psychology and anthropology, with phonetics and semantics, and its methods have been influenced, especially in recent years, by such recondite disciplines as mathematics and statistics.[3] It has even a connexion with geography, and this connexion is twofold. We have noted the recent resurgence of linguistic geography, in which language material is studied in terms of territorial distribution. The other connexion here is a parallel. Like geography, whose manifold links with other disciplines—with physics, botany, zoology, geology, economics, anthropology, history, statistics—are obvious, linguistics is widely related and has been moulded by its multiple relationships. Both geography and linguistics are by nature eclectic sciences: they explore more than one source of knowledge and seek to establish the connexion with several sets of facts. So far as linguistics is concerned, these facts come from the domains of physics, physiology, psychology, sociology, and history. But language, the subject of linguistics, touches, as medium or vehicle, all spheres of knowledge, and this leads to considerable complications and the paramount need for discrimination.

18. Because of its multiple uses, then, language has become a web of relationships, and this has obscured the investigation of it *per*

[1] e.g. *Language* (Baltimore) and *Word* (New York), and Z. S. Harris, *Methods in Structural Linguistics*, Chicago, 1951.

[2] J. Whatmough, *Language: a Modern Synthesis*, London, 1956.

[3] See G. Herdan, *Language as Choice and Chance*, Groningen, 1956.

se. Such investigation, however, the ideal of 'pure linguistics', can never be more than 'formal', i.e. phonetic and lexicological, and cannot be pursued with advantage by divorcing sound from sense as some 'structuralists' would have us do.[1] It is the coincidence of these elements in speech that is the very material of language. Sound without sense would result in glossolalia, not in recognizable repetition; for repetition of a signal is the key to a prearranged system of 'meanings'. This system is the vocal or symbolized language which we use in communication with others. Language is therefore a systematic relationship between sound and sense, not sound alone (*vox et praeterea nihil*), which is the province of acoustics. As such it is an abstraction and does not exist on the material plane. 'Sie existiert ja eigentlich nicht' is Hirt's paradox.[2]

III

19. With the foregoing sketch of the development of linguistics for preface and background, we can now approach the study of our subject. We are concerned with the historical grammar of Russian, which is, in a sense, synonymous with the history of the Russian language. In studying this we shall be confronted with both facts and conjectures, and to preserve accuracy and a balanced judgement we shall have to exercise due caution in not making the two sets of data interchangeable. The facts belong to the historical period of the language which extends over nine hundred years, i.e. from the eleventh to the twentieth century; the conjectures project our knowledge into prehistory and are often plausible and even probable, although not corroborated by records. We may accept them as an explanation of the state of Russian at the time of its earliest records, but at best they can be no more than surmise. This scrupulous discrimination between fact and fiction, record and reconstruction, is essential and unavoidable, if linguistic science is to remain scientific. It is the only 'opposition' that is valid in linguistics at all times.

20. The connexion of Russian with other Slavonic languages appears to have been realized long before the nineteenth century. It had come to the knowledge of even Western Europe in

[1] See J. Whatmough, op. cit., p. 40.
[2] H. Hirt and H. Arntz, *Die Hauptprobleme der indogermanischen Sprachwissenschaft*, Halle, 1939, p. 196.

the sixteenth, when J. J. Scaliger[1] defined his Slavonic group as the *Boge*-languages (§ 4). In the early nineteenth century its place in the Indo-European system was recognized by Bopp, the second part of whose *Vergleichende Grammatik* (1835) includes 'Altslawisch' in its table of contents. Since then Slavonic has been regarded as one of the dialectal subdivisions of Indo-European and has consequently figured in all the *Grundrisse* which have been published down to our own time. The twentieth century has seen attempts to define Common Slavonic, or 'Proto-Slavonic',[2] from which Russian and its cognates are said to derive. In the appropriate place (Chap. II) the definition will appear as an epitome of reconstructed data.

21. Because of the known linguistic connexions of Russian on the temporal plane we must begin its history before the Common Slavonic period. Common Slavonic, as we have learnt, is credibly regarded as a dialect of an even more remote and abstract linguistic system, to which the name 'Indo-European' is now commonly given in English. It is also known as 'Indogermanisch' in German and has sometimes been more briefly designated as 'Aryan'.[3]

22. Indo-European is the protoglossa (*Ursprache*), which summarizes the recorded data of the Indo-European languages. It is no longer considered as a language as by Schleicher, but rather as a set of 'starred' forms, sometimes difficult to pronounce, which summarize and symbolize the interrelations of cognate survivals. Thus IE **mātér* 'mother' represents the equation or correlation: Skt *mātár-*, Av. *mātar-*, Arm. *maír*, Gk μήτηρ, Alb. *motrë* 'sister', L. *māter*, Osc. *maatreis*, Umb. *matrer* (= L. *matris*), OIr. *māthir*, OI *móði*, OE *mōdor*, OHG *muoter*, OPr. *pomatre* 'mother-in-law', Lith. *mótė* (gen. *moters̃*) 'wife', OCS *mati* (gen. *matere*).

---

[1] Op. cit., pp. 119–22.
[2] A. Meillet, *Le slave commun*, 2nd ed. Paris, 1934. This has been revised by A. Vaillant. See also J. J. Mikkola, *Urslavische Grammatik*, i–iii, Heidelberg, 1913–50.
[3] H. Sweet, *The History of Language*, London, 1900. The term 'Aryan' is now sometimes synonymous with 'Indo-Iranian'.

I I

LINGUISTIC PREHISTORY

I. INDO-EUROPEAN

23. General. Consultation of standard reference-works such as
K. Brugmann and B. Delbrück's *Grundriss der vergleichenden Grammatik der indogermanischen Sprachen* (Strassburg, 1897–1916) and
A. Walde and J. Pokorny's *Vergleichendes Wörterbuch der indogermanischen Sprachen* (Berlin–Leipzig, 1926–32),[1] may leave the
student with the impression that the sum-total of our knowledge
of Common (or Proto-) Indo-European is contained in these
pages. But the discovery that Brugmann brought out a corrected
edition of his part of the *Grundriss* between 1897 and 1916 (see
§ 10, p. 6, n. 1) and especially that since the beginning of this
century two new sets of Indo-European languages—Tocharian A
and B and the Hittite group[2]—have been brought to light and
have provided stimulus and data to a great deal of research, which
has resulted, among other things, in the formulation of a revised
theory of linguistic relationships inside the Indo-European
group, will no doubt help him to realize that Indo-European
linguistics is not an unchanging body of fact and hypothesis, but
a domain of study in which the last word has not been said.

24. How, indeed, 'the last word' can be said here is altogether
difficult to imagine. The period of discovery is plainly by no
means over, for there remain unread inscriptions to decipher,[3]
and there may still be fresh material that will one day come to
light. But even if we had all the material that we can ever hope
to find at our disposal now, its nature would be such that with
its help we could not possibly arrive at more than a conjectural

---

[1] Julius Pokorny's *Indogermanisches etymologisches Wörterbuch* (Berne, 1948–) is a
successor to this work.

[2] E. Sieg, W. Siegling, and W. Schulze, *Tocharische Grammatik*[2], Berlin, 1931;
E. H. Sturtevant and E. Adelaide Hahn, *A Comparative Grammar of the Hittite Language*, i[2], New Haven, 1951; I. Gershevitch, *A Grammar of Manichean Sogdian*, Oxford,
1954.

[3] One of the latest decipherments is M. Ventris's reading of the Mycenean
Linear B. Syllabary. Cf. J. Chadwick, 'Mycenaean: A Newly Discovered Greek
Dialect' (*Transactions of the Philological Society, 1954*, Oxford, 1955, pp. 1–17); L. R.
Palmer, *Achaeans and Indo-Europeans*, Oxford, 1955; S. Ja. Lur'je, *Jazyk i kul'tura
mikenskoj Grecii*, Moscow–Leningrad, 1957.

solution of our problem. Indo-European linguistics, like all other branches of linguistic study, has the disadvantage of dealing with data which are disparate in time. In contrast to the relative antiquity of Vedic Sanskrit, Homeric Greek, and the Italic dialects, we have the relative modernity of Lithuanian and Albanian and the 'intermediate' medieval records of Armenian, Celtic, Germanic, and Slavonic. It must be obvious now that we are comparing languages sometimes separated by not inconsiderable periods of time and that the records of each are also spaced out in terms of centuries. This prevents investigation on a strictly 'synchronic' basis, and as our material is not even approximately contemporaneous, our conclusions will inevitably be distorted and our reconstructions will be made at the sacrifice of some degree of plausibility. Then there is a further difficulty which is very important. Our records are 'selective' and thus represent what we have a right to regard, in the light of modern dialect-study, as a fraction of the potential varieties of a language. The recorded dialects of Ancient Greek are particularly instructive in this respect. Dialectal differentiation in the early stages was probably the rule rather than the exception.

25. Comparison of our records of Indo-European language-types with due regard to the time factor enables us to infer that the rate of development in each type varies considerably. Thus Lithuanian in the sixteenth century and even today has conservative features which allow us to regard it, along with Sanskrit, as a key to the postulated Indo-European declension. But this conservativeness must not mislead us into thinking that a modern language, however slow its rate of development, can be more than the shadow of an ancient condition. It is in the nature of language to 'change', or to transform itself, as we know from the collation and study of the later with the earlier stages of recorded languages.

26. The comparative method as used in Indo-European linguistics involves the marshalling and investigation of data of historically disparate cognate languages as if these data were of uniform validity. It is true, of course, that since the time of Bopp, preference has been given to the earliest recorded languages, and the customary picture of Indo-European is still a palimpsest of Sanskrit and Greek with glosses from the remaining Indo-European language-groups, except perhaps the two latest.[1] Where a choice has to be made between Sanskrit and Greek evidence, either the one or the other is favoured, or alternative forms are posited (e.g. *-m/*-bh for the dative, ablative, and instrumental plural).[2] Where, on the other hand, there is considerable agreement among the various 'dialects' of Indo-European a statistically-vouched average form is reconstructed as simultaneous source and epitome. Such reconstructions are based not only on a phonetic likeness but on semantic congruence as well. Thus IE *bherō 'I carry' summarizes Skt bhárāmi, Av. baraimi, Arm. berem, Gk φέρω, Alb. bie, L. ferō, OIr. biru, Goth. baíra, OCS berǫ, all of which are similar in form and meaning. And here we may add Phrygian αββερετ 'attulit', Toch. A pärtär 'he carries', Messapian berain 'they may carry', and, with a difference of meaning, Lith. beriù 'I strew'.

27. The reconstructed Indo-European, which is still valid for practical purposes, although it must ultimately be revised to cover the relevant supplementary facts of Tocharian and especially of Hittite, is regarded by Indo-European scholars as the language of a people in a mixed pastoral-agricultural stage of development which had a central European habitat, extending from sea through forest to steppe and possessing an organized polity and religion. This assumption derives from linguistic evidence and seeks confirmation from the combined evidence of archaeology and anthropology. As Hirt[3] says: 'we shall be able to reconstruct only a fraction of Indo-European culture by linguistic comparison'. Chronology too can only be very approximate and must remain virtually hypothetical. Hirt, for instance, is inclined to fix the limits of Common Indo-European in the millennium between 3000 and 2000 B.C. Earlier dates, based on the Vedas, are qualified as 'fanciful'. At the time specified, Indo-European would appear to have been dialectally differentiated, and, as now, there must have been a greater affinity

---

[1] More recent studies (e.g. W. P. Lehmann, *Proto-Indo-European Phonology*, Austin, Texas, 1952) include these in their reconstructions.

[2] G. S. Lane, 'On the Present State of Indo-European Linguistics' (*Language*, xxv. 4, Baltimore, 1949, pp. 333–42). See also W. P. Lehmann, op. cit., pp. 1–6.

[3] H. Hirt and H. Arntz, op. cit., p. 30; also *Die Indogermanen, ihre Verbreitung, ihre Urheimat, und ihre Kultur*, Strassburg, 1905–7, and O. Schrader, *Die Indogermanen*[3], Leipzig, 1918.

between some dialects than between others. Thus later evidence permits us to illustrate this with the following diagram:[1]

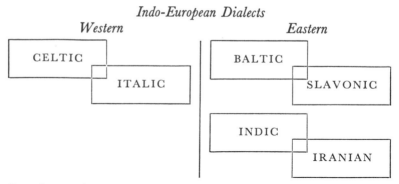

Indo-European Dialects

Western   *Eastern*

CELTIC   BALTIC

   ITALIC   SLAVONIC

                                             INDIC

                                                IRANIAN

Our figure, incomplete and tentative as it is, shows the closer, statistically supported affinities between some of the language-groups.[2] These affinities are binary in all cases. The validity of setting up such 'internal' groups may be questioned and has in effect been challenged in two cases out of three, the Indo-Iranian 'unity' being the only one that is unreservedly accepted. Its purpose is still more uncertain; for if we must posit 'starred' forms, it is in the interests of clarity and plausibility to have as few sets of these as possible. It may be ingenious and of practical value to reconstruct forms illustrating, say, Common Indo-European, 'Balto-Slavonic', and Common Slavonic, but all three sets of forms would obviously be abstractions; and although they might indicate a certain line of development, both line and forms could be no more than the articles of an act of faith. By leaving out the middle term—'Balto-Slavonic'—here, we not only do not distort the existing array of facts but have one abstraction the fewer to take on trust.

28. The foregoing diagram purports to show not only affinities but differences. The vertical line divides the western from the eastern dialects of Indo-European on the basis of a twofold development of the palatal plosives of Common Indo-European. Comparison of the Indo-European dialect-words for 'hundred'

---

    [1] 'Indic' (cf. G. Indisch) is preferable to 'Indo-Aryan', because it eliminates the ambiguous second element, and to 'Indian', because this term is applied to languages in the New World (Amerindian) as well as in the Old.
    [2] A. L. Kroeber and C. D. Chrétien, 'Quantitative Classification of Indo-European Languages' (*Language*, xiii, Baltimore, 1937, pp. 83–103).

enables us to put Greek (ἑ-κατόν), Italic (L. *centum*), Celtic (OIr. *cēt*), and Germanic (Goth. *hund*) into one group, in which IE *k̂- becomes a velar, and Indic (Skt *śatám*), Iranian (Av. *satəm*), Baltic (Lith. *šim̃tas*), and Slavonic (OCS сълто) into another, in which IE *k̂- becomes a sibilant. Latin *centum* and Avestic *satəm* are arbitrarily used to designate these two groups as *centum-* and *satəm-* languages. The corresponding geographical or territorial groups have lost some of their validity since the discovery of Tocharian, which has unexpectedly emerged as a *centum*-language instead of the *satəm*-language postulated by geography (cf. Toch. A *känt*).

29. The interrelationship of the well-authenticated Indo-European language-groups, as well as their geographical distribution, may be roughly indicated by the following diagram:[1]

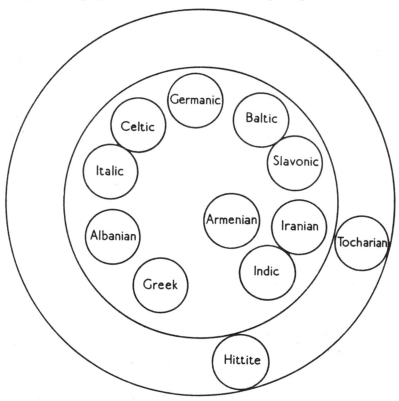

[1] This diagram was partly suggested by the one on p. 287 of H. Pedersen's *Sprogvidenskaben i det nittende Aarhundrede*, Copenhagen, 1924.

The less-known languages—Phrygian, Thracian, Illyrian, Messapian, Venetic, all of them *centum*-types, and of which we have only a very fragmentary knowledge—are not entered here. Their Indo-European character has not been seriously disputed, and their names help to pin-point some of the gaps in our mosaic. The diagram, moreover, shows the presence of Tocharian and Hittite, the new discoveries in the Indo-European area. They are represented as lying outside the inner circle which bounds the better-known types. This does not mean that they are not to be grouped with them, but rather that their relationship to the other Indo-European languages has not yet been completely worked out. Our statement applies more particularly to Hittite, which has given rise to a new theory.

30. In 1921 E. Forrer[1] advanced the view that Hittite had detached itself from the Indo-European complex before this had disintegrated. E. H. Sturtevant[2] accepts this view and presents it in the following scheme:

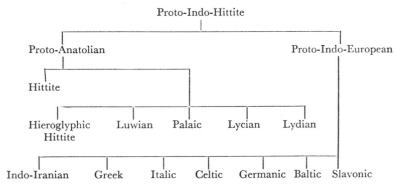

The Anatolian group, in contrast to its counterpart, possesses certain phonetic phenomena, viz. 'the laryngeals', which would appear, according to the author, to have been lost in Indo-European (cf. Hitt. *ḫuḫas* 'grandfather' with L. *avus*; Hitt. *ḫanti* 'in front' with Skt *anti*, Gk ἀντί, L. *ante*). The discovery of these 'laryngeals' or, better, laryngals has enabled Indo-European scholarship to penetrate further into prehistory. Sturtevant's Indo-Hittite theory, however, still lacks general acceptance.

---

[1] In *Mitteilungen der Deutschen Orient-Gesellschaft*, lxi, 1921, pp. 21 f.

[2] Op. cit., p. 163, also E. H. Sturtevant and E. Adelaide Hahn, *A Comparative Grammar of the Hittite Language*, New Haven, 1951, p. 9.

31. Common Indo-European, as now conceived,[1] is a system of sounds and forms representing correspondences among the recorded data of later times. Strictly speaking, Common Indo-European embodies not the first, but the second degree of abstraction: it prefigures, say, not Attic or even Homeric Greek, but the abstract 'Common Greek', which epitomizes the facts presented by the recorded Greek dialects, and whose reconstructed forms will perhaps be confirmed by 'Mycenean' (see § 24, p. 13, n. 3).

32. Phonology. It would seem that reconstructed Indo-European had a triangular system of vowel phonemes which appeared in two sets, distinguished by a difference of length:

$$*i \qquad\qquad *u \qquad\qquad\qquad *\bar{\imath} \qquad\qquad *\bar{u}$$
$$*e \ *\partial \ *o \qquad\qquad\qquad *\bar{e} \qquad *\bar{o}$$
$$*a \qquad\qquad\qquad\qquad *\bar{a}$$

The central vowel of the first set, sometimes called 'schwa indo-germanicum', is supposed to have existed in at least two variants, viz. $*\partial_1$ ('primum') and $*\partial_2$ ('secundum').

33. The diphthongal groups, like the primary vowels, were of two types, long and short, their second, non-syllabic element, or terminus of tongue movement, being represented by either $*i$ or $*u$, both of them 'semivowels' here (i, u). Thus there were six short and six long diphthongs in all, viz.:

$$*ei, *eu \qquad *oi, *ou \qquad *\bar{e}i, *\bar{e}u \qquad *\bar{o}i, *\bar{o}u$$
$$*ai, *au \qquad\qquad\qquad *\bar{a}i, *\bar{a}u$$

34. All these vowels and diphthongs could constitute syllables; but they did not have a monopoly of this function, because along with them we have also to consider the 'sonants', i.e. the 'liquid' and nasal syllabic consonants $*r̥$, $*l̥$, $*m̥$, $*n̥$, which, as some (e.g. de Saussure[2] and Walde) think, could be long as well as short.

35. The system of consonants includes these sonants, as well as a very large group of plosives—distinguished among themselves

[1] See W. P. Lehmann, *Proto-Indo-European Phonology*, Austin, Texas, 1952, pp. 99–102.
[2] *Mémoire sur le système primitif des voyelles dans les langues indo-européennes*, Leipzig, 1879.

by the presence or absence of voice and aspiration—two fricatives, and two 'semivowels':

	Bilabial	Dental	Palatal	Velar	Labio-velar	Laryngal
Plosive:						
Unaspirated	*p/*b	*t/*d	*ḱ/*ĝ	*k/*g	*kᵘ/*gᵘ	..
Aspirated	*ph/*bh	*th/*dh	*ḱh/*ĝh	*kh/*gh	*kᵘh/*gᵘh	..
Fricative	..	*þ, *s/(*z)	..	..	..	*h
Nasal	*m	*n	(*ñ)	(*ŋ)	..	..
Lateral	..	*l	..	..	..	..
Vibrant	..	*r	..	..	..	..
Semivowel	*u̯	..	*i̯	..	..	..

The symbols enclosed here in brackets are variants ('allophones') found only in limited phonetic environments: thus *z occurs before voiced consonants, *ñ before palatals, and *ŋ before velars, while *þ (θ) symbolizes the correlation Skt s, Gk τ, L. s in ṛkṣaḥ, ἄρκτος, and ursus 'bear' respectively, i.e. it follows IE *k.[1]

---

[1] Other consonants which have been assumed to have existed in IE are *ð (= IPA ð) and the aspirated *θh/*ðh (= IPA θh and ðh) as well as, in recent times, the so-called 'laryngeals' (laryngals), which some imagine to have survived into the earliest form of Indo-European (PIE). Four varieties of these have been assumed (see W. P. Lehmann, op. cit., pp. 98–99). Thus the correlation Hitt. išḫai 'to bind', Gk ζωστός, Av. yāsta- 'girt', Alb. ngjesh 'to gird', Lith. júostas 'girt', OCS po-jasati 'to gird', proposed by E. H. Sturtevant, presupposes an 'Indo-Hittite' initial *i̯ (see id. and E. Adelaide Hahn, *A Comparative Grammar of the Hittite Language*, i², New Haven, 1951, p. 5). Lehmann considers that the IH form was also Common Indo-European (op. cit., p. 77).

This author (op. cit., pp. 1–21, 109–14) incidentally attempts a 'structuralist' classification of Indo-European phonemes by recognizing the following minimum set:

'Obstruents'
    p   t   k   kʷ
  b   bh   d   dh   g   gh   gʷ   gʷh
       s

Vowels   e ē   a ā   o ō   i ī   u ū
'Resonants'   y w l r m n   •
'Laryngeals'   h x ɣ ʔ

Previous analyses of the Indo-European system of sounds have been primarily phonetic, hence the recognition of variants as well as phonemes. This, however, claims to be 'phonemic' (phonematic) and subsumes the variants under the phonemes. It will be noted that the vowel system particularly is impoverished by the denial of status to diphthongs. The new analysis rests entirely on facts provided by traditional scholarship, and the interpretations of them which Lehmann has made most use of are de Saussure's and Meillet's. These scholars, for instance, excluded the palatal series of consonants, which Brugmann, Hirt, and Kuryłowicz included in their lists. De Saussure's general tendency was to reduce the phonology of Indo-European to a minimum system, which adumbrates without itself being a 'structuralist' system.

36. This analysis of the system of Indo-European phonemes is complicated by the existence of certain fixed rules determining the relationship of vowels to one another in root and affix (formant). Here we have to do with one of the most difficult problems of Indo-European phonology, viz. the problem of vowel apophony or vowel gradation (G. *Ablaut*). The relationship of vowels to one another may be seen in the following examples, which present the vowels in three grades (G. *Stufen*)—normal (G. *Vollstufe*), long (G. *Dehnstufe*), and zero (G. *Schwundstufe*):

	Normal grade	*Long grade*	*Zero grade*
Short vowels	$*e/*o$ Gk πατέρα (acc.) 'father'	$*\bar{e}/*\bar{o}$ Gk πατήρ (nom.) 'father'	$-/-$ Gk πατρός (gen.) 'father's'
Long vowels	$*\bar{e}/*\bar{o}$ Skt sthā- 'to stand'		$*ə$ Skt sthitáḥ 'standing'

Where the long vowel represents the normal or basic grade, the long grade does not appear, and zero grade is represented by $*ə$.

37. The apophonic series (G. *Ablautsreihen*) in Indo-European have been extended by inclusion of the so-called 'reduced' grade (G. *Reduktionsstufe*), which is represented by shortened vowels ($*ĭ$, $*ŭ$). These shortened or 'reduced' vowels were originally due to loss of stress[1] and have either disappeared in some instances (cf. Skt ásti 'he is', L. est with Skt smás, L. sumus 'we are') or been preserved in others (e.g. OCS дьнь 'day', Gk τίθεμεν 'we put' < $*dhĭdhəmés$). Reduced grade and zero grade are often found together (cf. Gk ἐσμέν 'we are' with L. sumus). It would therefore seem that reduced grade, which is posited for the oldest period of Indo-European, gave way to zero grade, i.e. to the complete lapse of the unstressed vowel. Thus Common Indo-European $*\bar{e}$, $*\bar{a}$, $*\bar{o}$ became $*e$, $*a$, $*o$ respectively, and these changed into $*ĭ$, $*ŭ$ with loss of stress. The reduced $*ĭ$, $*ŭ$ disappeared under other conditions, especially after stress, and $*e$, $*a$, $*o$ became $*ə$ (zero grade).[2]

38. Besides rules governing apophony, Indo-European had rules distinguishing the use of sounds in final position from their use in other positions. Thus long diphthongs (e.g. $*\bar{a}u$)—including

---

[1] H. Hirt and H. Arntz, op. cit., pp. 149–50. Further members of this correlation are Arm. *arj*, Alb. *ari*, OIr. *art*.   [2] Ibid., p. 155.

combinations of a long vowel with a liquid or nasal (e.g. *$\bar{a}l$, *$\bar{a}m$)—might lose their second element (e.g. IE *$okt\bar{o}u$/*$okt\bar{o}$ may be postulated from Skt $a\d{s}\d{t}\acute{a}u$, Gk ὀκτώ, and IE *$a\hat{k}men$- from Skt $a\acute{s}man$ 'stone', Gk ἄκμων 'anvil'). Here Common Slavonic is of particular interest, as it appears to have lost all the consonantal endings of Indo-European flexion (cf. IE *$u\mathring{l}k^uos$ with OCS влькъ, Lith. $vi\tilde{l}kas$ 'wolf'; IE *$\hat{g}\mathring{r}nom$ with OCS зрьно, Goth. $ka\acute{u}rn$ 'grain'; IE *$bheroit$ and Skt $bh\acute{a}ret$ 'he may carry' with OCS бєрн 'take').

39. The coincident presence of tone and stress in the phonology of certain Indo-European languages, among them Sanskrit and Greek, has led to the postulation of a 'chromatic accent' as well as of dynamic stress in Common Indo-European. These two types of stress would seem to have prevailed at various times. Thus zero grade in Indo-European apophony must have resulted from the operation of a strong dynamic stress. The position of the stress appears to have been unrestricted, as it could fall on any syllable of a word. In later times, within the sphere of individual language-groups, the position of the stress was restricted either to one or to a few adjacent syllables. Thus Greek and Latin observed the 'three-syllable law' (G. *Dreisilbengesetz*), and Classical Sanskrit a four-syllable rule. In some later languages (e.g. Lithuanian, Latvian, Serbo-Croatian, Slovene) the 'chromatic accent' has survived, but in a modified form. The acute and circumflex, or *Stosston* (F. *intonation rude*) and *Schleifton* (F. *intonation douce*) respectively, are known in both Lithuanian and Serbo-Croatian in association with long syllables.[1] As de Saussure[2] has shown, the Indo-European long vowels are represented in 'Balto-Slavonic' by the acute (e.g. $\acute{i}$, $\acute{a}$, $\acute{u}$), and the diphthongs are normally circumflex (*$e\tilde{i}$, *$e\tilde{n}$, *$e\tilde{l}$). Where the circumflex is found with long vowels and the acute with diphthongs, we have to do with phonetic developments such as contraction and apocope (cf. Lith. $sesu\tilde{o}$ 'sister', which has lost final r, with Gk πατήρ 'father', in which r remained). Although Lithuanian has preserved its 'chromatic accent' or pitch-stress, it has completely transformed it: today the acute is a falling, not a rising, tone,

---

[1] Serbo-Croatian also has tonal differences in syllables with short vowels (cf. $\check{z}\grave{a}ba$ 'frog' with $\check{z}\grave{e}na$ 'wife').

[2] 'A propos de l'accentuation lituanienne' (*Recueil de publications scientifiques*, Paris, 1897).

as it was in Classical Greek and still is in Serbo-Croatian; and the originally falling circumflex has now an upward curve.[1]

40. Word-formation. Our next step in the survey of Indo-European is the investigation of 'words' and their components, formed by the phonemes which we have identified and classified (§§ 32–35). Word-formation in this language, as in its successors, consists of both composition and derivation (affixation). Sanskrit, Greek, and Germanic especially illustrate the former device, and Latin, Baltic, and Slavonic the latter. Both devices, however, exist in all Indo-European languages to a certain extent.

41. Composition involves the compounding of various semantically associated elements (e.g. Skt *kumbha-karáḥ* 'vase-maker', Gk ὁπλο-φόρος 'man-at-arms'; Skt *dvá-daśa*, Gk δώ-δεκα 'twelve'; Skt *tāmra-dhūmráḥ* 'dark-flame-coloured', Gk γλυκύ-πικρος 'bitter-sweet'), which have now been minutely studied and classified.[2] To do this, words had to be first reduced to their components by analysis.

42. Analysis of words into morphemes reveals the presence of the root (base) and of certain formants, which include the so-called 'root-determinatives' (e.g. *-s-*, *-m-*, *-p-* in IE *trese-*, *treme-*, *trepe-*; cf. Skt *trásati*, Gk τρέμει 'he trembles', L. *trepidus* 'trembling') as well as prefixes and suffixes. These two types of formants are well represented in Indo-European languages and are found in both noun and verb, but the use of flexional endings gives a preponderance to the suffix. The prefix is notably more frequent in verbal and the suffix in nominal forms (cf. the augment in Skt *á-bharam*, Gk ἔ-φερον 'he carried', which derives from the IE particle *e-* meaning approximately 'at that time', with the *-ter-/-tor-* suffix of the *nomina agentis*: Skt *dātar-* (nom. *dātā*), Gk δώτωρ, L. *dātor* 'giver').

43. Morphology. Indo-European morphology is the linguistic domain which has been investigated most after Indo-European phonology. Bopp devoted particular attention to it; it looms

---

[1] W. K. Matthews, 'The Affinities and Structure of Lithuanian' (*The Slavonic and East European Review*, xxxv. 84, London, 1956, pp. 62–64).

[2] K. Brugmann, *Kurze vergleichende Grammatik der indogermanischen Sprachen*, Strassburg, 1904, pp. 297–311.

large in Schleicher; and it was only after the phonetic researches
of the Neogrammarians that interest in it somewhat declined.
But phonology and morphology as understood by Indo-European scholarship are interdependent and complementary, and
the former inevitably prefaces the latter.

44. The contrast of noun and verb in Indo-European is an
archaic feature and depends not only on semantic but on formal
differentiation. The morphology of the noun, which includes
substantive, adjective, numeral, and pronoun, is determined by
the concepts of gender, number, and case. Indo-European gender would seem to have been the result of a double bipartition,
viz. animate/inanimate (neuter), with the former subdivided
into masculine and feminine. There were three numbers, including a dual, and an eight-case system, comprising the nominative,
vocative, accusative, genitive, dative, ablative, instrumental,
and locative. Hirt[1] thinks that the emergence of gender and
number was a relatively late development and attempts to show
that syncretism, or the formal coincidence of cases, existed in
Indo-European, where, say, the accusative stood for both the
case of the direct object and the 'directive' or allative case. He
proceeds from the 'casus indefinitus' (vocative), which has no
formal index, and finds it again in the locative; he postulates
the formal identity of nominative and accusative in early times;
and he derives the genitive from the nominative and the instrumental from the locative. This leaves the dative as the only
primitive case. If these views are tenable, the primitive Indo-
European case-system was probably much simpler than the
system, reconstructed on the basis of Sanskrit, Baltic, and
Slavonic, from which those of all recorded Indo-European languages are supposed to derive. The most feebly developed case-
system, we may note here, is in the dual, where there are usually
only three distinct forms, viz. nominative–vocative–accusative,
dative–ablative–instrumental, and genitive–locative.

45. The relative complexity of the Indo-European case-system
is increased by the variety of stems, both vocalic and consonantal, which we find especially in substantives and adjectives.
Substantival stems are particularly varied: they include stems
in *-a/*-i̯a, *-o, *-i, *-u, *-ī, *-ū, *-s, *-m, *-n, *-l, *-r, and an

---

[1] H. Hirt and H. Arntz, op. cit., pp. 54–71.

alternant stem in *-r/*-n, which have recently received added
support from Hittite (e.g. *wātar* 'water', gen. *weten-aš*).[1]

46. Indo-European adjectives, which are semantically subordinated to the substantives and generally congruent with them
in syntagmatic groupings, do not differ fundamentally from the
substantives; but they have a number of characteristic features
—the faculty of constructing generic forms from a common stem
(e.g. Skt *náva-ḥ*, *návā*, *návam* 'new'), comparison, and certain
idiosyncrasies of flexion, which give them independent status.
Their stem-forms are the same as those of substantives, the commonest being stems in *-o*, *-i*, *-u*, *-s*, and *-n*.

47. The comparative adjective is formed by adding the alternant suffix *-i̯es/*-i̯os (long grade *-i̯ēs/*-i̯ōs; zero grade *-s) to
the stem of the positive either directly or with the interposition
of the suffix *-i- (e.g. Skt *náv-yas-* < *náva-* 'new'; *svād-ī-yas-* <
svādú 'sweet').

48. The commonest suffix of the superlative adjective is *-isto-*,
whose first element *-is- may be the zero grade of the comparative suffix (e.g. Skt *svād-istha-ḥ*, Gk ἥδ-ιστο-s 'sweetest').

49. The Indo-European numerals 1–4 distinguish gender and
case. IE *oi̯-nos 'one' has a full system of declension; *d(u)u̯ō(u)/
*d(u)u̯oi 'two' is declined in the dual; and *trei̯es/*tri(i̯)ǝ and
*ku̯etu̯ores/*ku̯etu̯orǝ have a plural paradigm. The remaining
numerals are not declined. The first decade (1–10) contains the
primary forms of the numerals; the second (11–19) is constructed
by combining each of the primary nine with the word for 'ten'
(e.g. Skt *éka-daśa*, Gk ἕν-δεκα, L. *un-decim* 'eleven'); the word for
'twenty' has a dual ending, and the remaining decades (30–90)
are formal plurals. These are all derived from the primary
numerals by suffixing *-(d)ḱomt-/*-(d)ḱm̥t- 'decade', the element
found in *(d)ḱm̥tóm 'hundred' or 'a decade (of decades)'. Sanskrit
and the Classical languages seem to have preserved the Indo-
European word for 'thousand' (Skt *sa-hásram* < IE *sm̥-ĝheslo-m;
Gk χίλιοι, L. *mīlle* < IE *ĝhesl-i̯o-, *smī-ĝhsl-ī respectively).

50. Pronominal flexion differs from the strictly nominal in the
personal and reflexive series of pronouns, which have a charac-

[1] Cf. E. Benveniste, *Origines de la formation des noms en indoeuropéen*, Paris, 1935.
The author deals here with roots and 'root determinatives'.

teristic system of declension. In the first two persons of the personal pronoun and in the reflexive pronoun, gender is not recognized, and number has a different connotation than in the noun: 'we' and 'you' do not mean 'many Is' and 'many thous', but rather 'I and others' and 'thou and others', and this difference is expressed by the use of different stems or 'suppletive' forms (cf. Skt *áśvā* 'mare', pl. *áśvāḥ* with *ahám* 'I' and *vayám* 'we'). The anaphoric pronoun of the 3rd person, which is denominal in origin, and all the other pronouns with a 'normal' system of declension, viz. possessive, demonstrative, and relative, reveal in their case-forms the formal affinity of the pronoun to the other members of the Indo-European nominal category (cf. the declension of Skt *madíya-ḥ* 'my' with *náva-ḥ* 'new').

51. The Indo-European verb is assumed to have had all the complexity of the verb in Sanskrit and Greek. It is distinguished from the noun by a set of personal endings which, associated with number, give nine distinct formal types. Hirt[1] does not derive these endings from the personal pronoun, as Bopp and even Brugmann did, but regards them as particles attached to the verbal stem. Indeed, he goes further and derives verbal flexion from the nominal, basing his argument partly on the presence of a nominal element in the Indo-European verbal system, viz. on the presence of participles—which share declension with the adjectives—verbal nouns capable of government, and the infinitives. Bopp regarded the infinitive as being essentially a noun, although in the Classical languages it had been adapted to express the verbal concept of time. From such a standpoint it is easy to see the finite or conjugated verb as chronologically later than the verbal nouns, infinitives, and participles.

52. The finite verb expresses threefold voice (diathesis)—active, middle, and passive (this inadequately attested in Indo-European); mood (indicative, subjunctive, optative, imperative, and possibly an injunctive, expressing unreality); and tense (present, imperfect, aorist, perfect, pluperfect, and future). All three numbers are represented in the verb as they are in the noun. Active and middle voice have different personal endings. Compare, for instance, a fragment of the 'thematic' present-tense

[1] H. Hirt and H. Arntz, op. cit., pp. 72–81.

conjugation of IE *bherō 'I carry', as illustrated by Sanskrit and Greek:[1]

| | Active | | Middle | |
	Sanskrit	Greek	Sanskrit	Greek
Sg. 1	bhár-ā-mi	φέρ-ω	bhár-ē	φέρ-ο-μαι
2	bhár-ā-si	φέρ-εις	bhár-a-sē	φέρ-ῃ(<-ε-αι)
3	bhár-a-ti	φέρ-ει	bhár-a-tē	φέρ-ε-ται

Here we find thematic or stem vowels (Skt -a-, Gk -ε- < IE *-e-/*-o-) and the 'primary' endings, which occur in the present, future, and perfect of the indicative. These are contrasted with the 'secondary' endings of the augment-tenses—imperfect, aorist, and pluperfect. For illustration compare the forms of the imperfect with the partial paradigm given above:[2]

| | Active | | Middle | |
	Sanskrit	Greek	Sanskrit	Greek
Sg. 1	á-bhar-a-m	ἔ-φερ-ο-ν	á-bhar-ē	ἐ-φερ-ό-μην
2	á-bhar-a-ḥ	ἔ-φερ-ε-ς	á-bhar-a-thāḥ	ἐ-φέρ-ου(<ε-ο)
3	á-bhar-a-t	ἔ-φερ-ε	á-bhar-a-ta	ἐ-φέρ-ε-το

The Indo-European middle-voice endings, viz. primary *-mi, *-si, *-ti and secondary *-m, *-s, *-t in the singular, are based on the evidence of Sanskrit and Greek. Several other Indo-European languages, including Italic, Celtic, Tocharian, and even Hittite, point to the existence of a middle voice in -r, and this is considered to prove dialectal differentiation in the protoglossa (Ursprache).

53. In contrast to the indicative mood, the others have their own formal distinguishing marks, which may be either different endings or special modal indices. Thus the subjunctive, a relatively late formation, has a thematic vowel *e/*o to distinguish it from the corresponding indicative form (cf. Skt ás-a-ti 'he may be' with ás-ti 'he is', Gk φέρωμεν 'we may carry' with φέρομεν 'we carry').

54. The index of the optative mood is *-ịē- (zero grade *-ī-). This may be seen in L. s-ie-m/sim, s-ie-s/sīs, s-ie-t/sit 'I, you, he

---

[1] H. Krahe, Indogermanische Sprachwissenschaft, Berlin, 1943, p. 113.
[2] Ibid., p. 114.

may be', which should be compared to Sanskrit *s-yā-m*, *s-yā-ḥ*, *s-yā-t*.

55. The imperative mood in Indo-European had no modal index, but was to some extent distinguished from the indicative by its endings (cf. Gk 2nd sg. imp. φέρε with 2nd sg. indic. φέρεις; but 2nd pl. φέρετε is both indicative and imperative).

56. The Indo-European tense forms are responsible for a substantial part of the complexity of the verbal system, and the number of tenses must be multiplied by a considerable number of stem forms. But verbs are broadly classified on formal grounds into two types: (*a*) primary or original (e.g. IE **ei-mi* 'I go', **bher-ō* 'I carry'), and (*b*) derivative, the latter distinguished by characteristic suffixes (e.g. causative with suffix **-eịo-*: **sod-eịō* 'I make to sit'). Both Sanskrit and Greek again contribute to the reconstruction of three distinguishable tense forms in Indo-European, viz. present, aorist, and perfect. Each of these was capable of expressing the points of time known as past, present (achronic), and future. Moreover, the present tense expressed the notion of the past by the 'historic present' (*praesens historicus*); the aorist saw the present in the 'gnomic aorist' (*aoristus gnomicus*); and the perfect combined the notion of the past (as in Sanskrit and the Classical languages) with that of the present (cf. the Germanic preterite-present tenses).

57. Study of Slavonic aspect has led investigators to the conclusion that the Indo-European verb did not originally express time, but rather mode of action (G. *Aktionsart*) or aspect, i.e. the dichotomy of imperfective or durative and perfective or completive. This distinction inheres in the Greek tense-system and is also found elsewhere. In Slavonic and Germanic, for instance, prefixation makes an imperfective verb perfective. Hirt[1] inclines to the view that the initial contrast lay between the present as imperfective and the aorist as perfective.

58. The present stem gave rise to the imperfect, which survives in Sanskrit and Greek, is characterized by an augment (Skt *a-*, Gk *è-*), and constitutes a later development in Indo-European. It possesses, moreover, the imperfective force characteristic of the present-stem verb.

[1] H. Hirt and H. Arntz, op. cit., pp. 102–4.

59. The aorist, in contrast to the imperfect, is archaic and takes two distinct forms, viz. the radical, which is completely like the imperfect in structure, and the sigmatic, which contains the characteristic formant *-s- (cf. Gk ἔ-λαβ-o-ν 'I took' with ἔ-δειξ-α 'I showed' < ἔ-δεικ-σ-α).

60. As the Indo-European aorist was distinguished by its augment, the perfect was seemingly distinguished by reduplication, although this feature could on occasion be absent (cf. Skt véda, Gk οἶδα, Goth. wáit 'I know' with Skt ca-kára 'I have done', Gk λέ-λοιπα 'I have left', L. ce-cini 'I have sung').

61. The pluperfect, as an augment tense, shows the characteristics of both aorist (and imperfect) and perfect in having both augment and reduplication (e.g. Skt a-ca-cáks-am 'I had seen', Gk ἐ-πε-πράγ-μην 'I had made').

62. The future tense belongs to the present-stem group and seems, like the aorist and imperfect, to have been sigmatic, at least by the evidence of Sanskrit, Greek, and Lithuanian: the characteristic suffix *-si̯o-/*-əsi̯o- appears in Skt dā-syá-mi 'I shall give', Doric Gk δω-σέ-ω 'id.' (Att. δώ-σ-ω), and Lith. dúo-siu 'id.'

63. Of the nominal forms of the verb, we may note that Indo-European had numerous infinitives, which were characterized by the suffixes *-tu- (e.g. Skt kár-tum <√*kar- 'to do', L. supines in -tum, -tu; cf. also Balt. and Slav. locative-style infinitives in -ti), *-men- (e.g. Skt dámane, Hom. Gk δόμεναι 'to give' < IE *√do-), and *-s- (e.g. Skt jīváse 'to live', L. vīvere 'id'. < IE dat. *gʷii̯es-ai, loc. gʷī-i̯es-i respectively). The participles show other formants than *-i̯es/-i̯os-, viz. *-nt-, *-meno-, *-no-, and *-to-, which may be seen in Gk φέρων 'carrying' < φέροντ-, φερόμενος 'carried', OCS дѣланъ 'worked', and Gk στατός 'placed' respectively.

64. Syntax. Concentrating first on the morphology and then on the phonology of Indo-European, investigation tended to neglect syntax and give it no more than superficial attention, and it was not till Delbrück added the three volumes of his *Vergleichende Syntax der indogermanischen Sprachen* to Brugmann's *Grundriss* between 1893 and 1900 that Indo-European syntax won recognition. Since then it has received some attention,[1]

---

[1] J. Wackernagel, *Vorlesungen über Syntax*, i–ii, Bâle, 1920–4 (1928²); H. Hirt, *Indogermanische Grammatik*, vi–vii, Halle, 1934–7.

but its comparative neglect has led G. S. Lane[1] to describe it as the 'stepchild of linguistic science'.

65. Syntactic investigation has been centred mainly in the sentence, although other forms of syntagma, usually called 'phrases' in English, have not been neglected. This may be seen in the attention given, for instance, to the use of cases and to problems of congruence. The sentence itself, however, has furnished the background for these.

66. In Indo-European the sentence comprised certain autonomous elements called words, which were defined both phonologically and morphologically. The fundamental distinction in the sentence was based on the 'logical' opposition of subject and predicate or, in terms of their principal grammatical representatives, of noun and verb. The opposition of noun and verb, moreover, enables us to recognize nominal and verbal sentences. A nominal sentence, expressing, say, quality or possession, consists generally of two components or members connected by a copula, most often the verb 'to be'. A verbal sentence, on the other hand, indicates a process or state and may consist of a verb alone, in which the subject is implied as well as formally expressed in terms of person (cf. Gk λείπω with E. *I leave*). The subject noun may be qualified by adjectives, and the verb, in its turn, by noun complement or adverbial 'extension'. These are 'appositions' in the widest sense of the term; and apposition is a characteristic feature of Indo-European syntax. It may, for instance, bind nominal and verbal syntagmata into one sentence (e.g. L. *Caesarem appellant imperatorem* 'they name Caesar emperor', Gk τὸν Μῆδον ἴσμεν ἐλθόντα 'we know that the Mede came'), or it may lead to an accumulation of determinants or qualifiers. Accumulation of subjects and predicates is also possible, and here the conjunctive particles play their part: 'and' and 'or' are attested for Indo-European (cf. Skt *ca*, Gk τε, L. *-que* 'and', with Skt *vā*, Hom. Gk ἠέ < ἠ(ϝ)έ, L. *-ue* 'or').

67. As the words in the sentence are autonomous, they have to be connected by various devices. The simplest of these has just been mentioned. More complicated are the congruence of subject and verb in number and person, the congruence o determined (qualified) and determinant (qualifier) in number, gender, and case, government of noun or pronoun by verb, preposition or post-position, and appositional agreement in case. These congruences or concordances, whether total or partial, mould Indo-European sentence structure and determine its idiosyncrasy.

68. Where 'intrinsic' links exist between the components of the sentence, word-order as a bond between words will be of less account. In Indo-European accordingly word-order had rather an affective than a logically determined syntactic value, although habit tended to arrange words in a particular, if variable, succession. The variability in the position of words in the Indo-European sentence may be seen in the position of the verb, say, in Sanskrit and Old Irish. The verb closes the sentence in the former and opens it in the latter. It has been assumed that Ancient Greek practice, which places the principal or emphatic word first, is nearest to the conjectured Indo-European usage. The accessory words would then follow this word to form an enclitic group. Negation and interrogation do not appear to have demanded a special arrangement of words. Co-ordination took place mainly by means of the juxtaposition of co-ordinates, but particles would seem to have been present too, first to emphasize and then to conjoin (e.g. Gk μέν . . . δέ 'on the one hand . . . on the other').

69. Hirt[1] supposes that the archaic Indo-European had no hypotactic or subordinative constructions, but is willing to concede that they antedated the disintegration of the protoglossa. The earliest subordinate clauses would seem to have been relative, and, as E. Windisch[2] has shown, the relative pronouns appear to have grown out of the anaphoric (e.g. *i̯o). As for subordination by particle, it is reasonable to suppose that it may have followed subordination by participle, which in Indo-European was a well-articulated category. The participial construction would still help to vary the emergent relative clause as attribute or complement. But it may be plausibly conjectured that anaphoric indices were known and used in the early stages of development.

---

[1] H. Hirt and H. Arntz, op. cit., p. 192.
[2] *Altindische Studien*, ii. Referred to in op. cit. in n. 1.

70. The difficult subject of Indo-European word-order has been complicated by certain assumptions. Hirt,[1] for instance, is inclined to surmise that the Indo-European protoglossa had a rigid word-order before it developed its elaborate system of flexion. When this emerged it had a general relaxing effect, for sense was now determined partly by congruence and partly by juxtaposition. In his study of syntax, however, Delbrück[2] did not distinguish the characteristics of a possible earlier and later phase of Indo-European syntactic development and accordingly posited a general twofold word-order—regular and occasional, the latter being interpreted as a projection of the former. The verb, he surmised, must have had final place in the Indo-European sentence (e.g. L. *puer patrem amat* 'the boy loves his father'). In point of fact, the position of the verb in the Indo-European sentence, as disclosed by Indo-European language-types, varies considerably, and our Latin example containing three terms may theoretically have six permutations without the meaning of the sentence being affected.

71. There are similar free variations in the priority of determined and determinant (cf. Gk Διόσκουροι 'Dioscuri' [Castor and Pollux] with θυγάτηρ Διός 'daughter of Zeus'), but here a consensus of evidence—case and personal endings, apposition, derivation by suffix—would seem to suggest post-position of the determinant as the more characteristic, although possibly not for the earliest stage of Indo-European.

72. Vocabulary. Lexical concordance among Indo-European languages of various date helps the investigator to establish the nuclear vocabulary of the Indo-European protoglossa. The concordance must be both phonetic and semantic to be trustworthy, though where phonetic concordance exists allowance is made for semantic divergencies. The reverse, however, cannot be maintained.

73. Following the ancient Indian grammarians, the European etymologist tries to extract the radical part ($\sqrt{}$) common to the collated words. This has led to his recognition of 'roots'. Thus Skt *dhūmáḥ* 'smoke, vapour', Gk θυμός 'spirit', L. *fūmus* 'smoke', Lith. *dúmai* 'id.', OCS дꙑмъ 'id.', are traced back to an IE **dhū-mo-s*, in which the first element is the root, represented by

---

[1] H. Hirt und H. Arntz, op. cit., pp. 193–5.   [2] Ibid., p. 194.

the multiple correlation of *dhū-θū-fū-dū-dy*. Here, as we can see, the discrepancies are partly phonetic (cf. *dhū-* : *fū-*) and partly semantic (cf. 'smoke': 'spirit'). Yet both types of discrepancies can easily be reconciled. Such roots with various enlargements, viz. 'determinatives' and formants, are the kind of phonetic-semantic complexes which can at best be postulated for Indo-European and constitute its vocabulary.

74. Much importance has been attached to the semantic side of the vocabulary, and scholarship has succeeded in recovering the outlines of the Indo-European community and its culture by the collation of fragmentary lexical material. The vocabulary shared by this community consisted of relationship terms (e.g. the word for 'father': Skt *pitár-*, Arm. *hair*, Toch. A *pācar*, Toch. B *pātar*, Gk πατήρ, L. *pater*, OIr. *athir*, Goth. *fadar* < IE *pətér*); names of domestic animals (e.g. the word for 'sheep': Skt *áviḥ*, Gk ὄ(ϝ)ις, L. *ouis*, OIr. *ōi*, OE *ēowu* < IE *óuis*) and plants (e.g. the word for 'tree': Skt *dâru* 'wood', Av. *dāuru* 'id.', Hitt. *taru* 'id.', Gk δρῦς 'oak' and δόρυ 'shaft', OIr. *daur* 'oak', Goth. *triu* 'tree', Lith. *dervà* 'tree-stump'; 'tar', OCS дрѣво 'tree' < IE *doru/*drū-/*drou-/*dreu*); religious terms (e.g. the word for 'God': Skt *deváḥ* 'God', L. *deus*, pl. *dīuī* 'god[s]', Osc. *deívaí* 'dīuae', OIr. *dia*, OI *tīvar* 'gods', Lith. *diēvas* 'God' < IE *déiu̯os*); names of various objects (e.g. the word for 'wheel': Skt *ráthaḥ* 'chariot', Av. *raθa-* 'id.', L. *rota* 'wheel', OIr. *roth* 'id.', OHG *rad* 'id.', Lith. *rãtas* 'id.' < IE *reth-* 'to run'); names of parts of the body (e.g. the word for 'heart': Skt *hŕdayam*, Av. *zərəδaēm*, Hitt. *kardi-*, Gk καρδία, L. *cor(dis)*, OIr. *cride*, Goth. *haírtō*, OPr. *seyr*, Lith. *širdìs*, OCS срѣдьце < IE *k̑rd-*); colour adjectives (e.g. the word for 'red': Skt *rudhiráḥ*, Toch. B *rätre*, Gk ἐρυθρός, L. *rūfus*, OIr. *rūad*, Goth. *rauþs*, Lith. *raũdas*, OCS роудъ < IE *reudh-*); numerals (e.g. the word for 'five': Skt *páñca*, Av. *panča*, Arm. *hing*, Toch. B *piś*, Gk πέντε, L. *quīnque*, OIr. *cóic*, OW *pimp*, Goth. *fimf*, Lith. *penkì*, OCS пѧть < IE *penku̯e*); and names of certain acts and processes (e.g. the word for 'to sew': Skt *syūtáḥ* 'sewn', L. *suo* 'to sew', Goth. *siujan* 'id.', Lith. *siúti* 'id.', OCS шити 'id.' < IE *si̯ū-*).

75. This basic vocabulary must have been notably enlarged by loans resulting from the contacts of Indo-European with other language-groups. To some of these, viz. Semitic and Uralian, attempts have been made from time to time to bind it with genetic ties,[1] but such ties are inevitably altogether too slender to command acceptance at this stage. They are, in any case, very remote in time, being beyond the normal modest limits of the prehistory of Indo-European, which, as we have come now to realize, is a creation of synchronic linguistics by the telescoping of the time factor.

II. COMMON SLAVONIC

76. General. The foregoing sketch is the historical preface to an account of the structure of Common Slavonic (Proto-Slavonic), the conjectured protoglossa from which modern Russian and its Slavonic cognates may be said to derive. The unity of the Slavonic languages, summarized in this form, admits of no doubt. It is due to common origin and the parallel development which this has entailed. The development has been considerable in the historical period, yet in spite of notable divergences, the common characteristics have been preserved.

77. There are seven groups of Slavonic languages, viz. the East Slavonic (Russian, White Russian, and Ukrainian), Polish and Cassubian-Slovincian (Pomeranian), the two Lusatian languages (Upper and Lower), Czech and Slovak, Serbo-Croatian and Slovene, Macedonian and Bulgarian, and the extinct Polabian and Drevanian. The affinity of the Polish, Lusatian, and Czech groups on the one hand and that of the Serbo-Croatian and Bulgarian groups on the other permits the recognition of West and South Slavonic in contrast to East Slavonic. Historically the South Slavonic group is the most important of the three, not only because the oldest-recorded Slavonic language, Old Church Slavonic, is a South Slavonic language, originally the Thessalonican form of Macedonian, but because this literary language is usually regarded as having most of the characteristic features ascribed to Common Slavonic, at least in the later stages of this conjectured language, i.e. in and after the sixth century A.D., when as the result of tribal migrations dialectal differences were intensified.

---

[1] B. Collinder, *Indo-Uralisches Sprachgut. Die Urverwandtschaft zwischen der indo-europäischen und der uralischen—finnisch-ugrisch-samojedischen—Sprachfamilie*, Uppsala, 1934.

78. The earlier stages of Common Slavonic can be pieced together by collation of Old Church Slavonic with the evidence of the Baltic languages, especially Lithuanian.[1] The strong resemblance between Baltic and Slavonic has inclined some scholars to postulate a 'Balto-Slavonic' protoglossa[2] as an intermediate stage in the development of one dialect of Indo-European into Common Slavonic. The argument against such a procedure is that it leads to sterile refinements of essentially hypothetical data. It is sufficient to know Common Slavonic as we know, say, Common Greek, Common Italic, and Common Germanic and to see in these the result of divergent development from the even more hypothetical Indo-European protoglossa.

79. Phonology. The structure of Common Slavonic, to which data taken from all the recorded Slavonic languages have contributed, is, as we have seen, a later stage of the development of one type of Indo-European by the processes of simplification, levelling, and innovation. Its system of vowel phonemes comprises eleven items:

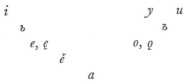

whose relation to the Indo-European system may be indicated diagrammatically as follows:[3]

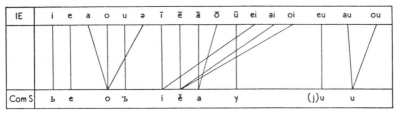

---

[1] See, for example, the comparative table in R. Ekblom, *Die frühe dorsale Palatalisierung im Slavischen*, Uppsala, 1951, pp. 84–85.

[2] W. K. Matthews, 'The Interrelations of Baltic and Slavonic' (*SEER*, xxxv, 85, London, 1957) and 'O vzaimootnošenii slavjanskich i baltijskich jazykov' (*Slavjanskaja filologija, Sbornik statej*, I, Moscow, 1958, pp. 27–44).

[3] This diagram has been adapted from the diagram on p. 46 of B. Rosenkranz, *Historische Laut- und Formenlehre des Altbulgarischen*, The Hague–Heidelberg, 1955, which in its turn was taken with modifications from p. 47 of H. Krahe, *Indogermanische Sprachwissenschaft*, Berlin, 1943.

As the diagram shows, Common Slavonic *i*, *u*, and *a* are each of twofold origin, and *ě* and *o* exhibit the coincidence of three Indo-European sounds. Common Slavonic *i* may go back, like *ě*, to Indo-European *$*ai$ (> *$*oi$), and this *i* may be distinguished from the product of Indo-European *$*ī$ and *$*ei$ as *i$_2$*, just as *ě*, resulting from Indo-European *$*ai$/*$*oi$ (cf. ComS *sněgъ* with Goth. *snaiws* 'snow'), may be distinguished from *ě*, which ascends to Indo-European *ē*, as *ě$_2$* (cf. ComS *sěmę* with L. *sēmen* 'seed'). One Indo-European source of *ę* is the syllabic nasals *m̨*, *n̨*, including their positional variants *n̨̥* and *m̨̥* (e.g. ComS *pa-mętь* 'memory' < IE *$*mn̥tis$; cf. L. *mens*, gen. *mentis* 'mind'). The other source of *ę*, as of *ǫ*, is the corresponding oral vowel followed by a nasal consonant, which is itself followed by a consonant (e.g. ComS *tętiva* 'bowstring' with Skt *tantúh* 'string'; ComS *zǫbъ* 'tooth' with Skt *jámbhah* 'tooth', Gk *γόμφος* 'bolt'). Indo-European syllabic *l̥* and *r̥* gave either *ъl* and *ъr* or *ьl* and *ьr*, according to whether they had a palatal or a velar quality respectively (cf. ComS *sьrdьce* 'heart' < IE *$*k̑r̥d$- with Lith. *širdìs*, and ComS *vьlkъ* 'wolf' < IE *$* u̯l̥k^{u}os$ with Gk *λύκος*). Alternatively, ComS *ьl*/*ьr* and *ъl*/*ъr* could be palatal or velar syllabic liquids (cf. OCS ль/рь and лъ/ръ). Our Slavonic combinations of vowel and liquid are paralleled in Lithuanian by *ir*/*il*, which help to define the phonetic quality of *ь* as ɪ. Other Lithuanian data enable us to interpret *ъ* as ω (cf. ComS *vьrхъ* 'top' with Lith. *viršùs*). Both these 'reduced' vowels appear to have been short and lax in articulation. The nasal vowels *ę* and *ǫ* were pronounced ɛ̃ and ɔ̃ respectively, and *ě* would seem to have been phonetically æ. All these values 'reappear' in Old Church Slavonic and are, indeed, derived from the latter.

80. The Common Slavonic consonantal system, as compared with that of Indo-European, is poorer in plosives and richer in fricatives. It may be represented by the following arrangement:

p/*b*	*t*/*d*			*k*/*g*
(*f*)/*v*	*s*/*z*	*š'*/*ž'*	*j*	*x*
	c'/*dz'*	*č'*/*dž'*		
m	*n*		*n'*	
			l	*l'*
			r	*r'*

These consonants, like the Common Slavonic vowels, may be

diagrammatically juxtaposed with the Indo-European so as to
show their origin.[1]

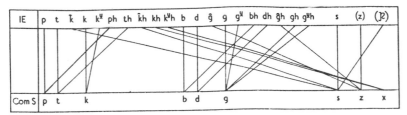

The labial and dental plosives are each derived from two sets of
Indo-European counterparts, viz. the simple and the aspirated:
thus Common Slavonic *d* goes back to both Indo-European *d
and *dh (cf. ComS *domъ* 'house' with Gk δόμος, and ComS *medъ*
'honey' with Skt *mádhu*). Of the velar plosives, *g* has four Indo-
European sources, for this language had velars and labio-
velars; but Indo-European *k* and *kᵘ gave Common Slavonic *k*,
whereas Indo-European *kh and *kᵘh developed into Common
Slavonic *x* (cf. ComS *kolo* 'wheel' with Gk κύκλος, ComS
soxa 'plough' with Skt *śakha* 'branch'). The hiss-sibilants too are
of various origins: thus Common Slavonic *s/z* derive not only
from Indo-European **s/*(*z), but also from *k̂/ĝ* (cf. ComS
sъrdьce 'heart' with Gk καρδία, and ComS *zǫbъ* 'tooth' with Gk
γόμφος 'bolt'). The hush-sibilants are of later origin than the
hiss-sibilants, being in fact derived from these. Other Common
Slavonic, as distinct from Indo-European, consonants are *x*
(< IE *s as well as from voiceless aspirated velars), *v* (< IE *u̯*),
and *f*, which appears first in foreign loans at a late period. Moreover, the presence of the palatal series *n'*, *l'*, and *r'* in Common
Slavonic is attested by Old Church Slavonic evidence.

81. The Common Slavonic system of phonemes accordingly
retains only the framework and not the details of the Indo-European system. Our diagrams show radical simplification in both
cases. The vowels no longer merely contrast long and short as in
Indo-European, but relative length is complicated by differences of quality, and a set of qualitatively distinct long vowels
is opposed to a set of equally distinct short (e.g. *ě/a* as against
e/o) and very short or 'reduced' vowels (e.g. *i/y* as against *ь/ъ*).

[1] The diagram here has been taken with modifications from the one on p. 69 of
H. Krahe, *Indogermanische Sprachwissenschaft*, Berlin, 1943.

But this opposition of vowels on the basis of length is also obscured by the parallel opposition on the basis of quality. Front (R. 'soft') vowels are contrasted with back (R. 'hard') in the following set of correlations:

$$i \quad \mathfrak{b} \quad e \quad ę \quad ě \quad (j)u$$
$$y \quad \mathfrak{z} \quad o \quad ǫ \quad a \quad u$$

These correlations, combined with those of length, permeate the entire system of Common Slavonic morphology as vocalic alternation or apophony (e.g. ComS berǫ 'I take', bьrati 'to take', sьborъ 'assembly'; ComS tręsti 'to shake', tręsъ 'earthquake', where we find the alternations e/ь/o and ę/ǫ respectively).

82. The Indo-European long diphthongs are treated in the same way as the short in Common Slavonic and may be said to be subsumed under these. They are invariably 'monophthongized': thus *ei > i, *ai, *oi > ě, *eu > (j)u, and *au, *ou > u. This applies also to the 'nasal diphthongs' (vowel + nasal consonant) which become the nasal vowels ę and ǫ in Common Slavonic (cf. ComS męti 'to crush' with Lith. mìnti, and ComS dǫga 'rainbow' with Lith. dangùs 'sky').

83. Simplification of 'liquid diphthongs' (vowel + l or r) leads to metathesis in some forms of Slavonic and to pleophony (R. polnoglasije) or flanking vowels in others: thus ol/or, el/er > la/ra, lě/rě in South Slavonic and olo/oro, elo, olo (< ele)/oro in East Slavonic (e.g. ComS gordъ 'town' > OCS градъ OR gorodъ; ComS volsъ 'hair' > OCS власъ OR volosъ; ComS melko 'milk' > OCS млѣко OR moloko; ComS dervo 'tree'>OCS дрѣво OR derevo). Pleophony, an East Slavonic feature, is graded chronologically as primary (see the above examples) and secondary and both represent the operation of the 'law' of open syllables.[1]

84. Initially v appears before ъ and y (cf. ComS vy- 'out-' with OE ūt), and prothetic j figures sporadically before front vowels and a (cf. the hesitation between a and ja in OCS агньць/ꙗгньць 'lamb'). These protheses are connected with the tendency to palatalize and to velarize, which finds other modes of expression

---

[1] W. K. Matthews, 'The Phonetic Basis of Pleophony in East Slavonic' (*SEER*, xxxvi. 86, London, 1957).

in Common Slavonic (§§ 86–89). In East Slavonic the reverse tendency may be seen in the substitution of *o* for initial *je-* and in the lapse of *j* in initial *ju-* (cf. OCS ѥзеро 'lake' with OR *ozero*; OCS юха 'broth' with OR *uxa*).

85. The Common Slavonic consonantal system is also simpler and more balanced than the Indo-European: there is no longer a preponderance of plosives, as in the latter; and the fricative series is much better represented, although there still remain unpaired types of phonemes, viz. *v*, *j*, and *x*, some of which acquire correlatives after the disintegration of Common Slavonic (e.g. *x* becomes part of the *x/γ* correlation). There is, moreover, greater variety among the dental–alveolar sonants. Compare, for instance, the two types of *l*, palatal and velar.

86. In contrast to the majority of the consonants in the Common Slavonic system, the hush-sibilants (F. *chuintantes*) *š'/ž'* and the affricates *c'/dz'*, *č'/dž'* (> *ž'*) are palatalized by nature. Some of them derive from the palatalization of velar *k*, *g*, *x* in certain phonetic environments. Three palatalizations are recognized in Slavonic scholarship and are thought to have taken place at chronologically different periods. The primary and oldest was regressive and gave rise to *č'*, *ž'*, and *š'* as the result of the action of *j* (iotacization) or of a front vowel (except *i₂*, *ě₂*) on a velar consonant (e.g. ComS nom. sg. *vьlkъ* 'wolf', voc. *vьlče*; ComS nom. sg. *bogъ* 'God', voc. *bože*; ComS nom. sg. *duxъ* 'spirit', voc. *duše*). The secondary palatalization shows the influence of *i₂* and *ě₂*, derived from Indo-European diphthongs, which converted *k*, *g*, *x* into *c'*, *dz'*, *s'* (e.g. ComS dat. sg. *rǫcě* < nom. sg. *rǫka* 'hand'; nom. pl. *bodzi* < nom. sg. *bogъ* 'God'; nom. pl. *dusi* < nom. sg. *duxъ* 'spirit'). The tertiary palatalization was progressive and was brought about by the influence of a preceding front vowel, viz. *i*, *ь*, *ę*, on a following velar consonant. It resulted in the same sibilant phonemes as the secondary palatalization (e.g. ComS *otьcь* 'father' < *otьkъ*; ComS *kъnędzь* 'prince' < Gc *kuning-*; ComS *vьsь* 'all' < *vьxъ* < *vьsъ*, cf. Lith. *visas* 'id.').[1]

---

[1] R. Ekblom (op. cit. p. 3) names our tertiary palatalization 'the second' and our secondary palatalization 'the third', but seems to prefer phonetic rather than numerical designations, so that our primary palatalization becomes 'the apical', our secondary 'the late dorsal', and our tertiary 'the early dorsal'. A. Vaillant (see *Grammaire comparée des langues slaves*, i, Lyons, 1950) thinks that the secondary and tertiary palatalizations were contemporaneous.

87. A form of indirect palatalization of velars is illustrated by the change of *kv/gv* before *i, ě* < IE *ai, *oi, into *cv/zv*. The palatalized group *zv* probably passed through the intermediate stage *dzv* (cf. Mac. sвезда 'star'). This form of palatalization is known only to South and East Slavonic (cf. OCS and OR *cvětъ* 'flower' with P. *kwiat*, Cz. *květ*; OCS and OR *zvězda* 'star' with P. *gwiazda*, Cz. *hvězda*).[1]

88. Of the palatalizing elements the most potent was *j* (iotacization), whose operation may be seen in the transformation of hiss-sibilants (F. *sifflantes*) into hush-sibilants (e.g. ComS *nošǫ* 'I carry' < *nosjǫ*; ComS *mažǫ* 'I smear' < *mazjǫ*) and of dentals as well as velars, and combinations of either with sibilants into affricates (e.g. ComS *svěča* 'candle' < *světja*; ComS *medža* 'border' < *medja*; ComS *pušča* 'waste' < *pustja*; ComS *ježdžǫ* 'I ride' < *jezdjǫ*; ComS *iščǫ* 'I seek' < *iskjǫ*; ComS *dъždžъ* 'rain' < *dъzgj-*). Here we may also mention the 'affrication' of *t* with a preceding *k/g* before *i* (e.g. ComS *noč̌ь* 'night' < *noktь*, cf. Lith. *naktìs*; ComS *moči* 'to be able' < *mogti*).

89. A divergent form of iotacization was the development of epenthetic *l* between a labial and *j* (e.g. ComS *spljǫ* 'I sleep' < *spjǫ*; ComS *ljubljǫ* 'I love' < *ljubjǫ*).

90. Simplification of consonantal groups is a feature of Common Slavonic, and the absence of geminates or reduplicated consonants is part of the same tendency. But simplification does not take place in all cases: thus the group *str* is possible in all positions, except finally (e.g. ComS *struja* 'stream', *sestra* 'sister', *ostrъ* 'sharp', cf. Lith. *aštrùs*). It will be seen here that the tolerated consonantal group exhibits a medial plosive which is flanked by a preceding sibilant and a following sonant. Where sibilant precedes plosive, the group remains, unless it is palatalized (e.g. *sp/zb*, *st/zd*, *sk/sg*). But where sibilant follows plosive, the latter tends to disappear (e.g. ComS aor. *rěxъ* 'I spoke' < *rěkxъ* < *rěksъ*) as it does before another plosive (e.g. ComS *greti* 'to row' < *grebti*) or before *l* (e.g. ComS *plelъ* 'woven' < *pletlъ*; ComS *moliti* 'to pray' < *modliti*). The simplification of consonantal groups contributed to the tendency to create open syllables, which is, as we have seen, a characteristic of Common Slavonic as compared with Indo-European. This state of things

[1] Cf. also Lith. *žvaigždė*, Latv. *zvaigzne* 'star'.

is reflected in tenth-century Old Church Slavonic, but gradually gave way to closed syllables in all the other forms of Slavonic, including Old Russian with its apocope of final ъ, ь (§§ 284). The emergence of open syllables in Common Slavonic is particularly noticeable in the final position (cf. ComS *vьlkъ* 'wolf' with Skt *vŕkaḥ*, Gk λύκος, L. *lupus*, Goth. *wulfs*, Lith. *vìlkas*). Furthermore, the process of simplification, even if it pursued a subtler line of development, often gave the same result. The change of, say, *tt/dt* into *st* is a familiar instance of dissimilation which, nevertheless, left the syllable open (e.g. ComS *pa-sti* 'to fall' < *pad-ti*, cf. *padǫ* 'I fall').

91. The phonological system of Common Slavonic is conceived as implying the presence of syllabic tone combined with stress ('chromatic accent'), which is posited for the language, because this feature occurs in Serbo-Croatian and Slovene as well as in modern Baltic (Lithuanian and Latvian), Ancient Greek, and Vedic Sanskrit. The position of this pitch-stress in Common Slavonic is determined mainly by reference both to East Slavonic, notably Russian, which has dynamic stress, and to the *ča*-dialect of Serbo-Croatian with its pitch-stress (cf. SCr. *vòda* 'water' with R. *vodá*, SCr. *ča*-dial. *vodã*). The place of Common Slavonic stress corresponds sometimes to that of Greek and Sanskrit (cf. R. *nébo*, SCr. *ča*- dial. *nȅbo* 'sky' with Skt *nábhas*, Gk νέφος 'cloud'), but such correspondences are often lacking and may be explained as due to intervening phonetic and morphological changes.

92. The long vowels of Common Slavonic are assumed to have had one of two tones, viz. a level-to-falling (G. *geschleift*), indicated by the circumflex accent, and a rising (G. *gestoßen*), indicated by the acute. These tones are represented in Serbo-Croatian by the pitch and length of syllables, in Czech by differences of length only, and in Russian by the position of the syllable bearing the stress. Compare, for instance, the following correspondences:[1]

ComS	SCr.	Slov.	Cz.	R.	Lith.
vôrnъ 'raven'	*vrân*	*vrân*	*vran*	*vóron*	*vaȓnas*
vórna 'crow'	*vrâna*	*vrána*	*vrána*	*voróna*	*várna*

[1] Cf. W. K. Matthews, 'The Phonetic Basis of Pleophony in East Slavonic' (*SEER*, xxxvi. 86, London, 1957, pp. 96–97).

Here the Lithuanian tones, which may be seen to coincide with those of Common Slavonic, are given their original values. In the modern language the values are reversed, the circumflex being a rising tone and the acute a falling tone.[1] The values of these accents in Slovene will establish those of Common Slavonic. (Note that Serbo-Croatian ˋ marks a falling tone on a short syllable, the Czech acute is the length-mark, and the same sign in Russian is the stress-mark.)

93. The Russian form *voróna* 'crow' in our table illustrates a shift of stress forward in the word, which is known as progressive metatony and is the outcome here of the greater energy of the acute accent as compared with that of the circumflex.

94. A different shift or metatony is shown by mobility of stress in the Russian paradigm of declension, for instance, nom. sg. *borodá* 'beard', acc. sg. *bórodu* (cf. nom. sg. *voróna*, acc. sg. *vorónu*). Here we have an instance of the so-called Fortunatov–de Saussure 'law' which explains the shift from the initial to the final syllable as due to the attraction of either a short syllable or a long circumflex syllable in Common Slavonic, as well as in Baltic, to a following long acute syllable (e.g. ComS *bordá*).[2]

95. Morphophonology. The morphophonological structure of Indo-European, which embodies the three *procédés* of vowel alternation, stressing, and affixation, is better preserved in Sanskrit and Greek than in Common Slavonic, in which simplification has changed the paradigm of the verb without producing a correspondingly radical change in the system of declension. Apophony and stress-variation survive in Common Slavonic; and of the two types of flexion to be found in Indo-European, the thematic, in which a characteristic vowel is appended to the root, easily predominates.

96. Common Slavonic apophony or alternation is both vocalic and consonantal. The former illustrates the correlations *i/y*, *i/ě*, *ь/ъ*, *e/o*, *ę/y*, whose distribution varies markedly: thus *ę/y* is found only finally (cf. ComS gen. sg. *ženy* < nom. sg. *žena* 'woman' with

---

[1] W. K. Matthews, 'The Affinities and Structure of Lithuanian' (*SEER*, xxxv. 84, London, 1956, p. 63).

[2] J. Kuryłowicz (see 'Le Problème des intonations balto-slaves', *Rocznik Slawistyczny*, Cracow, 1952, pp. 1–80) denies the applicability of the 'law' to Slavonic. But his thesis has not yet won general acceptance.

gen. sg. *zemlję* < nom. sg. *zemlja* 'earth'), and *i/ě* is more restricted in incidence than the remaining correlations (cf. ComS loc. sg. *koni* < nom. sg. *konь* 'horse' with ComS loc. sg. *gordě* < nom. sg. *gordъ* 'town'). The *ě/a* alternation is late and occurs only where *ě* is preceded by *j*, *č*, *ž*, *š* (cf. ComS *ležati* 'to lie' < *ležěti* with *viseti* 'to hang').

97. Some vocalic alternations point to quantitative distinctions, viz. *ъ/i* (< IE *i/*$\bar{\imath}$), *e/ě* (< IE *e/*$\bar{e}$), *o/a* (< IE *o/*$\bar{o}$), *ъ/y* (< IE *u/*$\bar{u}$) (e.g. ComS *dъxnǫti/dyxati* 'to breathe'), others to a diphthongal origin (e.g. *i/ě* < IE *ei/*oi in OCS цвисти 'to bloom'/ цвѣтъ 'flower'; *e/o* < IE *en/*on in ComS *tęgati* 'to tug'/*tǫgъ* 'tight'). The alternation of Indo-European *eu/*ou appears to have lapsed in Common Slavonic through the change of *eu > (*j*)*u* and of *ou > *u*: where *u̯* gave *v*, the preceding *e* tended to become *o* (cf. OCS плове́ 'I swim' with Gk πλέ($\digamma$)ω 'I sail'). The comparatively clear Indo-European system of vowel alternation has thus been considerably obscured in Common Slavonic, with concomitant complication of the apophonic series in word-formation and flexion.

98. Common Slavonic consonantal alternation was historically determined by the vowel system. We recall the two types of palatalization of velars, primary and secondary, and find the alternations that these gave rise to, viz. *k/č'/c'*, *g/ž'/dz'*, *x/š'/s'*, to be associated with those of vowels. The velars do not occur before front vowels (cf. ComS nom. sg. *vъlkъ* 'wolf' with voc. sg. *vъlče*, nom. pl. *vъlci*); the hiss-sibilants occur only before *i*, *ě*, which are of diphthongal origin (cf. ComS nom. pl. *vъlci* 'wolves' with Lith. nom. pl. *vilkaĩ*); and the hush-sibilants are not followed by *ě* in the late period (cf. ComS *slyšati* 'to hear' with *sěděti* 'to sit'). The dentals also exhibit alternation with sibilants and affricates, viz. *t/č*, *d/dž*, *s/š*, *z/ž* (e.g. ComS *světъ* 'light'/*svěča* 'candle'; ComS *nositi* 'to carry'/*nošǫ* 'I carry').

99. Word-formation. The system of Common Slavonic alternations shapes both word-formation and flexion. In word-formation it is apparent in root as well as in formant; in flexion it is naturally confined to the latter. As in Indo-European, word-formation here employs a threefold set of affixes. Among nouns in the widest sense of this word the suffix prevails; among verbs we find all three types, viz. prefix, infix, and suffix. Like Indo-

European again, Common Slavonic makes use of composition as well as derivation, but limits the process to nouns (cf. ComS *vodonosъ* 'water-carrier' with Gk ὑδροφόρος 'id.').

100. In nominal derivation some suffixes were productive in Common Slavonic (e.g. *-ьba*: ComS *borьba* 'conflict'), and others unproductive (e.g. ComS *-telь*: *datelь* 'giver'). The former included *-dlo* (e.g. ComS *ordlo* 'plough'), the diminutive formant *-k-* (e.g. ComS *učenikъ* 'disciple'), the adjectival *-n-* (e.g. ComS masc. nom. sg. *zimьnъ* 'wintry'), the abstract *-ostь* (e.g. ComS *bělostь* 'whiteness'), and the comparative (*-jьs-/-ьs-*), which appeared in the paradigm as *-jьš'-/ьš'* through palatalization (e.g. ComS fem. nom. sg. *mьn'ьši* 'less').

101. In the formation of Common Slavonic verbs the suffix is again in evidence, although the prefix, with some help from suffixes, is important in the construction of aspectual forms, and the infix is occasionally resorted to (e.g. *-n-* in ComS *sędǫ* 'I sit down' as compared with *sěsti* 'to sit down').

102. Derivation by suffix as well as by prefix occurs outside the major parts of speech, viz. in the particles (e.g. ComS *vъn-ǫtri* 'inside'). Here we often find flexional forms drawn upon to construct adverbs as well as prepositions (e.g. ComS *medžu* 'between'). Moreover, the neuter nominative–accusative forms of adjectives perform adverbial functions (e.g. ComS *bystro* 'quickly'); but other cases of adjective as well as of substantive, especially the instrumental and locative, are used also (e.g. ComS masc. instr. or acc. pl. *mǫžьsky* 'in manly fashion' < nom. sg. *mǫžьskъ* 'manly'; ComS loc. sg. *vьrxu* 'above' < *vьrxъ* 'top'). These are sometimes unrecognizable (e.g. ComS *doma* 'at home', cf. L. *domī*). Prepositional phrases also present a syntagmatic relationship or fixed congruence between preposition and noun, which may be treated as an adverbial unit (e.g. ComS *vъs-pętь* 'back').

103. Morphology. Flexion, unlike word-formation, belongs to this sector of linguistics, as it is controlled by the grammatical processes which express themselves in syntactic constructions. It may be nominal or verbal, as in Indo-European.

104. Nominal flexion assumes the form of declension, and here we have to note several types according to the part of speech involved. There is nevertheless a general major dichotomy: on the one hand, we have the substantival paradigms and, on the other hand, the pronominal. Adjectives, numerals, and participles show characteristics of both types of declension. The two types not merely present a case-system, but express threefold gender and number. It is customary to classify the substantives from the standpoint of flexion according to their stem forms. This gives us masculine and neuter o/jo-stems (e.g. ComS masc. *vьlkъ* 'wolf'/*konь* 'horse'; neut. *selo* 'settlement'/*pole* 'field' < *polje*), mostly feminine *ā/jā*-stems (e.g. ComS fem. *žena* 'woman'/*zemlja* 'earth'), masculine and feminine *i*-stems (e.g. ComS masc. *gostь* 'guest', fem. *kostь* 'bone'), exclusively masculine *u*-stems (e.g. ComS *synъ* 'son'), exclusively feminine *ū*-stems (e.g. ComS *svekry* 'mother-in-law'), and consonantal stems which are shared among all three genders (e.g. ComS masc. *n*-stem *kamy*, gen. *kamene* 'stone'; neut. *s*-stem *slovo*, gen. *slovese* 'word'; fem. *r*-stem *mati*, gen. *matere* 'mother').

105. The paradigms which each of these words helps to construct contain a maximum of seven cases, viz. nominative, accusative, genitive, dative, instrumental, locative, and vocative, multiplied by three numbers, including a dual. This would give a theoretical optimum of twenty-one distinct forms, but Common Slavonic does not seem to have had so many. Its successors, including Old Church Slavonic, show formal coincidences in all three numbers, and especially in the dual, whose seven cases furnish only three distinct forms. It may be plausibly assumed that stress was called in to distinguish homophones (e.g. ComS masc. acc. and instr. pl. *vьlky*; fem. gen. sg. and nom. pl. *ženy*), but that this was done in all cases of homophony can hardly be maintained (e.g. ComS neut. nom.–acc.–voc. sg. and pl. *seló/séla* respectively). It is characteristic of Common Slavonic that the 'extragrammatical' or concrete cases—dative, locative, instrumental—are less prone to confusion, except in the dual, than the rest. Accordingly, we find masculine nominative and accusative forms to be identical in the singular and different in the plural, and the same two cases of a feminine paradigm to be identical in the plural and different in the singular.

106. The adjective in Common Slavonic is not distinct in flexion from the substantive (cf. ComS masc.–fem.–neut. sg.

nᴜvъ/nova/novo 'new' with masc. *vъlkъ*, fem. *žena*, neut. *selo*), except at a later stage, when we find an attempt to distinguish between definite (determinate) and indefinite (indeterminate) by indicating the first with a suffixed demonstrative pronoun, as in Baltic (cf. ComS *novъ-jъ, nova-ja, novo-je* 'the new' with Lith. *naujàs-is, naujó-ji* 'id.'). It is the flexion of this pronoun which gives the definite or 'articulate' adjective its pronominal paradigm, whereas the declension of the basic or 'short' adjective is indistinguishable from that of the substantive. The typically pronominal system of declension is that of the demonstrative, possessive, interrogative, and indefinite group of pronouns. As with substantives, the cases here are not all formally differentiated: nominative and accusative are identical in the masculine and neuter singular (e.g. ComS *tъ, to* 'that'), and in the plural the genitive and locative show the same form (e.g. ComS *tĕxъ*) as indeed they do in the dual (e.g. ComS *toju*). The demonstrative pronoun *jъ–ja–je* is also the nucleus of the relative or anaphoric *jъ-že, ja-že, je-že*, and here it is declined as it is when functioning as the termination of the definite adjective.

107. Distinct from the pronominal group in paradigm are the personal pronouns, which are strictly confined to the first two persons and have suppletive forms as between singular on the one hand and dual and plural on the other (cf. ComS sg. *azъ* 'I', *ty* 'thou' with du. *vĕ* 'we two', *va* 'you two', and pl. *my* 'we', *vy* 'you'). The endings of the cases themselves are familiar from the nominal paradigm, but their distribution is different (cf. ComS gen.–acc. sg. *mene* 'of me, me' with *kamene* 'of stone'; dat. *mъnĕ* 'to me' with *ženĕ* 'to (the) woman'; instr. *mъnojǫ* 'by me' with *ženojǫ* 'by (the) woman'). The personal type of pronoun also differs from the larger demonstrative group by having enclitic forms which reduplicate some of the cases (e.g. ComS acc. *mene/mę* 'me', dat. *tebĕ/ti* 'to thee').

108. In the numerals, especially cardinal, gender and number are less clearly defined than case. This is inevitable, because apart from the trigeneric ordinals, which function as adjectives, they possess a substantival quality which helps to distinguish the cardinals from 'five' upwards in flexion as mostly feminine substantives (e.g. ComS fem. *pętь* 'five', *devętь* 'nine', *tysǫč'a* 'thousand'). As such they govern their substantives (e.g. ComS *pętъ ženъ* 'five women') instead of being governed by these like the first four numerals (e.g. ComS *jedinъ* 'one', *dъva* 'two', *trije* 'three', *četyre* 'four') which function as adjectives (e.g. ComS *četyri ženy* 'four women').

From the standpoint of case-flexion we may note that *jedinъ–jedina–jedino* has a full paradigm like the short adjective, *dъva/dъvě* is declined only in the dual, and *trije/tri* and *četyre/četyri* have a plural declension only. Incidentally, the cardinals from 'two' to 'four' inclusive have a common feminine and neuter form.

109. A second, more limited type of nominal flexion is the comparison of adjectives. This is found only in part of the category, viz. among adjectives of quality, and its formant has precedence over case-endings in declension. The formant is *-jъs-/-ъs-* which appears in all but the masculine and neuter nominative singular (cf. ComS masc. gen. sg. *bolьša* 'bigger' with nom. sg. *bol'ъjь*). In some adjectives the comparative suffix is preceded by *ě* (e.g. ComS masc. gen. sg. *nov-ě-jъša* 'newer'). The sibilant element has regularly lapsed in the masculine and neuter nominative singular (cf. ComS masc. sg. *novějь*, neut. *nov/je* with fem. *novějъši*). Comparative adjectives can be both definite and indefinite and like other adjectives have two kinds of declensional paradigms. As in other Indo-European languages some adjectives in Common Slavonic form their comparatives from other stems (cf. ComS *malъ* 'little' with *mьn'ъjь* 'less'). A specific superlative suffix is unknown, and this degree is indicated by prefixation (e.g. ComS masc. sg. *nainovějь* 'newest').

110. Verbal flexion expresses number and person and the more specifically verbal notions of tense, aspect, mood, and voice. The expression of gender in the verb is secondary and occurs only in complexes of finite and participial forms involving use of the indeclinable *l*-participle (cf. ComS masc. *dalъ jesmь* 'I have given' with fem. *dala jesmь*). The verbal paradigm is known traditionally as conjugation. This shares number with the noun and contrasts person with the nominal case-system. As with nouns, classification according to stem form is possible here.

111. Verbal stems are of two kinds in Common Slavonic—present and infinitive-aorist. These are the two formal pivots[1]

---

[1] J. J. Mikkola (*Urslavische Grammatik*, iii, Heidelberg, 1950, p. 96) refers to them as the 'Eckpfeiler' of the Slavonic verbal system.

of the Slavonic verb. The dichotomy is apophonic and easily apparent (cf. ComS pres. *berǫ* 'I take', with *bьrati* 'to take', aor. *bьraxъ* 'I took'). The Common Slavonic verbal system presents a threefold formal division[1] into athematic verbs (e.g. ComS *da-stъ* 'he gives'), 'semithematic' or *i*-stem verbs (e.g. ComS *vod-i-tъ* 'he leads'), and thematic, of which there are six subdivisions, viz. *-e-/-o-* stems (e.g. ComS *ved-e-tъ* 'he leads'), *-je-/-jo-* stems (e.g. ComS *děla-je-tъ* 'he does'), *-de-/-do-* stems (e.g. ComS *jь-de-tъ* 'he goes'), *-ve/-vo-* stems (e.g. ComS *ži-ve-tъ* 'he lives'), verbs with a nasal infix (e.g. ComS *sęd-e-tъ* 'he sits down'), and *-ne-/-no-* stems (e.g. ComS *dvig-ne-tъ* 'he moves').

112. The athematic verbs are a vestigial group of four verbs. Their inflexions are added immediately to the root (e.g. ComS *je-stъ* 'he is', *da-stъ* 'he gives, *ě-stъ/ja-stъ* 'he eats', *vě-stъ* 'he knows'). There is also a fifth verb, *jimatь* 'he has'/*jiměti* 'to have', which attaches its ending to a radical stem or base in *a/ě*.

113. In contrast to the athematic verbs, the semithematic and especially the thematic occur frequently. The semithematic verbs are either verbs of state or else denominals. They have *i* in the present tense and one of the correlatives *ě/a/i* in the infinitive (e.g. ComS *svьč'ǫ* < *svьtjǫ* 'shine', *svьtiši* 'thou shinest', *svьtěti* 'to shine'; *stojǫ* 'I stand', *stoiši* 'thou standest', *stojati/stojěti* 'to stand'; *gonjǫ* 'I drive', *goniši* 'thou drivest', *goniti* 'to drive').

114. The thematic verbs are by far the most numerous, and the principal subdivisions illustrate the fundamental alternation *e/o*, which has variants involving the prothesis of consonants such as *j, d, v, n*. As the principal type we have the *e/o* stems (e.g. ComS *vez-e-tъ* 'he carries'). In contrast to these primary stems, the *je/jo* stems are secondary formations from both verbal and nominal roots (cf. ComS *alč-e-tъ* 'he is hungry' with *gol-gol-e-tъ* 'he speaks'). The *de/do*, *ve/vo*, and nasal-infix stems are represented by a limited group of verbs each, whereas the *ne/no* type is more common.

115. The present-tense group includes the imperative and the present participles, active and passive (e.g. ComS imp. *beri* 'take', masc. act. part. *bery* 'taking', masc. pass. part. *beromъ* 'being taken'). The imperative form derives from the Indo-

---

[1] C. S. Stang, *Das slavische und baltische Verbum*, Oslo, 1942, pp. 21 ff.

European optative and is formed with the suffix *-oi-, which becomes Common Slavonic -i-/-ě- (e.g. ComS 2nd sg. vedi 'lead' < vedoi, 2nd pl. veděte < vedoite). The athematic verbs show the suffix -jь-/-i- (e.g. ComS 2nd sg. da-jь 'give', 2nd pl. da-i-te).

116. Morphological divergence from the present-tense group has united the stems of the infinitive and supine with those of the past participles and of the aorist. The infinitive and supine are nominal forms, representing a 'petrified' case-ending, viz. dative -ti, and accusative -tъ (cf. Skt infinitive in -tum and the Latin supine with the same ending). The past participles, both active and passive, show two types. The past active participle has a declinable form in -ъ/-(v)ъ, derived from the Indo-European perfect participle, and an indeclinable form in -l- (cf. ComS masc. nom. sg. nesъ 'carried' with neslъ); and the passive participle has semantically equivalent forms in -n- and -t- (< IE *-no-, *-to-). The -t- type is generally used when the root ends in a nasal sound (e.g. ComS masc. nom. sg. žę-tъ 'cut, harvested'), which makes the -n- suffix the more common of the two (e.g. ComS masc. nom. sg. vedenъ 'led').

117. The aorist itself also presents two types—a simple thematic and a sigmatic, i.e. with an s-infix (cf. ComS 1st sg. padъ 'I fell' with věsъ < věd-sъ 'I knew'). The sigmatic aorist is the later and more usual form, and shows the alternation x/s (cf. ComS 1st pl. daxomъ 'we gave' with 2nd pl. das-te 'you gave').

118. Semantically the aorist is a past tense; hence its formal opposition to the present. Another past tense, but of later origin, is the imperfect. The Indo-European imperfect, with its augment (cf. Skt á-bharat, Gk ἔ-φερε 'he was carrying' < IE *e-bher-e-t), was eliminated in Common Slavonic, and the new type belongs morphologically to the aorist-infinitive group of stems (cf. ComS 1st sg. aor. zъvaxъ 'I called' with 1st sg. impf. zъvaaxъ 'I was calling'). The formation of the imperfect shows mostly the presence of a stem in -ě- (e.g. ComS 1st sg. impf. veděaxъ 'I knew').

119. Collation of imperfect and aorist reveals that they express the distinction in past time between a continuous action or state and one that is not. Common Slavonic, like Baltic, illustrates this contrast in another way, that is, not through tense, but through aspect. As a system, aspect is primarily Slavonic and characterizes the later stages of development, especially in the eastern group. In Common Slavonic aspect is latent rather than explicit. The contrast is between perfective and imperfective, i.e. between completed and continuing action. The notions of both completion and continuity take different forms. Thus an imperfective action may be iterative (habitual, frequentative) as well as merely durative, and a perfective action may be punctual (momentaneous, semelfactive), ingressive (inceptive), or terminative. Morphologically perfective verbs are distinguished from their imperfective correlatives by prefixation (cf. ComS *pisati/napisati* 'to write').

120. Conjugation is restricted to the finite verb and takes place by means of personal endings. These can be both primary and secondary. The former occur in the present tense and show two varieties according to whether the verb is thematic or athematic: thus we have, for instance, the contrast of ComS 2nd sg. pres. *nes-e-ši* 'thou carriest' and *da-si* 'thou givest'. The secondary endings are those of the past tenses and the imperative. These differ from the present-tense endings in the singular and in the 3rd person plural (cf. ComS 1st–3rd pres. *vedǫ–vedeši̓–vedetь*, 3rd pl. *vedǫtь* 'I lead, &c.' with 1st–3rd aor. *vedoxъ–vede–vede*, 3rd pl. *vedošę* 'I led, &c.').

121. Syntax. It is thought that the structure of the sentence varied little between Indo-European and Common Slavonic. The distinction between noun and verb remained, and this led to the perpetuation of two types of sentences—nominal and verbal. Emphasis on the nominal element is seen in the development of the definite adjective and in the possibility of dispensing with the copula in the present (achronic) tense. In the syntagma the negative particle *ne* is closely connected with the verb and sometimes even written with it (e.g. OCS нѣстъ 'is not' < *ne* + *jestъ*). No Common Slavonic interrogative particle can be postulated, although such exist in the separate Slavonic languages.

122. The predicative nucleus of the Common Slavonic sentence is very often verbal. This may be seen in the use of purely verbal forms as logically complete sentences (e.g. ComS *jьdǫ* 'I go'). A subject, however, is frequently present and may be defined by an attribute. This is normally adjectival, although a qualifying substantive in the genitive case may also be found. Adjectives may precede or follow the words they qualify; genitives usually follow. Numerals always precede, whereas demonstrative adjectives usually precede when emphatic and follow when they are loosely connected with their substantive (cf. ComS *sъ rodъ* 'this clan' with *rodъ sъ* 'the clan'). General pre-position of the attribute is confirmed by the evidence of modern Slavonic speech.

123. Word-order in Common Slavonic does not appear to have been grammatically significant. In the two-term or binary sentence the verb may stand first or last. In narrative the verb often begins the sentence. Unstressed accessory words, whether pronouns or particles, usually follow the first autonomous word (e.g. ComS acc. *sę* 'self'; dat. *ti* 'to thee'; *li* 'or'; *bo* 'for'). Conjunctions serve to link the terms or members of a sentence as well as sentences in sequence. Asyndeton or absence of a conjunction is rare. Subordination is not a feature of the spoken language, and its use in writing presumably developed later. Participial usage in Common Slavonic does not show anything like the development this has undergone in Lithuanian. Absolute constructions into which participles enter as essential constituents are a literary growth and fall into the province of style.

124. Vocabulary. The Common Slavonic vocabulary was twofold, viz. (*a*) inherited Indo-European stock (§ 74) and (*b*) foreign loans. The latter were due to contacts of the Slavs with other peoples, including those of Indo-European speech, long after the disintegration of their protoglossa, viz. the Iranians and Greeks and the Germanic and Baltic tribes, as well as the alien Turkic tribes. Included in their 'fundamental' vocabulary of patriarchal relationship-terms, names of natural phenomena, parts of the body, living creatures, especially some domestic animals, numerals to 100, simple terms of processes, for instance 'to sew', 'to weave', 'to plough', to grind', and some abstract terms (e.g. ComS *vertmę* 'time'), the Slavs had a large assortment of dialect words which they shared with Baltic[1] (e.g. ComS *golva* 'head', *nesti* 'to carry'), and to all these they added in due course a cultural terminology borrowed at various times from Iranian

[1] R. Trautmann, *Baltisch-slavisches Wörterbuch*, Göttingen, 1923.

(e.g. ComS *bogъ* 'God'), Germanic (e.g. ComS *pъlkъ* 'host, army'), and Turkic (ComS *kapъ* 'image'). Some of the borrowings were calques or loan-translations (e.g. ComS *vojevoda* 'commander', cf. OHG *herizogo*). The Christian vocabulary is later and dialectal, but shows that Christianity had reached the Slavs before the missionary activity of St Cyril and St Methodius had begun (e.g. ComS *cьrky* 'church', *krьstiti* 'to baptize').

III

HISTORICAL BACKGROUND

125. Common Slavonic, as we have seen, was one of the Indo-European dialects, spoken, according to Lubor Niederle's[1] surmise, in an East European area bounded by the middle Vistula and the middle Dnieper and lying to the north of the Carpathians. This was the Slavonic habitat before the dispersion of the Slavonic-speaking tribes, which is recorded for us by alien historians from the sixth century A.D. onwards. Our first authentic information about the Slavs finds them under the name Venedi or Veneti in the first century of our era. This name occurs in the *Naturalis historia*[2] of Pliny the Elder (Secundus) and in the *Germania*[3] of Tacitus, and survives to this day in the German designation 'Wendisch', applied to Lusatian, and in Finnish 'Venäjä' and Estonian 'Vene', applied to Russia. The name reappears as Οὐενέδαι (Venedae) in Claudius Ptolemy's *De geographia* (Γεωγραφικὴ ὑφήγησις) in the second century A.D.[4] Ptolemy refers to the Baltic Sea as the Venedic Gulf (Οὐενεδικὸς κόλπος) and bears witness to the existence of the Venedae, who would seem to have lived at that time to the north of the Goths, to the west of the Baltic tribes—the Galindians (Γαλίνδαι) and Sudinians (Σουδινοί)— and to the south(-west) of the Finnic tribes. Jordanes (Jornandes),[5] writing in the sixth century, used the name Venetae in a general sense to include two others, viz. Antes (Antae) and Sclaveni. Both these names figure as Ἄνται and Σκλαβηνοί in the pages of *De bello Gothico* (Ὑπὲρ τῶν πολεμῶν v–viii)[6]

---

[1] *Rukovět' slovanské archeologie*, Prague, 1931.   [2] iv. 97.
[3] Cap. 46.   [4] iii. 5, 7.
[5] *De Getarum siue Gothorum origine et rebus gestis*, v, xxiii, xlviii.
[6] v. 27. 2. Procopius says, moreover (vii. 14, 29), that both tribes were 'in old times' (τὸ παλαιόν) called by a common name, viz. Spori (Σπόροι). This has been equated with Jordanes's Spali, who are surmised to have belonged to the Alan branch of the Sarmatian tribes. These, as is known, dominated the European steppe till they were defeated by the Goths in the third century A.D. It is thought that the Russian word *ispolin* 'giant' recalls the former Iranian masters of the Slavs in the Black Sea region (cf. (i)spol-in with Spal-i). See F. Dvorník, *The Slavs, their History and Civilization*, Boston, 1956, pp. 22–23.

by Procopius of Caesarea, a contemporary of the emperor Justinian. Jordanes and Procopius are agreed that the Antae (Ἄνται)[1] and Sclaveni (Σκλαβηνοί) spoke the same language and that their settlements were spread over a vast expanse of territory.

126. The name Sclaveni refers to the western and the name Antae to the eastern branch of the Slavs, who, according to Jordanes, occupied the area between the Dniester and the Dnieper. They appear to have come south after Attila's Huns had swept the Goths from the Black Sea area between the Dnieper and the Danube in the fifth century. The Avar invasion of the sixth century, breaking through the Bulgars in the eastern steppe, destroyed the name and cohesion of the Antae,[2] who resisted them, and led to the migration of their survivors northwards into a new habitat between the middle Dnieper and the Don, where, now as Slavs, they became subject to the Khazars in the seventh century. These held the south-eastern steppes up to the approaches of the Caucasus and had their centre of administration and trade at Itil' (the later Astrakhan') on the lower Volga. By the end of the seventh and the beginning of the eighth century they dominated the Crimea and had a governor (*tudun*) in Korsun' (Chersonesus taurica). They became for several centuries the rampart of Eastern Europe against incursions from the Asiatic steppes. In the middle of the ninth century, when Khazar authority had already been shaken by the Pechenegs (Patzinaks),[3] Constantine of Thessalonica, inventor of the Glagolitic alphabet (§§ 148–51), headed a delegation to them from Byzantium. That the Slavs paid tribute to the Khazars we know from the Old Russian 'Tale of Bygone Years' (*Povest' vremennych let*), and that they respectfully remembered

---

[1] Pliny the Elder (*Nat. hist.* vi. 13) mentions a people called Anti (Anthi), who lived between the Sea of Azov and the Caspian. It seems hardly possible to identify this people with the later Antes, Antae, who are known to have been Slavonic, unless we assume that the Iranian (Sarmatian) Anti formed a ruling class among those Slavs who were called Antes by Jordanes and Antae by Procopius, like the Varangian Rus' at a much later date.

[2] Menander Protector, *Historia*, frag. 5.

[3] Prince Svjatoslav Igorevič of Kiev (964–72), a Varangian like his ancestors, in spite of his Slavonic name (his Varangian name was Sveinald), completed the destruction of Khazaria by sacking Itil' after previously doing the same to Bulgar on the Kama. See A. Stender Petersen, 'Die Varägersage als Quelle der altrussischen Chronik' (*Acta Jutlandica*, vi, Aarhus, 1934).

Khazar authority is clear from the application of the title 'kagan', probably first learnt from the Avars, to Vladimir the Great by the Metropolitan Ilarion in the first half of the eleventh century. A century earlier the Arab traveller Al Mas'udī[1] speaks of heathen Slavs and Rus' in the service of the Kagan.

127. Mention of Byzantium and Rus' introduces us to the next phase in the history of the Eastern Slavs. When these are mentioned in the ninth and tenth centuries by Byzantine and Arab authors, they are no longer Antae. The postulated Russian 'Primary Chronicle' (*pervonačal'naja letopis'*),[2] which appears to have been completed by the beginning of the twelfth century (*c.* 1112), although the oldest manuscript embodying it—the Laurentian—is dated 1377, gives a detailed picture of East Slavonic settlement in the west and central Russian riverine areas in the ninth century. The chronicler does not use a common designation other than the alien term 'Rus'' to bind his Slavonic tribes, but enumerates and defines a multiplicity of tribal names. 'Rus'' was distinguished by both Arab (روس) and Greek ('Pῶς) from 'Slav', although both designations are mentioned often enough together. The Emperor Constantine VII in Chapter IX of his *De administrando imperio* (948–52) gives the names of the Dnieper cataracts in 'Russian' (ῥωσιστί) and in 'Slavonic' (σκλαβηνιστί), and the 'Russian' names are obviously Germanic (cf. OR 'Οστροβουνιπράχ, i.e. Островьныи прагъ with OSw. Ούλβοροί, i.e. Holmfors). The Russian *Povest' vremennych let* itself refers to Rus' not only as Rus' but as Varangians (OR *varjazi*) and goes on to tell us of the formation of East Slavonic principalities by Varangian rulers.

128. The political cohesion between Slav and Finn—the Slověne, Kriviči, Ves', and Vod'[3]—was provided by Varangian enterprise and organization in the Il'men'–Beloozero area in the middle of the ninth century (862). Rjurik (Run. Hrurikr,

---

[1] Cf. A. Ja. Garkavi (Harkavy), *Skazanija musul'manskich pisatelej o slavjanach i russkich*, St Petersburg, 1870.

[2] This has been reconstructed by A. A. Šachmatov in his critical edition of the *Povest' vremennych let*, Petrograd, 1916.

[3] Note the Old Russian use of collective names to designate alien groups. This puts Rus' on a par with Ves', Vod', Kors', Let'gola, and Litva. In contrast to these, the names of the Slavonic tribes, as well as of the Varangians, Germans, Greeks, and oriental peoples, appear in a plural form.

Hrørikr)[1] and his men-at-arms (OR *družina*) settled in Novgorod the Great (ON Holmgarðr), which became the first Varangian-Russian centre. Kiev, the future focus of East Slavonic polity, lay far to the south along the waterway 'from the Varangians to the Greeks' (OR изъ варягъ въ грекы), and it was natural that this principality should have been founded by Varangian 'colonists' from Novgorod, viz. Askol'd (ON Hǫskuldr)[2] and Dir (ON Dyri); for political unity followed trade, and this was plied and protected by Varangian armed merchants between the Gulf of Finland and the Bosphorus.

129. The principality of Kiev (ON Kœnugarðr) was geographically nearer to Byzantium than was Novgorod. This meant that Kiev was nearer to the source and centre of a great Christian civilization, and if only for geographical reasons it was destined to take the lead eventually among the early East Slavonic states. These, originally tribal, areas centred in towns, which were built on waterways and were the outcome and factors of trade and communication. They existed in number in the ninth century, and the Varangians, who had helped to develop them, named the territory served by the towns 'Garðaríki' (Land of Towns, 'Urbania'). This Garðaríki or Rus', as it came to be known in the ninth century, was not purely Slavonic. We have seen that the earliest Russian principality, Novgorod the Great, included Vepsian and Vodian subjects, and we shall learn subsequently that the Finnic element was well represented in the Novgorodian colonies (e.g. Dvinskaja zemlja, the basin of the Northern Dvina) and among the Vjatiči on the Oka. Thus, in his attack on Kiev, Oleg was aided by a mixed force, including Vepsians (Ves'), Merians (Merja), and even Estonians (Čud'). But the core of the Varangian state—the Kiev principality—was predominantly Slavonic, as the early disappearance of Russian-Germanic speech, which the testimony of Constantine VII shows to have existed side by side with East Slavonic,[3] leads us to suppose. The state of things linguistically

---

[1] V. Thomsen, *The Relations between Ancient Russia and Scandinavia*, Oxford–London, 1877, pp. 131–41.

[2] This name occurs as Ascalt in Irish annals. See J. H. Todd, *The War of the Gaedhil and the Gaill*, London, 1867, p. 233.

[3] *De administrando imperio*, cap. ix. See Gy. Moravcsik and R. J. H. Jenkins, *Constantine Porphyrogenitus, De administrando imperio*, Budapest, 1949, pp. 56–63.

in Garðaríki therefore was the same as that in the contemporary Scandinavian Duchy of Normandy, where Old Norse quickly succumbed to the massive inertia of Old French.

130. Varangian Slavonic Rus' in the ninth century was geographically at the point of intersection of three foci of trade and culture—a northern (Scandinavian), a southern (Byzantine), and an eastern (Khazarian). From two of these, Rus' was divided by seas, and her common frontier with Khazaria brought her into contact, both friendly and hostile, with the Kagan (Chacanus). Trade and war also took the Varangians to Byzantium, as two early tenth-century treaties—those of 911 and 944—between Rus' and Byzantium clearly show. But during that century Rus' appears to have been steadily permeated by Byzantine religious culture[1] and by the end of the century (988) had officially become Christian and had adopted the Bulgarian Cyrillic characters and religious literature. By this time too the tribal organizations of the Eastern Slavs, represented in the 'Primary Chronicle' by the Poljane, Derevljane, and Sever(jane) of the middle Dnieper, the Radimiči on the Sož, and the Vjatiči on the Oka, the Chorvaty, Duleby, Bužane (later Volynjane) in Galicia and Volynia, the Uliči and Tivercy on the Dniester, and the Poločane, Kriviči, and Slovene (or Novgorodians) in the river and lake area extending north-west of the Valday watershed, had become a group of principalities, controlled by the Rjurik dynasty from Kiev and centred in such towns as Galič, Turov, Vladimir Volynskij, Perejaslavl', and Novgorod Severskij in the south and Polock, Smolensk, Pskov, and Novgorod the Great in the north. Of these the last four were in the Scandinavian orbit and had originally paid tribute to the Varangians. The rest were closer to Kiev and had paid tribute to the Khazars. By the tenth century, when Constantine VII mentions some of these towns by name in his *De administrando imperio*, the Black Sea steppes between the Danube and Don were held by the Pechenegs (Patzinaks), and in the centuries to follow successive nomadic tribes, mainly Turkic in speech, displaced one another in this region. In the eleventh century, when we are able to read our first written records in

[1] In 864 Photius, patriarch of Constantinople, sent missionaries to Kiev and founded a short-lived bishopric there.

Russian (East Slavonic), the dominant power in the steppes was that of the Cumans or Polovecians, and these are the enemy in the only surviving piece of early Russian poetic literature 'The Lay of Igor'' (*Slovo o polku Igoreve*), which must have been composed after Prince Igor' Svjatoslavič's disastrous raid against the Polovecians in 1185.

131. In spite of the difficulties caused by the Turkic domination of the Black Sea steppes, Kiev Rus' flourished as a centre of East Slavonic culture for several centuries. Her prosperity and power were at first based almost exclusively on trade, and when this declined with the south and east, through the frequent blockading of the major trade-routes by hostile steppe-tribes, she reorientated herself increasingly towards agriculture. The growth of land tenure, the presence of a powerful military caste (*družina*), and the loose state-organization, based as this was on acknowledgement of the suzerainty of the Grand Prince of Kiev over the East Slavonic territories, led to the emergence of a political system which approximated in many ways to the feudal system of Western Europe. This Russian feudalism was the centrifugal force which prepared the destruction of Kiev as it was later to stimulate the acquisitive and centralizing instincts of Muscovy. By the end of the twelfth century internecine strife among the princes (see Prince Vladimir Monomach's *Poučenije* 'Admonition') had so diminished princely authority in Kiev that it required only the hostile presence of the steppe to destroy it utterly. This came with the invasion of the Tartars (Mongols) under Batu Khan, grandson of Genghis Khan, in the early thirteenth century (1237–40).[1] Kiev ceased to be a renowned centre of Christian culture, an emporium of trade, and a city resplendent with ecclesiastical art and architecture, and Rus' was to remain for a long time without a focus of authority, for the commercial and colonial power of Novgorod the Great, although it stood up to the German crusaders, was repeatedly weakened by internal dissensions.

132. Long before the collapse of Kiev, however, the Eastern Slavs of the middle Dnieper had begun to migrate north-eastwards into the frontier area originally occupied by the Vjatiči

---

[1] See the fragmentary lament *Slovo o pogibeli russkoj zemli* (*c.* 1238) and the chronicle accounts of the battle on the river Kalka and the devastation of Rjazan'.

and their East Finnic neighbours—the Muroma, Meščera, and Merja—as well as into the 'colonial' territories beyond these. Settlements were made even to the north of the upper Volga, and many of the names given to these, for instance Vladimir,[1] Perejaslavl', Vyšcgorod, Zvenigorod, Galič, and Starodub, recall the southern origin of the settlers. Among unfamiliar names, closely connected geographically with Vladimir, which was to become the new religious centre in 1299, were Tver', Rostov, Suzdal', and Rjazan'; and it is in the centre of the forested area occupied by these towns that Moscow arose as the capital of a small principality in the thirteenth century. With increasing migration from the south as the result of Tartar pressure, the Vladimir–Suzdal'–Rostov arc gradually emerged as a new focus of East Slavonic political power. For two centuries, however, Rus' had to pay tribute to and her princes to receive their titles from the Khan of the Golden Horde, whose seat was in the lower Volga region and whose authority far exceeded that of the Kagan of Khazaria. In this period a succession of astute princes in Moscow won for themselves the favour of the Khan and set about annexing piecemeal the towns and territories of neighbouring principalities. The process was initiated with the incorporation of the town of Kolomna and ended with the establishment of the Muscovite state.

133. While Muscovy, as the focal point of the new Russia Major and as the 'area of characterization' of the Russian language, was slowly taking shape in the north-east in the thirteenth and fourteenth centuries, Galič (Ukr. Halyč) in the south-west—founded about 1140—became, for a short time after the Tartar invasion, the second heir, as Russia Minor, to the power and culture of Kiev in the thirteenth century and extended its authority northwards into the Pripjat' country and beyond. This brought the princes of Galič into well-matched conflict with the Lithuanian grand-dukes. Galič suffered a second Tartar invasion at the end of the thirteenth century (1283), and after that the struggle which had begun between Galič and Lithuania for the possession of south-west Russia went entirely in favour of the latter. Lithuania indeed became an increasingly Slavonic principality through the conquests of

---

[1] Vladimir, in fact, superseded Kiev before its fall as the centre of political power.

Mindaugas (Mindowe, Mendog) in the thirteenth century, and by the end of the fourteenth had almost reached the Black Sea by annexing Volynia and Podolia. It is significant that the administrative language of the area was not only Latin but a form of White Russian.[1] In the meantime Poland had annexed Galič and her lands. The dynastic union of Poland and Lithuania in 1386 was the beginning of the gradual christianization and polonization of Lithuania proper and of the extension of Polish influence into western Russia (Ruthenia), which by this time was unmistakably showing its present-day linguistic cleavage into White Russian and Ukrainian, though neither of these names was as yet in use.

134. By the fourteenth century then there were two expanding powers in the East Slavonic area which strove for hegemony over it, viz. Poland–Lithuania in the west and Muscovy in the east. The rate at which these powers expanded was at first unequal. In the fourteenth century Muscovy could not vie in either territory or population with Poland–Lithuania. But at the battle of Kulikovo in 1380 the Muscovites inflicted a crushing defeat on the Tartars under Mamaj, and from that time onwards the political prestige of Muscovy grew as rapidly as that of the Golden Horde declined. It is a matter of no little interest that the forces not only of Poland–Lithuania but even of the Russian principality of Rjazan' were ranged against the Muscovite leader, Prince Dmitrij of the Don, in that battle (see *Zadonščina* 'Exploits beyond the Don' by Sofonij of Rjazan'),[2] and that Moscow was captured and burnt by the Tartars two years afterwards. Nevertheless, the legend of Tartar invincibility had been destroyed.

135. The process of territorial acquisition (*sobiranije zemel'*), characteristic of the earlier history of Muscovy, gained momentum under Ivan III, who had married a Greek princess of the Palaeolog dynasty and was inclined to regard himself as spiritual heir of the Byzantine emperors. He adopted the Byzantine symbol of the double-headed eagle as his device and referred to himself in official documents by the title of 'tsar', which till then had

---

[1] C. S. Stang, *Die westrussische Kanzleisprache des Großfürstentums Litauen*, Oslo, 1935.

[2] See also the 'hagiography' *O zitii i prestavlenii velikogo knjazia Dmitrija Ivanoviča*.

been applied in Russian only to the mightiest princes such as the Roman and Byzantine emperors and the khans of the Golden Horde, and his successors encouraged clerics and publicists to elaborate the theory of 'Moscow the Third Rome'.[1] The conquest and submission of Novgorod the Great and its vast colonial dependencies in the north-east were accomplished by treaty in 1478, and by the beginning of the sixteenth century Muscovy was territorially so large and the Golden Horde, from which the khanates of Crimea and Kazan' had already detached themselves, was so weak that the Muscovite rulers could turn their eyes confidently westwards. War with Poland–Lithuania and her northern neighbours, the Teutonic Order and Sweden, seemed now inevitable. Both Muscovy and Poland–Lithuania sought control over the White Russian and Ukrainian lands, and a strong Poland–Lithuania lay across the land route to the west, which since the fall of Byzantium (Constantinople) to the Turks in the fifteenth century (1453) had become the new source of culture, material and intellectual, if not spiritual. Wars were waged against Poland–Lithuania and the Teutonic Order under Ivan IV (see his correspondence with Prince Andrej Kurbskij), in whose person Muscovite autocracy reached its most flagrant expression. The goal was access to the Baltic and the sea-route to the west, and the prize was the Baltic provinces of the decaying Teutonic Order. But although Ivan's armies seized and devastated the country, superiority in military leadership—he was face to face at the end with King Stefan Báthory—and diplomatic subtlety wrested it from him in 1582, and Poland–Lithuania and Sweden shared what Muscovy lost.

136. Muscovite territorial gains in the later sixteenth century were made in the east at relatively small cost. The Tartar khanates of Kazan' and Astrakhan' had fallen before the Livonian war in the 1550's, and now Cossacks under Jermak in the service of the Stroganov family penetrated into western Siberia, following the route of the Russian conquerors of Yugria in the fifteenth century, and took possession of the Nogay khanate of

---

[1] This theory is ascribed to the monk Filofej of the Jeleazar Monastery in Pskov. See V. Malinin, *Starec Jeleazarova monastyrja Filofej i jego poslanija*, Kiev, 1901; Hildegard Schaeder, *Moskau das Dritte Rom. Studien zur Geschichte der politischen Theorien in der slavischen Welt*, Hamburg, 1929; O. Ohloblyn, *Moskovs'ka teorija III Rymu v XVI–XVII stol.*, Munich, 1951.

Sibir', which was to give its name later to almost the whole of Asiatic Russia (Siberia).

137. The reign of Ivan IV (1533–84) witnessed the struggle between the autocracy and the nobility or boyars, who were mainly the descendants of the ancient *družina* and petty princes. The boyars had become landowners in the Kiev period and cultivated their lands with the aid of serfs and hired labour. Their power had increased considerably in Muscovite times as their ranks increased with the inflow of princely immigrants from western Russia. The autocratic whim of the Muscovite princes could not brook a rival, and it fell to Ivan IV to break the power of the boyars mainly by creating his 'peculium' (*opričnina*) out of confiscated lands, which ultimately embraced half the territory of Muscovy and supported the men-at-arms (*opričniki*) who murdered large numbers of the disaffected princes.

138. It was in this century too that Muscovy created for herself a complicated bureaucratic system with chancelleries and archives to control every aspect of civil life; that the movements of the peasantry were restricted by law; that foreign craftsmen came to Moscow to practise their crafts; and that the Orthodox Church took decisive measures to overcome the 'judaist heresy' (*jeres' židovstvujuščix*) and the challenge of the 'Transvolgan monks' (*zavolžskije starcy*) to its vast material possessions.

139. The discontent of many sections of the population with Church and State anticipates the mood of one of the darkest periods in Russian history—the so-called 'troubled times' (*smutnoje vremja, smuta*)—when the cessation of the Muscovite dynasty led to rivalry among the boyars for the vacant throne and to the intervention of Poland, which brought two pretenders and supporting Polish armies to Moscow. The direct and insufferable interference of foreigners in Muscovite internal affairs ultimately provoked a series of national revolts, led by Church and nobility, which culminated in the expulsion of the Poles and in the election of a new dynasty.

140. The reigns of the first two Romanovs, Michael and Alexis, lasted for two-thirds of the seventeenth century, a period of defence and retrenchment, of territorial expansion to the Pacific Ocean, and of notable advance in the spheres of material and intellectual culture. Moscow had become an archiepiscopal see, after the Metropolitan left Vladimir in 1328, and a patriarchate towards the end of the sixteenth century (1589), some years after the death of Ivan IV in 1584. In 1652 Nikon, bishop of Novgorod, became patriarch, and it was under him that the liturgical books, which had accumulated scribal errors in the course of several centuries of recopying in spite of the radical changes made by South Slavonic scholars since the end of the fourteenth century and by Maksim Grek in the early sixteenth, were revised and corrected by collation with the Greek originals. The revision of the books was approved by the Patriarch of Constantinople, but it was one of the causes of the ecclesiastical schism (*raskol*) that led to the emergence of the sect of Old Believers (see Avvakum's *Žitije*, 1672–3).

141. Immediately after the end of the 'troubled times', the progressive elements in Muscovy felt the need of direct contact with the West, as they had during the reigns of Ivan IV and Boris Godunov; and accordingly we find Moscow becoming the centre of a large colony of foreign merchants, craftsmen, artisans, and professional men, and some Muscovites adopting Western dress and manners (see *Stoglav*, 1551, fol. 52). Foreign books were translated in increasing numbers, extracts were made at the Ambassadorial Office (*posol'skij prikaz*) from foreign newspapers, and the printing press, already introduced abortively in the early 1550's, was re-established in Moscow after the lapse of a century and began to devote its activities to the dissemination of secular as well as ecclesiastical literature. Cultural influences of various kinds now reached Moscow not only from Greece, the Balkans, and Western Europe, but also from the partly polonized White Russia and the Ukraine, which stood on a higher level of culture than Muscovy. It was from these two regions that Classical scholarship and literature found their way at long last to the Russian-speaking area. This was made possible in part through the territorial acquisitions of Tsar Alexis, which included the Smolensk and Novgorod Severskij lands and part of the 'Left Bank' Ukraine, with the city of Kiev, where the Mohyla Academy had been founded at the end of the sixteenth century as an Orthodox centre of learning. The annexation of a large part of the Ukraine was the outcome of a ten years' war with

Poland (complete mistress of the Lithuanian lands since 1569), in which the Cossacks of the Dnieper (Zaporižžja), jealous of their independence, took hopeful and active part on the side of Muscovy.

142. Muscovy gave place to Imperial Russia in the reign of Peter the Great which extended to 1725. This reign saw an acceleration in the momentum of europeanization, whose beginnings we have already observed in the reign of Ivan IV. Peter the Great's commanding personality and enormous energy played a notable part in the change (see Feofan Prokopovič, *Slovo na pogrebenije Petra Velikogo*). He was a military leader as well as a reformer and innovator, and the aims and demands of his costly wars made his domestic reforms both far-reaching and permanent. Among these were the forcible introduction of Western dress as the culmination of the victory of Western manners; the europeanization of the calendar (1700), which had remained pre-Christian till 1699; the reform of the bureaucracy, now regulated by the 'table of ranks' (*tabel' o rangach*, 1722), which subordinated wealth and social status to service; the fostering of industry; the delimitation of the spheres of influence of Church and State and the subordination of the first to the second; and, more important than these from our point of view, the establishment of school and newspaper (*Vedomosti*, 1703–27), the introduction of the 'civil alphabet' (*graždanskaja azbuka*) in 1710, and the impetus which the Tsar gave to translations, mainly technical, from other languages. These cultural reforms, 'educational' in the widest sense of the term, influenced the written use of Russian, separated it visibly from the 'Slavonic' of the Church, and contributed to its modernization. They had, with one exception, already been anticipated by his predecessors, and what they owed to him was born of his active and vivid temperament. Of particular interest is the encouragement which Peter the Great gave to the translator and lexicographer. This was the outcome of his conviction that the West had a great deal to teach Russia and of his normal attitude to foreigners from the West, to whose quarter in Moscow (*nemeckaja sloboda*) he was a frequent and welcome visitor.

143. Peter the Great's Germanophil proclivities are especially evident in the dynastic alliances of his family. In the course of the eighteenth century we find Germans in control of the government both as favourites of empresses (e.g. Biron) and on the throne itself (Catherine II), and we see them dominating the Imperial Academy of Sciences, which Peter the Great himself had planned, but which was established only after his death. They even exercised some influence on the curriculum of Moscow University, which was founded in 1755. The presence of Germans in high places, however, did not lead to the spread of German in Russia, but rather of French, the language of 'polite society' in the 'Age of Enlightenment'. Accordingly we find that it was French influence which shaped the modern Russian language and literature in post-Petrine times right up to the early nineteenth century. In this connexion too we may note that the eighteenth-century trend in Russia, as elsewhere in Europe, was aristocratic, and the class cleavage, which Peter the Great had harnessed to state service, became more marked through the accumulation of privileges by the gentry (*dvorjanstvo*).

144. Meanwhile Russia, which had become a great power under Peter the Great, had continued to extend her frontiers to the enclosed seas in Europe and Asia, and by the nineteenth century, after suffering the Napoleonic invasion, she was able to influence policy in Western Europe. But before this had happened, the autocratic State had undergone several minor crises, which were the result of the disintegrating ideas of French revolutionary liberalism. These ideas were primarily social and economic, and provided food for much thought and little action in the course of the nineteenth century. By this time education in Russia had become largely russianized, as may be seen from the membership of the St Petersburg Academy of Sciences, and intellectual ideas were moulded by conservative national as well as by liberal and socialist foreign influences. The former helped to preserve the autocratic State till its collapse in 1917 and the latter to define the new Soviet Russia, with its militant 'proletarian' ideology. Liberalizing measures in the interim were the emancipation of the serfs in 1861 and the introduction of a representative institution (*duma*) after the revolution of 1905.

145. This revolution was largely the outcome of the disintegrating effect of an unsuccessful war with Japan, as the revolution of 1917 was the legacy of an unsuccessful war with Germany,

and both were the unintended sequel to foiled imperialistic
designs. The Russian Empire, the dream and creation of Peter
I who had assumed the imperial title in 1721, had not yet
reached its farthest limits. Before the territorial gains of 1945
there were some territorial sacrifices to make, especially along
the western frontier. These went with a period of retrenchment
and rehabilitation within the newly-shrunken periphery, and
they brought to the knowledge of the West fragments of that
national and linguistic mosaic which has been Russia since the
Muscovite expansion of the sixteenth century.

146. This kaleidoscope of history is recorded in its essential as
well as inessential details in the development of the Russian
language, which we shall study here presently. Since the time
of Peter the Great Russian was inevitably accepted, occasionally
perhaps under protest, all over the East Slavonic area till the
emergence of nineteenth-century nationalism in the wake of
the French revolution and the Napoleonic wars; and even in the
nineteenth century its prestige was so great that it enabled historians of the language to conjure up and perpetuate the myth
that White Russian and Ukrainian were dialects of Russian.
Today, a volte-face in Russian scholarship justly accounts them
independent languages, each with a literature of its own and a
literary tradition ascending to the eleventh and twelfth centuries. Knowledge of this has led the modern investigator to
make more scrupulous discriminations in assessing the linguistic
nature of medieval documents belonging to the East Slavonic
area. We shall therefore not consider the writs or charters originating, say, in Smolensk and Polock in the thirteenth century
or the literary remains directly associated with Kiev, Černigov,
and Galič, as material for the study of the history of Russian,
but rather as material which helps to define the early stages of
White Russian and Ukrainian respectively. With this caution
we can now proceed to fill in the background to the historical
grammar of the language.

IV

ALPHABET AND SPELLING

147. We must now retrace our steps to the tenth century, when a written language seems to have come into being on the territory of Rus', for we cannot know the historical beginnings of Russian until we have familiarized ourselves with its first written words. Soviet linguistic scholarship, still influenced to some extent by the emotions of the war years, is inclined to give too easy credence to investigators whose patriotism is stronger than their scruple for truth and the value of authentic evidence, and who in some instances are historians and archaeologists rather than linguists (e.g. D. S. Lichačov and A. C. Arcichovskij). These scholars and others, using fancy and the flimsiest 'evidence', have sketched a detailed picture of prehistoric East Slavonic writing, and one of them, S. P. Obnorskij,[1] does not consider it 'overbold' to assume that even the Antae possessed an alphabet of their own in the sixth and seventh centuries. The traditional account of the origin of the Slavonic alphabets, which is still unanimously accepted in the West and upheld by some Soviet scholars (e.g. A. M. Seliščev), has been challenged by Russian patriotism, which appears to discard it for another based chiefly on a statement in the *Memoria et Vita Constantini philosophi*. Interpretation of the statement (§ 148) along lines suggested by V. I. Grigorovič in the nineteenth century and by N. K. Nikol'skij in the 1920's[2] makes Tauris (later the Crimea) the place of origin of Glagolitic, the older of the two Slavonic alphabets.

148. Here we must turn to the traditional exposition of our problem. The oldest Slavonic manuscripts are written in one or other of two parallel alphabets, Glagolitic and Cyrillic, both of which survive to this day. The former, in a somewhat changed 'Croatian' form, is used in a few places on the north Dalmatian

---

[1] *Kul'tura russkogo jazyka*, Moscow, 1948.
[2] 'K voprosu o russkich pis'menach upomjanutych v Žitii Konstantina Filosofa' (*Izvestija po russkomu jazyku i slovesnosti Akademii Nauk SSSR*, i. 1, Leningrad, 1928).

littoral (e.g. near Zadar) and islands (e.g. Krk, Cres, Rab, Lošinj); and the latter, as Neocyrillic in two styles of typeface,— an ecclesiastical and a secular— is current among the Orthodox Slavs. Written record, represented by the anonymous 'Pannonian Legends' or Slavonic biographies of the brothers Constantine and Methodius of Thessalonica[1] and by the monk Chrabr's disquisition on the Slavonic characters (*O pismenech*), all of them extant only in late transcripts, is the source of our knowledge of the invention of Slavonic writing, but it does not tell us which of the two alphabets is in question. A consensus of opinion among scholars inclines to give the Glagolitic alphabet priority and to regard Cyrillic as a subsequent and secondary development. If this view is adopted, the Greek Constantine the Philosopher (later St Cyril) must have devised it before his departure with his elder brother Methodius on their semi-political missionary journey to Moravia at the invitation of the local Slavonic prince Rastislav in 863. Both brothers appear to have had a good knowledge of the Macedonian form of Slavonic, which was spoken in the environs of their native Thessalonica (Slav. Solun'); and Constantine, as a notable linguist and connoisseur of several alphabets, may have been tempted by the stimulating phonetic exercise of devising one for the still illiterate Slavs. He may have received some incentive to do this when he set out on his journey to Khazaria in 860–1, as we are told in the *Memoria et vita* (cap. viii). The relevant passage, taken from the oldest manuscript (fifteenth century), reads: 'He (Constantine the Philosopher) found there the Gospels and Psalter written in Russian characters, and he found a man who spoke that speech, and spoke with him and acquired the force of (his) speech, and comparing it with his own, resolved the characters —vowels and consonants—and invoking God in prayer, soon began to read and to discourse, and men marvelled at him, praising God.' 'Russian' here has been read as 'Gothic'[2] and as 'Slavonic'.[3] F. Dvorník[4] accepts the Gothic thesis, pointing out

---

[1] F. Pastrnek, *Dějiny slovanských apoštolů Cyrilla a Methoda*, Prague, 1902; F. Dvorník, *Les Légendes de Constantin et de Méthode vues de Byzance*, Prague, 1933.

[2] G. A. Il'inskij, 'Odin epizod iz korsunskogo perioda žizni Konstantina Filosofa' (*Slavia*, iii, Prague, 1924).

[3] A. A. Vasiliev, *La Russie primitive et Byzance*, Paris, 1930.

[4] *Les Slaves, Byzance et Rome au ixe siècle*, Paris, 1926; *Les Légendes de Constantin et de Méthode vues de Byzance*, Prague, 1933.

that the Goths had a Christian hierarchy from the end of the fourth century A.D., that St John Chrysostom had consecrated Wulfila (Οὐλφίλας) as their bishop and taken special interest in them, that there were four episcopal sees in the Crimea and the Caucasus in the seventh century, and that the Goths had Scriptural texts, of which the late fifth-century Codex argenteus, among others, is surviving evidence. Dvorník argues that 'Russian' (originally 'Varangian') was used by the anonymous hagiographer for 'Gothic', because the new name was in use over the area from which the Tauric Goths had come. The characters 'resolved' by Constantine therefore were those which Wulfila had adapted from the Greek to represent his Moesian (Danubian) Gothic. On the other hand, if they were Slavonic, as some Russian scholars have thought and still think, they must have been either Glagolitic or Cyrillic. Some Soviet scholars appear to be convinced that the characters were Glagolitic, although there is not the slightest evidence for this, and the Ukrainian bishop Ilarion (I. Ohijenko) and the late A. A. Vasiliev (Vasil'jev) would have us believe that they were Cyrillic, although the evidence here is also non-existent. The *Memoria et Vita* does say that Constantine 'compared' the language of the sacred books which were shown to him in Korsun' (Chersonesus taurica) with his own, but the statement probably means that he collated the characters of the other language with the Greek characters. This would mean that the characters were manifestly Greek in style, which excludes Glagolitic, but not Gothic or Cyrillic.

149. Before deciding between Glagolitic and Cyrillic as the original alphabet, we must consider here the evidence offered by Chrabr, which we shall find in a thirteenth- to fourteenth-century Bulgarian manuscript, although Chrabr wrote at the turn of the ninth century.[1] The passage from *O pismenech* reads: 'Now at first the Slavs had no books, but read and riddled with the help of strokes and notches, being heathens. When they had been baptized, however, they were obliged (to write) Slavonic with Roman and Greek characters unsystematically. But how is it possible to write adequately with Greek characters богъ or животъ or ѕѣло or цръковь or чааниѥ or широта or ѩдъ or

---

[1] See W. Vondrák, *Kirchenslavische Chrestomathie*, Göttingen, 1910, pp. 107–8.

жд̑оу (for ιжд̑оу) or юность or азыкъ (for ιазыкъ) or other (words) like these. And so things stayed for many years. Then God, who loves man and orders everything and does not leave mankind without wisdom, but leads everything to wisdom and salvation, had mercy on men, sending them St Constantine the Philosopher, called Cyril, a righteous and noble man, and he made for them thirty-eight characters, some on the Greek model, others according to the Slavonic language. He began with the first (character) in the Greek manner—they with alpha, he with азъ. Both (alphabets) begin with азъ. And as they (i.e. the Greeks) improved on the Hebrew characters, so did he on the Greek.' Like other writing of this kind, Chrabr mingles fact with fancy and patriotic fervour, and we have to read him with care. The cogent parts of the extract we have quoted are that the Slavs used Latin and Greek characters unsystematically; that the Greek alphabet was incapable of coping with a Slavonic phonematic system (Byzantine possessed no equivalents for b, g, $\check{z}$, dz, x, c, $\check{c}$, $\check{s}$, ϱ, ρ), and that Constantine's Slavonic alphabet was modelled on the Greek. Now, if the first statement is as true as the other two obviously are, the books referred to in the *Memoria et Vita* (cap. viii) could not have been in a Slavonic language at all, for the organization of the Slavonic alphabet by Constantine was apparently preceded by a state of chaos in spelling. The importance of our passage from the *Memoria et Vita* resides in the implication that Constantine may have been interested in the possibility of using the Greek alphabet to represent an illiterate alien language. His linguistic feat is of minor importance in comparison, as it is paralleled in the same chapter by a reference to the rapidity with which he mastered Samaritan after having learnt Hebrew in Korsun'. This indeed is probably little more than hagiographic commonplace and may be ignored in favour of the more significant reference to the invention of the Slavonic alphabet. The formal proximity of this to the Greek, indirectly suggested by the list of 'keywords' for the supplementary 'invented' set, might imply that Chrabr had the Cyrillic alphabet in mind. Moreover, there is a trend of opinion, represented, for instance, by the Bulgarian scholar E. Georgiev,[1] which recognizes Cyrillic as the original Slavonic alphabet and Glagolitic as a subsequent stylization of it, apparently, if we

---

[1] *Načaloto na slavjanskata pismenost' v Bǎlgarija, Stǎrobǎlgarskite azbuki*, Sofia, 1942.

may trust Brückner, to mask the Byzantine origin of Cyrillo-Methodian Christianity in the Roman sphere of influence.[1] The dependence of one on the other and of both on Greek is obvious from a study of the following comparative table, especially if the 'binary' system of alphabetic numeration is also taken into account.

Glagolitic	Numerical value	Cyrillic	Numerical value	Greek	Latin-style transliteration	Phonetic transcription
Ⰰ	1	а	1	A	a	a
Ⰱ	2	б			b	b
Ⰲ	3	в	2	B	v	v
Ⰳ	4	г	3	Γ	g	g
Ⰴ	5	д	4	Δ	d	d
Ⰵ	6	є	5	E (ϵ)	e	ε
Ⰶ	7	ж			ž	ʒ
Ⰷ	8	ѕ, ѕ	6	(ζ)	dz	dz
Ⰸ	9	з, з	7	Z (ȝ)	z	z
Ⰹ Ⰺ	10	і, ї	10	I	i	i
Ⰻ	20	н	8	H	i	i
Ⰼ	30	(ꙉ)			g'	ɟ
Ⰽ	40	к	20	K	k	k
Ⰾ	50	л	30	Λ	l	l
Ⰿ	60	м	40	M	m	m
Ⱀ	70	н	50	N	n	n
Ⱁ	80	о	70	O	o	ɔ
Ⱂ	90	п	80	Π	p	p
Ⱃ	100	р	100	P	r	r
Ⱄ	200	с	200	C	s	s
Ⱅ	300	т	300	T	t	t
Ⱆ	400	оу	400	(OY)	u	u
Ⱇ	500	ф	500	Φ	f	f
Ⱈ	600	х	600	X	x/ch	x
Ⱉ	700	ѡ	800	(ω)	o	o
Ⱋ	800	щ			št	ʃt
Ⱌ	900	ц	900		c	ts
Ⱍ	1,000	у	90		č	tʃ
Ⱎ		ш			š	ʃ
Ⱏ		ъ			ŭ/ъ	ɵ

[1] A. Brückner. *Die Wahrheit über die Slavenapostel,* Tübingen, 1913.

Glago-litic	Nume-rical value	Cyrillic	Nume-rical value	Greek	Latin-style trans-literation	Phonetic tran-scription
ⰟⰊ		ЪІ			y	i
Ⱏ		ь			ĭ/ь	ι
Ⰱ		ѣ	900		ě	æ
Ⱃ		ю			ju	ju
Ⱄ		ꙗ			ja	ja
		ѥ			je	jε
ⰵ		ѧ			ę	ε̃
ⰶ		ѫ			ǫ	õ
ⰶ		ѩ			ję	jε̃
ⰶ		ѭ			jǫ	jõ
		ѯ	60	(ξ)	ks	ks
		ѱ	700	Ψ	ps	ps
		ѳ	9	Θ	t/f	t/f
Ⰹ		ѵ	400	Υ	υ	ι

150. The priority of the Glagolitic alphabet, as commonly accepted, has been demonstrated by competent scholarship, not only because of its more 'archaic' appearance, which is not indeed a sound argument here, as we are dealing with two distinct sets of characters, but also because of linguistic evidence, which is. The argument of 'archaism' may be valid where two variants (*ductus*) of the same alphabet are in question. Thus the angular 'Croatian' Glagolitic is more stylized and therefore later than the curvate 'Macedonian' Glagolitic. But it is impossible to compare the latter with early Cyrillic, which is an alphabet of an altogether different type. The linguistic argument, on the other hand, confronts the language of the Glagolitic Kiev Missal, Codex Zographensis, and Codex Marianus with that of the Cyrillic Codex Suprasliensis and 'Book of Savva' (R. *Savvina kniga*) and finds that the language of the first group is older than the language of the second, and certainly older in some respects than that of the 'Ostromir Gospels' (R. *Ostromirovo jevangelije*). Glagolitic Old Church Slavonic, for instance, has many examples of uncontracted adjectives (e.g. -аꙑего, -оуꙑемоу), the 2nd and 3rd person dual endings of the imperfect -ꙑнета, -ꙑшете (cf. Sav. -ста, -сте), forms of the simple aorist (e.g. ведъ 'I led'), unknown to the Codex Suprasliensis and the Book of Savva, and a primitive stratum of words (e.g. братръ 'brother', искрь 'near', ашютъ/ашоутъ 'in vain').[1] The linguistic argument receives confirmation from the cogent palaeographic observation that palimpsests containing both alphabets show Cyrillic superimposed on Glagolitic. Moreover, the numerical value of the Glagolitic characters (§ 149) harmonizes with their alphabetical sequence, whereas in Cyrillic we do not find complete harmony (e.g. б has no numerical value).

151. Of the two Slavonic alphabets, the one with any adequate claims to being an 'original invention' is obviously the Glagolitic,[2] and accordingly this is regarded by most scholars as the prototype. We may accept the customary view without undue reserve and therefore assume that Chrabr, who ascribes the invention of the Slavonic alphabet to Constantine, must have had Glagolitic in mind. V. Jagić[3] thinks that either Glagolitic or Cyrillic could have been implied. P. A. Lavrov[4] and A. I. Soboleveskij,[5] however, are convinced that it was Cyrillic.

152. Both alphabets appear to have reached Rus'; but Glagolitic is very scantily represented there, and so offers no material support to the contention of P. Ja. Černych[6] that Constantine discovered Glagolitic in the Crimea on his mission to the Khazars. The occurrence of Glagolitic characters in many Russian Cyrillic manuscripts may well represent the copyists' curiosity in the other Slavonic alphabet, of which they may be presumed to have had some knowledge, as later Russian copyists had of St Stefan's Old Permian alphabet.[7] That the Glagolitic alphabet was known in Rus' is attested *inter alia* by the Novgorod priest Upyr' Lichoj, who in 1047 had transliterated the Glagolitic text of all the Sixteen Prophets into Cyrillic. His work, extant

[1] J. Vajs, *Rukověť, hlaholské paleografie*, Prague, 1932, p. 16.
[2] G. Dobner (*Abhandlungen der Böhmischen Gesellschaft der Wissenschaften*, ii, Prague, 1785, p. 103) regarded Glagolitic as Constantine's 'wahre Erfindung, weil dessen rohe, ungestaltete, mit keinen andern Lettern übereinkommende Schriftzüge ein wahres neues Erfindungswerk anzeigen'.
[3] *Entstehungsgeschichte der kirchenslavischen Sprache*[2], Berlin, 1913.
[4] 'Paleografičeskoje obozrenije kirillovskogo pis'ma' (*Enciklopedija slavjanskoj filologii*, iv. 1, Petrograd, 1914).
[5] *Slavjano-russkaja paleografija*[2], St Petersburg, 1908.
[6] 'Jazyk i pis'mo' in N. N. Voronin, M. K. Karger i M. A. Tichanova, *Istorija kul'tury drevnej Rusi*, ii, Moscow–Leningrad, 1951, pp. 114–38.
[7] V. I. Lytkin, *Drevnepermskij jazyk*, Moscow, 1952, pp. 75–76.

in fifteenth- and sixteenth-century manuscripts, contains the statement that he copied his text 'from the Cyrillic' (ис коурило-вицѣ), which suggests that he regarded Glagolitic as the invention of St Cyril (Constantine). The Glagolitic inscriptions on the walls of the St Sophia Cathedral (R. Sofijskij sobor) in Novgorod the Great are too fragmentary to be more than a scribal curiosity and in any case appear to go back only to the turn of the eleventh century.

153. The Glagolitic alphabet, as history records, received papal sanction in the ninth century, and Soviet scholars like L. P. Jakubinskij[1] have been inclined to use this fact to explain the neglect of Glagolitic in Rus'. The alphabet may very well have reached Kiev from Moravia in the late ninth or early tenth century. In any case it must have been 'overlaid' in the tenth century by Cyrillic, which, because of its manifest resemblance to the Greek alphabet, was approved as being a more suitable symbolization of Byzantine Christian literature, and, moreover, it had not been used in missionary fields exposed to the influence of Rome. This seems rather far-fetched and certainly recalls the view held by Brückner,[2] according to which Glagolitic was devised by Constantine to conceal the Greek provenance of his alphabet with Byzantine sanction (§ 149). Brückner's view is as political as Jakubinskij's and echoes, perhaps unintentionally, J. Dobrovský's dictum (1783) that the Glagolitic alphabet was a transformation of Cyrillic by 'monastic cunning'.[3]

154. What we do find in Rus' by the eleventh century is the extensive use of the Cyrillic alphabet for both religious and secular purposes. Cyrillic must have reached the East Slavonic area earlier, possibly in the course of the tenth century and in any case before the official recognition of Christianity under Vladimir the Great in 988. That it was known in the tenth century seems to be proved by the text of Oleg's treaty with Byzantium in 911. According to the *Povest' vremennych let*, which quotes it *in extenso*, that treaty was set down 'in writing'; and, as another treaty concluded by the same prince with Byzantium in 944 tells us, parchment (OR харатиа) was used.

---

[1] *Istorija drevnerusskogo jazyka*, Moscow, 1953, p. 109.
[2] Op. cit.
[3] J. Vajs, op. cit., p. 24.

155. There is also a curious, baffling word of those times carved on an amphora (OR кърчага), which was found at Gnezdovo near Smolensk and has been known since 1949. This is now referred to as the Gnezdovo Inscription, and recent attempts have been made to decipher it. M. N. Tichomirov[1] reads it as гороухща, which is meaningless. Černych[2] suggests гороушна and interprets it as meaning (зьрна) гороушьна 'mustard (seeds)'. The latter's reading of the word is unsound, because tenth-century East Slavonic had not lost its unstressed ь (cf. the evidence furnished by Constantine VII). Moreover, the reading is arbitrary, inasmuch as it transposes letters to force an interpretation, for if ш was written above the line as an afterthought, it would have been more accurately placed. We may suggest Гороунша, which may be an Old Russian diminutive name in -ша. But such an interpretation is no more than tentative. The object on which the word is cut out may be an importation along with the Arab coins (dirhems), which helped the archaeologists to date the Gnezdovo finds.

156. We are now thrown back on certainties, and these take us into the eleventh century. Our certainties are of two kinds, viz. copies of Old Church Slavonic liturgical texts made on parchment or vellum in Rus', chiefly in the Novgorod area, and the recently discovered 'Novgorod Birch-bark Writs' (*Novgorodskije berestjanyje gramoty*).[3] The characters used in both cases are Cyrillic uncials. Those engrossed on parchment often possess calligraphic merit, for instance the 'Ostromir Gospels'; those scratched on birch-bark are crude, though legible. The alphabet in the more extensive monuments contains the full complement of characters and is identical with that used in Bulgaria.

157. Bulgaria was the only possible source of Russian Cyrillic; for it was there that the alphabet had been devised to represent the phonemes of Thessalonican Macedonian, which Constantine and Methodius had inevitably chosen as the 'Slavonic' of their Scriptural and liturgical translations from the Greek. The

---

[1] 'Drevnejšaja russkaja nadpis'' (*Vestnik AN SSSR*, iv, Moscow, 1950).
[2] Op. cit.
[3] A. V. Arcichovskij i M. N. Tichomirov, *Novgorodskije gramoty na bereste (iz raskopok 1951 g.)*, Moscow, 1953; V. I. Borkovskij (ed.), *Paleografičeskij i lingvističeskij analiz novgorodskich berestjanych gramot*, Moscow, 1955.

alphabet symbolized a mainly ecclesiastical and partly secular literature which was imported into Rus' along with the rudiments of Christian doctrine apparently in the tenth century. Alphabet, Old Church Slavonic, and Christianity came together as an undivided trinity. The alphabet underwent considerable modification in the course of nearly a millennium and was soon adapted to other than ecclesiastical uses; Old Church Slavonic gradually took on an East Slavonic aspect; and the Christian religion is still closely linked in the formulas of prayer and liturgy with an alien, though related, Slavonic language and symbolized in a stylized 'archaic' character.

158. The tendency to substitute Russian for Macedonian-Bulgarian sounds, and therefore a Russian for a Macedonian-Bulgarian spelling, is seen in the earliest dated manuscript. The 'Ostromir Gospels', which appears to have been copied by deacon Grigorij from a Bulgarian original in 1056–7, contains a great many involuntary substitutions in spelling (e.g. the Russian spellings ѥсть 'is' for ѥстъ, ꙗзыкъ 'tongue' for ѩзыкъ, боюсѧ 'I fear' for боѭсѧ, створи 'he made' for сътвори, вълкъ 'wolf' for влъкъ, цьркы 'church' for цръкы, прѣже 'before' for прѣжде). Study of these and of similar 'errors' in other, dated or undated, manuscripts of the eleventh century will enable us to tabulate the changes in the Cyrillic alphabet as it was adapted to the phonology of Old East Slavonic. The evidence of the substitutions or 'errors' has been recently confirmed to some extent by the oldest and best preserved of the 'Novgorod Birch-bark Writs' (No. 9), which archaeologists seem now inclined to date back, after their first flush of enthusiasm and under the sobering influence of the palaeographers, to the end of the eleventh or the beginning of the twelfth century.[1]

[1] Cf. A. V. Arcichovskij, 'Novyje otkrytija v Novgorode' (*Voprosy istorii*, 12, Moscow, 1951, pp. 77–87) with A. V. Arcichovskij i M. N. Tichomirov, op. cit., pp. 9, 15.

As the result of fresh excavations in Novgorod in 1954–5, fifty-three new writs on birch-bark were brought to light, and A. V. Arcichovskij has ascribed eight of them, on stratigraphic and palaeographic grounds, to the eleventh century (Nos. 84, 88, 89, 90, 109, 120, 121, 123), one to the turn of the eleventh and twelfth centuries (No. 119), and twelve to the twelfth century. V. I. Borkovskij ('Fonetiko-morfologičeskije zametki o gramotach na bereste iz raskopok 1953–1954 gg', *Voprosy jazykoznanija*, 4, Moscow, 1957, pp. 74–78) thinks that No. 109 belongs to the twelfth century at the earliest.

159. The Russian recension of the Old Church Slavonic alphabet admits of not a few variants. Thus the absence of nasal vowels in Old East Slavonic—they were unknown in the tenth century—made the two *jusy* (symbols of nasal vowels) superfluous and they were given the value of oral vowels. The major *jus* (ѫ) was discarded in the twelfth century and replaced by оу (ȣ); the minor *jus* (ѧ), pronounced like 'ьa' (i.e. a following a palatal or palatized consonant), became the prototype of modern Russian я. These and other, mainly vocalic, variants (e.g. є, ѥ, ѣ > е; н, ı > и; о, ѡ > о) figure in the following table, which brings together the typographically modernized Old East Slavonic (Old Russian) eleventh-century alphabet with its twentieth-century Russian counterpart in parallel columns.

Old Russian	Modern Russian	Old Russian	Modern Russian
а	А	х	х
б	Б	ѡ	
в	В	ц	ц
г	Г	ү	ч
д	Д	ш	ш
є	Е, Э	щ	щ
ж	Ж	ъ	ъ
ѕ		ъı	ы
ҙ	3	ь	ь
н	И	ѣ	
ı, ï		ю	ю
к	К	ıa	я
л	Л	ѥ	
м	М	ѧ	
N	Н	ѫ	
о	О	ıѧ	
п	П	ıѫ	
ρ	Р	ѯ	
с	С	ѱ	
т	Т	ѳ	
оү (ȣ)	у	ѵ	
Ф	Ф		

160. The Old Russian alphabet in its eleventh-century form survived almost in its entirety until the sixteenth century, when the ligatured cursive script (*skoropis'*) finally replaced the semi-uncials, which in their turn had replaced the archaic uncial script in the fourteenth. The sixteenth-century cursive used з for з, и for н, ш for т, ы for ъı, the thirteenth-century у for the earlier оу, ȣ, and v for eleventh-century у, and had no equivalents for ѥ, i/ï, ѩ, ѫ, ѭ, and ѱ. Of these ѩ and ѭ are confined, like ѫ, to mainly eleventh-century manuscripts.

161. In these manuscripts the difference between hard (non-palatalized) and soft (palatalized) consonants is indicated by special vowel-characters.[1] Hard consonants are followed by a, o, ъı (> ы), оу/ȣ, ъ, and soft consonants by ѩ/ѧ, є (> е)/ѥ/ѣ, н (> и), ю, ь. But certain consonants, as we shall see later (§ 190), were palatalized 'by nature': accordingly their symbols ж, ц, ɣ (> ч), ш, щ (> щ), were normally followed by the 'softening' vowel-characters (e.g. дажь 'give'; отьци 'fathers'; ночь 'night'; *Ost.* 1056–7: исправльше 'having corrected'). One exception here was permitted by a convention of Old Church Slavonic in the eleventh century, viz. а, and not ѩ, usually appears after the above-mentioned symbols (e.g. *Ost.* 1056–7: почахъ 'I began' for почѩхъ). In addition to this, оу/ȣ is sometimes found for ю (e.g. *Ost.* 1056–7: dat. abs. прѣдрьжѧщоу 'holding'). The Old Church Slavonic syllabic 'liquids' (sonants) лъ, ръ, ль, рь often occur 'in reverse', i.e. with the vowel character preceding the consonant character. This was in accord with the design of the Old Russian phonological system, which admits of no syllabic consonants. And finally the interchange of ѣ and е/ѥ was an Old Russian feature unknown to Old Church Slavonic (§ 162).

162. In the twelfth century and particularly in the thirteenth ѳ was regularly replaced by ф, but it was revived in the sixteenth century and not finally discarded till the spelling reform of 1918. The use of the *i*-ligatured vowel-characters ѩ and ѥ was restricted in the twelfth century, but the latter was not abandoned till the fourteenth, and the former survived to the seventeenth. The *jery* (ь/ъ) were at first carefully distinguished (cf. Colophon

---

[1] N. S. Roždestvenskij, 'Kratkij očerk istorii russkogo pravopisanija' in A. B. Šapiro, *Russkoje pravopisanije*, Moscow, 1951, pp. 160–98.

to *Ost.* 1057), but in weak position the complete lapse of the 'reduced' vowels, which they represented, and their 'clarification' (*projasnenije*) into e/o in strong position (e.g. *Nov. min.*, 1095: желѣзною 'with an iron-' for желѣзьноѭ; *Ost.* 1056–7: кꙑнигꙑ 'books' for къниꙑгꙑ) began to cause difficulty to some scribes, especially outside the properly Russian area (e.g. the 'White Russian' Smolensk Writ, 1229, in which we find the interchange of e/ѣ/ь and of o/ъ: берьгомь 'with the coast' for берегомь; вѣдомъ 'known' for вѣдомо; будѣте 'will be' for будеть). Other writs of the thirteenth century, besides this prototype of White Russian, show the same features, although in a less obvious form. By the fourteenth century strong ь and ъ had been systematically replaced by e and o respectively. From the sixteenth ь was no longer the symbol of a vowel, but merely a mark of palatalization, the 'soft sign' (*mjagkij znak*), and ъ had come in effect to be regarded as the corresponding 'hard sign' (*tvjordyj znak*), although it tended to be omitted sporadically if in weak position (e.g. I. Peresvetov, *Vtoraja čelobitnaja*, 16th century: бьет челом холоп твой 'thy servant petitions'). Lapse of the *jery* by apocope or syncope led to a rift between the spelling and pronunciation of consonants. The various types of assimilation which now supervened were seldom shown in spelling (e.g. *Ipat.*, *c.* 1425: празной 'empty' for праздной; *Domostroj*, 16th cent.: лошки 'spoons' for ложьки).

163. The phonetic interpretation of vowels remained undisturbed until the first appearance of *akan'je* (*a*-articulation or the substitution of **a** and **ə** for unstressed *o*) in the fourteenth century. The confusion of *a* and *o* became more common in the fifteenth and sixteenth centuries; but traditional rules, grounded in *okan'je* (*o*-articulation or the preservation of the unstressed rounded vowel), rigidly resisted the tendency in Muscovy, where only a few *a*-type pronunciations insinuated themselves into the spelling (e.g. завтракъ 'breakfast' for завтрокъ; стаканъ 'tumbler' for стоканъ; крапива 'nettle' for кропива).

164. The symbol ѣ, although it was identified with e in Old Russian pronunciation from the earliest times, was fairly consistently kept apart from it in writing under Church Slavonic influence until the fifteenth century, when a period of confusion in the use of the two characters set in. In the period from the eighteenth century to 1918 the differentiation between ѣ and e was arbitrary and artificial as well as sometimes etymologically wrong (e.g. сѣкира 'axe' for секира). The spelling reform of 1918 removed ѣ from the alphabet as the bugbear of Russian schoolchildren, for whom even mnemonic verses containing words written with this character had been found necessary.

165. Old Russian spelling underwent certain arbitrary changes in the fourteenth century as the result of the orthographic reforms introduced by the Metropolitan Kiprian, who was a Bulgarian. These were patently reactionary, aiming as they did to impose earlier South Slavonic usage. They included the substitution of Old Church Slavonic лъ, рь, ръ for Russian ъл, ьр, ър, the reintroduction of ѕ for ҙ in some cases, of ж for оу/ѕ (оу was initial, ѕ medial), а for ꙗ/ѧ (ꙗ was initial, ѧ medial), і for и before all vowels (a rule unknown before), and the restoration of ѳ, ѯ, and ѵ in Greek loan-words and of 'tricornute' ѡ for 'acute' o initially and occasionally in other positions. These trivialities are enumerated subsequently in Church Slavonic grammars like that of the Ukrainian Meletij Smotryc′kyj (*Grammatiki slavenskija pravilnoje sintagma*, Evje, 1619), who complicated matters by introducing other pedantries such as the rule requiring the endings -и, -ѧ, -ѧ in the masculine, feminine, and neuter plural of the adjective respectively (e.g. свѧтїи, свѧтыѧ, свѧтаѧ 'holy'). Smotryc′kyj's grammar, which was reprinted anonymously in Moscow in 1648, deals also with word-division and the use of capitals. Before the sixteenth century manuscripts did not divide the text into words. In 1564 a book printed in Moscow, viz. *Apostol* 'Acts of the Apostles', was careful to do this, but not systematically (e.g. вковарьствѣ 'in cunning' for в коварьствѣ). It was only at the end of the sixteenth century that systematic word-division first appears in printed books. By the seventeenth century word-division, though subject to rules like those enumerated by Smotryc′kyj, is general, except in manuscripts, which still continue to be written as in previous centuries. As regards the use of capital letters, there is a notable difference in practice between copyist and printer. Until the sixteenth century this use was hindered by the nature of the initial characters: they occur in manuscripts only at the beginning of each book, chapter, or—more rarely—paragraph. After the introduction o printing they also begin fresh sentences and are occasionally used for proper names. Smotryc'kyj extends the use of these to the names of 'dignitaries' (e.g. Царь 'tsar'), of the 'arts' (c.g. Грамматика 'grammar'), and of parts of speech (e.g. Глаголъ 'verb'). He also approved of the use of the stress mark and the abbreviation mark (*titlo* 'tittle').

166. This was the state of printed Russian, ecclesiastical and secular, before the Petrine reform of the alphabet in 1710. The reform, prepared in part by seventeenth-century typographical selection (which had abandoned ж) and in part by cursive practice, drew a sharp line between ecclesiastical and secular usage by instituting a new 'civil alphabet' (R. *graždanskaja azbuka*). This had discarded the following characters[1]—ε, ѡ, ѧ, ѯ, ѱ, while retaining ѕ, ï, ѵ (alongside of у), ѣ, ѳ, and v, the last three of which were to disappear together with dotted i only in 1918. The reform knew nothing of either stresses (*sily*) or 'tittles' (*titla*). Moreover, the outward aspect of the characters which were retained was also changed by substituting a 'ductus' conforming to Latin models. When the Imperial Academy Press was founded in 1727 the Petrine reform of the alphabet was standardized.

167. But although the alphabet had been modified, spelling was left untouched, and here usage appears to have been chaotic even in the later eighteenth century. A. P. Sumarokov's treatise 'On Orthography' (*O pravopisanii*) declares that 'writers today have lost all sense of proportion and write not only without any sense of shame, but look to lower example; and the audacity of ignorance has surpassed all measure'. Spelling was a leading topic with Russian scholars in the eighteenth and nineteenth centuries. V. K. Trediakovskij's 'Dialogue between a Foreigner and a Russian about the Old and the New Spelling' (*Razgovor meždu čužestrannym čelovekom i rossijskim ob ortografii starinnoj i novoj*, 1747) precipitated the discussion. It is a defence of Peter the Great's 'civil alphabet' against the old (Church Slavonic) 'ductus' and a plea for the application of the phonetic principle to spelling. 'That orthography is quite correct which pays attention only to sounds (*zvony*)', he writes. But in spite of Trediakovskij's insistence on phonetic spelling he is not consistent in practice

---

[1] See S. P. Obnorskij i S. G. Barchudarov, *Chrestomatija po istorii russkogo jazyka*, ii. 1, Moscow, 1949, pp. 151–3, where Peter the Great's own corrections are reproduced.

and makes no concessions to *akan'je*, which was general in eighteenth-century educated Russian. He also has his own eccentricities (e.g. the use of i and s for и and з respectively, шч for щ, and one o for two to avoid haplology, so that he writes, say, вобшче for вообще). M. V. Lomonosov, on the contrary, upheld the traditional morphological principle of spelling against him in his 'Russian Grammar' (*Rossijskaja grammatika*, 1755) in the interests of etymology.[1] Like Trediakovskij he preferred шч to щ, but wrote e for э (e.g. етотъ 'this'), e for iô (Sumarokov has ьо and N. M. Karamzin was to write ё towards the end of the century), and i only before vowel characters; and while admitting that ѣ and e 'are hardly distinguishable at all in ordinary speech', he retains the former to help distinguish homophones in writing (e.g. лечу 'I fly' from лѣчу 'I heal'). Lomonosov also continues to write ъ, using it as a 'hard sign', occasionally after phonetically 'soft' ч and щ (e.g. кирпичъ 'brick', овощъ 'vegetable'). His use of ь as the 'soft sign' is mainly consistent with morphological needs (e.g. nom. sg. речь 'speech', gen. речи), but he sometimes makes concessions to phonetic principles (e.g. верьхъ 'top'). He adheres to Church Slavonic tradition in writing -аго/-яго for -ого/-его, but hesitates between the Russian adjectival endings -ой/-ей and the corresponding Church Slavonic -ый/-ий. Lomonosov was attacked by Sumarokov in a series of treatises, including *O pravopisanii*, for damaging the Russian language by 'converting the Moscow dialect into that of Kolmogory (*sic* for Cholmogory)', his supposed birthplace in northern Russia. In spite of the obvious interest and importance of the subject, the government, however, took no action in the matter of regulating the orthography, and it was left to the reformers to bring order by degrees into the prevailing chaos. The Imperial Academy of Sciences in its 'Dictionary' (1789–1794) and its 'Russian Grammar' (1802) found itself able to frame more precise rules by continuing to adhere to Lomonosov's morphological principle. Yet even at the turn of the century there was still considerable inconsistency and variation, and Karamzin[2] could declare: 'You will scarcely find in the entire country some hundred persons who have a

---

[1] In § 112 we read: '. . . that all trace of the derivation and composition of words may not be lost.'

[2] 'Zapiski o drevnej i novoj Rossii' (*Aonidy*, 2, Moscow, 1797).

complete knowledge of spelling.' Puškin himself was no exception (cf. his spellings здаровъ 'well', большова 'of the big', щастье 'happiness', грѣшной 'sinful', цалую 'I kiss').

168. Nineteenth-century Russian grammarians, for instance A. Ch. Vostokov, N. I. Greč, I. I. Davydov, and F. I. Buslajev, did a great deal to normalize Russian spelling, but in the middle of the century V. G. Belinskij still considered their rules to be arbitrary and confusing.[1] In 1873 Ja. K. Grot published his capital treatise 'Debatable Questions of Russian Orthography from Peter the Great till Today' (*Spornyje voprosy russkogo pravopisanija ot Petra Velikogo donyne*).[2] Its declared purpose was 'to explain to the thoughtful reader the present state of Russian spelling from the historical point of view and to contribute towards a greater uniformity of the written form'. As a practical manual he published his 'Russian Orthography' (*Russkoje pravopisanije*) in 1885. This became an indispensable guide to both school and press and ran through some twenty editions, but it was not unanimously accepted and followed. Although Grot was mainly a traditionalist, he sometimes pitted himself against tradition (cf. the inconsistency of свистнуть 'to whistle' and хлеснуть 'to lash'). His traditionalism is most evident in the retention of ъ and ѣ and in the catalogue of all radicals containing the latter.[3]

169. The simplification of Russian spelling was widely discussed in the middle of the nineteenth century. In the course of 1862–3 conferences were convened in St Petersburg to elucidate the complicated problem. Some forty years later a project of spelling reform was prepared by P. N. Sakulin for the Moscow Pedagogical Society. It included the elimination of i, ъ, ѣ, ѳ, ѵ from the alphabet; ь was to be used as a 'separative' (e.g. объем 'volume' for объемъ); ы and o were to appear after ж, ц, ч, ш, щ; ь was to be omitted in such words as мощь, ночь, рожь, тишь; the adjectival endings -ово/-ево were to be used for -аго/яго, её for ея, and они for онѣ; з was to be retained in the prefixes без-, воз-, низ-, раз-, через- in all positions, and unstressed е was to be substituted for и in the locative of words like Василий and здание and in the dative-locative of words like Мария. But

[1] *Sočinenija*, ix, Moscow, 1860.
[2] Reprinted in *Filologičeskije razyskanija*[3], St Petersburg, 1885.
[3] Cf. his statement: 'it was difficult to learn to distinguish ѣ from e' (*Sočinenija*, x, St Petersburg, p. 421).

Sakulin's project was turned down by the government in 1903. In the following year the Imperial Academy set up its own Orthographical Commission to deal with the problem, which by this time had become pressing. The Commission decided to recommend the exclusion of the characters ъ, ѣ, ѳ, and either i or и. This and other suggestions were incorporated in the report of a subcommittee, which included not only Sakulin but Baudouin de Courtenay, Korš, Sobolevskij, and Šachmatov. The final 'resolution' (*postanovlenije*) of this subcommittee was published in 1912. The Imperial Academy accepted a modified form of it, summarized under thirteen points. These thirteen points were: (1) e for ѣ, (2) ф for ѳ, (3) ъ only as a 'separative sign' (e.g. съемка 'taking'), (4) и for i, (5) the desirability of ё, (6) the prefixes без-, вз-, воз-, низ-, раз-, роз-, через-, чрез- to be spelt бес-, &c., before symbols representing voiceless consonants, (7) the adjectival acc.–gen. sg. endings -ого/-его for -аго/-яго (cf. Sakulin's more phonetic -ово/-ево), (8) the endings -ые/-ие for feminine and neuter nom.–acc. pl. -ыя/-iя, (9) они for онѣ in the feminine nom. pl., (10) одни for однѣ also in the feminine nom. pl., (11) ee (её) for ея, (12) syllabification to recognize indivisibility of the last consonant of a group and the following vowel, of й and the preceding vowel, of an initial consonant-group and the following vowel, and the separation of prefixes (e.g. под-ходить 'to step up to'), and (13) either the composite or the separate writing of compound adverbs (e.g. в-стороне 'aside'). This reform, however, was not carried into effect until December 1917; but, even then, points five and thirteen, possibly because they were not so categorically worded as the rest, were left out. It is interesting to note in this connexion that point five is now being increasingly implemented in printing.

170. Among the problems of Russian spelling which remain unsolved are (1) the writing of compound adverbs, (2) double consonants in loan-words from foreign languages, (3) the spelling of individual words (e.g. мачеха/мачиха 'stepmother'), and, more important than any of these, (4) the solution of the pressing, but eschewed, problem of *akan'je*. This last as well as the makeshift -ого/-его (contrast Sakulin's -ово/-ево) shows that the morphological principle remains latent in Russian spelling to this day.

V

SOURCES

171. Enumeration and study of the written material, on which the history of Russian must unavoidably be based,[1] belongs to the field of philological bibliography rather than to that of literary aesthetics, for this material *in toto* can be described as literature only in the widest sense of the term. It consists of all kinds of writing, some of it, especially in the earlier phases, as far removed from the notion of belles-lettres as it is possible to imagine. But writing is not our only source of the Russian language. For at least two generations now there have been phonetic recordings of spoken Russian and of many of its dialects, and these recordings, although not of uniform merit, have helped to establish the vital relationship between orthography and pronunciation in recent times, to give precision to the notion of dialectal differences, and to recreate, by the projection of present knowledge into the past, types of Russian pronunciation which time has obliterated. These are of considerable significance for the historical investigation of Russian; but we must always be alert to the secondary value of such evidence, for in restoring a 'dead' or obsolete pronunciation we are doing an exercise in conjecture. As we follow the line of development traced out by a selection of the more important 'milestones' of the language, we shall find ourselves, except in the latest stage, entirely engrossed in manuscripts and books. The manuscripts are chronologically the earlier material; but they continue to be produced well into the period of printing, and the earliest books, mainly of the seventeenth century, fall within the period of the older language.

172. Old Russian, as we learn to know it in the eleventh century, is contained in inscriptions on stone, coins, and domestic utensils, and in manuscripts written on parchment and birch-bark. The inscriptions are short and of very small linguistic

---

[1] See also W. K. Matthews, 'The Russian Language before 1700' (*SEER*, xxxi. 77, London, 1953, pp. 364–87).

value. Some of them are close in language to Old Church Slavonic, for instance, the inscriptions on the coins of Vladimir the Great (981–1015), Svjatopolk (1015–19), and Jaroslav the Wise (1019–54), and others, like the Tmutorokan' Inscription (1068) on a slab of marble, telling how Prince Gleb Svjatoslavič of Tmutorokan' measured the distance across the strait of Kerč on the ice, are more obviously Old Russian.

173. From the beginning, then, we are confronted with the presence of two languages, although we shall sometimes be hard put to it to distinguish them, as they share a large common vocabulary and not a few common constructions. The contrast between them is clearer when the material is more abundant; and here we must turn to the manuscripts. In the eleventh century there are for the most part Russian copies of Old Church Slavonic originals, and their tenor is almost exclusively ecclesiastical. These are the 'Ostromir Gospels', engrossed on parchment for Ostromir, burgomaster (*posadnik*) of Novgorod the Great, by deacon Grigorij in 1056–7, the 'Archangel Gospels' (*Archangel'skoje jevangelije, c.* 1092), the 'Novgorod Liturgical Menaea' (*Novgorodskije služebnyje minei*, 1095–7), the 'Turov Gospels' (*Turovskoje jevangelije*, 11th cent.) or leaves of an evangeliarium (or evangelistarium), the two 'Svjatoslav Miscellanies' (*Sborniki Svjatoslava*, 1073–6), a Russian adaptation of the Bulgarian encyclopaedia of Tsar Symeon the Great (893–927), and a small number of psalters, hagiographies, homilies, pandects, and a patericon (*Sinajskij paterik*). The language of these manuscripts, all written on parchment, is substantially Old Church Slavonic, but in a Russian recension. This explains the numerous errors of the copyists, which help us to reconstruct the Russian pronunciation of the time. A better notion of this, however, emerges from the earliest of the newly-discovered Novgorod writs on birch-bark. This (No. 9) appears to be a private note of a few lines from one Gostjata to Vasilij on a legal issue. The language resembles that of later writs, viz. those of the twelfth century, and uses the Old Church Slavonic characters with Russian values (e.g. ѧ in съдаѧли 'they gave', pronounced 'съдаюали'; мѧ 'me', pronounced 'миа'). Like the Tmutorokan' Inscription, it drops the auxiliary verb быти 'to be' in the third person of the perfect tense and uses this tense instead of the aorist. These features would seem to have characterized Old Russian morphologically at the literary beginnings of the language.

174. In the succeeding centuries both inscriptions and manuscripts multiplied, and the Russian element in the specifically ecclesiastical material becomes more marked or, to put it differently, the Church Slavonic element becomes more corrupt. The twelfth century is notable for the variety of its ecclesiastical genres—gospels (e.g. *Mstislavovo jevangelije, c.* 1117; *Jur'jevskoje jevangelije, c.* 1120), homilies, menaea, hymnaries (viz. *stixirari, kondakari, oktoixi, triodi*), legal codices or nomocanons (*kormčije*), and hagiographies (e.g. *Skazanije i strast' i pochvala svjatuju mučeniku Borisa i Gleba*). Some of these items are contained in such characteristic miscellanies (*sborniki*) as the 'Assumption Miscellany' (*Uspenskij sbornik*) and the 'Golden Fount' (*Zlatostruj*),[1] in both of which, for instance, we find the martyrological 'Legend of Boris and Gleb'. In a number of cases the materials are dated; in others we have to make use of palaeographic evidence. This is, on the whole, a more reliable guide than archaeology, which, as in the case of the 'Novgorod Birch-bark Writs', tends to be erratic and dates its undated documentary finds by the datable objects (e.g. coins) with which they were unearthed, although these objects might well have been heirlooms in some instances rather than actually received at the time when the particular document was written.

175. More valuable for the study of twelfth-century Russian than the Russian copyists' errors in copying Old Church Slavonic are the earliest lengthy writs (*gramoty*), viz. the deed of gift (*darstvennaja gramota*) of Princes Mstislav and Vsevolod to the St George Monastery in Novgorod the Great (*c.* 1130) and the deed of deposit (*vkladnaja*) of Varlaam, founder of the Chutyn' Monastery (*c.* 1192), in both of which we note the influence of Church Slavonic on certain formulas and constructions. The inscriptions like those on the Steržen' Cross (1133), on the bowl (*čara*) of Prince Vladimir Davidovič of Černigov (*c.* 1151), and on the gold cross of Princess Jevfrosinija of Polock (*c.* 1161) are on the whole a trifle longer and accordingly more informative

---

[1] These manuscripts are sometimes relegated by chronologists to the early thirteenth century.

than the Tmutorokan′ Inscription; but the two latter illustrate peculiarities of Ukrainian and White Russian respectively.

176. In the thirteenth century we have our earliest extant copy of the Old Russian legal code (*Russkaja pravda, c.* 1282), contained in the 'Novgorod Nomocanon' (*Novgorodskaja kormčaja*). Another translated nomocanon, viz. that of Photius, emanates from Rjazan′ (1284), and there are numerous ecclesiastical works, executed in a variety of provincial scriptoria, especially in the north (e.g. Novgorod, Rostov, Rjazan′). The diversity of such centres is also impressed on the bibliographer by the writs which by this time have notably risen in number. These, like the ecclesiastical manuscripts, are associated mainly with northern centres, for instance Novgorod and Tver′, as well as the 'White Russian' Smolensk and Polock; and the fourteenth century extends the area of literary production to Pskov, Jaroslavl′, Moscow, and Rjazan′. All these items are written on parchment in a language which recalls that of the eleventh-century 'Novgorod Birch-bark Writs' (e.g. No. 9) and the items in the *Russkaja pravda*. It is essentially Old Russian, though it is inevitably impure in parts, because of the prevailing influence of the slowly-decaying Church Slavonic. Besides the writs on parchment the period from the twelfth to the fourteenth century, as we have seen, also presents a number of writs on birch-bark, whose linguistic value, however, is minimized by their fragmentariness.

177. The fourteenth century continued to proliferate ecclesiastical literature with less care than the thirteenth until the period of South Slavonic influence set in and recovered older practice. We have already seen that as the result of Archbishop Kiprian's reforms several obsolete characters, including ѕ, ѡ, ѫ, ѳ, were revived (§ 165) and certain non-Russian combinations of extant characters substituted for Russian usage (e.g. preconsonantal лъ, ръ for ъл, ър). The ecclesiastical manuscripts of this century, as of the next, present therefore on the whole an archaic aspect. The interest of these fourteenth-century manuscripts, however, does not reside in this, but rather in their historical and, to a less extent, in their literary significance, for they include the dated Laurentian Manuscript (*Lavrent′jevskij spisok*) of the *Povest′ vremennych let* (1377), the oldest extant copy of a composite chronicle (*letopisnyj svod*) after the palaeographically dated in part late-thirteenth-century First Novgorod Chronicle. This Laurentian Manuscript gives us specimens of tenth-century Russian treaties, viz. those of 911, 944, and 971, as well as Prince Vladimir Monomach's *Poučenije* (under 1096). Other fourteenth-century manuscripts contain the homilies of Kiril, bishop of Turov, and of Serapion, bishop of Vladimir (cf. *Zlataja cep'*). Here accordingly we have three distinct kinds of writing, with the *Poučenije* constituting a sort of link between the extremes of secular and ecclesiastical style, represented by the treaties and the homilies respectively.

178. The fourteenth century in some respects marks a turning-point in the history of Russian philological bibliography, for it witnessed not only the beginnings of South Slavonic influence but changes in the materials used for writing and in the 'ductus' of the copyist. It was in the middle of the fourteenth century that the use of paper was first introduced, though paper was not preferred to parchment till the fifteenth century. The uncial character, which had predominated from the beginning to the middle of the fourteenth century, was now exposed to the competition of the semi-uncial character. In the fifteenth the ligatured cursive was introduced, and this hand became customary in the following two centuries.

179. The fifteenth century is still part of the manuscript age, and its manuscripts possess a notable variety of interest. Chief among them is the Hypatian redaction (*Ipat'jevskij spisok, c.* 1425) of a fourteenth-century code of annals, which may be compared with the Laurentian Manuscript from the linguistic point of view. Such comparison shows its language to have, on the whole, less of the Church Slavonic veneer which may be seen in the Laurentian. A similar contrast is offered by the language of the Novgorod homilies of Luka Židjata (belonging historically to the eleventh century, though palaeographically to the turn of the fourteenth), and that of the homily 'On the Law and Grace' (*Slovo o zakone i blagodati*) of his contemporary, Ilarion, metropolitan of Kiev, which has survived in a sixteenth-century manuscript. To the fifteenth century too belong the earliest manuscripts of 'Exploits beyond the Don' (*Zadonščina*) of Sofonij of Rjazan', a military narrative (*voinskaja povest'*) closely related in language and spirit to the 'Lay of Igor" (*Slovo o polku Igoreve*), that unique twelfth-century prose-poem, which unfortunately survives only as a nineteenth-century printed text, and, more interesting still, the manuscript of the 'Itinerary beyond Three Seas' (*Choženije za tri morja*, 1466–72) of the Tver' merchant Afanasij Nikitin, who tells of his experiences in Mogul India in simple unaffected Russian. This style of writing, however, was not generally cultivated in the fifteenth century, which is better represented by the pompous logomania (*pletenije sloves* or *izvitije*) of the hagiographer Jepifanij the Most Wise (cf. his *Žitije Stefana Permskogo* and *Žitije Sergija Radonežskogo*), who, while following earlier models (e.g. the thirteenth-century *Molenije Daniila Zatočnika*), was perhaps more under the influence of contemporary South Slavonic pedantry.

180. The fifteenth-century manuscripts, like those of the fourteenth, issue from a diversity of provincial centres, which include Ustjug (in the basin of the Northern Dvina) and Moscow itself. The earliest Moscow manuscripts, like those of Jaroslavl' and Rjazan', date from the middle of the fourteenth century, but they do not become either numerous or typical until the sixteenth. By that time the art of printing had reached Eastern Europe, and an *Apostol* (Acts of the Apostles) had been printed in Moscow by Ivan Feodorov in 1564.[1] But as it was at first an ecclesiastical monopoly and subject to adverse political influences, its progress was restricted, and it was not until the middle of the seventeenth century that it produced its first secular books (e.g. *Učenije i chitrost' ratnogo strojenija pechotnych ljudej*, 1647).

181. The sixteenth-century manuscripts of linguistic interest, as well as of historical and sociological value, are the correspondence of Ivan IV and Prince Andrej Kurbskij (1563–79), the 'Book of Household Management' (*Domostroj*) by the priest Sil'vestr, the 'Centicapitular Protocol' (*Stoglav*, 1551), Ivan Peresvetov's 'Legend of Sultan Mahomet' (*Skazanije o Magmetesaltane, c.* 1547), and the legal codes (*sudebniki*) of Ivan IV (1550) and Feodor (1589), which go back to that of Ivan III (1497).

---

[1] It would seem that printing in Muscovy antedates Feodorov's activities by a decade. Ivan IV's correspondence contains a reference to the printer M. Nefed'ev in 1556.

This century also saw the literary activity of Maksim the Greek (Maksim Grek), whose work of revising the Scriptures generally follows the conservative practice of the South Slavonic scholars of the two preceding centuries.

182. The seventeenth century is remarkably rich in bibliographical material. The copying of early manuscripts continued in spite of the development and secularization of printing in the second half of the century, and the art of copying, as we already know, survived into the eighteenth century, which was nevertheless predominantly an age of the printed word in Russia. One reason for the plethora of written sources which we encounter in this century of political transition is a growing acquaintance with the culture, material as well as intellectual, of Western Europe. The contacts between East and West, whether hostile or amicable, had begun in the sixteenth century, and a live interest in Western Europe may be seen in the time of Ivan IV (1533–84). The channel of Western influence on Muscovy was her nearest western neighbour Poland, especially the eastern and south-eastern provinces of that country—White Russia and the Ukraine—parts of which had been ceded to Tsar Alexis in 1667. The level of culture here was notably higher than in Muscovy, and this enabled their scholars to play an outstanding part in the promotion and development of Russian education, church life, and literature, particularly towards the end of the century. Relations with the West led to the cultivation of the translator's art, and this in its turn contributed materially to the formation of a unified literary language. Translation covered several fields, including the literary (e.g. *Povest' o Bove koroleviče*[1] through White Russian, and *Velikoje zercalo* and *Rimskije dejanija* through Polish) and the technological, in which the originals were mainly West European, as we observe towards the end of the century under Peter the Great (e.g. K. N. Zotov's *Svetil'nik morskoj* from the Dutch). But translations were accompanied and excelled in quality and number by original works in both verse (e.g. *Povest' o Gore-zločastii*; Simeon Polockij's *Vertograd mnogocvetnyj*, 1678) and prose, which covered history (e.g. Prince I. M. Katyrev-Rostovskij's *Letopisnaja kniga*, 1626), hagiography

[1] The remote original of this was the romance of Bevis of Hampton, which reached Muscovy in an Italian version, where Bevis becomes Buovo.

(e.g. *Povest' o Julianii Lazarevskoj*), romance (e.g. *Povest' o Frole Skobejeve*), satire (e.g. *Prazdnik kabackich jaryžek*), memoirs (e.g. G. Kotošichin's *O Rossii v carstvovanije Alekseja Michajloviča, c.* 1664), and autobiography (e.g. Avvakum's *Žitije*, 1672–3). It will be seen here that the medieval and the modern, the ecclesiastical and the secular, genres of literature were cultivated side by side. And in addition to these we have administrative and judicial documents and private correspondence (e.g. the letters and papers of Peter the Great), which help to widen the conception of literature for bibliographer and philologist.[1]

183. The early part of the eighteenth century, which introduces the modern period of the language, is characterized by much the same sort of writing as the later seventeenth century. The ecclesiastical and secular styles had now been effectually separated as distinct languages, viz. Church Slavonic and Russian, and the Petrine reform of the alphabet (1710) had left each with a different outward appearance. The literature of translations continued, especially in the technological and scientific fields, with the Tsar's personal encouragement (e.g. B. Varenius's 'Geography' in the version of F. Polikarpov, 1718). It was he too who countenanced the first steps in journalism (e.g. *Vedomosti*, 1703–27) and left behind a voluminous body of private correspondence, papers, and decrees. All such modes of writing fall obviously outside the proper sphere of original imaginative literature, which in its turn advanced by leaps and bounds in all the classical genres as the eighteenth century ran its course. An attempt to differentiate styles of writing (*stili*) belongs to the polymath Lomonosov, whose work has already been noticed in orthography and grammar (§ 167). Lomonosov, with his encyclopaedic mind, was a characteristic product of the eighteenth-century thirst for knowledge and is also in the direct line of development of Russian literature. Others in this line were Deržavin in verse and Karamzin chiefly in prose in the eighteenth century and Puškin in both in the nineteenth.

184. The characteristically modern style of writing Russian, especially prose, emerged in the second half of the nineteenth century, which saw many significant contributions not only

---

[1] W. K. Matthews, 'Observations on the Study of Seventeenth-Century Russian (*SEER*, xxxiv. 83, London, 1956, pp. 487–90).

to the novel, but to scholarship, journalism, and thought. All these and other spheres of intellectual activity, which continue along new lines in the period after 1918, provide the historian of language with an enormous quantity of written material for the study of the development, chiefly in vocabulary and idiom, of the modern type of Russian. In addition we have at our disposal, from the end of the eighteenth century to date, a series of dictionaries, grammars, and linguistic works; and, since the end of the nineteenth century, studies in the dialectal varieties of spoken Russian provide the *apparatus criticus* for contemporary scholarly and systematic commentary on the extant material. It must be obvious that as we approach recent times the abundance of sources makes selective investigation necessary. No longer, as in the eleventh and twelfth centuries, have we to deal with a language limited to a body of material which can be easily incorporated in a modest list. The bibliography of modern Russian, then, and this includes both manuscript and printed material since the beginning of the eighteenth century, can only be suggested with no more than an allusion to the variety of genres and disciplines into which it would have to be classified for cataloguing.

VI

CHARACTERISTICS OF OLD RUSSIAN

185. General. Before we can begin our study of the development of Russian, we must have in mind as clear an outline of the structure of Old Russian as it is possible to trace at the present time, and to do this we must consider the language in its various aspects, i.e. as an organized complex of phonology, morphology, syntax, vocabulary, and style, based on the examination of the rather scanty materials of the eleventh and twelfth centuries.

186. For the phonological aspect we can also draw on still earlier and scantier material[1] of Byzantine and Arab origin as well as on our familiarity with the structure of Old Church Slavonic,[2] whose influence on Old Russian was considerable and confusing. The evidence of Old Russian loan-words in peripheral languages such as Baltic and West Finnic is generally unsatisfactory, because these languages were recorded in writing as late as the sixteenth century and, like all other languages, must therefore have undergone some development in the interim. Moreover, the discoveries of the modern phonetic sciences, although vital to our study, are nevertheless grounded in a knowledge of living languages, in this case of Modern Russian, between which and Old Russian there extends a space of some nine hundred years. We have accordingly to proceed here warily by combining fact with conjecture, but we shall try to keep the latter within the realm of probability.

187. Phonology. By collation of relevant medieval data and its interpretation with the aid of modern phonology we can set up the following systems of vowels and consonants for Old Russian

[1] W. K. Matthews, 'The Pronunciation of Medieval Russian' (*SEER* xxx. 74, London, 1951, pp. 87–111) and 'The Phonemes of Tenth-Century East Slavonic in the Light of Byzantine Evidence' (*Slavistična revija*, x. 1–4, Ljubljana, 1957, pp. 160–71).
[2] W. K. Matthews, 'The Old Bulgarian Language-Type' (*Archivum Linguisticum*, i. 2, Glasgow, 1949, pp. 157–80).

in the eleventh and twelfth centuries, or the oldest recovered period of the literary language.

188. The vowel system appears in the form of a triangle which differs little from its modern counterpart and may be conveniently presented in the modern Cyrillic character.

	Front		Central		Back	
Close . . .	и				ы	у
Half-close . .		ь	ъ			
Half-open . .		e			o	
Open. . .			a			

The front vowels are unrounded, and the 'characteristic' back vowels are rounded. The back vowel ы, though associated as a variant with the phoneme и (cf. 12th cent. в ынѣхъ обласѣхъ 'in other parts' for инѣхъ), is phonetically different as it is in modern Russian. Its presence in the back series in both Russian and White Russian today is noteworthy and appears to be the result of a tendency towards maximum differentiation as well as of the possible influence of Old Church Slavonic, where it apparently constituted a separate phoneme. Its blurring in the related Ukrainian and Polish and its lapse elsewhere confirm its close association with и. The inaccurately named 'semivowels' (*jery*), ь and ъ,[1] survive in Old Russian as distinguishable vowels, although their distribution has been interfered with. Their final loss, except in strong positions, led to the emergence of the modern Russian phonological system with its five 'alphabetic' vowel phonemes, viz. *i, e, a, o, u*. But even in the eleventh and twelfth centuries there are instances of the change (*projasnenije* 'clarification') of ь and ъ into e and o respectively. This demonstrates their original qualitative difference from the 'closer' и and y (cf. OCS *ĭ* and *ŭ*). The half-open vowels e and o appear to have been much as they are now, although there are indications that they may have been closer (i.e. phonetically **e, o**) in the North Russian (Novgorod) dialect; but even there o is found transcribing unstressed Greek *a* (e.g. Ондроникъ < Ἀνδρονίκος). The graphic

---

[1] For the phonetic value of this vowel, see the signature of Anna, daughter of Prince Jaroslav the Wise and Queen of France, in a Latin writ of 1063, viz. Ａna Pъина, where ъ stands for ə.

confusion of e and ѣ (this was æ in OCS) suggests a common pronunciation which may be phonetically indicated by half-open ε. *Jat'* (ѣ), however, is also found in alternation with a in final position (e.g. gen. sg. землѣ/земля 'earth'), and this leads us to conclude that it may also have had a variant pronunciation æ.[1] The vowel a was intermediate in character, i.e. neither front nor back, and therefore in suitable consonantal environments may have been heard as either.

189. The characters of the alphabet which reached Russia from Bulgaria in the tenth century must be kept strictly apart from our symbols for the Old Russian phonemes. Cyrillic ι, i, ï, и (also consonantal *j* in diphthongs) represent и; the character ѣ, as we have seen, stands for e (which is written є) and is synonymous with ꙗ (our я) when final; the phoneme a is written a; ω is an alternative representation of o: the character ъı is normally written for our ы, and y usually figures as oy or ȣ and sometimes as the major *jus* (ѫ). As we have hinted already (§ 81), some vowel characters representing 'hard' (normal) vowels are paralleled by symbols for 'soft' vowels, i.e. vowels preceded by palatalized consonants: thus the phonemes e, a, y in palatalized contexts appear as ѥ, ꙗ/ѧ/ꙗ, ю/ѭ, i.e. as ligatures preceded by ι ('pre-iotacized' characters).

190. The Old Russian consonantal system would seem to have already possessed its modern dualism of 'hard' and 'soft' (palatalized) types, but the hush-sibilants (F. *chuintantes*) and affricates were always palatalized (we indicate this with a top post-literal stroke), and the velar group (к, г, х) was always 'hard' or non-palatalized. This may be seen from our table, in which the unmodified symbols represent the 'hard' types.

		Bilabial	Labio-dental	Dental	Alveolar	Palatal	Velar
Occlusive	plosive	п/б		т/д			к/г
	nasal	м		н			
Constric-tive	fricative		(ф)/в	с/з	ш′/ж′	й	х/[γ]
	affricate			ц′	ч′ •		
	lateral				л		
	vibrant				р		

---

[1] W. K. Matthews, 'The Phonetic Value of *Jat'* in Old Russian' (*Ramovšev zbornik, Slavistična revija*, iii. 3–4, Ljubljana, 1950, pp. 256–62).

All the consonantal phonemes scheduled above, except the velars, the already 'soft' й (ĵ), the hush-sibilants, and the 'unpaired' affricates, may appear in a palatalized form in suitable contexts, i.e. when they are immediately followed by the front vowels и and e or by back vowels preceded by ĵ (which is indicated in Old Russian by the *i*-ligature). The quality of the 'soft' consonants was an inherent quality in the old language, although, as its spelling suggests, this was probably the outcome of palatalization, or the influence of front vowels and ĵ. Accordingly the total number of Old Russian phonemes must be increased by the addition of the palatalized counterparts of the normal consonants, viz. п′/б′, т′/д′, м′, н′, ф′/в′, с′/з′, л′/р′, thus making a grand total of thirty-two.

191. Examination of our table shows that the phonological feature of voice divides all the plosives and most of the fricatives into correlative pairs. The pair ф/в is not very secure, because the first is a foreign phoneme, figuring in loan-words mainly from Byzantine Greek, and x is solitary. This phoneme, however, has a voiced correlative (γ) dialectally (e.g. probably in Kiev Russian and in the dialects of the present-day South Russian and White Russian areas). Where γ appears, the к/г correlation is reduced to the simple member к. Subsequently, the hardening (velarization) of ш′/ж′ and ц′, and the 'softening' (palatalization) of the velars reconstruct the Russian consonantal system in its contemporary form.

192. The writing of the Old Russian consonants differs little from the modern Cyrillic characters, except in style: ѕ, ӡ, з all represent з; ɴ is written for modern н (which was и in Old Russian); ѵ stands for ч and ш for щ. The 'ductus' used in the Old Russian manuscripts was a bold-face uncial, later a semi-uncial down to the fifteenth century (§ 160), whereas present-day printing is normally based on any but bold-face founts.

193. Having picked out the phonemes of Old Russian we must now study their distribution. Phonemes combine into syllables and words. In some instances syllable and word are synonymous (e.g. я(зъ) 'I', и 'and', о 'concerning'). The distribution of phonemes in a syllable invariably implies the presence of a nuclear vowel or diphthong, of which the second component is й (e.g. край 'edge'). With this nucleus either one or several consonants may be associated, and the position of these may be either initial (before the vowel) or final (after the vowel). If we use the Roman capitals V and C to represent 'vowel' and 'consonant' respectively, we can symbolize the representative syllabic groups of Old Russian as follows: V (e.g. a 'but'), VC (e.g. изъ 'out of'), VCC (e.g. утрь 'inside'), VCCC (e.g. остръ 'sharp'), CV (e.g. до 'till'), CCV (e.g. при 'at'), CCCV (стрый 'uncle'), CVC (e.g. даръ 'tribute'), CVCC (e.g. вьршь 'corn'), CCVC (e.g. стѣнь 'shadow'), CCVCC (e.g. простъ 'simple'), CCCVC (e.g. стругъ 'vessel'), CCCVCC (e.g. страсть 'passion'). Our illustrations here are all monosyllables, because by the end of the eleventh and the early twelfth century final ь and ъ had disappeared, leaving the preceding consonant final, but presumably voiced, and not voiceless as it is in the modern language. In words of more than one syllable we have medial position, where consonantal complexes may occur, but these are decomposable by the inherited tendency of Old Russian to leave a syllable open wherever possible (e.g. непрѣбрьдомый 'impassable' and достойно 'it is fitting', which are divided не-прѣ-брь-до-мый and до-стой-но respectively). Nevertheless there are many closed syllables in the language as the result of the loss of the weak *jery* (e.g. донь-де-же 'while', жадь-ный 'thirsty', кърмь-чий 'steersman', прѣ-сък-ну-ти 'to desiccate').

194. Apart from phonemes and their combinations (phonological syntagmata) we have to recognize a prosody or phoneme-attribute in Old Russian, which, as in the modern language, takes the form of stress. This appears to have had phonematic value in both phases of Russian. The examination of modern Russian stress reveals that it is defined by two qualities, viz. it is irregular in incidence and it is mobile in the paradigm (e.g. Mod. R. замо́к/за́мок 'lock/castle' and nom. рука́/acc. ру́ку 'hand'). Old Russian stress can be surmised by the projection of the modern or at least of the 'known' sixteenth-century system into the medieval 'unknown'. This procedure, the only one available to us, may be reinforced by the results of the comparative study of Slavonic stress and of the dialects of modern East Slavonic languages, but there is nothing at our disposal to verify its accuracy. The fourteenth-century 'Čudovo New Testament' (*Čudovskij Novyj Zavet*) appears to be the earliest Old

Russian accented text; but, as Sobolevskij[1] says, it combines the 'living stress of the scribe's Russian dialect with the traditional [South Slavonic] stresses of the ecclesiastical text'. Other fourteenth- and fifteenth-century monuments would seem to go back originally to Middle Bulgarian and therefore probably reflect the practice of Bulgarian scribes. Only when we reach the sixteenth century do we obtain a distinct picture of Russian stress, for sixteenth- and especially seventeenth-century manuscripts usually include stress in spelling. Moreover, the books published in the middle of the seventeenth century by the ecclesiastical presses of Moscow invariably indicate stress, and this practice has been continued in works printed in Church Slavonic, although Peter the Great's reform of the Russian alphabet deliberately abandoned it.

195. As between now and the sixteenth century there have been changes in stressing after an intermediate period of hesitation:[2] thus sixteenth-century плóди 'fruits', мóсты 'bridges', óрли 'eagles' became плодь́, мость́, орль́. And the modern instances of metatony or shift of stress (e.g. пóд носом 'under one's nose', зá руку 'by the hand', пó двору 'outside', нá берег 'to the shore') have parallels in the fourteenth century (e.g. *Čud.* нá горы 'on to the hills', нá брѣзѣ 'ashore', вó имя 'in the name'). The evidence of modern Russian dialects and of the stresses in the fourteenth-century 'Čudovo New Testament' enables us to see that sometimes final ь and ъ, which were to lapse in weak or unsupported position (e.g. дьнь 'day', ночь 'night', густъ 'dense'), were stressed in Old Russian (e.g. дьнь́сь 'today', ночь́сь 'tonight', ономь́-дни 'on that day', густь́й 'the dense'). In the 'Čudovo New Testament' we also find родóсь 'this people' (< OR родъ), мирóсь 'this world' (< OR миръ). All this seems to show an early metatony from the ending to the stem of certain words (cf. OR ночь́ 'night', вьрхъ́ 'top', звѣрь́ 'beast' with Lith. *naktìs, virsùs, žvėrìs*). The 'Čudovo New Testament' moreover demonstrates a preference for final stress in the feminine nom.–acc. pl. of substantives (cf. жень́ 'women', сестрь́ 'sisters') and this is preserved in the seventeenth-century 'Code of Tsar Alexis' (*Uloženije Alekseja Michajloviča*, 1649), since when there has been a shift of stress to the stem (e.g. Mod. R. жёны, сёстры).

---

[1] *Lekcii po istorii russkogo jazyka*[4], Moscow, 1907, p. 267.
[2] V. Kiparsky, *O kolebanijach udarenija v russkom literaturnom jazyke*, i, Helsinki, 1950.

196. Morphophonology. The grammatical or morphological value of phonemes is realized in the morpheme or formal unit. This includes such formants as affixes of various kinds which are attached to the root or radical morpheme. Both prefixes and suffixes in some instances are shared by Russian with Old Church Slavonic (cf. OR and OCS прѣд- 'before', дѣт-ьство 'infancy'). This also applies to other formants, such as endings (e.g. OR рѣ-хъ 'spoke') and link-vowels (e.g. OR благ-о-дать 'grace'). In all these instances the overwhelming influence of Old Church Slavonic furnished the prototype; but in others again, viz. case and personal endings generally, we have to do with coincidence resulting from a common origin.

197. Old Russian morphemes may be monosyllabic (e.g. на- 'on', вьсь 'all') or disyllabic (e.g. dat. sg. матер-и 'mother'). To such bases several affixes may be added which sometimes produce words of many syllables (e.g. воз-ворот-и-ти 'to give back', въс-по-мя-ну-ти 'to remember').

198. The intersection of phonology and morphology is particularly evident in morphophonological alternations which may be both vocalic and consonantal and which have their origin in Common Slavonic. The vowel alternations comprise the correlation of vowels in stem and formant, as shown in declension and conjugation as well as in word-formation: (e.g. o/e instr. собою/gen. себе 'self'; несохъ/несе 'I carried/thou didst carry'; ъ/ь городъ 'town'/мужь 'man'; a/я жена 'woman'/земля 'earth'; e/ь деру/дьрати 'I flay/to flay'; ы/у дышати/духъ 'to breathe/spirit'). Consonantal alternation in Old Russian involves among other things the correlation of velar with 'sibilant' broadly understood (e.g. к/ч' in nom. sg. вълкъ/voc. вълче 'wolf'; г/з in nom. sg. другъ/loc. друзѣ 'friend'); the correlation of dental with 'sibilant' (e.g. т/ч' in летѣти/лечу 'to fly'/'I fly'; д/ж' in видѣти/вижю 'to see'/'I see'); the correlation of labial with labial + л' (e.g. любити/люблю 'to love'/'I love'); the correlation of т/щ (e.g. in питати/пища 'to feed'/'food'); and the correlation of н/zero (cf. к нему with ему 'to him'). The velar–sibilant correlation is twofold, being the outcome of three historical palatalizations,[1] viz. the apical (first), the early dorsal (second), and the late dorsal

---

[1] R. Ekblom, *Die frühe dorsale Palatalisierung im Slavischen*, Uppsala, 1951, p. 3.

(third). The first results in the Old Russian pairs к/ч′, г/ж′, х/ш′, as illustrated by a collation of the nominative forms with the vocatives вълче 'wolf', друже 'friend', душе 'spirit', and the other two in the velar–hiss-sibilant pairs к/ц′, г/з′, х/с′, as we see from a collation of the nominatives with the corresponding locatives вълцѣ, друзѣ, дусѣ. Similar alternations are to be found outside nominal formations (e.g. in the verb: могу/можеши 'I can'/'thou canst'). These and other alternations of phonemes in morphological contexts provide the morphophonemes which are part of the operation or processes of declension and conjugation.

I. MORPHOLOGY

199. This field of study is apportioned here between the processes of declension and conjugation, which constitute flexion, and the process of word-formation, which expresses itself in the modification of root by affix.

200. Declension. Old Russian declension is an operation which involves the various subdivisions of the noun (*nomen*), viz. substantive, adjective, numeral, and pronoun. Three main classes of declension are distinguished: (1) nominal (types I and II), (2) composite (type III), and (3) pronominal (type IV). The first is binary, with correlative stems (e.g. *o/jo*, *ā/jā*) and comprises mostly nouns, i.e. substantives, indefinite (short) adjectives, and certain pronouns (e.g. каковъ 'what sort', коликъ 'how many'), and numerals. This type also includes a unitary declension restricted to substantives (viz. *i*-stems, *u*-stems, and consonantal stems) and to some cardinal numerals (e.g. пять 'five', осмь 'eight'). The binary composite declension is confined to the definite adjective and participle, which combine a basic nominal paradigm with the declension of the postpositive personal pronoun, viz. и, я, e 'he, she, it'. The binary pronominal declension, which resembles the composite declension in many details, is unproductive, having reached saturation point in its development. It includes the generic pronouns and numerals (e.g. тъ–та–то 'that', одинъ–одьна–одьно 'one') as well as the non-generic interrogatives (e.g. кто 'who', чьто 'what'), but not the personal pronouns of the first and second person and the reflexive pronoun, all of which have a divergent type of declension. None of the declensions, however, except the last, is exclusive, and this accounts for the intersection and miscegenation of paradigms in the course of the development of Russian.

201. All our declensional types exhibit case distinctions, giving a maximum paradigm of seven cases, which are distributed among three numbers, including a dual. The paradigms also provide for the expression of three genders, which are for the most part not too rigidly associated with specific stems. Generic distinction, moreover, offers a criterion for broadly classifying declinable words into those with immanent gender, such as the substantives and cardinals, and those with syntactic gender, such as the adjectives and ordinals. The association between stem-form, already noted in our examination of the declensional types, and gender evinces a lack of symmetry. Of the eleven varieties of stem-form, which may be grouped under six headings, viz. $\bar{a}/j\bar{a}$, o/jo, u, i, $\bar{u}$, and various consonant stems (n, s, t, r), some are associated with one or other of the three genders: thus u-stems are exclusively masculine, $\bar{u}$-stems and the two r-stems exclusively feminine, and the few s-stems exclusively neuter.

202. The cases—two of them 'direct' (nominative and accusative) and the rest 'oblique' (genitive, dative, instrumental, locative)—serve to indicate a set of relations between the declined word and the remainder of the syntagma or phrase. Masculine and feminine substantives, moreover, may appear in a special vocative-case form in the singular, whereas in the dual and plural the vocative form is identical with the nominative. This case indicates the isolation of the word from its syntagma, and the same function is performed in the other numbers by prosodic (in this case intonational and accentual) devices. The theoretically numerous case-forms are not always phonetically distinct (e.g. the nom. and acc., the gen. and loc., the dat. and instr. of all genders in the dual; the nom., acc., and voc. of the neuter in all numbers; and the nom. and acc. pl. of the feminine).

203. The concept of gender, as illustrated in Old Russian, is complex and shows the intersection of three lines of cleavage, viz. stem-form, sex, and animateness. Of these the first has already been considered. The fundamental distinction in terms of sex expresses itself in the allocation of animate substantives to one or other of the three generic categories: thus богъ 'God', мужь 'man', and конь 'horse' are masculine; богыни (богыня) 'goddess', жена 'woman', and корова 'cow' are feminine; and дѣтя 'child', теля 'calf', утя 'duckling'—the names of sexually immature creatures—are neuter, i.e. neither masculine nor feminine. But, as we can see here, the generic distinctions are comprised in formal categories which follow another line of cleavage, so that *o/jo*-stems are masculine and neuter, whereas *ā/jā*-stems are predominantly feminine.

204. The nature of animateness comes out in certain case distinctions. Thus the occasional use of the masculine genitive singular for the accusative singular brings the masculine formally into line with the paradigmatic differentiation of the nominative and accusative singular in the feminine (cf. masc. nom. sg. конь/gen.–acc. коня 'horse', with fem. nom. sg. корова/acc. корову 'cow') and enables the language to distinguish animate from sex gender in the object. But the animate category is a late and still imperfect development in Old Russian, for we also find the corresponding accusative form functioning as an 'undifferentiated' animate (e.g. masc. nom.–acc. конь 'horse').

205. Distinctions of number—singular, dual, and plural—are made in most declinable words. The exceptions are few and generally easy to account for. Some collective and abstract substantives (e.g. челядь 'servants', правьда 'truth') appear only in the singular. *Pluralia tantum* comprise a small group of substantives (e.g. людие 'people', ворота 'gates'). And the reflexive pronoun (acc. ся), the interrogative pronouns къто 'who', чьто 'what', and the cardinal numerals, except одинъ 'one', десять 'ten', съто 'hundred', and тысяча 'thousand', do not distinguish number. The dual is used not only for paired objects (e.g. nom. руцѣ 'both hands'), but to express the notion of duality (e.g. nom. женѣ 'both women').

206. The distribution of stem-form, gender, and number in the Old Russian paradigms of declension may be conveniently summarized and generalized in the following tables which illustrate five declensional types, viz. (1) the binary nominal, (2) the unitary nominal, (3) the binary composite, (4) the binary pronominal, (5) the personal and reflexive pronominal.[1]

207. TYPE I. BINARY NOMINAL DECLENSION. Under this heading

[1] N. S. Trubetzkoy, *Altkirchenslavische Grammatik*, Vienna, 1954, pp. 116–18.

we distinguish two complementary types of declension according to stem-form, viz. masculine and neuter substantives with stems in *o/jo*, masculine substantives in *u*, and feminine substantives with stems in *ā/jā*. Further, both types of stem figure in the paradigms of short or non-composite adjectives; and the soft type dominates the declension of the comparative adjectives and active participles. Specimens of each are given below.

(*a*) *Masculine and Neuter Substantives with Stems in* o/jo

Hard stems in *o*: masc. столъ 'throne', neut. лѣто 'year'. Soft stems in *jo*: masc. конь 'horse', neut. поле 'field'.

	o-stems					
	Singular		*Dual*		*Plural*	
	Masc.	*Neut.*	*Masc.*	*Neut.*	*Masc.*	*Neut.*
Nom.	столъ	лѣто	стола	лѣтѣ	столи	лѣта
Acc.					столы	
Gen.	стола	лѣта	столу	лѣту	столъ	лѣтъ
Dat.	столу	лѣту	столома	лѣтома	столомъ	лѣтомъ
Instr.	столъмь	лѣтъмь			столы	лѣты
Loc.	столѣ	лѣтѣ	столу	лѣту	столѣхъ	лѣтѣхъ
Voc.	столе					

	jo-stems					
	Singular		*Dual*		*Plural*	
	Masc.	*Neut.*	*Masc.*	*Neut.*	*Masc.*	*Neut.*
Nom.	конь	поле	коня	поли	кони	поля
Acc.					конѣ	
Gen.	коня	поля	коню	полю	конь	поль
Dat.	коню	полю	конема	полема	конемъ	полемъ
Instr.	коньмь	польмь			кони	поли
Loc.	кони	поли	коню	полю	конихъ	полихъ
Voc.	коню					

Observations. (1) Stems in к, г, х are treated in twofold fashion in this declension: (*a*) in the voc. sg. they are replaced by ч, ж, ш respectively (e.g. вълче < nom. sg. вълкъ 'wolf'; друже < nom. sg. другъ 'friend'; душе < nom. sg. духъ 'spirit'); (*b*) in the loc. sg. and loc. and nom. pl. by ц, з, с (e.g. вълцѣ, вълцѣхъ, вълци; друзѣ, друзѣхъ, друzи; дусѣ, дусѣхъ, дуси).

(2) Only the masculine paradigm has a distinct form for the vocative case in the singular. Moreover, the vocalic endings of the hard and the soft stem are in a unique correlation (е/ю). (Cf. also § 202.)

(3) The acc. sg. of animate substantives sometimes takes the gen. form (e.g. коня for конь, мужа for мужь 'man'). This brings the differentiation of the two cases into line with that of the *ā/jā*-stems (§ 204).

(4) Among the *jo*-type words there are some ending in -и (= -*j*) in the nom. sg. (e.g. краи 'edge', изгои 'outlaw' < гои 'peace').

(5) The endings of the oblique cases are shared by the two genders in all three numbers.

(6) Unlike the *ā/jā*-declension, this shows the formal identity of the nom. and acc. in the masc. sg. and their divergence in the pl. The neuter *o/jo*-declension has common endings with the *ā/jā*-declension in the nom.–acc. du. All three genders have a common zero form in the gen. pl., which in the masc. *o/jo*-declension is identical with the form of the nom. sg.

(7) The instr. sg. endings -ъмь/ьмь occasionally have the variants -омь/емь. The ending -ъмь in the masc. substantives may reflect the influence of the *u*-stem.

(8) The correlative vocalic endings here are the same as for the *ā/jā*-stems. There is also the correlation ы/и in the instr. pl. (cf. Obs. 2).

(9) The numeral съто 'hundred' belongs to this declension and has a paradigm like that of лѣто.

(b) *Masculine Substantives with Stem in* u

Hard-stem type: сынъ 'son'.

	Singular	*Dual*	*Plural*
Nom.	сынъ	сыны	сынове
Acc.	сынъ	сыны	сыны
Gen.	сыну	сынову	сыновъ
Dat.	сынови	сынъма	сынъмъ
Instr.	сынъмь	сынъма	сынъми
Loc.	сыну	сынову	сынъхъ
Voc.	сыну		

Observations. (1) A small number of masculine nouns belongs to this declension (e.g. волъ 'ox', домъ 'house', родъ 'clan', медъ 'honey', полъ 'half', вьрхъ 'top', рядъ 'row', чинъ 'rank', and several others).

(2) The element of binariness, viz. the presence of a correlative soft stem (*ju*), is apparent in this declension in certain case-forms, for instance in the dat. sg. and in the nom. and gen. pl. (e.g. dat. sg. врачеви < врачь 'leech, healer', nom. pl. врачеве, gen. pl. врачевъ).

(3) The paradigm is in part theoretical, as some case-forms are not attested. Moreover, there has been miscegenation with the masculine *o/jo*-stem paradigm, with which the *u*-stems appear to have originally shared only two forms, viz. the nom.–acc. sg. and the instr. sg. (cf. столъ, столъмь with сынъ, сынъмь).

(4) It is quite possible that the more common ending of the instr. sg. in the paradigm of the *o/jo*-stems, viz. -ъмь, may be due to the influence of the *u*-stems (see Obs. 3).

(5) Intermixture with the *o/jo*-stems has resulted in the emergence of parallel forms in both paradigms (e.g. gen. sg. сына for сыну; dat. sg. вълкови for вълку).

(6) The *u*-stem paradigm has influenced even the *jo*-stems (e.g. dat. sg. коневи for коню; nom. pl. змиеве for змии 'serpent'). Such instances are not necessarily proof that a soft counterpart of the *u*-stems existed.

(c) Feminine Substantives with Stems in ā/jā

Hard stem in *ā*: жєна 'woman'.
Soft stem in *jā*: зємля 'earth'.

	ā-stem			*jā*-stem		
	Singular	*Dual*	*Plural*	*Singular*	*Dual*	*Plural*
Nom.	жєна	женѣ	жены	зємля	зємли	зємлѣ
Acc.	жєну			зємлю		
Gen.	жєны	жєну	жєнъ	зємлѣ	зємлю	зємль
Dat.	женѣ	жєнама	жєнамъ	зємли	зємляма	зємлямъ
Instr.	жєною		жєнами	зємлєю		зємлями
Loc.	женѣ	жєну	жєнахъ	зємли	зємлю	зємляхъ
Voc.	жєно			зємлє		

Observations. (1) Velar stems in к, г, х substitute their sibilant correlates ц, з, с respectively before the front vowels ѣ and и, thus dat. and loc. sg. and nom.–acc. du. руцѣ (< nom. sg. рука 'hand'), нозѣ (< nom. sg. нога 'foot'), мусѣ (< nom. sg. муха 'fly').

(2) Most of the *ā/jā*-stems are feminine, but a few masculine substantives also belong to this declension (e.g. слуга 'servant', воєвода 'commander', уноша 'youth').

(3) The nominatives of some *jā*-stems may end in -и (e.g. the feminine substantives богыни 'goddess', рабыни 'bondwoman', пустыни 'wilderness', and the masculines судии 'judge', кърмчии 'steersman', ловчии 'huntsman').

(4) Nominative and accusative are formally distinguished in the singular, but not in the other numbers.

(5) Note the correlative vocalic endings in the paradigm: о/є, ъ/ь, ы/ѣ, ѣ/и, у/ю, also the 'neutrality' of ѣ, whose hardness or softness depends on its correlate (cf. ы/ѣ with ѣ/и).

(6) The numeral тысяча 'thousand' belongs to the *jā*-stem type of declension.

(d) Short Adjectives in All Three Genders
(i) Hard stems in *o* and *ā*: masc. новъ, neut. ново, fem. нова 'new'.

	Singular			Dual			Plural		
	Masc.	*Neut.*	*Fem.*	*Masc.*	*Neut.*	*Fem.*	*Masc.*	*Neut.*	*Fem.*
Nom.	новъ	ново	нова	нова	новѣ		нови	нова	новы
Acc.			нову				новы		
Gen.	нова		новы	нову			новъ		
Dat.	нову		новѣ	новома		новама	новомъ		новамъ
Instr.	новомь		новою				новы		новами
Loc.	новѣ			нову			новѣхъ		новахъ

(ii) Soft stems in *jo* and *jā*: masc. синь, neut. сине, fem. синя 'blue'.

	Singular			Dual			Plural		
	Masc.	*Neut.*	*Fem.*	*Masc.*	*Neut.*	*Fem.*	*Masc.*	*Neut.*	*Fem.*
Nom.	синь	сине	синя	синя	сини		сини	синя	синѣ
Acc.			синю				синѣ		
Gen.	синя		синѣ	синю			синь		
Dat.	синю		сини	синема		синяма	синемъ		синямъ
Instr.	синемь		синею				сини		синями
Loc.	сини			синю			синихъ		синяхъ

Observations. (1) Like the substantives with stems in *o/jo* and *ā/jā*, the short or non-composite adjective is of binary type in declension. The masculine and neuter forms illustrate the *o/jo*-stems, and the feminine forms the *ā/jā*-stems.

(2) This type of adjective is contrasted with the long or composite (also known as the 'articulate') type, whose complexity is the result of fusing the short form with the personal pronoun (§ 200).

(3) The existence of both types of adjective is determined by the need of congruence with the substantive, whose characteristics—case, gender, number—they reproduce without comparable irregularities of stem-form.

(4) The short or non-composite ordinals (e.g. пьрвъ–пьрво–пьрва 'first') follow this paradigm.

(5) A number of short indefinite pronouns belong here (e.g. каковъ–каково–какова 'what kind'; толикъ–толико–толика 'so much'; етеръ–етеро–етера 'a certain').

(6) The paradigm is also that of the short passive participles, present and past (e.g. pres. pass. несомъ–несомо–песома 'being carried'; past pass. нессиъ–несено–несена 'carried', also взятъ–взято–взята 'taken').

(e) Short Comparative Adjective in All Three Genders

Soft stems in *jo* and *jā*: masc. болии, neut. боле, fem. больши 'more'.

	Singular		
	Masc.	*Neut.*	*Fem.*
Nom.	болии	боле	больши
Acc.	большь		большу
Gen.	больша		большѣ
Dat.	большу		больши
Instr.	большемъ		большею
Loc.	больши		

	Dual		
	Masc.	*Neut.*	*Fem.*
Nom.	больша	больши	
Acc.			
Gen.	большу		
Dat.	большема		большама
Instr.			
Loc.	большу		

	Plural		
	Masc.	*Neut.*	*Fem.*
Nom.	больше	больша	большѣ
Acc.	большѣ		
Gen.	большь		
Dat.	большемъ		большамъ
Instr.	больши		большами
Loc.	большихъ		большахъ

Observations. (1) This paradigm is exclusively of the soft-stem type.

(2) There are two comparative suffixes in use, viz. -ьш- and the more common -ѣиш- (e.g. новѣи–новѣе–новѣиши 'newer'). Some adjectives ending in -окъ/-ъкъ in the masculine singular (e.g. глубокъ 'deep') do not incorporate this suffix in declension (e.g. глублии–глубле–глубльши 'deeper'), but others do (e.g. крѣпъкъ 'strong', comp. крѣпчаи–крѣпчае–крѣпчаиши).

(3) The masculine nom. sg. and the neuter nom.–acc. sg. forms generally lack the characteristic suffix which appears in the feminine. But the neuter is sometimes found to use a form with this suffix in the nom.–acc. sg. (e.g. больше for боле; cf. the participles).

(4) In the masculine acc. sg. the nom. form seems to be the more common, unless the comparative adjective qualifies an animate substantive.

(5) A genitive-type acc. form is used in congruence with animate substantives in the masc. sg.

(f) Short Active Participle in All Three Genders

(i) Present: masc. неса, neut. неса, fem. несучи 'carrying'.

	Singular			Dual			Plural		
	Masc.	*Neut.*	*Fem.*	*Masc.*	*Neut.*	*Fem.*	*Masc.*	*Neut.*	*Fem.*
Nom.	неса	неса	несучи	несуча	несучи	несучи	несуче	несуча	несучѣ
Acc.	несучь	неса	несучу	несуча	несучи	несучи	несучѣ	несуча	несучѣ
Gen.	несуча	несуча	несучѣ	несучу	несучу	несучу	несучь	несучь	несучь
Dat.	несучу	несучи		несучема	несучема	несучама	несучемъ	несучемъ	несучам̃
Instr.	несучемь	несучею		несучема	несучема	несучама	несучи	несучи	несучами
Loc.	несучи	несучи	несучи	несучу	несучу	несучу	несучихъ	несучихъ	несучахъ

(ii) Past: masc. несъ, neut. несъ, fem. несъши 'carried'.

	Singular			Dual			Plural		
	Masc.	*Neut.*	*Fem.*	*Masc.*	*Neut.*	*Fem.*	*Masc.*	*Neut.*	*Fem.*
Nom.	несъ	несъ	несъши	несъша	несъши	несъши	несъше	несъша	несъшѣ
Acc.	несъшь	несъ	несъшу	несъша	несъши	несъши	несъшѣ	несъша	несъшѣ
Gen.	несъша	несъшѣ	несъшѣ	несъшу	несъшу	несъшу	несъшь	несъшь	несъшь
Dat.	несъшу	несъши	несъши	несъшема	несъшама	несъшама	несъшемъ	несъшемъ	несъшамъ
Inst.	несъшемь	несъшею	несъшею	несъшема	несъшама	несъшама	несъши	несъши	несъшами
Loc.	несъши	несъши	несъши	несъшу	несъшу	несъшу	несъшихъ	несъшихъ	несъшахъ

Observations. (1) Both participles have a declension of the soft-stem type. The hard–soft correlation appears only in the masc. nom. sg. (e.g. pres. веда 'leading'/зная 'knowing'; past ведъ 'led'/хваль 'praised').

(2) There is a contrast between masc. nom. sg. and neuter nom.–acc. sg. on the one hand and the rest of the paradigm on the other (cf. pres. masc. nom. sg. неса with acc. sg. несучь and fem. nom. sg. несучи; past masc. nom. sg. несъ with acc. sg. несъшь and fem. nom. sg. несъши).

(3) The presence of the endings -a and -y, instead of -я and -ю respectively, was an orthographic convention and did not indicate the hardness of the preceding sibilants ч, ш, which were soft by nature in Old Russian.

(4) The present participle has a neut. nom.–acc. variant in несуче for неса (cf. the neuter comparative adjective больше for боле).

208. Type II. Unitary Nominal Declension. Under this heading we examine a relatively limited number of substantives and cardinal numerals having only one form of declension, i.e. one which does not imply the possible existence of a correlate. There are, however, two types of paradigm, one regular and the other anomalous. Like the paradigm of the masculine *u*-stems, the latter was no longer productive at the outset.

(*a*) *Masculine and Feminine Substantives with Stems in* i
Masc. путь 'way', fem. кость 'bone'

	Singular		Dual		Plural	
	Masc.	*Fem.*	*Masc.*	*Fem.*	*Masc.*	*Fem.*
Nom.	путь	кость	пути	кости	путие	кости
Acc.					пути	
Gen.	пути	кости	путью	костью	путии	костии
Dat.			путьма	костьма	путьмъ	костьмъ
Instr.	путьмь	костью			путьми	костьми
Loc.	пути	кости	путью	костью	путьхъ	костьхъ
Voc.						

Observations. (1) The masculine substantives of this declension are few in number and include, among others, such words as гость 'guest', зять 'son-in-law', тесть 'father-in-law', тать 'thief', медвѣдь 'bear', голубь 'pigeon'. The majority of the substantives are feminine.

(2) This declension appears to have the smallest number of distinct case-forms, viz. eight in the feminine out of a theoretically possible twenty-one.

(3) The cardinal numerals трие/три 'three', пять 'five', шесть 'six', седмь 'seven', осмь 'eight', девять 'nine' follow this paradigm, the first being declined only in the plural and the rest only in the singular. All except трие/три, which has three-fold syntactic gender, are feminine substantives.

(4) Variants, with ь for и, are found in the masc. nom. pl. and in the gen. pl. of both genders (e.g. путье, костьи).

(b) Consonant Stems of All Three Genders

Masc. камы 'stone', neut. слово 'word', fem. мати 'mother'.

	Singular		
	Masc.	Neut.	Fem.
Nom.	камы	слово	мати
Acc.	камень		матерь
Gen.	камене	словесе	матере
Dat.	камени	словеси	матери
Instr.	каменьмь	словесьмь	матерью
Loc.	камене	словесе	матере
Voc.	камени		мати

	Dual		
	Masc.	Neut.	Fem.
Nom. Acc.	камени	словесѣ	матери
Gen.	камену	словесу	матеру
Dat. Instr.	каменьма	словесьма	матерьма
Loc. Voc.	камену	словесу	матеру

	Plural		
	Masc.	Neut.	Fem.
Nom.	камене	словеса	матере
Acc.	камени		матери
Gen.	каменъ	словесъ	матеръ
Dat.	каменьмъ	словесьмъ	матерьмъ
Instr.	каменьми	словесы	матерьми
Loc.	каменьхъ	словесьхъ	матерьхъ
Voc.			

Observations. (1) The restricted membership of this group includes mostly neuter stems in *n* (e.g. имя 'name', gen. sg. имене), *s* (e.g. тѣло 'body', gen. sg. тѣлесе), and *t* (e.g. теля 'calf', gen. sg. теляте), two feminine substantives in *r*, the second being дъчи 'daughter' (gen. sg. дъчере), and a few masculines in *n* (e.g. дьнь 'day', gen. sg. дьне). The feminine vowel stems in *ū* also belong to this declension (e.g. цьркы 'church', acc. sg. цьркъвь, gen. sg. and nom. pl. цьркъве).

(2) Certain masculine plural forms of a mixed (binary–unitary) nominal declension follow this paradigm (e.g. горожане 'citizens', учителе 'teachers').

(3) Here too we must include the numerals четыре/четыри and десять 'ten'. The first of these has syntactic gender like трие/три, and десять has a full paradigm (e.g. gen. sg. десяте, nom. du. десяти, gen. pl. десятъ).

(4) Our paradigms are 'basic' and do not show variants: thus камы has -и in the loc. sg. and -ью in the gen.–loc. du.; слово has -и in the nom.–acc. du. as well as -ѣ; мати has -и in the loc. sg. and nom. pl. as well as -ью in the gen.–loc. du. Other words following these three paradigms exhibit the same variants.

(5) The feminines in *r* and *ū* are the only ones which distinguish nom. and acc. in the plural paradigm, but they too have a variant in -и in the nominative case.

(6) Confusion of masculine *jo*-stems and feminine *jā*-stems with *i*-stems has resulted in the creation of hybrid types similar to those which emerged from the miscegenation of masculine *o/jo*- and *u*-stems (e.g. огнь 'fire' has gen. sg. огня as well as огни; кость has dat. pl. костямъ as well as костьмъ; учитель has gen. pl. учитель as well as учителъ).

209. Type III. Binary Composite Declension. This type comprises the long or 'articulate' adjectives, ordinal numerals, and participles both active and passive. Semantically the long form was originally contrasted with the short or 'basic' form as definite or determinate, hence the use of the Russian term 'articulate' (*člennaja forma*). The synthesis of the composite form is still mostly transparent: thus the long nom. sg. of новъ–ново–нова 'new' results from the addition of the personal pronouns и–е–я, in that order, and this gives the новыи (< новъи)–новое–новая of our paradigm. The oblique forms are also fairly easy to analyse, especially if we collate them with the corresponding unabbreviated Old Church Slavonic forms (cf. masc. instr. sg. новымь with OCS новъі-илib).

(a) Long Adjectives in All Three Genders

(i) Hard stems in *o* and *ā*: masc. новыи, neut. новое, fem. новая 'the new'.

	Singular			Dual			Plural		
	Masc.	*Neut.*	*Fem.*	*Masc.*	*Neut.*	*Fem.*	*Masc.*	*Neut.*	*Fem.*
Nom.	новыи	новое	новая	новая	новѣи		новии	новая	новыѣ
Acc.			новую				новыѣ		
Gen.	нового		новоѣ	новою			новыхъ		
Dat.	новому		новои	новыма			новымъ		
Instr.	новымь		новою				новыми		
Loc.	новомь		новои	новою			новыхъ		

(ii) Soft stems in *jo* and *jā*: masc. синии, neut. синее, fem. синяя 'the blue'.

	Singular			Dual			Plural		
	Masc.	*Neut.*	*Fem.*	*Masc.*	*Neut.*	*Fem.*	*Masc.*	*Neut.*	*Fem.*
Nom.	синии	синее	синяя	синяя	синии		синии	синяя	синѣѣ
Acc.			синюю				синѣѣ		
Gen.	синего		синеѣ	синею			синихъ		
Dat.	синему		синеи	синима			синимъ		
Instr.	синимь		синею				синими		
Loc.	синемь		синеи	синею			синихъ		

Observations. (1) Our paradigms here have many variants. The masc. acc. sg. has the alternative genitive-type forms нового, синего for animate substantives which have alternative gen.–acc. forms, viz. мужь 'man', къназь 'prince'. The more primitive gen. sg. forms новаго, синяго (masc.), новыѣ (fem.) figure frequently in the oldest manuscripts, more often indeed than the forms in our paradigm, and are the result of Old Church Slavonic influence. Also the unabbreviated forms новыимь (instr. sg.), новыима (dat.–instr. du.), новыихъ (gen.-loc. pl.), новыимъ (dat. pl.), новыими (instr. pl.) are common in the eleventh century. In the loc. sg. the forms новѣмь (masc. and neut.) and новѣи (fem.) are even nearer to their earlier 'unfused' counterparts, viz. новѣ-емь, новѣ-еи.

(2) The long ordinals are represented here too (e.g. пьрвыи 'the first' < short ordinal пьрвъ+и; въторыи 'the second'; десятыи 'the tenth; дъвадесятьныи 'the twentieth'; сътьныи 'hundredth'; тысячьныи 'thousandth').

(3) The long participles, active and passive, belong to this declension. Here are some specimens of the more characteristic forms which are based on the short forms already cited, viz. pres. act. несаи (masc.), несучее (neut.) несучия (fem.); pres. pass. несомыи (masc.), несомое (neut.), несомая (fem.); past act. несъи (masc.), несъшее (neut.) несъшия (fem.); past pass. несеныи (masc.), несеное (neut.), несеная (fem.), and взятыи (masc.), взятое (neut.), взятая (fem.). Of this set the participial forms with a sibilant suffix follow the soft-stem declension (e.g. pres. act. masc. and neut. gen. sg. несучего; past act. fem. nom.–acc. pl. несъшѣѣ).

210. Type IV. Binary Pronominal Declension. Like Types I and II, this is a binary type of declension and differs from the other nominal types in being almost exclusively pronominal. Its only divergent members are two numerals.

(i) Hard stems in *o* and *ā*: masc. тъ, neut. то, fem. та 'that'.

	Singular			Dual			Plural		
	Masc.	*Neut.*	*Fem.*	*Masc.*	*Neut.*	*Fem.*	*Masc.*	*Neut.*	*Fem.*
Nom.	тъ	то	та	та	тѣ		ти	та	ты
Acc.			ту				ты		
Gen.	того		тоѣ	тою			тѣхъ		
Dat.	тому		тои	тѣма			тѣмъ		
Instr.	тѣмь		тою				тѣми		
Loc.	томь		тои	тою			тѣхъ		

(ii) Soft stems in *jo* and *jā*: masc. и 'he', neut. е 'it', fem. я 'she'.

	Singular			Dual			Plural		
	Masc.	Neut.	Fem.	Masc.	Neut.	Fem.	Masc.	Neut.	Fem.
Nom.	и	е	я	я	и		и	я	ѣ
Acc.			ю				ѣ		
Gen.	его		еѣ		ею			ихъ	
Dat.	ему		еи		има			имъ	
Instr.	имь		ею					ими	
Loc.	емь		еи		ею			ихъ	

Observations. (1) The masc. acc. sg. in the above two para-digms has an alternative genitive-type form for the animate object of transitive verbs, viz. того, его. The normal accusative form also has an enclitic variant нь which is fused with preposi-tions (e.g. нань 'on him/it').

(2) This declension includes the numerals одинъ–одьно–одьна 'one' and дъва/дъвѣ 'two'. The latter has the same nom. sg. form in the neuter and feminine, and this feature distin-guishes the quantitative pronoun оба/обѣ 'both', which also belongs here. Both оба/обѣ and дъва/дъвѣ are declined only in the dual.

(3) The pronouns which follow this declension comprise the demonstrative (e.g. онъ–оно–она 'that'), possessive (e.g. мои–мое–моя 'my'), and indefinite groups (e.g. инъ–ино–ина 'an-other').

(4) The confusion of pronominal and composite stems ac-counts for the declension of кыи (< къи)–кое–кая 'which' and its derivatives (e.g. нѣкыи 'a certain').

(5) There are certain anomalies attaching to вьсь–вьсе–вься 'all' and сиць–сице–сица 'such', both of which are declined according to the soft-stem paradigm, except in the masc. and neut. instr. sg., and in the dat.–instr. du., and the gen., dat., instr., and loc. pl. of all three genders (e.g. dat.–instr. du. вьсѣма; gen.–loc. pl. сицѣхъ).

(6) The interrogative pronouns and their non-generic deriva-tives нѣкъто 'a certain', ничьто 'nothing at all' are declined only in the singular. къто 'who' has a genitive-type accusa-tive form and чьто 'what' has the normal nominative-type

accusative. Both are provided with the invariable particle -то in the nominative case. Their paradigm is as follows:

Nom.	къто	чьто
Acc.	кого	
Gen.	кого	чего
Dat.	кому	чему
Instr.	цѣмь	чимь
Loc.	комь	чемь

It will be noticed here that the instrumental form of къто illustrates the second palatalization, which will be found also in such pronominal forms as, for instance, the instr. sg. тацѣмь < такъ 'this sort'. чьто has two variants in the gen., viz. чесо, чьсо.

(7) The personal pronoun was replaced in Old Russian by a demonstrative in the nominative case, viz. by онъ–оно–она, but retained its oblique forms in declension. Its old nominative forms, enlarged by the particle -же, figure usually as anaphoric (relative) pronouns.

(8) A similar emphatic particle -жьдо appears in other pronouns, for instance in кыи-жьдо 'each'. This particle, like -то and -же, is invariable.

211. TYPE V. PERSONAL AND REFLEXIVE PRONOUNS. These are non-generic, limited in number, and anomalous in terms of declension. Only three sets appear in our paradigms, two illustrating the first two persons of the personal pronoun (i.e. speaker and interlocutor), and the third the reflexive pronoun, which is restricted to the singular and has no nominative case.

	Singular			*Dual*		*Plural*	
	1st pers.	*2nd pers.*	*Reflexive*	*1st pers.*	*2nd pers.*	*1st pers.*	*2nd pers.*
Nom.	язъ/я	ты		вѣ	ва	мы	вы
Acc.	мене/мя	тебе/тя	себе/ся	на		насъ/ны	васъ/вы
Gen.	мене	тебе	себе	наю	ваю	насъ	васъ
Dat.	мънѣ/ми	тобѣ/ти	собѣ/си	нама/на	вама/ва	намъ/ны	вамъ/вы
Instr.	мъною	тобою	собою			нами	вами
Loc.	мънѣ	тобѣ	собѣ	наю	ваю	насъ	васъ

Observations. (1) In spite of anomalies, this declension has formally many features which correlate it with other declensional types (cf. gen. sg. мене with камене; instr. and loc. sg. мъною, мънѣ with женою, женѣ; dat. and instr. pl. намъ, нами with женамъ, женами).

(2) Some of the variants are given above, but there are still others, viz. dat. and loc. sg. тебѣ, себѣ for тобѣ, собѣ.

(3) The shorter forms in each case are enclitics (cf. masc. acc. sg. of и, § 227). We may remark here that the dual and the plural forms на, ва, ны, вы cause confusion by being both accusative and dative in sense.

212. Conjugation. Not all the many forms of the verb in Old Russian are affected by the process of conjugation, which is limited to the finite verb and its characteristic feature of person. The declensional category of the participles (§ 207, *f*, i–ii) and invariable categories like the infinitive and supine, which imply the absence of person, are also part of the totality of verbal forms. All these constitute a complex system which may be classified in terms of congruence. This system is triadic: (*a*) forms with personal congruence (finite verbs), (*b*) forms with generic congruence (participles), and (*c*) forms without congruence (infinitive and supine). The formal categories and their ramifications may be tabulated as below:[1]

Finite verbs				Declinable participles				Invariables	
	Indicative			Active		Passive			
	Non-preterite	*Preterite*		*Present*	*Past*	*Present*	*Past*	*Infinitive*	*Supine*
Imperative	Present (future)	Imperfect	Aorist						

213. The verbal system recognizes the categories of aspect and voice and of mood and tense. The invariables lie outside all these categories; the declinable participles are subject to voice and tense; and the finite verb, which is the most independent and articulate of the three, illustrates all the categories and has a form—the imperative—which shares the achronic feature of

---

[1] N. S. Trubetzkoy, op. cit., pp. 156–61. Trubetzkoy's tabular epitome (p. 157) has been simplified in arrangement and detail.

the invariables. As we have already dealt with the declinable participles under declension (§ 207), we shall confine ourselves here to the conjugated finite verbs and their invariable dependents.

214. The finite verbs of the indicative mood have theoretically nine forms, i.e. three persons multiplied by three numbers, and these are for the most part individually represented in conjugation but for minor coincidences of form. Among such coincidences are the common forms of the 2nd and 3rd persons dual in all tenses of the indicative as well as the forms shared by these persons in all tenses save the present. The imperative paradigm too is restricted by formal coincidence. This gives the present tense a maximum of eight distinct forms and the imperative (without its 1st person singular) a set of five. Compare with these figures the coincidences in nominal declension, where hardly more than half of the theoretically possible forms are represented, viz. 10–12 out of 21.

215. The link with aspect in the finite verb may be seen in the frequent derivation of the imperfect tense, with its durative sense, from the imperfective verbs, and the aorist, with its sense of finality, from perfective verbs. The parallelism of tense and aspect in past time (preterite) made the transition from Old Russian to the modern verbal system easier. But in principle as well as in practice the two past-tense forms could be derived from either aspect.

216. Most finite verbs in Old Russian exhibit the presence of two groups of stems in their conjugation, viz. (*a*) the present-stem group, comprising the present indicative and imperative and the present participles, and (*b*) the aorist-stem (or infinitive) group, comprising the aorist, past participles, infinitive, and supine. The stem of the imperfect coincides sometimes with that of (*a*) and sometimes with that of (*b*).

217. The present-tense endings fall into two classes, viz. (*a*) the endings of the singular: 1st pers. -у, -ю, 2nd pers. -ши, 3rd pers. -ть (also used in the plural) and (*b*) the dual and plural endings: 1st pers. du. -вѣ, 2nd and 3rd pers. du. -та; 1st pers. pl. -мъ, 2nd pers. pl. -те. Some athematic verbs have -мь in the first person (e.g. юсмь 'I am', дамь 'I give', вѣмь 'I know') and -си in the second (e.g. юси 'thou art', даси 'thou givest', вѣси 'thou knowest'). The ending of the 3rd pers. sing. was sometimes dropped.

218. The present-tense group of forms shows (a) a unitary and (b) a binary type of conjugation.[1]

219. (a) UNITARY CONJUGATION.

Infinitive любити 'to love'.

	Present tense			Imperative			Present participle	
							Active masc. nom.	Passive masc. nom.
	1	*2*	*3*	*1*	*2*	*3*		
Sin-gular	люблю	любиши	любить		люби		любя	любимъ
Dual	любивѣ	любита		любивѣ	любита		любяча	любима
Plural	любимъ	любите	любять	любимъ	любите		любяче	любими

Observations. (1) The present tense has variant forms for the 2nd pers. sg. (любишь), the 1st du. (любива), and the 1st pl. (любимо). Of these the first form has survived and the other two have disappeared in the course of historical evolution.

(2) The imperative endings are identical with those of the indicative, except in the 2nd and 3rd sg., which have the bare stem or 'zero ending'. The identity of the written forms probably misrepresents existing phonological distinctions (cf. the difference of stress in the modern forms, viz. 2nd pl. indic. лю́бите and 2nd pl. imp. люби́те).

(3) The operation of consonantal alternation has resulted in the contrast of plosive and sibilant stems (cf. вижю 'I see' and видиши 'thou seest').

220. (b) BINARY CONJUGATION.

I. *Present Tense.*

(i) Hard stem: infinitive нести 'to carry'.

	Present tense			Imperative			Present participle	
							Active masc. nom.	Passive masc. nom.
	1	*2*	*3*	*1*	*2*	*3*		
Singular	несу	несеши	несеть		неси		неса	несомъ
Dual	несевѣ	несета		несѣвѣ	несѣта		несуча	несома
Plural	несемъ	несете	несуть	несѣмъ	несѣте		несуче	несоми

[1] N. S. Trubetzkoy, op. cit., pp. 161–3.

(ii) Soft stem: infinitive знати 'to know'.

	Present tense			Imperative			Present participle	
	1	*2*	*3*	*1*	*2*	*3*	*Active masc. nom.*	*Passive masc. nom.*
Singular	знаю	знаеши	знаеть		знаи		зная	знаемъ
Dual	знаевѣ	знаета		знаивѣ	знаита		знаюча	знаема
Plural	знаемъ	знаете	знають	знаимъ	знаите		знаюче	знаеми

Observations. (1) Variants like those of the present tense and imperative of любити (e.g. 1st pl. pres. несемо, знаемо; 1st pl. imp. несѣмо, знаимо).

(2) The alternation ѣ/и between hard and soft stems appears in the imperative dual and plural forms (cf. несѣвѣ/знаивѣ, несѣмъ/знаимъ).

(3) The orthographic contrast e/ѣ between present and imperative forms in all three numbers does not appear to have been borne out by the pronunciation.

(4) Velar stems show assibilation before -и and ѣ (e.g. 2nd and 3rd sg. imp. берези 'take care', 2nd pl. березѣте).

221. II. *Past Tense*

	Imperfect			Aorist		
	1	*2*	*3*	*1*	*2*	*3*
Singular	несяхъ	несяше		несохъ	несе	
Dual	несяховѣ	несящета		несоховѣ	несоста	
Plural	несяхомъ	несящете	несяху	несохомъ	несосте	несоша

Observations. (1) The ending -ть appears sometimes in the 3rd pers. sg. and pl. of the imperfect (e.g. несяшеть, несяхуть).

(2) Certain verbs occasionally take the form of uncontracted stems in the imperfect (e.g. 1st sg. несяахъ for несяхъ).

(3) The ending -a is found for -ѣ in the 1st du. of both imperfect and aorist (e.g. несяхова, несохова).

222. (*c*) ANOMALOUS CONJUGATION. A small group of unproductive athematic verbs, comprising быти 'to be', дати 'to give',

Ѣсти 'to eat', вѣдѣти 'to know', and имѣти 'to have', present a number of striking anomalies.
Infinitive быти 'to be'.

	Singular			Dual		
	1	*2*	*3*	*1*	*2*	*3*
sent indicative .	есмь	еси	есть	есвѣ	еста	
ure indicative .	буду	будеши	будеть	будевѣ	будета	
perfect indicative .	бяхъ	бяше		бяховѣ	бяста	
rist indicative . .	быхъ	бы		быховѣ	быста	
perative . .		буди		будѣвѣ	будѣта	
	Masculine		Neuter			
sent participle .	са	саи	са	сучеѥ		
t participle . .	бывъ	бывыи	бывъ	бывъшеѥ		

	Plural		
	1	*2*	*3*
Present indicative .	есмъ	есте	суть
Future indicative .	будемъ	будете	будуть
Imperfect indicative .	бяхомъ	бясте	бяху
Aorist indicative . .	быхомъ	бысте	быша
Imperative . .	будѣмъ	будѣте	
	Feminine		
Present participle .	сучи	сучия	
Past participle . .	бывъши	бывъшия	

Observations. (1) Variants in the personal endings occur especially in the present tense (e.g. есми for есмь, е for есть, есмы (-о, -е) for есмъ, and есва for есвѣ). In the future—the only future form in the language different from the present—we find буде for будеть, and будева for будевѣ; in the imperfect бяшеть 3rd sg. for бяше, бяхова for бяховѣ, and бяхуть for бяху; and in the aorist бысть 3rd sg. for бы, and быхова for быховѣ.

(2) There was an alternative, formally mixed, paradigm of the imperfect indicative, viz. бѣхъ, бѣ, бѣховѣ, бѣста, бѣхомъ, бѣсте, бѣша. This was of Old Church Slavonic origin.

(3) It will be noted that the athematic verbs have -мь, not -у/-ю, in the 1st sg. and -си for -ши in the 2nd sg. (cf. ѥсмь, ѥси with несу, несеши), except for имѣти, 2nd sg. имаши.

(4) The verbs дати, ѣсти have the 2nd and 3rd sg. imperative forms дажь, ѣжь.

223. Compound Conjugation. This consists mostly of combinations of the generic, indeclinable past-participle in *l* with forms of the verb быти 'to be', which functions here as an auxiliary. Other auxiliaries combine only with the infinitive in the formation of the compound future tense. They are: начати, почати, учати 'to begin', хотѣти 'to want', имѣти 'to have', яти 'to take' (e.g. учьну, хочю, имамь/имѣю, иму нести 'I shall carry'). In this use the future of быти is unknown to Old Russian. The perfect tense of our specimen verb нести is formed with the ѥсмь paradigm, the pluperfect with the бяхъ or бѣхъ paradigm, the future perfect (*futurum exactum*) with the буду paradigm, and the conditional or subjunctive with the быхъ paradigm (cf. OCS бимь). As the *l*-participle distinguishes both gender and number, this multiplies the theoretically possible forms by nine. Thus we have the following forms: 1st sg. есмь неслъ–несло–несла; 1st du. есвѣ несла–неслѣ; 1st pl. есмъ несли–несла–неслы 'I/we two/we have carried'. Бяхъ неслъ means 'I had carried'; буду неслъ 'I shall have carried'; быхъ неслъ 'I should have carried'.

224. Invariable Verbal Forms. In Old Russian these were the infinitive and the supine, both of them nominal forms resulting from the 'petrification' of case-forms. The infinitive is considered to be derived from a dative, and the supine from an accusative original. The normal ending of the infinitive is -ти and that of the supine is -тъ (e.g. нести, нестъ). Where the stem ends in a velar we find the infinitive ending in -чи and the supine in -чь (e.g. жечи < *žeg-ti 'to burn' (transitive) and жечь 'in order to burn').

225. Conjugational Classes. These correspond in the nominal sphere to declensions according to stem-form, but the compari

son between the two categories, verbal and nominal, should not
be pushed too far. A major subdivision of verbal stems is that
between the thematic and athematic (§ 222). By relegating the
latter to a Class V, we can distribute the remainder among four
other formal classes, of which the first three will include stems
ending in *e* in the 3rd person singular of the present indicative,
and Class IV will include the *i*-stems (e.g. любити 'to love').
The *e*-verbs are represented by Class I (e.g. нести, 3rd sg. нес-е-
ть), Class II (e.g. двинути, 3rd sg. двин-е-ть), and Class III
(e.g. знати, 3rd sg. зна-ю-ть). These verbs are classified according to the presence or absence of one or other of two characteristic phonemes, *n* and *j*, preceding the *u*-ending of the 1st
person singular and 3rd person plural, and the *e*-ending of the
remaining persons. Class I may have, for instance, the hard consonant *s* (or a variety of other stem consonants) which is
palatalized before *e* (e.g. 1st sg. несу, 2nd sg. несеши); Class II
has the infix *n* (e.g. 1st sg. дви-н-у, 2nd sg. дви-н-еши); Class III
has *j*-, the index of iotacization (e.g. 1st sg. знаю, 2nd sg. зна-ю-
ши = *zna-j-u, zna-j-eši*). These are primary stem distinctions
which can be multiplied by the admission of further details
obtained from a comparison of the present and the aorist or
infinitive stems: thus in Class I we find зову 'I call'/зъвати
'to call' and им-у 'I take, seize'/я-ти 'to take' which may
be contrasted with нес-у/нес-ти. Similar variations have been
observed in the other classes, even in the athematic verbs (e.g.
вѣс-ть 'he knows' < *vĕd-tь, вѣд-ѣ-ти 'to know'). The formal
classes of the verb do not therefore completely coincide with the
conjugational, but rather vary them. Thus from the standpoint
of conjugation, as we have already seen, Classes I to V represent
three distinct types, viz. the *e*-type, the *i*-type, and the athematic type. Using the imperative conjugation as a criterion, moreover, we can bring our five classes under two heads, viz. the
hard *ĕ*-type and the soft *i*-type (e.g. 1st pl. несѣмъ, двинѣмъ,
знаимъ, любимъ, будѣмъ). Such a classification finds links
between the five classes and rearranges them as a dichotomy.

226. Aspect. The formal classes of aspect make use, among
other things, of the alternation of root vowels as a criterion.
Among root alternations e/o is perhaps the most common, the
back correlate indicating durativeness or imperfectiveness (e.g.

нести/носити 'to carry'; вести/водити 'to convey'). Another alternation is represented by ѣ/a (e.g. летѣіи/лѣтати 'to fly'). Moreover, the conjugational classes in Old Russian can also indicate differences of aspect: thus Class III contains iterative verbs with the suffix -ва- (e.g. бывати 'to be') and Class II the corresponding punctual types with the suffix -ну- in the infinitive (e.g. тълкнути 'to shove'). Prefixation is another device here (cf. pfv. на-писати 'to write down' with impfv. писати 'to write'). Sometimes prefixated verbs are reinforced by suffixes to differentiate aspect (cf. pfv. усъх-ну-ти 'to dry up' with impfv. усыхати, and pfv. отъпустити 'to let go' with impfv. отъпущ-а-ти).

227. Word-formation. The methods used in forming words in Old Russian are normally four: (*a*) suffixation (e.g. учи-тель 'teacher', горож-анинъ 'burgess'), (*b*) prefixation (e.g. по-вѣсть 'story', на-волокъ 'water meadow'), (*c*) composition (e.g. бог-о-словъ 'theologian', человѣк-о-любьць 'anthropophil'), and (*d*) apophony, both vocalic and consonantal (e.g. усъхнути 'to dry up'/сухъ 'dry'; коньць 'end'/чинъ 'order').[1]

All these methods can function in one combination or another or they may be applied separately. Suffixes are mainly used in nominal and prefixes in verbal formations. Some suffixes are synonymous with infixes (e.g. н in на-н-ь 'on him/it'). Prefixes may be either prepositional (e.g. отъ-рядити 'to send off', на-сельникъ 'inhabitant') or they may be special morphemes, sometimes called 'preverbs' (e.g. въз- 'up-', роз- 'dis-'). They may occasionally be used only with nouns (e.g. наи-новѣи 'the newest', су-пругъ 'yoke-fellow'). Our last examples here illustrate composition. This was introduced into Russian from Old Church Slavonic, which followed Greek models (e.g. благо-изволение 'benevolence' < εὐδοκία, where the first component is plainly an Old Church Slavonic form, for which Old Russian would have had бологo-). The practice of composition was at first mainly confined to the ecclesiastical style and made use of many Old Church Slavonic calques (e.g. прѣ-водъ 'metaphor', ино-словиѥ 'allegory', въспято-словиѥ 'ἀντίφρασις').

228. A survey of the morphemes used in forming the various parts of speech may begin with these in their traditional order i.e. with the substantives coming first. Many of the substantive

[1] N. S. Trubetzkoy op. cit., pp. 181–2.

have petrified suffixes, which can no longer be used to form new words (e.g. бор-ьба 'struggle', жив-отъ 'life', прав-ьда 'truth'); but other suffixes are still productive in Old Russian (e.g. мыт-ьникъ 'toll-taker', лов-чии 'huntsman', рус-инъ 'Russian', учи-тель 'teacher', лют-ость 'cruelty', здоров-иѥ 'health'). Still other suffixes are found in hypocoristic personal names (e.g. Добр-ило, Тѣш-ата, Василь-ко).

229. Adjectives may be formed from substantives by the addi-tion of the suffixes -ьн- (e.g. мѣд-ьнъ 'copper-'), or -ьск- (e.g. человѣч-ьскъ 'human'). There appears to be a difference of meaning between the two formants (cf. бѣсьнъ 'possessed' with бѣсовьскъ 'diabolical'), but it is not always clearly drawn (cf. небесьнъ/небесьскъ 'celestial'). Another adjectival suffix is -ив-, which derives from abstract substantives (e.g. милост-ивъ 'gracious' < милость 'grace'), competes with -ьн- by giving rise to contrasted planes of meaning (cf. лъж-ивъ 'lying' with лъж-ьнъ 'false'), and appears to be productive, as it may figure in calques (e.g. богочьстивъ 'devout'). The suffixes -ат-, -ит- -овит- are normally attached to concrete substantives (e.g. бород-атъ 'bearded', плод-овитъ 'fertile'). The suffixes -ок-/ек-, -ък-/-ьк- lack the 'attenuative' force in adjectives which they have in nouns (e.g. выс-окъ 'high', дал-ѐкъ 'distant', льг-ъкъ 'light', гор-ькъ 'bitter').

230. Possessive adjectives show two sets of derivative types, viz. those due to palatalization of hard and of non-apical soft consonants (e.g. орьль 'eagle's' < орьлъ 'eagle', пророчь 'prophet's' < пророкъ 'prophet', къняжь 'prince's' < къня зь 'prince', творьчь 'creator's' < творьць 'creator'), and those formed with -ов-/-ев- or -ин- (e.g. учител-евъ 'teacher's', воѥвод-инъ 'commander's'). Of the last two formants -инъ is used only with ā/jā-stems, whether masculine or feminine. With these possessive adjectives we find the common formants -ьн- and -ьск- associated either as alternatives (e.g. отьчь and отьнь 'father's, paternal') or as substitutes (e.g. пророчьскъ 'pro-phetic', бѣсовьскъ 'diabolical').

231. The comparative degree of adjectives, as we have already noticed, makes use of the suffixes -ьш- and -ѣиш- (§ 207*e* (2)), and the superlative relies on the prefixes наи- and прѣ-, the former of which is added to the comparative and the latter to the positive form of the adjective (e.g. наи-новѣи 'the newest', прѣ-мудрыи 'the most wise').

232. Ordinal numerals are distinguished from the corresponding cardinals by contrasting hard endings with soft (cf. пятъ 'fifth' with пять 'five'). The suffix -ьн- also functions among the ordinals as the formant of decades (e.g. седмьдесятьнъ 'seventieth'). For multiplicatives -як- is used (e.g. дво-якъ 'twofold'); -еро (also -оро) is found in some collectives (e.g. пят-еро 'quintet'); and трь-, used as a prefix with certain adjectives, has superlative force (e.g. трьсвятъ 'thrice holy').

233. Pronominal derivation shows the presence of such suffixes as -ов-/-ев- (e.g. так-овъ 'such-like' < такъ, сиц-евъ 'such-like' < сиць) as well as -лик- (e.g. то-ликъ, се-ликъ 'so much').

234. The nature of verbal stems and the formation of verbal aspects have already been noted elsewhere (§§ 225–6). Here we need only mention the use of characteristic suffixes in the derivation of verbs from nouns. Among the most productive of these are those in *-a-*, *-ě-*, and *-i-* (e.g. глагол-а-ти 'to speak' < глаголъ 'word'; укрѣп-ѣ-ти 'to grow strong' < крѣпъкъ 'strong'; гостити 'to trade' < гость 'merchant'). Conversely, we have deverbal formations among nouns (e.g. послушьнъ 'obedient' < послушати 'to obey'; дьрзъкъ 'bold' < дьрзнути 'to dare').

235. Adverbial forms comprising pronominal stems with characteristic suffixes constitute a series of well-established types. Among the suffixes -амо/-ямо, -де/-дѣ, -уду/-юду are notable (e.g. ин-амо 'elsewhither', къ-дѣ 'where', and вьс-юду 'everywhere'). These are the 'basic' local types of adverbs, with which the temporal adverbs are closely connected in root and suffix (e.g. инъ-гда 'sometimes', къ-гда 'when', вьсе-гда 'always'). Other adverbs consist of prepositional syntagmata (e.g. на-зади 'behind') or of petrified case-forms (e.g. муж-ьскы 'in manly wise').

II. SYNTAX

236. The structure of the sentence must be contrasted first with the structure of the phrase, which may be incorporated in the sentence: thus при С(вя)тославѣ князи 'under Prince Svjatoslav' and русьскы землѣ 'of the land of Rus'', which occur in the 'Svjatoslav Miscellany' (1076), are phrases. If we add коньчяхъ книжькы сия 'I finished this little book', which precedes these in the scribe Ioan's colophon, we shall have an expanded simple sentence. The nucleus of it is the association or nexus of a nominal and a verbal element, or, more simply, of a subject and a predicate. These are represented here in the one word коньчяхъ 'I finished', a finite verb (cf. коньчяти 'to finish') in the 1st person singular. Another scribe (Dŭmka), who was responsible for copying the 'Novgorod Liturgical Menaea' (1095–7), writes in the margin of his manuscript: азъ грѣшьныи рабъ б(о)жии недостоиныи Дъмъка написахъ кънигы сия 'I, Dŭmka, sinful and unworthy servant of God, wrote this book', where we find the subject (азъ) and the finite verb (написахъ) separately expressed. This is possible in the 1st singular when there is emphasis on the subject, otherwise Ioan's practice is followed. When the subject is in the 2nd singular, however, it may be represented by a vocative (e.g. Г(оспод)и помози рабу св(о)ему Дъмъкѣ 'Lord help thy servant Dŭmka'.

237. We have here two types of sentence, viz. an indicative type (e.g. написахъ кънигы) and an imperative type—here optative —(помози рабу), of which the first is by far the more common in Old Russian. A typically imperative sentence may be seen in нѣмчина не сажати в погребъ Новѣгородѣ (e.g. *Nov. gram.*, c. 1195: 'the German is not to be cast in jail in Novgorod', where the verb takes the form of the infinitive). In optative sentences (e.g. *Ost.* 1056–7: слава тебѣ г(оспод)и ц(а)рю н(е)б(е)сьныи 'glory to Thee, Lord, the King of Heaven') the verb may be absent. That it is 'understood' here is a convenient fiction.

238. The simplest sentences are elementary, logically complete syntagmata in which there is a nexus of subject and predicate, either in one word (e.g. написахъ, помози) or in two separate words (e.g. *Mst., c.* 1130: кто запъртить 'whoever shall damage'). Both elements may be 'expanded', viz.

Subject	*Predicate*
Самъ же Изяславъ кънязь	правляаше столъ о(ть)ца своего Ярослава Кыевѣ (*Ost.* 1057)
'Now Prince Izjaslav himself	reigned on the throne of his father Jaroslav in Kiev.'

Here the nucleus of the sentence is Изяславъ правляаше. Examination of the subject portion shows the presence of apposition, whose elements are bound by generic concord (самъ–Изяславъ–кънязь). Other possible attributes are (*a*) adjectival, as in азъ грѣшьныи рабъ б(о)жии недостоиныи Дъмъка (*Nov. min.*, 1097), where we find three adjectives associated with a complex of three appositions (азъ–рабъ–Дъмъка), or (*b*) participial, as in се азъ Мьстиславъ Володимирь с(ы)нъ дьржа русьску землю въ своіе княжениіе (*Mst., c.* 1130) 'Lo I, Mstislav, son of Volodimir, ruling the land of Rus' as prince', where дьржа (lit. 'holding'), qualifies the subject Мьстиславъ, or (*c*) they may assume the form of the genitive case of a substantive (e.g. *Nov. min.*, 1095: огньныхъ слугъ славьны видьчь[1] 'glorious witness of fiery servants').

239. The predicate portion sometimes shows the absence of the verb, especially when one has been used in a previous sentence; but this does not make the verbless sentence a logically incomplete syntagma (e.g. *Skazanije o Borise i Glebe*, 12th cent.: къде бо ихъ жития и слава мира сего 'where indeed (are) their lives and the glory of this world'). The absence of the verb is counterbalanced by the presence of a complement in the general sense of this word. Thus in а то за нимъ (*Nov. b. gram.* No. 9, 11th cent.) 'and that (is) in his possession', we have то 'that' put in a syntagmatic relationship with за нимъ, literally 'behind him'. This relationship is enough to establish a predicative nexus here. Complements, if nominal, may, like the subject-word, be expanded by attributes. Where, for instance, a direct object appears, it may be qualified by adjectives and their equivalents, and the object may be in apposition to another (e.g. *Nov. min.*, 1097: Г(оспод)и простите мя грѣшьнаго убогаго унылаго недостоинаго раба своего Якова а мирьскы Дъмъка 'Lord, forgive me, Thy sinful, poor, unhappy, and unworthy servant Jakov, or Dŭmka in the world'). Other complements include adverbial syntagmata (e.g. Tmutorokan' Inscription, 1068: въ лѣто 6576 ... Глѣбъ князь мѣрилъ мо(ре) по леду от Тъмуторо-каня до Кърчева 'in the year 1068 ... Prince Gleb measured the sea on the ice between Tmutorokan' and Kŭrčev', where we find three adverbial modifications). When the complement includes

---

[1] For видьцъ. This is an example of *cokan'je* (*c*-articulation) which was characteristic of Novgorod Russian as it is today of certain types of North Russian.

nominal parts of speech there is formal concord between them, as we have observed in the foregoing examples.

240. The simple sentence, to whatever extent it may have been 'expanded', may be contrasted with the compound and the complex sentence. The former exhibits juxtaposition of independent nexuses, whereas the latter establishes a 'hierarchy' of dependence. Such sentences are possible in Russian Church Slavonic, especially when they are copied from Bulgaro-Byzantine models. The complex sentence, which is hypotactic or subordinative by definition, appears even in purely Russian material. Thus in 'Prince Mstislav's Writ' (*c.* 1130) we read, among other things, а се я Всеволодъ далъ ѥсмь блюдо серебрьно, въ 30 гр(и)внъ серебра, с(вя)т(о)му же Георгиеви велѣлъ ѥсмь бити въ нѥ на обѣдѣ коли игуменъ обѣдаѥть 'and lo I, Vsevolod, have given a silver dish, of (the value of) thirty silver marks, and have ordered St George to strike it at dinner when the abbot is dining.' Here we have a compound and a complex sentence in one. The sentence containing the perfect велѣлъ ѥсмь, which is construed here[1] with the dative святому же Георгиеви, ends in a temporal clause of nexus type. But the 'typical' complex sentence should contain the relative or anaphoric pronoun, and this we find in the 'Ostromir Gospels' (e.g. никъто же бо не можеть знамении сихъ творити, яже ты твориши 'no one can do the miracles which thou doest'). Here яже 'which' is neuter plural, agreeing with знамения 'miracles'.

241. The links between individual clauses in a complex sentence, as we have seen, are provided by connectives, which include the copulatives а 'and, but', и 'and', and да 'that'. In No. 9 of the 'Novgorod Birch-bark Writs' we have ѥже ми отьць даялъ и роди съдаяли а то за нимъ, а нынѣ водя новую жену, а мънѣ не въдасть ничьто же 'what my father has bequeathed to me and my relations have bequeathed is in his possession; and now, marrying a new wife, he will give me nothing.' Here 'а' appears at the beginning of the second sentence as a copulative. Elsewhere it is slightly adversative. On the

---

[1] Another interpretation might be to ignore the punctuation after серебра and to place a comma after Георгиеви. This would give a more 'rational' reading, while doing no violence to the text.

other hand, и is a 'neutral' link-word. Да figures in да судить
кему Б(ог)ъ въ д(ь)нь пришьствия своюго и тъ с(вя)тыи
Георгии (*Mst.*, *c.* 1130) 'may God judge him in the day of his
coming, and the said St George'. Apart from these connectives
and others like бо 'for' and the contrastive -же (cf. Gk μέν, δέ),
нъ 'but', and то 'then', and specifically adverbial conjunctions
such as коли 'when' and аче/аще 'if', a very common one in
Old Russian is ce 'lo', which is found in many 'writs' (*gramoty*),
especially deeds of gift (e.g. *Vkladnaja Varlaama*, *c.* 1192: ce
въдале Варлааме[1] с(вя)т(о)му сп(а)су землю и огородъ и
ловища рыбьная и гоголиная 'Lo I, Varlaam, have deposited
with (the monastery of) the Holy Saviour (this) land and
orchard and fishing and game preserves'). Nevertheless, we
occasionally find paratactic constructions with the connective
conspicuously absent (e.g. *Skaz. B. G.*, *c.* 12th cent.: онъ же съ
радостию въставъ иде рекъ се готовъ юсмь 'and he arose joy-
fully (and) went (and) said: Lo, I am ready').

242. Examination of the various sentence structures in the
Russian of the eleventh and twelfth centuries reveals the presence
of a number of salient features. There is first the predicative
accusative or genitive–accusative for the modern instrumental
(e.g. *Nov. Writ, c.* 1195: а кого б(о)гъ поставить князя а с
тѣмъ мира потвердить 'whatever prince God appoints (it is)
with him (that) the treaty (lit. 'peace') must be confirmed', or
оже явится пр(о)ст(о)волоса 'if she appears with head un-
covered'). Next we have the placing of the attribute. This may
be either before or after the qualified substantive. In Russian
Church Slavonic the post-position of the adjective is favoured,
but in more specifically Russian texts the attribute precedes (cf.
Svjat., 1076: избьрано из мъногъ книгъ княж(иихъ) 'selected
from many of the prince's books' with *Nov. gram., c.* 1195: съ
всемь латиньскымь языкомь 'with all the Latin nation').[2]

243. The existence of definite (long) and indefinite (short)
adjectives in Old Russian arose from a desire to identify and
emphasize. No doubt originally the definite adjectives were
used exclusively in this way, but by the eleventh and twelfth

---

[1] For въдалъ Варлаамъ. Perhaps въдале stands for въдалъ ю. Варлааме is
the vocative form.
[2] Here the merchants of the Holy Roman Empire.

centuries they appear to be used entirely as in modern Russian, i.e. as attributive and predicative forms respectively. A few instances here will show Old Russian usage (e.g. *Skaz. B. G.*, 12th cent.: отъ неяже родися сии оканьныи [*sic*] С(вя)тополкъ 'of whom this accursed Svjatopolk was born'; призъвавъ Бориса . . . бл(а)женааго и скоропослушьливааго 'sending for Boris . . . the blessed and obedient'; иде рекъ се готовъ юсмь 'went (and) said: Lo, I am ready'; *Žitije Nifonta*, 1219: путь юже видѣ тѣсныи скърбьнъ юсть 'the strait way thou sawest is sorrowful').

244. A frequently occurring feature is the repetition of prepositions with each substantive or pronoun (e.g. *Var., c.* 1192: аще кто . . . цьто[1] хочеть от(ъ)яти от(ъ) нивъ ли от(ъ) пожьнь ли или отъ ловищь 'if anyone should take away something from these fields, or from these meadows, or from these preserves'; *Nif.*, 1219: при князи при Васильцѣ при с(ы)ну Ко(н)стянтиновѣ а внуцѣ Всеволожи 'under the Prince, under Vasil'ko, under the son of Constantine and grandson of Vsevolod'). As to some extent a contrast to the plethora of prepositions is their possible absence with the locative case (contrast *Nif.* 1219: въ градѣ Ростовѣ 'in the town of Rostov' with *Nov. gram. c.* 1195: аче будеть судъ князю новгороцкъму Новѣгородѣ 'if the Novgorod prince holds assizes in Novgorod').

245. Among other nominal features in Old Russian syntax we find a nominative object with an infinitive, expressed or implied, as in то за обиду гривьна (*Nov. gram., c.* 1195) 'one mark (to be paid) for the injury', where the accusative гривьну might have been expected in the light of modern practice. In contrast to this we find a genitive object with negative verbs (e.g. *Skaz. B.G.*, 12th cent.: не обрѣтъшю супостатъ своихъ 'not having found his enemies'), which is a characteristic of the Slavonic and the Baltic languages. Another feature of Old Russian syntax with parallels in these language-groups is the predicative instrumental (e.g. ibid.: сего мати преже бѣ чьрницею 'his mother was formerly a nun').

246. Nominal forms are also involved in abbreviated constructions with participles (e.g. *Svjat.*, 1076: идеже криво братию

[1] For чьто. An instance of *cokan'je* (*c*-articulation).

исправивъше чьтѣте 'wherever it is wrong, brethren, having amended (it), read on'). The dative absolute, which figures largely in ecclesiastical writing and imitates the Greek genitive absolute, was a favoured construction for many centuries even in secular prose (e.g. *Skaz. B.G.*, 12th cent.: сущю самодрьжьцю вьсеи русьскѣи земли Володимиру с(ы)ну Святославлю, вънуку же Игореву 'Volodimir, son of Svjatoslav and grandson of Igor', being the autocrat of all the land of Rus'").

247. Among verbal features in Old Russian syntax which deserve notice here are (*a*) the occasional use of the supine to express purpose (e.g. *Ost.*, 1056–7: азъ же посълахъ вы жятъ 'and I sent you forth to reap'), with the infinitive sometimes functioning as a substitute; (*b*) the use of conditional constructions (e.g. *Var., c.* 1192: аще кто . . . цьто хочеть от(ъ)яти от(ъ) нивъ . . . а буди ему противень с(вя)тыи сп(а)съ 'if anyone should take away something from (these) fields . . . may the Holy Saviour oppose him'); (*c*) the competition of the perfect tense, with or without the auxiliary of the 3rd person singular, with the simpler past tenses, especially the aorist (cf. *Tmut.*, 1068: Глѣбъ князь мѣрилъ мо(ре) по леду 'Prince Gleb measured the sea on the ice' with *Ost.*, 1057: написахъ ev(ан)г(е)лие се 'I copied these Gospels', or with *Svjat.*, 1076 (col.): коньчяшя ся книгы сия рукою грѣшьнааго Иоана 'this book was finished by the hand of sinful Ioan'); (*d*) the use of the reflexive verb with a detached and mobile pronoun (cf. the foregoing example with *Mst., c.* 1130: кто ся изоостанеть [*sic*] въ манастыри 'whosoever is left in the monastery'); and (*e*) the reliance on difference of aspect in expressing future meaning with present-tense forms (e.g. *Nov. b. gram.* No. 9, 11th cent.: а нынѣ водя новую жену, а мънѣ не въдасть ничьто же 'and now, marrying a new wife, he will give me nothing').

248. Still another Old Russian feature is the lack of discrimination between direct and indirect speech and the consequent sudden transitions from one to the other. An early example of this, although it survives in a late recension (1377), is the sentence relating to Prince Oleg in the *Povest' vremennych let*, viz. и повелѣ оседлати конь, а то вижю кости его 'he ordered his horse to be saddled, so that I might see its (i.e. the dead horse's) bones'.

249. Furthermore, there is the occasional lack of concord between subject and verb, especially when the former is an 'unindividuated' collective (e.g. *1 Nov. let.*, 13–14th c.: ходиша вся русьска земля 'the whole land of Rus' went (pl.)') or where several subjects are connected by prepositions and only one is in the nominative (e.g. *Nov. gram., c.* 1195: се язъ Ярославъ Володимѣричь, сгадавъ с посадникомь с Мирошкою и с тысяцкымь Яковомъ и с всѣми новгородьци потвердихомъ мира старого с посломь Арбудомъ и с всѣми нѣмьцкыми с(ы)ны 'Lo I, Jaroslav Volodimĕrič', in consultation with the burgomaster Miroška and the prefect Jakov and all Novgorodians, confirmed the old treaty with the ambassador Arbud and all German sons').

250. Word-order in Old Russian was flexible; but examination of stereotyped sentences shows that certain positions in the sentence were reserved for the major 'members' or constituents. As the sentence is normally part of something larger, its inclusion in the larger group is reflected by the presence of certain particles as well as in 'shifts' from the 'normal' position. Let us study the distribution of the constituents in a number of 'neutral' sentences to begin with.

(*a*) азъ Григории диякон(ъ) написахъ ev(ан)г(е)лие се (*Ost.*).
'I, Grigorij the deacon, copied these Gospels.'

(*b*) г(оспод)и помози рабу св(о)ему Михаилу (*Nov. Men.*).
'Lord, help thy servant Michail.'

(*c*) се я Всеволодъ далъ юсмь блюдо серебрьно (*Mst.*)
'Lo I, Vsevolod, have given a silver dish.'

(*d*) сь убо Володимиръ имѣяше с(ы)новъ 30 (*Lgd B. G.*).
'This Volodimir had some thirty sons.'

In all the above instances we find the subject preceding the verb as well as occasionally preceded by a particle. The functions and arrangement of particles and of other invariables in larger groupings may be seen in the following example from the colophon to the 'Ostromir Gospels'.

Написахъ *же* евангелие се рабу божию, наречену сущу въ кр(ь)щении Иосифъ, *а* мирьскы Остромиръ, близоку сущу Изяславу кънязу, Изяславу *же* кънязу тогда прѣдрьжящу объ власти, и о(тъ)ца своего Ярослава и брата своего Володимира; самъ же Изяславъ кънязь правляше столъ о(тъ)ца своего Ярослава Кыевѣ, а брата своего столъ поручи правити близоку своему Остромиру Новѣгородѣ. Мънога же лѣт(а) даруи Б(ог)ъ сътяжавъшуму Ev(ан)г(е)лие се на утѣшение мъногамъ д(у)шамъ кр(ь)стиянскамъ.

'And I copied these Gospels for the servant of the Lord called Iosif in baptism and Ostromir in the world, the companion of Prince Izjaslav; for Prince Izjaslav then held both principalities, both his father Jaroslav's and his brother Volodimir's. Now Prince Izjaslav himself reigned on the throne of his father Jaroslav in Kiev and he gave the governance of his brother's throne to his companion Ostromir in Novgorod. May God grant many years to the one who commissioned these Gospels for the comfort of many Christian souls.'

Although Russian Church Slavonic practice is notable here, especially in the forms used (which we have partly obscured outwardly by normalization), it is nevertheless a passage which fairly represents eleventh-century Old Russian, even in several of its idiosyncrasies. It will be observed that the links between some of the clauses are rather loose (cf. the dative absolute at the end of the first sentence) and that a and enclitic -же are in evidence and the latter overworked. In the above sentences too the normal subject-verb sequence is sometimes reversed for emphasis, and the constituent which is given prominence appears at the head of the sentence (e.g. а брата своего столъ поручи правити . . . Остромиру 'and he gave the governance of his brother's throne to . . . Ostromir'; мънога же лѣт(а) даруи Б(ог)ъ сътяжавъшуму Ev(ан)г(е)лие се 'may God grant many years to the one who commissioned these Gospels'). The postposition of adjectives, an Old Church Slavonic device, will be remarked in our example as well as the presence of non-Russian forms (e.g. сущу for сучю, сътяжавъшуму for сътяжавъшему).

251. As a contrast to the language of the Colophon let us quote here a passage from a Novgorod writ (c. 1195), which illustrates the ancient legal style, viz.

Послалъ єсмь посла своєго Григу на сеи правдѣ, первоє ходити новгородцю послу и всякому новгородцю въ миръ въ . . . нѣмечьску землю и на гъцкъ берегъ, такоже ходити нѣмьчьмь[1] и г(ъ)тяномъ въ Новъгородъ безъ пакости.

'I have sent my ambassador Griga on these terms, first that the Novgorodian ambassador and any Novgorodian shall travel in peace to the German land and to Gothland, and also Germans and Gothlanders shall travel to Novgorod unmolested.' In this short passage there is no sign of Church Slavonic influence, and the grammar and terminology are Russian.

III. VOCABULARY

252. We recognize Old Russian not only by its characteristic phonology and grammatical system but by its vocabulary, and in this domain we observe the intersection of diverse elements, revealing its contacts with other languages. Its 'fundamental' vocabulary is an abundant inheritance from Common Slavonic, which, as we have already seen (§ 124), was not entirely without the leaven of earlier borrowings. The Common Slavonic elements of Old Russian are certain categories of words covering: (*a*) natural phenomena, animate and inanimate (e.g. небо 'sky', съльньце 'sun', звѣзда 'star', дьнь 'day', ночь 'night', земля 'earth', вода 'water', вѣтръ 'wind', дерево 'tree', трава 'grass', звѣрь 'beast', рыба 'fish', пъта 'bird', человѣкъ 'man'); (*b*) simple actions, states, and qualities (e.g. дѣлати 'to do', видѣти 'to see', ѣсти/ясти 'to eat', ити 'to go', рѣчи 'to speak', жити 'to live', быти 'to be', съпати 'to sleep'; добръ 'good', унъ 'young', красьнъ 'beautiful'); (*c*) parts of the body (e.g. тѣло 'body', голова 'head', рука 'hand', нога 'foot'); (*d*) terminology of a settled material culture (e.g. орати 'to plough', пасти 'to graze', прясти 'to spin'; домъ 'house', стѣна 'wall', токъ 'threshing-floor'; конь 'horse', овьца 'sheep', пьсъ 'dog'; сукно 'cloth', ножь 'knife', гърнъ 'pot'); (*e*) relationship terms (e.g. отьць 'father', мати 'mother', сынъ 'son', дъчи 'daughter', братъ 'brother', сестра 'sister'); (*f*) terms pertaining to social organization (e.g. родъ 'clan', племя 'tribe', вѣче 'witan', староста 'elder', рабъ 'slave', челядь 'servants'); (*g*) military vocabulary (e.g. рать 'war', лукъ 'bow', стрѣла 'arrow', копиѥ 'pike'); (*h*) religious terms (e.g. вълхвъ 'sorcerer', баяти 'to bewitch'); (*i*) various culture terms (e.g. зъдъчии 'builder', гусли 'zither', плясати 'to dance'); and

---

[1] Another instance of *cokan'je* (*c*-articulation).

(*j*) abstract vocabulary (e.g. мысль 'thought', умъ 'reason', истина 'truth').

This elementary vocabulary, as we know, had a great many words in common with Baltic,[1] pointing at least to an earlier symbiosis of the peoples speaking one or other of these groups of languages (cf. OR корова 'cow', ледъ 'ice', бѣгати 'to run', вести 'to lead' with Lith. *kárvė*, *lẽdas*, *bė́gti*, *vèsti*). And it had been notably increased through contacts with the Iranian- and the Germanic-speaking peoples. The Iranian terminology appertained in part to religion (cf. богъ 'God', хърсъ 'sun-god', раи 'paradise', святъ 'holy', миръ 'peace' with Av. *baghō*, *hvarə*, *rắy*, *spentō*, *miθrō*, respectively) and may have entered the Old East Slavonic vocabulary from the language of the Scythians and Sarmatians. The Germanic element is seen in several Slavonic word-categories (e.g. кънязь 'prince' < Gc *kuning*-; истьба 'house' < OHG *stuba*, E. *stove*; блюдо 'dish' < Goth. *biuþs*; гобьзъ 'abundant' < Goth. *gabigs*; хлѣбъ 'bread' < Goth. *hlaifs*, E. *loaf*; льсть 'cunning, fraud' < Goth. *lists*).[2] Moreover, the Germanic contribution held Latin and Greek secular and ecclesiastical elements in suspension (e.g. цѣсарь/цьсарь 'emperor' < *Caesar*, цьркы 'church' < Gk τό (δῶμα) κυριακόν).

253. At the beginning of the Old Russian period we observe that the language is already provided with loan-words derived from three distinct sources—Old Swedish, Byzantine Greek, and Turkic—representing three distinct foci of influence, or, in geographical terms, the north-west, the south, and the south-east. The loans from Scandinavia and Khazaria came directly into Old Russian; but the Greek loans arrived mainly through the intermediary of Old Church Slavonic. This language was the principal formative influence on Old Russian, as Old French was on Middle English; but unlike the influence of Old French on the English vocabulary, the influence of Old Church Slavonic on the Russian vocabulary is much more difficult to recognize. It is a relatively simple thing for the educated speaker of English to pick out the Romance from the Germanic 'half' of the English vocabulary; but the affinity of Old Russian to Old Church Slavonic makes many words, especially those of daily

---

[1] R. Trautmann, op. cit.

[2] V. Kiparsky, *Die gemeinslavischen Lehnwörter aus dem Germanischen*, Helsinki, 1934.

occurrence, identical, at least in their written forms. The differences become clearer, as we have noticed, when there are
phonetic discrepancies between the two languages—when, for
instance, we have forms illustrating the Old Church Slavonic
nasal vowels (cf. OCS пѫть 'way' with OR путь; OCS пѧть
'five' with OR пять) or Old Russian pleophony (cf. OR городъ
'town' with OCS градъ; OR молодъ 'young' with OCS младъ).
It requires only a modicum of linguistic knowledge to sift
out such formally distinct Old Church Slavonic loan-words in
Russian, especially outside the limits of the abstract vocabulary.

254. This last may be considered *a priori* to be predominantly
borrowed and as such, in many instances, translated from
Hellenistic and Byzantine Greek. *Calques* or loan-translations
are particularly common, as a few random Old Church Slavonic examples will show (e.g. беззаконниѥ 'trespass' < ἀνομία,
изьбьрати 'to select' < ἐκλέγειν, прьстень 'ring' < δακτύλιος,
прѣждевъзеганиѥ 'priority at table' < πρωτοκλισία, прѣ-
стѫпити 'to pass by' < παρέρχεσθαι, сънити 'to come down'
< καταβαίνειν, тысѫщьникъ 'chiliarch' < χιλίαρχος). These
were taken wholesale into Russian and figure prominently in
religious writing, and some (e.g. гражданинъ 'citizen') must
have been in daily use as they are today. It could not have been
otherwise, of course, for sacred literature became early an essential part of Russian culture along with the language it was
written in and the alphabet which had been devised for that
language. Old Russian therefore acquired its Greek *calques* from
Old Church Slavonic and together with these a notable body of
untranslated Greek loan-words as well as specific non-Greek
words in the Byzantine vocabulary, which the Macedonian and
Bulgarian translators had been prompted for one reason or
another to adopt unchanged (e.g. OCS идолъ 'idol' < εἴδωλον,
стихиꙗ 'principle' < στοιχεῖον, икона 'image' < εἰκών,
монастырь 'monastery' < μοναστήριον, диаволъ 'devil' <
διάβολος, ѥрєи 'priest' < ἱερεύς).

255. Other loan-words came into Old Russian through Old
Church Slavonic from Latin (e.g. коляда 'Christmas' < *calendae*, оцьтъ 'vinegar' < *acetum*, ол(ъ)тарь 'altar' < *altare*, пас-
тырь 'shepherd' < *pastor*, поганъ 'heathen' < *paganus*, къметь

'vassal' < *comes* 'companion'), mostly in a Greek form (e.g. names of months) but occasionally direct from the original.

256. The two languages by virtue of their common origin and early contact with much the same foreign influences also show loan-words of various age from Germanic (e.g. хлѣбъ 'bread') and Turkic (e.g. санъ 'rank', клобукъ 'headgear'). But unlike Old Church Slavonic, Old Russian possessed by the eleventh and twelfth centuries an accumulation of distinct and independent borrowings from Old Scandinavian (Nordic), chiefly of the Swedish type, and, as the late testimony of the 'Lay of Igor" (*Slovo o polku Igoreve*) shows, from Turkic as well in one or other of its dialectal varieties.

257. The Scandinavian loans in Old Russian are a compact group with, as we should naturally expect, predominantly trading, shipping, military, and administrative bias. Varangian influence had led to the organization of trade and life in Rus' and had provided the armed protection necessary to a community that lived by trade. Accordingly we find such loan-words as пудъ (< *pund* < L. *pondus*) 'pood'; бьрковьскъ (for пудъ бьрковьскъ < OSw. place-name *Biærkö*, mod. *Björkö*) 'unit of weight, viz. ten poods'; аскъ/яскъ (OSw. *asker*) 'basket'; ларь (OSw. *lar*) 'box'; якорь (< OSw. *ankari*) 'anchor'; шьгла (< OSw. *sigla*) 'mast'; стягъ (< OSw. *stang*) 'flag'; крюкъ (< OSw. *króker*) 'hook'; вира (cf. ON *verr* 'man') 'fine'; ти(в)унъ (cf. ON *þiónn* 'attendant') 'steward' (cf. E. *thane*); ябетьникъ (< OSw. *æmbiti*) 'official'; гридь (cf. ON *griði* 'servant') 'warrior, companion'.[1] No doubt other words current in the ninth and tenth centuries have since been lost, so that the group has been impoverished; but the old personal names persist to this day, viz. Рюрикъ (< Run. Hrurikr, Hrørikr)), Игорь (< Ingvarr), Олегъ (< Helgi), Ольга (< Helga), and Глѣбъ (< Guðleifr).

258. Our Turkic loan-words from the 'Lay of Igor" (e.g. босый 'dun', челка 'horsetail tassel', яруга 'ravine'), however, are less significant, as they have passed through a long period of evolution to find themselves in a book published in 1800 from a

---

[1] Clara Thörnqvist, *Studien über die nordischen Lehnwörter im Russischen*, Uppsala–Stockholm, 1948.

presumably sixteenth-century manuscript which was destroyed during the Napoleonic invasion of Russia. On the contrary, the title 'Kagan' (*chacanus*), given to Vladimir the Great, Grand Prince of Kiev, is ancient and apparently of Turkic origin, for it was applied to Avar leaders of the seventh century and was later used among the Khazars, from whom some of the Russian grand princes took it as an exalted appellation for themselves. This word is now 'khan' (R. хан). The Turkic origin of another title бояринъ 'boyar' is not now seriously disputed, although there is still no consensus of opinion about its source. Some scholars have connected it with Turkic *bajar* 'magnate'; others conjecture that its alternative боляринъ is the 'basic' form.[1] In any case it resulted in the modern, pre-revolutionary баринъ 'gentleman', which is first recorded in 1780.[2]

259. Loan-words, as we have seen, are either permanent or impermanent according to their ability to adapt themselves to the changing demands of community life. Many of the words we have enumerated above are now obsolete; others still survive. Rulers and modes of government tend to pass into history where their names and immortality are guaranteed. But objects of daily use, whose foreign names were assimilated at the time of their acquisition (e.g. кровать 'bed' < Gk κραββάτι(ον), уксусъ 'vinegar' < Gk ὄξος, парусъ 'sail' < Gk φάρος, огурьцъ 'cucumber' < Gk ἄγουρος, вишня 'cherry' < Gk βυσσινιά, севкла, later свекла, 'beet' < Gk σεῦκλον/σεῦτλον, to name only medieval Greek examples), are now part of the 'fundamental' vocabulary of common things.

IV. STYLE

260. The syntactic structure of Old Russian, which we have examined above and whose materials we have dealt with, depends on the style used; and from the beginning styles varied considerably. We recall that a ready-made literature, primarily ecclesiastical and very largely translated, reached Rus' with Christianity from Bulgaria. This literature adhered closely to Greek models in the construction of sentences, as may be most clearly seen in versions of Biblical and patristic texts. The character of the literature demanded it (cf. Wulfila's Gothic version

[1] K. H. Menges, *The Oriental Elements in the Vocabulary of the Oldest Russian Epos, The Igor' Tale*, New York, 1951, pp. 18–20.
[2] P. Ja. Černych, *Očerk russkoj istoričeskoj leksikologii*, Moscow, 1956, p. 122.

of the fourth century as presented in the sixth-century Codex argenteus). How close the text of the russianized 'Ostromir Gospels' (simplified here in spelling) is to its Hellenistic Greek original may be seen from a short extract (St. John ix. 1–7) from both (i–ii), followed by the English version (iii), viz.

(i) Τῷ καιρῷ ἐκείνῳ παράγων ὁ Ἰησοῦς εἶδεν ἄνθρωπον τυφλὸν ἐκ γενετῆς. καὶ ἠρώτησαν αὐτόν οἱ μαθηταὶ αὐτοῦ λέγοντες Ῥαββί, τίς ἥμαρτεν, οὗτος ἢ οἱ γονεῖς αὐτοῦ, ἵνα τυφλός γεννηθῇ; ἀπεκρίθη ὁ Ἰησοῦς, Οὔτε οὗτος ἥμαρτεν οὔτε οἱ γονεῖς αὐτοῦ, ἀλλ' ἵνα φανερωθῇ τὰ ἔργα τοῦ Θεοῦ ἐν αὐτῷ. ἐμὲ δεῖ ἐργάζεσθαι τὰ ἔργα τοῦ πέμψαντός με ἕως ἡμέρα ἐστίν· ἔρχεται νὺξ ὅτε οὐδεὶς δύναται ἐργάζεσθαι. ὅταν ἐν τῷ κόσμῳ ὦ, φῶς εἰμὶ τοῦ κόσμου. ταῦτα εἰπὼν ἔπτυσεν χαμαὶ καὶ ἐποίησεν πηλὸν ἐκ τοῦ πτύσματος, καὶ ἐπέχρισεν τὸν πηλὸν ἐπὶ τοὺς ὀφθαλμοὺς τοῦ τυφλοῦ,[1] καὶ εἶπεν αὐτῷ Ὕπαγε νίψαι εἰς τὴν κολυμβήθραν τοῦ Σιλωάμ (ὃ ἑρμηνεύεται Ἀπεσταλμένος). ἀπῆλθεν οὖν καὶ ἐνίψατο, καὶ ἦλθεν βλέπων.

(ii) Въ врѣмѧ оно, мимоидыи I(су)съ, видѣ чловѣка слѣпа отъ рожьства и въпросишѧ и оченици юего гл(аго)лѭще, рауви, кꙑто съгрѣши, сь ли или родителѧ юего, да слѣпъ родисѧ? Отъвѣща Iи(су)съ ни сь съгрѣши ни родителѧ юего, нъ да явѧть сѧ дѣла божия на нюемь. мьнѣ подобаюеть дѣлати дѣла посълавшааго мѧ доньде же дьнь юесть; придеть же нощь, юегда никꙑто же не можеть дѣлати. юегда же въ мирѣ юесмь, свѣтъ юесмь миру. си рекъ, плинѫ на землю, и сътвори брьниюе отъ плюновения и помаза юему очи брьниюемъ, и рече юему, иди умыи сѧ въ кѫпели силуамьстѣ, юже съказаюеть сѧ посъланъ. шьдъ же и умы сѧ и приде видѧ.

(iii) '(At that time), as Jesus passed by, he saw a man which was blind from his birth. And his disciples asked him, saying, Master, who did sin, this man, or his parents, that he was born blind? Jesus answered, Neither hath this man sinned, nor his parents: but that the works of God should be made manifest in him. I must work the works of him that sent me, while it is day: the night cometh, when no man can work. As long as I am in the world, I am the light of the world. When he had thus spoken, he spat on the ground, and made clay of the spittle, and he anointed the eyes of the blind man with the clay, And said unto him, Go, wash in the pool of Siloam, (which is by interpretation, Sent.) He went his way therefore, and washed, and came seeing.

---

[1] A variant here reads: καὶ ἐπέθηκεν αὐτοῦ τὸν πηλὸν ἐπὶ τοὺς ὀφθαλμούς.

Collation of the Slavonic with the Greek text shows the translators following the original closely, as if intent on being utterly faithful to Holy Writ. This is what the early translators were apt to do; and here Wulfila anticipated Cyril and Methodius by many centuries. Study of the divergences from the Greek text in the Slavonic translation shows that the essential differences between the two languages sporadically emerges in idiom (e.g. на землю for χαμαί, въ кѫпели for εἰς τὴν κολυμβήθραν), grammar (e.g. ѥсмь for both ὦ and εἰμί), and style (e.g. use of же); but the framework of the prototype is so rigid that the translator has to follow the ins and outs of the word-order.

261. Rather later translators, especially of other than sacred subjects, feel freer in relation to the original text, and their versions accordingly are often less faithful than those of the pioneer translators of Scriptural passages into Slavonic. Among these latter too there are some whose literalness defeats itself. Comparison, for instance, of parallel passages in the 'Svjatoslav Miscellanies' of 1073 and 1076—symposia originally prepared for the Bulgarian tsar Symeon—shows both confusion and variations in detail. The passage we might consider here is the exhortation of the monk Nilus to the monk Agathius. The Greek title (Νείλου μοναχοῦ ἐκ τοῦ πρὸς Ἀγάθιον μοναχόν), translated as Нила чрьньца отъ того ѥже къ Агаѳиу чрьньцю in the 1073 version, is reduced to Нила чрьноризьца three years later. The servility of the first translator leaves his version incomprehensible without reference to the Greek text. But even here something extraneous has been interpolated, viz. ѥже in the sense of 'that is to say', which is misleading. Both texts, however, do not stray from their original. The Greek passage reads: οὕτως τῷ Κορνηλίῳ ἐν οἰκίᾳ προσευχομένῳ ἐπιφοιτήσας ἄγγελος ἔλεγεν· αἱ προσευχαί σου καὶ αἱ ἐλεημοσύναι σου ἀνέβησαν εἰς μνημό-συνον ἔμπροσθεν τοῦ Θεοῦ. 'Thus there appeared to Cornelius as he was praying in his house an angel who said, Thy prayers and thine alms have ascended into remembrance in the presence of God'. This is Biblical in its source (Acts x. 4) and simplicity, and reveals the transfiguring touch of imaginative expression. The Authorized Version translates the end of the passage closely but idiomatically as 'are come up for a memorial before God'. In the Slavonic version (and the two variants tally here, with

one curious exception) the simplicity is preserved, but the
originality is lost: the words 'have ascended into remembrance
in the presence of God' has become възидоша на памѧть прѣдъ
Б(ог)а 'have risen in memory before God'. But there is variation
in the interpretation of the next clause: in τί τοίνυν τὸν Κορνήλιον
ἔβλαψεν ἡ ἐν τῷ οἴκῳ προσευχή 'how indeed did praying in his
house harm Cornelius?' ἔβλαψεν becomes вереди in one case
(1073) and не врѣди in the other (1076). The two interpretations are directly opposed in grammar.

262. Greek usage, outside the simple directness of Biblical
Greek, favoured complex rather than simple sentences, subordination rather than co-ordination, participial constructions
(e.g. the genitive absolute) rather than finite clauses; it normally
placed its attribute after the qualified word; it frequently
resorted to antithesis and other figures of rhetoric; and it
evinced a predilection for pronounced rhythmical patterns.[1]
Old Church Slavonic reproduces these features partly from its
own resources (e.g. the corresponding dative absolute)—and
Old Russian follows its Slavonic prototype here almost to the
letter—and partly by literal translation.

263. In contrast to the involved prose of the ecclesiastical style,
which Old Russian had inherited from Old Church Slavonic
and which is represented, among others, by Ilarion's eleventh-
century homily 'The Law and Grace' (*O zakone i blagodati*)
and those of Kiril of Turov, we have the relative simplicity of
the Old Russian administrative style (R. *delovci jazyk*), which
intrudes into the chronicles and other narratives. This style
uses the simple sentence, co-ordination, and direct speech (e.g.
Lavr., 1377: и повелѣ осѣдлати конь, а то вижю кости ѥго 'he
ordered his horse to be saddled, so that he [lit. I] might see its
[the dead horse's] bones'), but on occasion introduces such
bookish constructions as the postpositive adjective (see next
example), the dative absolute (e.g. *Skaz. B. G.*, 12th cent.: сущю
самодрьжьцю вьсеи русьскѣи земли Володимиру с(ы)ну
Свѧтославлю 'Volodimir, son of Svjatoslav, being autocrat of
all the land of Rus"), the abstract neuter plural (*Kir. Tur.*,

[1] W. K. Matthews, 'The Russian Language before 1700' (*SEER*, xxxi. 77
London, 1953, pp. 376–7).

Slovo na antipaschu, 13th cent.: днесь ветхая коньць прияша 'today the old things have come to an end'), and concordant participial attributes (e.g. *1 Nov. Let.*, 13-14th c.: а вы плотници суще, а приставимъ вы хором рубити 'as you are carpenters we shall set you to build a house'). The purest administrative style, to be sure, is mostly free from such turns of speech; but in spite of its relatively greater nearness to the contemporary spoken language, it is nevertheless a form of written expression, and to that extent artificial.

264. Between the administrative and the ecclesiastical style, as polarities, we find interposed, as it were, an 'intermediate' style represented by the language of what may be termed 'literary works'. All three styles—the ecclesiastical, the administrative, and the literary—are illustrated, for instance, by Ilarion's Homily, the *Russkaja pravda* (Russian Code), and the 'Lay of Igor" in that order. But the value of these illustrations is somewhat diminished by their occurrence in late manuscripts. Chronologically better, if less pertinent, examples may be found in the twelfth-century writs and the contemporary 'Assumption Miscellany' (*Uspenskij sbornik*), which contains specimens of both the ecclesiastical and the literary style.

265. As an example of forensic language let us take an excerpt from the treaty concluded by Prince Jaroslav Vladimirovič of Novgorod with German ambassadors about 1195:

Оже тяжа родится бес крови снидутся послуси, и русь и нѣмци, то вергуть жеребеѥ. кому ся выимьть, ротѣ шедъ, свою правду възмуть. оже ѥмати скотъ варягу на русинѣ или русину на варязѣ, а ся ѥго заприть, то 12 мужь послухы идеть ротѣ, възметь своѥ.

'If a litigation arises without blood-letting, witnesses shall assemble, Russian and German, and shall cast lots. Whoever draws one shall take his due on oath. If a Varangian has a claim on a Russian or a Russian on a Varangian and it is not satisfied, twelve witnesses shall take oath, and he shall have his due.'

Here we find the antithetic logic of the forensic style, ellipses, concision, and the absence of ecclesiastical models. To persons acquainted with this style, to legislators, merchants, and officials, its language would occasion no impediment, for the background of reference (Bronisław Malinowski's 'context of situation')[1] would provide immediate understanding, and the ellipses would be resolved at first hearing. Like the ecclesiastical style, however, the forensic, from a modern point of view, is a relatively loose structure, as may be seen, for one thing, from the defective character of the punctuation. The clauses seem to be strung together into a roughly patterned succession of words. A sense of order and fitness does not preside over either style. Consecutiveness is left to a crude logic and is apt to be disturbed by verbal associations.

266. Even the style that we have designated 'literary' shares these defects. Although originating as an 'intermediate' style, it does not reflect a 'golden mean'. It is the creation of monks, moving within the confines of the ecclesiastical philosophy and formulas of Old Church Slavonic. The ecclesiastical style is still the dominant element here, as we can see from its choice of words. But the spoken language is free to assert itself too, and we sometimes find it intruding as a refreshing experience into a sequence of stilted elaborations. A lucid instance of the literary and ecclesiastical style in one comes from 'The Legend of Boris and Gleb' (*Skazanije o Borise i Glebe*), which survives in what is conjectured to be a thirteenth-century manuscript. It reads:

Въ то же время бяше пришелъ Борисъ изд[2] Ростова, печенегомъ же о онуду пакы идущемъ ратию на Русь. Въ велицѣ печали бяаше Володимиръ, зане не можааше изити противу имъ, и много печаляашеся. И призвавъ Бориса, юму же бѣ имя наречено въ с(вя)тѣмь кр(е)щении Романъ, бл(а)женааго и скоропослушьливааго, прѣдавъ воѣ мъногы въ руцѣ юго, посъла и противу безбожьнымъ печенѣгомъ. онъ же, съ радостию въставъ, иде, рекъ — се, готовъ юсмь предъ очима твоима сътворити юлико велить воля с(ь)рдца твоюго.

'At that time Boris came from Rostov, as the Pechenegs from over there were again advancing to make war on Rus'. Volodimir was in great distress, because he could not go out against them, and he was very troubled. And calling Boris, who was named Roman in holy baptism, and who was full of grace and obedient, he gave him the command of many warriors and sen▪

---

[1] Cf. Supplement I in C. K. Ogden and I. A. Richards, *The Meaning of Meanin*▪ London, 1927.

[2] Here an intrusive (epenthetic) consonant in syntagmatic junction.

him against the godless Pechenegs. Rising gladly, he (Boris) went (to him) and said: "Lo, I am ready to do before your eyes as much as the desire of your heart commands."'

This is distinctly 'literary' in manner; but here and there in the hagiography we encounter such 'asides' of the story-teller as прочая же юго добродѣтели инде съкажемъ, нынѣ же нѣсть время 'we shall tell of his other virtues elsewhere; there is no time now', or again нъ се остаану много глаголати, да не (въ) многописании въ забыть вълѣземъ 'but I shall not say more here, so that in writing much we do not lose our argument'.

267. Twelfth-century Russian was therefore not a uniform written language, but admitted the practice of several styles. All these had to some extent been exposed to the influence of Old Church Slavonic which provided both literary incentive and specimens of usage even then possessing some flexibility. Yet in its origins, we must remember, Old Church Slavonic was, like Wulfila's Gothic and like pioneering missionary efforts generally, a deliberate and artificial creation.

PART II

VII

PERIODIZATION OF THE HISTORY OF RUSSIAN

268. Although in the preceding chapter we considered Old Russian as a static language-type, necessarily generalized and representing approximately the literary language of a period covering a century and a half, we also adopted it as our point of departure in the examination of historical data in process of evolution. These data, in chronological terms, correspond to a space of nine hundred years and more, from the year 1056, when Grigorij the deacon began to copy the 'Ostromir Gospels' in Novgorod, down to the enormous production of books in the U.S.S.R. today, and they illustrate a vast array of written records, to which a sense of order, the limitations of memory, and a habit of comparison have attempted, from time to time, to set artificial and arbitrary bounds.

269. In studying languages as temporal phenomena, the historian of language, like the historian of society in his own domain, resorts generally to periodization, and the practice in dealing with the languages, as with the history, of Western Europe has been to recognize a succession of three vaguely defined areas of time which are labelled 'old', 'middle', and 'new' or 'modern'. Other terms meaning much the same as these have been known and used, for instance 'early' and 'late'; and these adversative notions are sometimes used to subdivide and thus to multiply by two the usual 'old'–'middle'–'modern' sequence. The practice is followed particularly in the investigation of the Germanic languages, where it was introduced by Jacob Grimm. This linguistic scholar applied the tripartition of European history into 'ancient', 'medieval', and 'modern' to the history the German language, and since his time the terms 'Althochdeutsch', 'Mittelhochdeutsch', and 'Neuhochdeutsch', and corresponding terms for the other Germanic languages, have been widely used. French scholarship on the contrary has till recent times preferred a simpler division of time by recognizing an older and a more modern period with a frontier separating the sixteenth from the seventeenth century. But more recently we find that the German practice is being followed in France, for instance by M. Cohen in *Histoire d'une langue: le français* (Paris, 1947); and accordingly we now have *le moyen français* (14th–16th cent.) interpolated between *l'ancien français* (11th–13th cent.) and *le français moderne* (since 1589). The insufficiency of the trichotomy of time is tacitly admitted by Western historians of language by their resort to subdivisions. An English example is very much to the point here. H. C. Wyld in his *A Short History of English*[3] (London, 1927) accepts the three periods, but adds an awkward fourth, and finds it necessary to make elaborate refinements. The outcome of this procedure is a complicated chronological picture, viz. 'Old English' is subdivided into 'Earliest Old English' (end of the 7th cent.), 'Early Old English' (8th–9th cent.), and 'Late Old English' (from 900 to 1050); then comes 'Early Transition English' (1050–1150), followed by 'Middle English', which subdivides into 'Early Middle English' (1150–1250), 'Central Middle English' (1250–1370), and 'Late Middle English' (1370–1400), and at length by 'Modern English' with its 'Early Modern' (1400–1500), 'Seventeenth-century', 'Eighteenth-century', and 'Present-day' periods. The magic spell of three is broken, and the subdivisions here are 'practical' rather than symmetrical. Cohen, too, encounters difficulty in subdividing his major periods, especially the latest, and uses political criteria to do so: the last but one is significantly headed 'Le français et le régime bourgeois du suffrage universel, 1848–1936', and apparently *le français contemporain* begins in 1936.

270. These vagaries of the historians of language demonstrate only too clearly their helplessness and subjectivity in the arbitrary periodization of linguistic history. And yet a chronology appears to be necessary, for we live in an exaggerated consciousness of the time factor, and our minds have perfected a bent for classification. While admitting that the purpose of our chronology is chiefly mnemonic, we can, without applying the traditional Germanic tripartition to the history of Russian, as is done in W. J. Entwistle and W. A. Morison's *Russian and the Slavonic Languages* (London, 1949), recognize a period of time in which a type of language we non-committally designate 'Old Russian' prevailed and a later period when another type of the 'same' language called 'Modern Russian' began to assume a shape which is substantially akin to the structure of the present-day language. Reference to Entwistle and Morison's book will show that the authors begin their historical period at 1100, a round figure of no chronological significance. Before that date the term 'Proto-Russian' is used for a period of time, partly recorded, with a fluid frontier separating it from Common Slavonic, which has an imaginary frontier with the more tenuous 'Proto-Slavonic'. This in its turn confines on a nebulous 'Primitive Slavonic', which the authors' elaborate periodization brings in contact with the hypothetical 'Balto-Slavonic',[1] a limbo interposed between the certainties of historical record and the 'starred' forms of our Indo-European reconstructions. This is, of course, all retrospect and surmise; but with Old Russian we are on firmer ground. Our authors see it as extending from 1100 to 1500, which appear to coincide with the Kiev period and the 'interregnum' between the fall of the principality on the Dnieper and the rise of Muscovy in the fifteenth century. The inexpressive date 1500 marks the supposed onset of 'Middle Russian', which covers the sixteenth and seventeenth centuries. 'Modern Russian' begins in the middle of the Petrine Age with the arbitrary date 1700. B. O. Unbegaun also, in his unfinished study of early sixteenth-century Russian,[2] uses the dates 1500–50 to contain his material, but these dates are equally ineloquent. Round numbers, no doubt, are very convenient in themselves, to delimit periods, but at the same time they reveal the essential artificiality of the chronology.

271. Perhaps after all it might be more expedient to resort to vaguer designations which allow some latitude to the working out of the processes of linguistic development. Novgorod the

[1] W. K. Matthews, 'The Interrelations of Baltic and Slavonic' (*SEER* xxxv. 85, London, 1957).
[2] *La Langue russe au XVIe siècle* (1500–50). I. *La Flexion des noms*, Paris, 1935.

Great, Muscovy, and Europeanized Russia might be terms to call to mind the recognized cultural periods and their linguistic aspects, but they nevertheless represent in another nomenclature the familiar trichotomy of time and the areas it covers. There is nothing essentially wrong in such tripartition: it may show and has been shown to represent historical phases, but linguistic development cannot be fitted into these without some violence. The development of Russian since the days of Novgorod the Great shows no break. Its indebtedness to Kiev, like that of all other parts of feudal Russia, did not end with the fall of Kiev and the subsequent inclusion of that city in Poland-Lithuania, nor did it end with the establishment of another centre of literary usage in the north. The Byzantine civilization of Novgorod, which had radiated there from Kiev, now took on more pronounced regional characteristics, and these in course of time modified and were mirrored in the autocratic Muscovite civilization, into which Novgorodian culture was absorbed.

272. The Byzantine civilization of Kiev, seriously damaged by Tartar inroads, continued under West Slavonic hegemony and assumed a different, europeanized aspect unknown to that of Muscovy. The common literary language of the eleventh and twelfth centuries now began to show more clearly the dialectal features that had from earliest recorded times distinguished Novgorod, Smolensk,[1] and Kiev, which were to become later the centres of Russian, White Russian, and Ukrainian sentiment and culture respectively. In our study so far we have steadily kept these facts in mind and have limited ourselves to purely Novgorodian or novgorodianized Kievite material, which in point of fact predominates in the surviving literature of the first three centuries, viz. from the eleventh to the thirteenth. In view of this we cannot draw a linguistic line as we draw a historical line between Kiev–Novgorod on the one hand and Muscovy on the other. The language of the period beginning with the fifteenth century in the north and ending with the onset of the

---

[1] After its absorption in Muscovy in 1514 this White Russian centre gradually lost its more salient native characteristics, and its comparative nearness to Moscow exposed it to strong Russian influence. It is not included in the White Russian S.S. Republic today, although it lies inside the linguistic boundaries of White Russian. The new centre is Minsk, which was annexed to Russia as the result of the second partition of Poland in 1793.

Petrine Age is connected more intimately with the old than with the new. It must have been easier for, say, a seventeenth-century Russian to understand twelfth-century Russian than it is for a Russian of today to understand seventeenth-century Russian. The line of cleavage runs through the borderlands of the seventeenth and eighteenth centuries. A dichotomy rather than a trichotomy of the historical period in the evolution of Russian appears to meet existing facts best of all. And indeed it has been the habit of historians of the Russian language who have written in Russian to distinguish Old Russian (*drevnerusskij jazyk*) from Modern Russian (*sovremennyj russkij jazyk*) as historians of the French language till recently have distinguished *l'ancien français* from *le français moderne*.

VIII

PHONOLOGICAL CHANGES

I. SOUNDS

273. General. Taking the synchronic and normalized characterization of eleventh- and twelfth-century Old Russian in Chapter VI as our point of departure, we can now consider such changes as the language has undergone century by century to the present time. In what follows we shall be principally concerned with data which have already been used as illustrations elsewhere. These and other data, however, will now be viewed in historical perspective and for ease of reference will be presented systematically under the familiar headings of phonology, morphology, syntax, vocabulary, and style in that order.

274. Although in our synchronic study of Old Russian we directed our attention to the mainly twelfth-century language, because earlier material was scanty, we shall find it necessary here, in order to preserve strict diachronic sequence, to begin with the earliest or eleventh-century records. These were mainly copies of Old Church Slavonic originals, and accordingly we shall have to pick out any 'revealing' errors made by the Russian scribes—Grigorij, Dŭmka, Ioan, and others—in copying them. These errors, supported by the evidence of the eleventh- and twelfth-century writs (*gramoty*), will establish the character of eleventh-century Russian phonology as compared with that of the primarily Bulgarian type of Old Church Slavonic.

Eleventh Century

275. Vowels. In the domain of vowel sounds we observe: (*a*) the absence of nasals, (*b*) pleophonic forms, (*c*) ь/ъ before liquids, (*d*) initial ло-/ро-, (*e*) the frequency of o for ѥ initially, (*f*) confusion of e and ѣ, (*g*) the development of strong ь/ъ into e/o, and (*h*) their lapse in weak positions.

276. The absence of nasal vowels in Old Russian is proved by even earlier evidence, viz. that of Constantine VII's *De* *administrando imperio* (cap. ix), which was written in 949. A form like Νεασήτ (cf. OCS неꙗсъіть, OR неясыть 'pelican') is a case in point, if the traditional interpretation of the word is correct. Nevertheless, by the middle of the next century we already find the not infrequent interchange of the characters ж/ѭ with у/ю and ѧ/ꙗ with а/я in the 'Ostromir Gospels' and in the later eleventh-century manuscripts, which unmistakably proves the absence of nasal vowels in the speech of the Russian copyists (*Ost.*, 1056–7: acc. sg. воду 'water' for OCS водѫ, dat. pl. инждеомъ 'to the Jews' for OCS июдѣомъ, nom. pl. овьца 'sheep' for OCS овьцѧ, gen. sg. морѧ for OCS морꙗ). To these we add the testimony of the oldest 'Novgorod Birch-bark Writs' (e.g. No. 8: acc. sg. по корову 'about a cow' for по коровж; No. 9: даллъ 'he gave' for даялъ).

277. Primary pleophony (*polnoglasije*), a capital feature of East Slavonic, with its characteristic groups *telot/teret* and *tolot/torot* for the Old Church Slavonic (South Slavonic) *tlět/trět* and *tlat/trat* respectively,[1] is represented by 'accidental' forms in the eleventh-century ecclesiastical manuscripts as well as by 'natural' forms in the writs. In the 'Ostromir Gospels' we encounter перегнжвъ 'having bent' for OCS прѣгънжвъ and acc. sg. Володимира 'Vladimir' for OCS Владимира, which may be supplemented by gen. sg. ворога 'of enemy' for OCS врага in the 'Svjatoslav Miscellany' (1076). The evidence of the birch-bark writs also supports the existence of such forms (e.g. No. 8 корова 'cow').

278. Secondary pleophony, viz. forms of the type *tъrъt, tъlъt/tъrъt*, where primary pleophony shows *telot/teret, tolot/torot*, is well in evidence in the 'Ostromir Gospels' (e.g. зьрьно 'grain' for OCS зрьно, мълъния 'lightning' for OCS млънии). It will be noted that there are no examples here for *tъlъt* as there are none for *telet* in Old Russian. These secondary pleophonic forms are apparently 'compromise' forms between the characteristically Old Church Slavonic post-liquid ь/ъ (viz. ль/рь, лъ/ръ) and the corresponding Old Russian pre-liquid forms (viz. ьл/ьр, ъл/ър) to be dealt with in the next paragraph.

279. The apparent metathesis or transposition of liquid and

---

[1] The letter *t* in these groups of sounds conventionally represents a consonant (*c*): thus *telot/teret* may be indicated more suitably as *CeloC/CereC*.

vowel in Old Russian as compared to what obtains in Old Church Slavonic is in effect due to the late development of syllabic liquids in the South Slavonic and in some of the West Slavonic (viz. Czech and Slovak) languages. The Old Russian forms are therefore actually nearer to Common Slavonic, and their presence in the 'Ostromir Gospels', for instance, indicates the scribes' pronunciation (e.g. цьркы 'church' for OCS црькъı, испълнь 'full' for OCS исплънь).

280. Initial ла/ра in Old Church Slavonic are sometimes given their Old Russian equivalents, viz. ло/ро (e.g. *Svjat.*, 1073: роздѣли 'divide' for раздѣли).

281. Old Church Slavonic initial ю is replaced by o in the Russian recension of Church Slavonic manuscripts (e.g. *Ost.*, 1056–7: gen. sg. олѣя 'oil' for OCS юлѣꙗ; *Pandekty Antiocha*, 11th cent.: Оклесиастъ 'Ecclesiastes'). Many of our examples are personal names (e.g. *Nov. stichirar'*, c. 1163: gen. sg. Олены 'Helen's'), and these occur in the western types of East Slavonic (e.g. *Nadpis' na kreste Jevfrosinii Polockoj*, 1161: Офросинья 'Euphrosyne'; *Dobrilovo jev.*, 1164: gen. sg. Овгенья 'Eugene's') as well as in Old Church Slavonic itself (cf. *Codex Suprasliensis*: Оуктимонъ/Єуктимонъ '*Εὐκτήμων*').[1]

282. The Old Church Slavonic distinction between e and ѣ is not carefully observed even in the 'Ostromir Gospels', where we find несть 'is not' for OCS нѣстъ. More examples are provided by the 'Svjatoslav Miscellany' (1073) with веруꙗ 'believing' for OCS вѣроуꙗ, руце 'hands' for OCS рѫцѣ, съвѣдетель 'witness' for OCS съвѣдѣтель; the 'Novgorod Menaeum' (1095) with обретъ 'found' for OCS обрѣтъ; the 'Novgorod Menaeum' (1097) with на тѣле 'on the body' for на тѣлѣ, посреде 'amidst' for OCS посредѣ; and the 'Archangel Gospels' (1092) with юсти 'to eat' for OCS ѣсти. The conclusion we may draw from these substitutions is that the two characters were phonetically synonymous in Old Russian.

283. Positionally 'strong' ь and ъ, i.e. either stressed or followed by unstressed *jery*, are sporadically 'clarified' to e and o

---

[1] K. H. Meyer, *Altkirchenslavisch-griechisches Wörterbuch des Codex Suprasliensis*, Glückstadt–Hamburg, 1935, p. 75.

respectively (e.g. *Ost.*, 1056–7: смоковьница 'fig-tree' for OCS
смокъвьница).

284. The lapse of weak ь and ъ in Old Russian, recorded by
Constantine VII in the tenth century (e.g. Νεασήτ and -πραχ
for неясыть and -прагъ), is one of the most significant and far-
reaching changes in the phonology of the language. Already in
the 'Ostromir Gospels' as well as in the other eleventh-century
manuscripts we find frequent omission of the two characters in
unstressed position (e.g. *Ost.*, 1056–7: dat. pl. книгамъ 'to the
books' for OCS къниглмъ; *Svjat.*, 1073: створи 'created' for
OCS съткори, кнѧзь 'prince' for OCS кънѧзь; *Svjat.*, 1076:
книжькы 'little book' for OCS кънижькъі). The 'Tmutorokan'
Inscription' (1068) provides князь again for кънязь.

285. Consonants. In the domain of Old Russian consonants
we observe (*a*) the correspondence of ч/ж to Old Church
Slavonic шт/жд, (*b*) the palatalization of к, г, х, (*c*) the interchange of к and х, and two North Russian dialectal features,
viz. (*d*) the change of жд into жг and (*e*) *cokan'je* or *c*-articulation.

286. The correspondence of Old Russian ч/ж and Old Church
Slavonic шт/жд results from differential treatment in the first
palatalization of the dentals т/д and of certain consonantal
groups like кт/гт. Old Russian ч/ж appear in the 'Ostromir
Gospels' (e.g. клевечуть 'they slander' for OCS клекештѫтъ,
and прѣже 'before' for OCS прѣжде) and in the 'Svjatoslav
Miscellany' of 1073 (e.g. трепечуще 'trembling' for OCS
трепештѫште).

287. The substitution of the character и for ы in Old Russian is
a consonantal rather than a vocalic phenomenon, for 'soft
quality' in consonants was indicated by vowel symbols. The
Common Slavonic velars were hard, as we have seen; and the
beginnings of their palatalization in Old Russian may be observed sporadically in the eleventh century. An early example
occurs in the 'Svjatoslav Miscellany' of 1073 (e.g. acc. pl. фуники
'figs' for OCS фуникъі). It will be noted that this form of
palatalization did not result in assibilation as did the three
Common Slavonic palatalizations.

288. The interchange of к and х is confined only to the word
крьстъ 'cross' and Христосъ 'Christ' and is probably due

semantic as well as to phonetic factors. In the colophon to the
'Ostromir Gospels' we find dat. pl. душамъ крьстияньскамъ
'for Christian souls'; and the 'Svjatoslav Miscellany' (1073) has
Крнстосъ, хрьстъ, and хрьстити for Христосъ, крьстъ, and
крьстити 'to baptize' respectively.

289. The change of жд into жг is a peculiarity of the Novgorod
and Pskov types of Russian and is met with in the late eleventh
century (e.g. *Nov. min.*, 1095: дъжгъ 'rain' for дъждь; *Nov. min.*,
1096: gen. sg. пригважгаюма 'crucified' for пригваждаюма).
Pskov examples occur much later.

290. *Cokan'je*, a general term for the confusion of the affricates ч
and ц, is a dialectal phenomenon found in Novgorod and Pskov
manuscripts as well as in Old White Russian writs from
Smolensk and Polock. It occurs, for instance, in the 'Novgorod
Menaea' of 1095–7 (e.g. црево 'womb' for чрѣво, чвѣтъ 'flower'
for цвѣтъ, видьчь 'witness' for видьць, пѣвьчь 'singer' for
пѣвьць).

291. We have here a composite fragmentary picture of the
phonological tendencies of Old Russian proper, i.e. the lineal
ancestor of modern literary language, for our data are insuffi-
cient to enable us to fill in all the details. Nevertheless, some of
the tendencies have been recorded, and they will be seen to be
operative in the ensuing centuries.

Twelfth Century

292. The manuscripts of this century preserve the main phonological features of the preceding century as we have noted them
above.

293. Vowels. Instances of the change of initial ѥ into o still
occur sporadically (e.g. *Sinodal'naja korm.*, 12th cent.; voc.
Офреме 'Ephraim' for Ѥфреме).

A new phenomenon which appears in the twelfth century
is the change of original e and the same sound derived from ь
into o after palatalized consonants, whether the vowel occurs in
a stressed or in an unstressed syllable (e.g. *Slovo ob Antichriste*,
12th cent.: съкажомъ 'let us say' for съкажемъ, dat. pl.
бывъшомъ 'to those that have been' for бывъшемъ; *Žitije Jepifanija kiprskogo*, 12th cent.: instr. sg. врачомъ 'by the physician'

for врачьмь, dat. pl. имущомъ 'to the possessors' for имущемъ).

294. The confusion of e and ѣ is well illustrated in this century throughout the East Slavonic area, especially in the north (e.g. *Nov. stich.*, 1157: gen. sg. семене 'of seed' for сѣмене, тесныи 'narrow' for тѣсьныи, loc. sg. на дрѣве 'on the tree' for на дрѣвѣ).

295. There are still few instances of the change of strong ь and ъ into e and o (e.g. *Var., c.* 1192: противень 'adverse' for противьнь, за Волховомъ 'on the other side of the Volchov' for за Волховъмь).

296. Our last example here also illustrates the loss of the unstressed *jery*. This was a very common phenomenon by the twelfth century (e.g. *Var., c.* 1092: божница 'church' for божьница, пожни 'meadows' for пожьни; *Mst., c.* 1130: кто 'who' for къто, князь 'prince' for кънязь).

297. Consonants. Palatalization of the velars is extended in this period (e.g. *Jur. jev.*, 1120: великии 'great' for великыи; *Lestvica*, 12th cent.: аки 'as if' for акы; 12th cent.: паки 'again' for пакы).

A document we have had occasion to cite several times, viz. Varlaam's 'Deed of Deposit' (*c.* 1192), contains one rare feature. This is the presence of x for c in the form of the pronoun вьсь 'all'. It occurs in the passage вху (for вьсю) же ту землю хутын(ь)скую вдале [*sic*] 'I have given all the ground in Chutyn". As the example is almost unique (another occurs in the 'First Novgorod Chronicle', 13–14th c.), it can hardly be made the basis of a theory, and, moreover, the unusual form вху may have been influenced by the syllable of the name beginning with xy-, which must have been in the scribe's mind as he wrote the passage. Nevertheless, we may posit an alternative form вьхъ for вьсь (cf. *1 Nov. let.*, 13–14th c.: нельга 'it is not allowed' with нельзя).

Thirteenth Century

298. General. By this time dialectal features become everywhere more prominent in the manuscripts, as in the turmoil of internecine strife and foreign intervention new centres arose for the maintenance and proliferation of written literature. The manuscripts of the thirteenth century enable us to establish two major dialect-areas for Russian, viz. (*a*) a northern (Novgorod, Pskov) and (*b*) a central or eastern (Rostov, Rjazan'). The northern dialect is distinguished most clearly by its characteristic *cokan'je* and the central by its differentiation of e and ѣ. The western dialect of Smolensk and Polock is also represented now and has features (besides northern *cokan'je*) which warrant its being regarded as the direct ancestor of modern White Russian much in the same way as we consider the dialectal features of manuscripts emanating from Galicia and Volynia as well as from Černigov and Kiev to be early indications of Ukrainian.

299. Vowels. Examples of the confusion of e and ѣ multiply at this time, and some Novgorod manuscripts interchange the characters at will (e.g. *Nov. gram.*, 1265: на цѣмь 'on which' for на чемь; *1 Nov. let.*, 13–14th c.: всѣ 'everything' for вьсе). In the central dialect the Kiev practice of discriminating between the two characters is on the whole adhered to, although we occasionally find the substitution of ѣ for e in unstressed syllables (e.g. *Rjaz. korm.*, 1284: бѣседа 'conversation' for бесѣда).

300. The tendency to change e into o after palatalized 'sibilants', especially in unstressed syllables, continues to prevail (e.g. *Triod' Moiseja Kijevljanina*, 13th cent.: dat. sg. приюмшому 'having received' for приюмшему, dat. pl. стоящомъ 'standing' for стоящемъ; *Nif.*, 1219: dat. sg. умьршому 'to the dead (one)' for умьршему; *Rjaz. korm.*, 1284: ащо 'if' for аще).

301. A multitude of examples illustrate the change of ь/ъ into e/o respectively in weak position, where their lapse may have produced difficulties in pronunciation (e.g. *Nov. korm.*, *c.* 1282: тревога 'alarm', стекло 'glass', for трьвога, стькло; *Psalt.*, 1296: броня 'armour', блоха 'flea', вдохнувъ 'having inhaled' for брьня, блъха, въдъхнувъ).

302. Elsewhere we find the weak *jery* disappearing, as they began to do sporadically even a great deal earlier (e.g. *Nif.*, 1219: gen. sg. грѣшного 'of the sinful' for грѣшьного; *Nov. korm.*, *c.* 1282: кииждо 'each' for кыижьдо).

303. Consonants. The palatalization of velars continues apace in the thirteenth century, but there are still noticeable hesitations in spelling (e.g. *Nov. korm.*, *c.* 1282: въ Киѥве 'in Kiev' for въ Кыѥвѣ; *Psalt.*, 1296: acc. pl праздьники 'holidays' for праздьникы).

304. Palatalization of originally hard consonants other than velars is sporadically attested (e.g. *Miljatino jevangelije*, 1215: прискрьбьнъ 'sorrowful' for прискърбьнъ; *Psalt.*, 1296: ропьщють 'they murmur' for ропщють).

305. There are sporadic examples also of the opposite phenomenon of velarization (e.g. *Pantelejmonovo jevangelije*, 13th cent.: животъный 'pertaining to life' for животьный; *Nov. paremejnik*, 1271: чтутъ 'they honour' for чьтуть).

306. The loss of weak ь and ъ, which we noticed in the twelfth century, led to changes in the distribution of consonants in the thirteenth. These changes were the outcome of certain processes of assimilation—voicing and unvoicing. Besides these changes there were others involving dissimilation.

307. Contacts between consonants which had been separated by the weak *jery* led to instances of voicing where the following consonant was voiced (e.g. *Nif.*, 1219: гдѣ 'where' for къде; *Nov. prol.*, 1262: здравъ 'well' for съдравъ; *Rjaz. korm.*, 1284: здѣ 'here' for сьде).

308. The unvoicing of final consonants is first recorded at the end of this century (e.g. *Nov. korm.*, *c.* 1282: gen. pl. калантъ 'calendae' for каландъ; *Psalt.*, 1296: отинуть 'completely' for отъинудь).

309. Consonantal changes which emerge specifically in the thirteenth century include: (*a*) the change of x(в) into ф (e.g. *Rjaz. korm.*, 1284: Амфилофий for Амфилохий) and vice versa (e.g. *Nov. prol.*, 1262: въ колохонѣ 'in the colophon' for въ колофонѣ; *Nov. korm.*, *c.* 1282: просхура 'wafer' for просфора), (*b*) the interchange of в and y which is also found in specifically White Russian material (e.g. *Nov. korm.*, *c.* 1282: уторникъ 'Tuesday' for въторникъ), and (*c*) instances of dissimilation (e.g. *Nov. korm.*, *c.* 1282: уларь 'horarium' for орарь).

Fourteenth Century

310. General. The dialectal features in manuscripts become more numerous in the course of this century, and each of the three East Slavonic languages now takes on a distinguishable physiognomy. The systems of unstressed vowels, which will lead ultimately to the creation of a regional dichotomy with a central area of *akan'je* (*a*-articulation) flanked by a northern (Russian) and a southern (Ukrainian) area of *okan'je* (*o*-articulation), are now in process of formation. Divergences in the unstressed vocalism, where *akan'je* shows itself, are, however, only a fraction of the dialectal differentiation that took place at this time. The fourteenth century indeed—a century of political fragmentation like its predecessor—is the age of dialectal development *par excellence* in the East Slavonic area. For the first time now we have secular manuscripts illustrating new dialectal types, viz. those of Pskov, Tver', the Northern Dvina area, and Moscow. The Pskov manuscripts are mostly ecclesiastical, but the others are mostly writs. Linguistically, the former are of considerably smaller interest than the latter; but from a phonological point of view they offer sufficient evidence, supported by that of the Pskov writs, that the Pskov dialect was transitional between the Novgorod (North Russian) dialect and the Smolensk–Polock (White Russian) dialect, for it shares *cokan'je* with Novgorodian and, like the Old White Russian of Smolensk and Polock, it has bilabial *ų* (**w**) before a consonant. *Cokan'je* is also present in the dialect of the Northern Dvina area, which represents a northerly colonial extension of the Novgorod dialect.

311. Apart from the North Russian dialects of Novgorodian type, we have in the fourteenth-century specimens of Moscow Russian a dialect of the central or eastern type like those of Rostov and Rjazan', to which the Suzdal' dialect of the Laurentian MS of the *Povest' vremennych let* may also be said to belong. Moreover, Moscow Russian is of particular importance to us, because it was the dialect-type which, like that of London in fourteenth-century England, was to become the foundation of the spoken κοινή and of the literary language. Compared with the dialects we have just passed under review, it has no very distinctive features: there is no *cokan'je* to couple it with, say, the Novgorod dialect and no bilabial *ų* (**w**) or fricative *ğ* (**ɣ**) to range it with the White Russian type. The phonology of Moscow Russian shows o from e before a hard consonant, especially when e follows a hush-sibilant or affricate (e.g. *Duchovnaja kn. Ivana Kality*, 1327: на шолку for на шелку 'in silk'), и for ѣ (e.g. ibid.: со всими 'with all' for съ вьсѣми), and cases of *akan'je*, which is illustrated by the confusion of a and o (*Mos. jev.*, 1393: к Симану 'to Simon' for къ Симону, gen. sg. запода 'of the west' for запада).

312. Vowels. The changes of the Russian vowel system in the fourteenth century are dominated by the final disappearance of weak ь and ъ and the transformation of the strong varieties into e and o respectively, together with all the other phonological as well as morphological consequences which this entailed.

313. The change of mainly unstressed e into o after soft 'sibilants', which began in the twelfth century, is abundantly illustrated now even under stress (e.g. *Mos. jev.*, 1358: gen. pl. жонъ 'women' for женъ; ibid., 1393: шодъ 'gone' for шедъ < шьдъ, instr. sg. одежою 'with clothes' for одежею; *Lavr.*, 1377: доступившо 'having reached' for доступивше; *Čud. Novyj Zavet*, 14th cent.: instr. sg. жолчью 'in anger' for желчью; *Mos. Par.*, 14th cent.: instr. sg. пищою 'with food' for пищею; *Sil'vestrov sbornik*, 14th cent.: тяжокъ 'heavy' for тяжекъ).

314. By the fourteenth century the difference between e and ѣ had been completely lost in North and Central Russian. Generally, however, Church Slavonic practice was followed. This was revised by the South Slavonic scholars who came to Muscovy from the Balkans at this time and left their reactionary impress, as we have seen, on Russian spelling. Accordingly ecclesiastical manuscripts are not a very reliable indication of the changes taking place in the language.

315. Reference has already been made to *akan'je* above, and Moscow examples of it have been quoted. The oldest manuscript (*Mos. jev.*, 1339) with traces of this pronunciation goes back to the early part of the century. It appears to have been copied from a Galician[1] original, and therefore the facts of *akan'je* stand out prominently (e.g. кака 'how' for како, дивна 'wonderful' for дивно, в апустѣвшии земли 'in the depopulated country' for въ опустѣвъшии земли). These examples, however,

---

[1] Galician, as one ancestor of modern Ukrainian, retained the feature of *okan'je* or spelling pronunciation.

are of sporadic occurrence, and we have to wait till the end of the century for more abundant evidence.

316. Consonants. Instances of the palatalization of velars, shown by the writing of и after к, г, х, are more numerous in the fourteenth century than in the preceding two, and it is usually assumed that by this time the process was complete and the use of и for ы had become traditional. The writing of ы, however, in this position occurs sporadically even in the fifteenth century.

317. Velarization of formerly palatalized or soft consonants, which appears at the end of the preceding century, seems to be a regular feature in this (e.g. *Mos. jev.*, 1339: пиѥтъ 'drinks'for пиѥть, исцѣлитъ 'will cure' for изцѣлить; *Perejaslavskoje jev.*, 1354: стоитъ 'stands' for стоить; *Nov. prol.*, 1356: acc. sg. гнѣвъную 'enraged' for гнѣвьную; *Mos. jev.*, 1355: просятъ 'they ask' for просять; ibid., 1393: gen. sg. богатъства 'of riches' for богатьства, слѣзетъ 'will come down' for слѣзеть; *Taktikon Nikona Černorizca*, 1397: церковъ 'church' for церковь).

318. Consonantal assimilation, both voicing and unvoicing, whose beginnings we have observed in the thirteenth century, becomes a common and varied phenomenon in this (e.g. *Kal.*, 1327: с опча 'together' for съ обьча; *Lavr.*, 1377: instr. pl. з дѣтьми 'with children' for съ дѣтьми, dat. sg. свадбѣ 'for the wedding' for сватьбѣ, gen. sg. тадбы 'of theft' for татьбы, acc. sg. тчерь 'daughter' for дъчерь).

319. Dissimilation may be seen in the change of к/г into х before a following к (e.g. *Lavr.*, 1377: dat. pl. хъ киевскимъ 'to the Kievite' for къ кыевьскыимъ; *Čud.*, 14th cent.: gen. sg. мяхка 'of soft' for мягка) and of р into л (e.g. *Nov. prol.*, 1356: Илинархъ 'Irinarch' for Иринархъ).

320. Lapse of consonants, especially at the beginning and the end of words,[1] is well illustrated at this time (e.g. *Kal.*, 1327: стоканъ 'tumbler' for дъстъканъ; *Lavr.*, 1377: полтора 'one and a half' for полъвътора; *Mos. jev.*, 1393: серце 'heart' for сърдьце).

321. Interpolation (epenthesis) of consonants, which occurs sporadically in the thirteenth century (e.g. *Nov. korm.*, c. 1282),

---

[1] Cf. L. A. Bulachovskij, *Istoričeskij kommentarij k literaturnomu russkomu jazyku*, Char'kov–Kiev, 1937, p. 81. Достоканъ occurs in the seventeenth century.

is illustrated in the fourteenth, for instance, by the emergence of
т between с and р (e.g. *Triod'*, 1311: пострамити 'to shame'
for посрамити; *1 Nov. let.*, 13–14th c.: устрѣтоша 'they met'
for усрѣтоша).

322. The sporadic appearance of в before vowels initially and
medially is to be seen in some Russian manuscripts of this time
(e.g. *Kal.*, 1327: въ ворду 'to the Horde' for въ Орду; *Lavr.*,
1377: Вольга 'Ol'ga' for Ольга, Фаравонъ 'Pharaoh' for
Фараонъ, Левонъ 'Leon' for Леонъ; *Per. jev.*, 1354: ютери
вотъ насъ 'some of us' for ютери отъ насъ).

323. The unvoicing of voiced final consonants, which is first
recorded in the previous century, offers further 'accidental'
examples in this (e.g. *Lavr.*, 1377: порупъ 'cell' for порубъ,
Андронигъ 'Andronicus' for Андроникъ). The confusion of
г and к in the last example implies final unvoicing.

324. Among the most important features of Modern Russian is
the 'hardness' of ш, ж, and ц. The earliest examples of 'hardened'
sibilants occur in the fourteenth century (e.g. *Duch. kn. Dmitrija
Donskogo, c.* 1389: imp. жывите 'live' for живите, держыть
'holds' for держить). After the fourteenth century combinations
of these characters with ы, indicating the hardness of the sounds
they represent, is no longer rare.

Fifteenth Century

325. General. In the course of the fourteenth and fifteenth
centuries and in the early part of the sixteenth (1328–1523) the
gradual and forcible unification of the northern and central
tracts of European Russia was gradually taking place under the
direction of the princes of Moscow or Muscovy, as we can now
call their territory: Novgorod the Great and its dependencies
had been annexed in 1478 and Novgorod Severskij, to the
south-west, in 1523. It was natural therefore that a new type of
literary Russian should have begun to take shape under the
influence of the Moscow dialect, whose features have already
been noticed. The west and south of the East Slavonic area
(White Russia and the Ukraine) were now finally under Polish–
Lithuanian suzerainty and had, indeed, been under non-Russian
influence since the end of the fourteenth century as a result of

the conquests of the Lithuanian prince Algirdas (Olgierd). From the fifteenth century on we are accordingly concerned with the evolution of literary Russian in its new, Muscovite guise.

326. Vowels. The changes in the phonology of this language will be examined here in the already familiar order; but particular items will not now appear, because certain processes of development, viz. lapse of weak ь and ъ, the change of their strong counterparts into e and o respectively, and the coincidence of e and ѣ were now complete. We are left therefore with the change of e into o and the progress of *akan'je*.

327. The velarization or 'hardening' of e into o had begun as early as the twelfth century after the palatalized sibilants ш, ж, ч, ц; but there is evidence from a later period (e.g. *Nov. jev.*, 1270: дньотъ 'this day' for дьнь-тъ) which shows that it could also take place after other palatalized consonants (e.g. *Nov. jev.*, 1362: gen. sg. Ѥлеоны 'Helen's' for Ѥлены; *Nov. gram.*, 1392: на сомъ 'on this' for на семь). Similar spellings continue to appear in the fifteenth century (e.g. *Dvinskije gram.*, 14th–15th cent.: за моромъ 'overseas' for за моремь, озора 'lakes' for озера, gen. pl. рубловъ 'of roubles' for рублевъ; *Nov. ber. gram.*, No. 10, 15th cent.: межу нобомъ 'between heaven' for межю небомь; *Ipat'jevskij spisok, c.* 1425: в Кановѣ 'in Kanev' for въ Каневѣ). In all these cases we note that the change of e into o takes place in stressed syllables. At first the influence of stress on the change of e into o, as we have observed, was not important; while the sibilant and palatalized character of the preceding consonant was. Later both stress and the character of the following consonant or final position established the requisite conditions. These account for the change of sg. озера 'lake' to pl. озёра, or of все 'all' to всё. Analogy explains идёте 'you go', which has been influenced by идёшь (with hardened ш) and идём. Words with original ѣ rarely illustrate the change (cf. лес 'forest' < лѣсъ with звёзды 'stars' < звѣзды), also learned words mainly of Church Slavonic origin (e.g. член 'member', житие 'life of a saint'), words with secondary pleophony (e.g. верх 'top' < верьхъ), and words combined with the negative particle (e.g. недоросль 'minor in years'). We have already seen that the presence of *jo* (now written ё) in the language exercised the ingenuity of the eighteenth-century orthographers in finding a suitable symbol to represent it.

328. *Akan'je,* which is a Central Russian feature, never took root in the north, except in an enclave to the north of Kostroma.[1] Its rise, as we have seen, was late, and its progress not very rapid. In the fifteenth century confusion of a and o in Russian manuscripts is not infrequent (e.g. *Kolomenskaja paleja,* 1406: погарять 'to burn' for погорять, задовити 'to smother' for задавити). The slowness of *akan'je* to spread in writing (and incidentally it also occurs in Pskov manuscripts of this period, e.g. *Pskovskij izmaragd,* 1500: gen. sg. великаго Новограда 'of Novgorod the Great' for Новаграда) was due to the prevalence of a rigid orthographic system.

329. Consonants. Consonantal changes in fifteenth-century Russian are confined to assimilative features, unvoicing of final consonants, lapse, and velarization.

330. Assimilation (unvoicing here) is found in a number of fifteenth-century manuscripts (e.g. *Kol.,* 1406: рѣтка 'rarely' for рѣдко; *Duch. kn. Vasilija Dmitrijeviča, c.* 1424: acc. sg. коропку 'box' for коробку).

331. The unvoicing of final voiced consonants is seen in the Hypatian MS (*c.* 1425), where we find, among others, Серпь 'Serbians' for Сербь, Трубѣшь 'Trubež' for Трубежь, дошть 'rain' for дождь. These, as usual, are sporadic, for the traditional orthography was too strong a force to be seriously disturbed, especially in the hands of the South Slavonic scholars whose influence dominated Muscovite copyists in this century.

332. Lapse of final л after a consonant in the masculine singular of the indeclinable past participle becomes more common at this time (e.g. *Mos. gram.,* 1490: тако рекъ 'so said' for тако реклъ).

333. Instances of the simplification of consonantal groups occur sporadically (e.g. *Kol.,* 1406: безна 'abyss' for бездъна; *Ipat., c.* 1425: звѣзное 'starry' for звѣздьное). The initial cause of this was lapse of the weak *jery.*

---

[1] W. K. Matthews, 'Modern Russian Dialects' (*Transactions of the Philological Society,* Oxford, 1951, pp. 112–48), also *The Structure and Development of Russian,* Cambridge, 1953, pp. 86–106.

334. Records of the velarization or hardening of consonants continue throughout this century (e.g. *Kol.*, 1406: gen. sg. зимъныя 'of winter' for зимьныя, dat. sg. умъному 'to the wise' for умьному).

Sixteenth Century

335. General. By the sixteenth century the State of Muscovy was already firmly established in the Russian-speaking areas, viz. Muscovy proper, Novgorod and its dependencies, Rostov and Suzdal', from which the original minor appanage of Moscow had been detached, and Rjazan' to the south. At the end of this century the Moscow κοινή had apparently succeeded in effacing regional differences from the literary language, but until then they were still very much in evidence. The divergences are phonological as well as morphological, and the former may be seen in the Novgorod *cokan'je* and confusion of e and ѣ, Moscow *okan'je*, and Rjazan' *akan'je*. The inroads of *akan'je* on the purely Moscow pronunciation have been remarked already; but we may assume that, for instance, Ivan the Terrible pronounced his unstressed *o*'s as **o**. The tsars and aristocracy resorted to *akan'je* only in the middle of the next century.

336. Vowels. Instances of *akan'je*, in spite of the rigidity of traditional orthography, appear in the manuscripts now and then (e.g. *Vjazemskoje jev.*, 1527:[1] въ карабли 'in the ship' for въ корабли, не удалѣютъ 'shall not prevail' for не одолѣютъ, gen. sg. никаго for никого, да седмьдесятъ 'up to seventy' for до седмьдесятъ, какошь 'hen' for кокошь; *Sbornik Sinodal'noj biblioteki*, 16th cent.: изобличихамъ 'we showed them up' for изобличихомъ, митраполитъ 'metropolitan' for митрополитъ, gen. sg. арла 'of the eagle' for орла).

337. Consonants. Of consonantal peculiarities in sixteenth-century manuscripts we may mention here instances of unvoicing, lapse, substitution, and dissimilation.

338. Unvoicing is seen in the following examples (viz. *Dom.*, 16th cent.: лошки 'spoons' for ложькы, изрѣтка 'rarely' for изрѣдъка, обрѣски 'scraps' for обрѣзъкы).

---

[1] Written in the village of Novoje near Vjaz'ma.

339. Lapse or syncope of consonants continues to be recorded (e.g. *Dom.*, 16th cent.: лѣсница 'ladder' for лѣстьница, чесно 'honestly' for честьно, pl. посные 'pertaining to fasting' for постьные).

340. Cases of the substitution of ш for ч before н are found (e.g. *Dom.*, 16th cent.: обышный 'customary' for обычьный, пшенишный 'wheaten' for пшеничьный) as well as of the substitution of в for г in inflexions (e.g. *Dom.*, 16th cent.: gen. sg. тово 'of it' for того, одново 'of one' for одьного).

341. Dissimilation, especially of adjacent liquids, whose beginnings we noted in the thirteenth century, continues to be illustrated sporadically till the sixteenth and the early seventeenth (e.g. *Kijevskij pomjannik*, 16th cent.: верблюдъ 'camel' for вельблюдъ, cf. OCS вельблѫдъ).

Seventeenth Century

342. General. This century witnessed the intensification of the tendencies already observed in the language of the sixteenth. By this time the Moscow pronunciation was supreme in colloquial Russian, and in spite of the conservative influence of Ukrainian *okan'je* which came in with the immigrant Ukrainian scholars and churchmen, it gradually acquired its characteristic modern *akan'je*. As a result of this there was for a time no accepted norm of pronunciation in Muscovy in the second half of the seventeenth century. The lack of a norm is seen in Tsar Alexis's decree of 1675,[1] which provided, for instance, that if the author of a petition, ignorant of the proper spelling, should write another's name or surname with '*o* for *a* and *a* for *o* . . . according to the custom of the town he was born in and his own mode of speaking or writing, he shall not be held in reproach'.

343. Vowels. *Akan'je* appears now and then in Tsar Alexis's correspondence[2] and in his 'Legal Code' (*Sobornoje uloženije*) of 1649 (e.g. *Pis'ma Al. Mich.*, 17th cent.: gen. pl. утакъ 'of ducks' for утокъ, instr. sg. звать Никулаю 'to be called Nicholas' for Никулою; *Ulož.*, 1649: галанцомъ 'to the Dutch' for голландьцемъ, салдаты 'soldiers' for солдаты; Avvakum., *Žitije*, 1672-3: нечева 'nothing' for нечего).

---

[1] *Polnoje sobranije zakonov*, i, St Petersburg, 1830, 597, p. 1000.
[2] *Sobranije pisem carja Alekseja Michajloviča*, Moscow, 1856.

344. Other features of seventeenth-century vocalism include the change of stressed e into o, the differentiation of e and ѣ, the latter appearing under stress, and the substitution of ы for и.

345. The prerequisite for the change of e into o here is the hardness of the following consonant in a stressed syllable (e.g. пришолъ 'he came' for пришелъ, gen. pl. пчолъ 'of bees' for пчелъ, съ ключомъ 'with the key' for съ ключемъ).

346. The differentiation of e and ѣ was apparently purely orthographic as ѣ was used mechanically under stress (e.g. *Ulož.*, 1649: loc. sg. рекѣ 'in the river' for рѣкѣ, nom. pl. рѣки).

347. The back-vowel symbol ы appears for the expected и to indicate the hardness of the preceding consonant (e.g. *Ulož.*, 1649: въ ыное государство 'into another country' for въ иное государство, с ыноземцы 'with foreigners' for съ иноземьци). This is an instance of progressive, as distinct from the more usual regressive, assimilation.

348. Consonants. The consonantal system is now more settled: the hush-sibilants and the affricate ц, as we have seen, tend to be hard (velarized), Moscow шп for чн is confirmed by several examples, assimilations are general, prevocalic в appears again, as well as в for г, and final -мъ for -мь in the instr. sg. and -тъ for -ть in the 3rd pres. have prevailed.

349. Instances of hard ш, ж, ц are frequent enough (e.g. *Avv.*, 1672–3: pl. грѣшъные 'sinful' for грѣшьные, отцы 'fathers' for отьци).

350. The deaffrication of ч before н results in ш, as recorded earlier (e.g. *Ulož.*, 1649: однолишно 'individually' for одноличьно, nom. pl. лавошные 'shop-keepers' for лавочьные, instr. sg. пушешнымъ 'by gun' for пушечьнымъ).

351. Assimilations at this time include both voicing and unvoicing (e.g. ibid.: здѣлаемъ 'we shall make' for съдѣлаемъ, зъ бою 'from battle' for съ боя, исъ правилъ 'from the rules' for изъ правилъ, испортимъ 'we shall spoil' for изпортимъ).

352. Prevocalic в appears in numerous examples (e.g. ibid.: вотчинъ 'father's' for отьчинъ, восмь 'eight' for осмь, gen. pl. вострыхъ 'of sharp' for острыхъ).

353. For final hard -мъ and -тъ in the instr. sg. and the 3rd pres. respectively many examples will be found, as they are accepted by the orthography of the time. They also represent modern practice (e.g. ibid.: умышлениемъ 'deliberately' for умышлениемь, возложитъ хулу 'shall slander' for возложить хулу).

Eighteenth Century

354. General. The study of Russian phonology in the eighteenth century has to rely in the main on the existence of numerous printed books in all fields of writing. These, like the seventeenth-century publications, adhere for the most part to a set fashion of spelling, which was not substantially disturbed by the Petrine alphabetic reform. Moreover, seventeenth-century books, whether ecclesiastical or secular, marked the stressed syllables with accents if they were published by the ecclesiastical presses, and are accordingly a guide to the accentuation of the contemporary language. On the contrary, secular publications, especially after the Petrine reform of 1710, abandon this salutary custom; for we find, say, the first newspaper *Vedomosti*, which began to appear at the end of 1703, discontinuing accentuation of words in the course of 1709. Since 1710 printed books in Russian have been unaccented, except in rare cases for pedagogical purposes, and, unless they are in verse, they are entirely unhelpful for a study of changes in Russian accentuation.

355. The phonology of eighteenth-century Russian may be studied at the beginning of this period in the private correspondence and official papers of Peter the Great[1] and in the middle of it in the data pertaining to the three styles recommended by Lomonosov.

356. Peter the Great's private letters are written in a not too careful spelling with the consequence that certain aspects of his pronunciation are clearly recorded. We observe that he used the *a*-articulation (*akan'je*), as his father Tsar Alexis appears to have done (e.g. *K carice Natalii Kirillovne*, 14. viii. 1693: гасударынѣ 'to my lady' for государынѣ; *eidem*, 1693: instr. sg. малитвами 'by your prayers' for молитвами; *Punkty poslam*,

[1] A. F. Byčkov, i dr., *Pis'ma i bumagi imperatora Petra Velikogo*, i–x, St Petersburg–Moscow, 1887–1956.

1697: вѣдамасть 'news' for вѣдомость; *К Anis'je Kirillovne Tolstoj i Jekaterine Aleksejevne*, 29. xii. 1708: насить 'to wear' for носить).

357. Of consonantal features we may note here the indication of final unvoicing, examples of assimilation and the substitution of в for г, ш for щ, and the hardness of the sibilant in the reflexive ending -ся.

358. Peter the Great's predilection for the character ѳ helps us to assume that he pronounced his final consonants voiceless (e.g. *К carice Natalii Kirillovne*, 20. iv. 1689: чтопъ 'in order to' for чтобъ; *Punkty poslam*, 1697: gen. pl. капитаноѳъ 'of captains' for капитановъ, поручикоѳъ 'of lieutenants' for поручиковъ, маляроѳъ 'painters' for маляровъ).

359. Consonantal assimilations are frequently indicated (e.g. *К carice Natalii Kirillovne*, 1693: натсажать 'to superimpose' for надсажать, gen. pl. нискихъ 'of low (ones)' for низкихъ), and there are instances of syncope or lapse (e.g. *Žalovannaja gram. Ivanu Tesengu*, 10. ii. 1700: instr. sg. голанскимъ языкомъ 'in Dutch' for голландскимъ языкомъ).

360. Substitution of в for г in speech must have been as common as it is today, though, as now, it was masked by the orthography, but Peter the Great seems to prefer the phonetic spelling (e.g. *К F. M. Apraksinu*, 28. iv. 1707: gen. sg. ево 'his' for его).

361. His writing of ш for щ on occasion proves that he used the long palatalized Moscow ʃʃ (e.g. *К kn. A. I. Repninu*, 19. v. 1705: аше 'if' for аще).

362. Also there are indications that he pronounced -ся as -sə (e.g. *Rezoljucii na dokladnyje stat'i A. Ju. Kreveta*, 1697: найматса 'to be engaged' for на(н)иматься).

363. Not only from Peter the Great but from many other contemporary sources we may gather evidence of the 'hard' pronunciation of the short hush-sibilants and of the affricate ц (e.g. *Junosti čestnoje zercalo*, 1719: прігожство 'handsomeness' for пригожьство, чістишъ 'thou cleanest' for чистишь; *Apoffeg-mata*, 1716: Цыникус 'Cynicus' for Цiникусъ) as well as of the presence of long ʃʃ in Moscow Russian (e.g. *Apoff.*, 1716: gen. pl. неудобрѣщителных 'complex', where щ figures for ш).

364. The influence of printers' spelling throughout the eighteenth century left little latitude for individual peculiarities as the production of manuscripts had done in previous centuries. From now onwards the official orthography is no adequate guide to pronunciation, especially as it adopts certain Church Slavonic features (e.g. the masc. and neut. gen. endings -aro/ -яго), and we have to rely here chiefly on the evidence of metre, notably of rhythm and rhyme. But in contrast to books, manuscript material, which is not unplentiful in the eighteenth century, is, as we have already seen, a valuable aid in the study of Russian phonology at this time. Thus we find such slips as твая 'your' for твоя in F. Prokopovič's *Pochval'noje slovo o flote rossijskom* (1720); надеясъ 'hoping' for надеясь in *Istorija o Petre zlatych ključej* (an early 18th-cent. MS); въ Галандію 'to Holland' for въ Голландию, Санктпетербурхъ 'St Petersburg' for Санктпетербургъ, во Франциую 'to France' for во Франциию; *Povest' ob Aleksandre* (18th-cent. MS): instr. pl. з драгоценными 'with valuables' for съ драгоцѣнными, свидетелствуюсь, что 'I bear witness that' for свидѣтельствуюсь, что; *Povest' o rossijskom kupce Ioanne* (18th-cent. MS): изволишъ 'thou wishest' for изволишь, любовъ 'love' for любовь, расъ 'one' (in counting) for разъ.

365. The second half of the eighteenth century is even more dominated by the printed word, although manuscripts are available for the study of the pronunciation of individual authors. Moreover, V. K. Trediakovskij's printed works are particularly valuable because of his keen interest in problems of Russian orthography (e.g. *Razgovor ob ortografii*, 1748): thus his spellings шч and iô for traditional щ and e respectively are phonologically significant. From him also come the historically important statements, viz. (*a*) that 'ъ and ь are not letters', i.e. do not indicate sounds, but only the attributes of sounds, and (*b*) that 'ѣ and e do not represent different sounds'. Then there is the admission that words like плодъ 'fructus' and плотъ 'ratis' are undifferentiated in pronunciation. Further, in Part III of this work Trediakovskij expressly tells us that 'all unstressed o's are pronounced like a in Moscow speech'; that 'some

unstressed a's are pronounced like e in common speech, i.e. часы́
is said for часы́'; that 'stressed e mostly changes to diphthongal
iô' (e.g. зовіôтъ 'calls' for зоветъ); that 'radical and mostly
unstressed i often changes in our pronunciation to e' (e.g.
пѣвчей 'singing' for пѣвчій); that 'mostly unstressed я in our
present pronunciation changes into e' (e.g. кнѣіня 'princes' for
княгіня); that 'radical unstressed e frequently changes in vulgar
pronunciation into i' (e.g. сказываітъ 'says' for сказываетъ);
and that 'radical ы in our language often changes into о' (e.g.
которой 'which' for который). Other valuable comments of
Trediakovskij's relate to the pronunciation of final consonants
(cf. his random examples бопъ 'bean' for бобъ, Петрофъ
'Peter's' for Петровъ, вретъ 'harm' for вредъ, мушъ 'husband'
for мужь, обрасъ 'image' for образъ, рохъ 'horn' for рогъ) and
to consonantal assimilations (e.g. офца 'sheep' for овца,
пріежжій 'new arrival' for пріезжій, вошшествіе 'ascension'
for восшествіе, персіцкій 'Persian' for персідскій, шчастіе
'happiness' for счастіе, хъ кому 'to whom' for къ кому).

366. Much less valuable for later eighteenth-century Russian
phonology are the writings of M. V. Lomonosov, particularly
his *Rossijskaja grammatika* (1755) and *O pol'ze knig cerkovnych v
rossijskom jazyke* (1757), which show him to be more interested
in grammatical phenomena. Nevertheless, his first work contains useful pointers to pronunciation, for instance his mention
of the confusion of e and я in spelling, which results in such 'un-
forgivable' blunders as тену 'I pull' for тяну and яму 'to him'
for ему (cf. *Ross. gramm.*, § 116) and the difficulty of differentiating between e and ѣ in spelling (cf. *Ross. gramm.*, § 117). Furthermore, his own practice occasionally yields evidence of his own
type of pronunciation (e.g. сверьхъ 'besides' for сверхъ). Here
we may observe that his second work *O pol'ze knig cerkovnych v
rossijskom jazyke*, in which he develops his theory of the 'three
styles of discourse', is not connected merely with stylistics (see
Chap. XII), but has its grammatical and even phonological
aspect. Thus his 'Grammar' limits the use of иô (= ë) to the
'low' style and gives a list of words for which he recommends the
pronunciation of e as ë (e.g. медъ 'honey', семга 'salmon', овесъ
'oats', орелъ 'eagle', пестръ 'motley', Петръ 'Peter', Феодоръ
'Theodore', Семенъ 'Simon'). In the 'high style', however,

the Church Slavonic pronunciation was obligatory. (In this connexion it should be pointed out that A. S. Šiškov,[1] writing in the early nineteenth century, regarded the contemporary pronunciation of e before hard consonants as 'unbecoming to the nobility and purity' of literary Russian). But in the 'middle style' as in the 'low', the pronunciation of $(j)o$ for $(j)e$ was canonized only by Karamzin's introduction of the character ë towards the end of the century.

367. Lomonosov's remark that his own Maritime (*primorskij*) dialect was 'near to the Old Slavonic' suggests that he used the *o*-articulation (*okan'je*) in public speaking and reading aloud (cf. *Ross. gramm.*, § 100). But *akan'je* was recognized by the 'Academy Grammar' (1802) which formulated the rule as follows: 'the letter o, when unstressed, is pronounced in many words like the letter a in ordinary conversation, in order to soften articulation'. The 'high style' also distinguished e and ѣ phonetically in accordance with the Church Slavonic pronunciation of the two characters, the second being pronounced *ie*.[2] This incidentally is confirmed by Trediakovskij in his treatise on contemporary spelling (*Razgovor ob ortografii*), in which he regards confusion of the sounds represented by these characters as 'immeasurably faulty'. But Lomonosov and Sumarokov both confessed to being unable to distinguish them phonetically, and, as we have already seen, the two characters were phonetically synonymous as early as the eleventh century.

368. The pronunciation of r as a fricative, which is peculiar to South Russian today, was evidently unusual in Lomonosov's 'high style'. Trediakovskij, writing of this pronunciation in his treatise, says that 'all of us Russians pronounce our r like Latin *h*'. This is really not quite accurate phonetically, because the German and the Polish *h*, which he mentions in this connexion, are not identical, the first being glottal and the second velar, whereas South Russian r is a strongly fricative velar. Lomonosov in his 'Grammar' (§ 99) limits the fricative pronunciation to Church Slavonic words (e.g. господъ 'Lord', гласъ 'voice', благо 'the good') and their compounds, thus conveying the

---

[1] *Sobranije sočinenij i perevodov*, i, St Petersburg, 1818, p. 253.
[2] Cf. *Technologija* (MS. 1725), where we read: 'the letter ѣ is pronounced as *ie* . . . for ѣ it is not possible to write and pronounce e or i'.

impression that this was their original pronunciation. This is a tribute to White Russian and Ukrainian scholarship which introduced it into Muscovy. Lomonosov himself, as a North Russian, no doubt adhered to the plosive pronunciation of r. But the 'high style' pronunciation of this character survives into the early nineteenth century.[1]

Nineteenth Century

369. General. The end of the eighteenth and the beginning of the nineteenth century saw the phonetic fixation of the literary language in accordance with the norms of the Moscow pronunciation. Karamzin had recognized the existence of $(j)o$ in the 'polite' as well as the 'vulgar' pronunciation and had devised the character ë to represent it as early as 1797,[2] and Greč[3] contrasted the Church Slavonic pronunciation of единого, моего, and Петръ with the Russian единава, маево, Пётръ, which had been accepted, save for the 'high' and 'middle' styles, in the eighteenth century. Now in the nineteenth the isolation of Church Slavonic pronunciation is complete, and the Russian phonetic norms are paramount in the literary language.

370. Greč's 'Grammar' is explicit on other subtle points too, for instance the pronunciation of чн as шн, which indicates the primacy of Moscow pronunciation in the literary language. In his correspondence with Ja. K. Grot, the poet P. A. Pletnjov[4] says that Puškin and Delvig were proud of having been Muscovites, because 'a Russian not born in Moscow could not be a judge of what was a good Russian pronunciation'. Greč draws attention to the difference between speech and writing by giving a series of significant examples, viz. што 'what' for что, скушно 'tedious' for скучно, чесы 'clock' for часы, шелунъ 'mischiefmaker' for шалунъ.

371. Between the 1830's and the last decade of the nineteenth century we have the researches of such grammatical scholars as Grot[5] to guide us on the pronunciation of the time as well as the

[1] Cf. A. S. Šiškov, op. cit., iii, pp. 31–40.
[2] *Aonidy*, 2, Moscow, 1797.
[3] *Praktičeskaja russkaja grammatika*, Moscow, 1827, p. 421.
[4] *Sočinenija i perepiska*, iii, St Petersburg, 1885, p. 400.
[5] e.g. *Filologičeskije razyskanija*[4] (St Petersburg, 1899), *Russkoje pravopisanije*[22] (Petrograd, 1916).

far from negligible evidence of metre; but there were no accurate phonetic studies till the work of Šachmatov and especially
of Ščerba, whose work covers the first half of the present century.
But as the testimony of modern scholarship proves, the norms
of Russian pronunciation prevailing in the nineteenth century
remained undisturbed until the revolution of 1917.

372. Towards the end of the nineteenth century changes in
pronunciation were recorded and penalized by normative grammarians, among them F. Je. ˈKorš, who appears to have chris-
tened his students питухи, because they pronounced pretonic
e as *i*. The old-fashioned *e*-pronunciation was still recommended
in the 1930's by D. N. Ušakov,[1] and even some present-day
scholars[2] appear to be disinclined to accept the pronunciation
of pretonic e/я as pure ι, in spite of the prevalence of this pronunciation during the last two generations and more. The
normalizers incidentally are grammarians rather than phone-
ticians.

373. The type of literary pronunciation prevalent during the
second half of the nineteenth century and the early twentieth,
i.e. to about 1917, was that of the city of Moscow and is known
as the 'old Moscow norm'. Its characteristics will have been
gathered from the preceding part of this study, and it remains
for us now to summarize them. Moderate *akan'je* in the vowel
system, with a strong pretonic **a** (e.g. вода **vaˈda** 'water') and
mainly ι/ə in the weak syllables, both pretonic and posttonic, of
palatalized ('soft') and velarized ('hard') contexts respectively
(e.g. язык **jiˈzɨk** 'tongue', возле **ˈvoz̧lι/ˈvoz̧lə** 'beside', соро-
ковой **sərəkʌˈvoj** 'fortieth', город **ˈgorət** 'town`) and a con-
sonantal system with parallel hard and soft series of phonemes,
two unpaired affricates, and paired hush-sibilants, which are
distinguished by duration as well as by quality (cf. шептать
ʃəˈptat, 'to whisper' with щепать ʃʃιˈpat, 'to snap off' and
пожать pʌˈʒat, 'to press lightly' with уезжать ωjιˈʒ̧ʒ̧æt, 'to
leave'). Furthermore, the endings -ся/-сь are pronounced un-

---

[1] Cf. the Introduction to *Tolkovyj slovar' russkogo jazyka*, i, Moscow, 1935,
col. xxxii, where the *e*-sound is qualified as 'obscure'.

[2] For example R. I. Avanesov, *Russkoje literaturnoje proiznošenije*[2], Moscow, 1954,
pp. 42–44. The author transcribes the first vowel of неделя with ие instead of
with и, though he admits the frequency of *ikan'je*. This phenomenon is regarded as
'vulgar' (p. 42).

palatalized (c.g. мылся **'milsə** 'he washed', мылась **'miləs** 'she washed'), but there is generally a higher percentage of palatalization than there is in present-day Russian, which tends to follow spelling more closely and to affect the 'hard' Leningrad (St Petersburg) pronunciation of foreign loan-words.

374. Since the revolution of 1917 considerable changes have taken place in Russian educated speech because of the influence of the literary language, which encourages a bookish pronunciation, and mainly because of the influx of heterogeneous dialect-speakers into Moscow. The old Moscow norms maintain themselves 'as an ideal' on the Russian stage.[1] This pronunciation, as we have seen, is described in Ušakov's 'Dictionary';[2] but even there changes are noted which show a shift in pronunciation, for instance, the assertion of the historical spelling-value of щ as a consonantal group **ʃtʃ**, instead of the prerevolutionary long palatalized **ʃʃ**; the abandonment of the long voiced hush-sibilant **ӡӡ**, (as in вожжи **'voӡӡι** 'reins'); the further reduction of Moscow palatalization (e.g. верх **γeгх** 'top', nom. pl. лавки **'laʃķι** 'shops' for which **γεrx** and **'laʃķι** are preferred); the lapse of **γ** in a small group of words (e.g. Богъ 'God', благодарю 'thank you', Господь 'Lord'); and the already noticed Leningrad-type addiction to the 'hard' pronunciation of borrowed West European words (e.g. темп 'tempo' which tends to be pronounced **tεmp**).

375. The present-day language[3] possesses forty phonemes, of which five are vowels, viz. the 'alphabetic' types *i, e, a, o, u*. The sound *y* (ы) is a variant of *i*. Consonants are far more numerous than vowels, partly because they comprise two parallel series, one of which is 'hard' or non-palatalized, viz. *p/b, t/d, k/g, f/v, s/z, š/ž, j, x, c, m, n, l, r*. It will be noted that seven consonants here are unpaired. All the consonants enumerated have their palatalized counterparts, except *š/ž, c, j*. In addition to this set, viz. *p'/b', t'/d', k'/g', f'/v', s'/z', x', m', n', l', r'*, we also have *č* which has retained its palatalized quality since the eleventh century, unlike *c* and the hush-sibilants which have 'hardened' in course of time.

---

[1] G. Vinokur, *Russkoje sceničeskoje proiznošenije*, Moscow, 1948, p. 28.

[2] *Tolkovyj slovar' russkogo jazyka*, i, Moscow, 1935, cols. xxx–xxxiv.

[3] V. V. Vinogradov, Je. S. Istrina i S. G. Barchudarov, *Grammatika russkogo jazyka*, i, Moscow, 1953, p. 51.

II. STRESS

376. An essential element of Russian phonology is stress,[1] which, as we have gathered from previous statements, was not recorded systematically till the seventeenth century. Before that time only certain manuscripts, notably the fourteenth-century 'Čudovo New Testament' and a number of other fourteenth- and fifteenth-century monuments, which derive from Middle Bulgarian originals and disclose South Slavonic features, are stressed. Late sixteenth-century manuscripts like *Domostroj* and the version of Donatus are not consistently stressed, and many words lack the stress-mark. But manuscripts of the ensuing century such as the 'Chronograph' (*Kronograf*), begun in Moscow at the command of the Tsar in the sixteenth century, offer considerable material, and so do the publications of the ecclesiastical presses, whether ecclesiastical or secular (e.g. *Učenije i chitrost' ratnogo strojenija pechotnych ljudej,* 1647; *Grammatika slovenskaja,* 1648; *Sobornoje Uloženije,* 1649).

377. It is obviously impossible as a result of this state of things to determine the details of Old Russian pronunciation before the sixteenth century. But by using the evidence of the 'Čudovo New Testament', of the 'Chronograph', and of later recorded material, as well as the methods of comparative-historical linguistics and our knowledge of the phonetics of modern literary Russian, its dialects, and immediate cognates, and by drawing on the data of the typologically more remote Slavonic as well as the extra-Slavonic Indo-European languages, we can reconstruct the earlier prehistoric and historical accentuation. But of course these reconstructions will be at best only very plausible conjectures.

378. As we can pursue the accentuation of Russian with some confidence as far back as the fourteenth century, we are led to observe that the earlier type of Russian resembled the modern language in at least three essentials: (*a*) the dynamic quality of its stress, which makes it different from what we know of stress in Vedic Sanskrit and Ancient Greek, in modern Serbo-Croatian and Lithuanian, with their 'musical' or pitch accents; (*b*) the irregularity of stress-incidence in contrast to the protosyllabic

---

[1] Cf. A. I. Sobolevskij, *Lekcii po istorii russkogo jazyka*[4], Moscow, 1907, pp. 267–78.

stress of Czech, Slovak, and Latvian, or the penultimate stress of Polish; and (c) the mobility of stress in the paradigm as in Lithuanian (cf. R. nom. sg. рукá 'hand', acc. рýку with Lith. nom. sg. rankà, acc. rañką).

379. The absence of still earlier evidence is naturally serious, and here Old Church Slavonic provides no data, because it has no stressed manuscripts.[1] But as the loss of ь and ъ came quite early in the history of Russian, we are warranted in assuming that Russian stress in the eleventh and twelfth centuries was broadly the same as it is in the modern language.

380. Comparison of fourteenth- with twentieth-century Russian stress reveals striking similarities as well as differences. The modern instances of metatony or stress-shift such as нá пол 'on to the floor', пóд носом 'under one's nose', нé был 'he was not' find parallels in the 'Čudovo New Testament' (e.g. нá горы 'on to the hills', пó ряду 'in order', дó вечера 'till the evening', вó имя 'in the name'), where the phenomenon is less restricted than in the modern language. In both cases, however, we note that metatony takes place only when normally the first syllable of the following word is stressed. English, incidentally, also provides a set of parallels here (cf. *Čud.* нá вы with 'ón you', which is a translation of the 14th-cent. Russian). The metatonic tendency is recorded in seventeenth-century manuscripts (e.g. *Lečebnik*: зá локоть 'by the arm', lit. 'elbow', нá полы 'on to the floors'; cf. here the Middle Bulgarian 'Chludov Psalter', 15th cent.: въ земли 'in the earth', дó вѣка 'to eternity', and the Mod. B. нá глава 'on the head'). Shift of stress is also illustrated by the obsolete Russian forms днесь 'today', ночéсь 'tonight', ономé-дни 'that day', which derive from the Old Russian acc. sg. дьнь сь, ночь сь, loc. sg. онъмь дьне(-и). In all these cases we find indications of the overwhelmingly regressive metatony which we observed in our earlier examples. They also show, unexpectedly, that the final (later 'mute') syllable could be stressed. We assume on the evidence of such forms as градóсь 'this town', родóсь 'this clan', and мирóсь 'this world' in the 'Čudovo New

---

[1] The supraliteral marks in the Kiev Missal (*c.* 10th cent.) can in some cases be interpreted as stress and even pitch marks (cf. N. K. Grunskij, *Pamjatniki i voprosy drevne-slavjanskoj pis'mennosti*, i, Jur'jev, 1904, pp. 34–59); but these have so far not been adequately studied, nor have the conclusions so far reached won general acceptance.

Testament' that the final syllable of similar words, for instance, ночь 'night', звѣрь 'beast', медъ 'honey', сынъ 'son', originally carried the stress (cf. Lith. *naktìs, žvėrìs, medùs, sūnùs*) and that subsequently this was shifted to the root syllable.

381. The archaisms in stressing which we find in the modern language, for instance в печи́ 'in the oven' (cf. в пе́чи), зачаст-у́ю 'often' (cf. fem. acc. sg. ча́стую 'frequent'), удало́й 'bold' (cf. уда́лый 'id.'), спроста́ 'simply' (cf. спро́ста), высоко́ 'high' (cf. высо́ко), and many more, show a regressive metatony if we compare them with the corresponding 'unrestricted' or alternative forms. It will have been noticed that the archaic forms are mostly confined to adverbialized phrases.

382. Besides metatony involving a shift to one place back in the word there are cases of it where it jumps one syllable. These occur in the so-called 'pleophonic' forms (e.g. бе́регъ 'bank, shore', го́лодъ 'famine'). Here the original stress would appear to have been on the last syllable, viz. берегѣ, голодѣ, for Modern Bulgarian has such forms as брегѣ́т 'the shore', гладѣ́т 'the famine', and we can also compare the stress of со́лодъ 'malt' with that of Lithuanian *saldùs* 'sweet'. Another pertinent example is the modern Russian adjective вороно́й (sc. конь) 'raven (horse)', which suggests that the early stress of the word во́ронъ 'raven' was on the last, 'mute' syllable, represented by ъ (thus воронѣ). Such a supposition is proved by бо́рошно 'rye meal', which figures in the 'Čudovo New Testament' as брашьно́ and as бра́шьно (cf. also де́рево 'tree' with the *ča*- dialect form of Serbo-Croatian древо̀).

383. The predicative adjectives ду́рен 'bad', чу́ден 'wonderful', че́стен 'honest', and others like them have a variant stress on the last syllable which would seem to be archaic. This earlier stress may be compared with such forms as дурно́й, чудно́й, честно́й. Here again the metatony is regressive.

384. Case-forms like instr. sg. сы́ном 'as the son' appear, in the light of comparative-historical evidence, to represent shifted stress. Lithuanian *sūnùs*, for instance, has instr. sg. *sūnumì*. Accordingly it has been assumed that the earlier Russian form may have been stressed сынъмѣ́ (cf. instr. pl. дверьми́ 'with doors', also горючими слезьми́ 'with bitter tears 'in Russian folk-songs).

385. Archaically stressed case-forms survive in some personal names, viz. Благовó, Дурновó, Суховó, Хитровó (cf. gen. sg. благóго, дурнóго, сухóго, хи́трого < благóй 'gracious', дурнóй 'wicked', сухóй 'dried up', хи́трый 'cunning'). We find genitive singular forms like добрóго 'of the good', мудрóго 'of the wise', чистóго 'of the clean', in the work of the 'russianized' Croat Križanič, a ča-dialect speaker.

386. The evidence of the 'Čudovo New Testament' points to the end-stressing of feminine substantives in -á in the nominative-accusative plural, although this is contrary to modern usage (e.g. женьí 'women', бѣдьí 'cares', сестрьí 'sisters', рѣкьí 'rivers', слугьí 'servants', овьця́ 'sheep'). Feminines in -ь also preserve end-stress in many other case-forms (e.g. gen. sg. плоти́ 'of the flesh', ярости́ 'of fury'; dat. по плоти́ 'according to the flesh'; loc. въ кротости́ 'in humility'). Comparative adjectives were often stressed on the last syllable (e.g. fem. nom. sg. бо́льши́ 'bigger', менши́ 'less'; cf. the masc. nom. sg. forms in contemporary usage—бо́льшо́й, мснь́шо́й). The 2nd plural present indicative had end-stress (cf. живсте́ 'you live', можете́ 'you can', ядите́ 'you eat' with the corresponding modern forms живёте, мо́жете, еди́те). The infinitive too occasionally stressed its ending contrary to later usage (cf. взяти́ 'to take', кляти́ ся 'to swear', помощи́ 'to help' with Modern Russian взять, кля́сться, помо́чь), and we find the same stress in participles, present and past, definite and indefinite (cf. nom. pl. несуще́ 'carrying' and nom. sg. видящи́ 'seeing' with modern dialectal несучи́ 'carrying', идучи́ 'going').

387. Accordingly we are now warranted in stating that there have been noteworthy changes in the incidence of stress in the systems of both declension and conjugation at least since the fourteenth century, and probably also since the eleventh, as we have found it reasonable to suppose that the system of eleventh-century Russian stress was substantially the same as what we know of Russian stress in the fourteenth century.

388. We are now in a position to examine the later evidence on Russian stress, viz. that of the sixteenth and seventeenth centuries and of the early eighteenth. Our sixteenth-century material is contained in the Russian version of the Latin grammar of Donatus, in *Domostroj*, and in a manuscript dealing with the art of bookbinding (*O knižnom pereplete*),[1] and the seventeenth-century data are drawn from the pirated Moscow version (1648) of Meletij Smotryc'kyj's 'Church Slavonic Grammar' (*Grammatiki slavenskija pravilnoje sintagma*, Ev'je, 1619), Tsar Alexis's 'Legal Code' (*Uloženije*, 1649), and the news-sheets (*kuranty*) of the Moscow Ambassadorial Office (*Posol'skij prikaz*), which began to be excerpted from the contemporary foreign press of the seventeenth century.[2] As for the early eighteenth century, the first Russian newspaper *Vedomosti* presents useful material for the period between 1703 and 1709, and this may be supplemented with data from, say, L. Magnickij's *Arifmetika, sireč' nauka čislitel'naja* (Moscow, 1703) and F. G. Polikarpov-Orlov's *Leksikon trejazyčnyj* (Moscow, 1704), a 'Church-Slavonic–Greek–Latin Dictionary', as well as with the metrical data of early eighteenth-century poetry (e.g. V. K. Trediakovskij's *Telemachida*, with its numerous stress-marks, and all the syllabo-tonic verse-writing of this period, notably M. V. Lomonosov's).

389. Examination of this material may be summarized under two headings: (*a*) differential stress and (*b*) instances of metatony. The first presupposes comparison with modern Russian stress, which often shows a regressive shift in the corresponding example (cf. *Donatus menšej*, 16th cent.: степéнь 'degree' with modern стéпень, илѝ 'or' with ѝли, 2nd pl. pres. ind. любѝте 'love' with лю́бите; *Dom.*, 16th cent.: nom. pl. игры́ 'games' with и́гры, беречѝ 'to keep' with берéчь, возлé 'beside' with вóзле, nom. pl. винá 'wines' with вѝна; *O kniž. per.*, 16th cent.: протѝвъ 'opposite' with прóтив, равнó 'equal' with рáвно; *Gramm. slav.*, 1648: учѝтъ 'teaches' with у́чит, честны́й–честнóе–честнáя 'honest' with чéстный–чéстное–чéстная, fem. sg. обрáзная 'figurative' with óбразная, держѝтся 'holds' with дéржится; *Kur.*, 17th cent.: в нощѝ 'in the night' with в нóчи, neut. sg. утаéно 'concealed' with утáено; *Ulož.*, 1649: оружьé 'arms' with орýжье). The contrary is also true, and we find progressive metatony in the modern forms (cf. *Dom.*, 16th cent.: loc. pl. чáстех 'in the parts' with частя́х, óбразѣхъ 'figures'

---

[1] Contained in P. K. Simoni, *Opyt sbornika svedenij po istorii i technike knigopereplet-nogo chudožestva na Rusi* (St Petersburg, 1903).

[2] Manuscripts of translations from leaflets and newspapers in manuscript have been preserved in Russia from the fifteenth century.

with образа́х, у́ченъ 'taught' with учён; *Dom.*, 16th cent.:
gen. sg. мо́ста 'of the bridge' with моста́, сѣмена 'seeds' with
семена́; *O kniž. per.*, 16th cent.: fem. sg. е́ловая 'white deal'
with ело́вая; *Gramm. slav.*, 1648: зна́менуетъ 'signifies' with
знамену́ет, и́мать 'has' with име́ет, instr. pl. ча́стицами 'with
particles' for части́цами; *Ulož.*, 1649: во́ровски 'thievishly'
with воровски́, къ Мо́сквѣ 'to Moscow' with к Москве́,
на́чнетъ/у́чнетъ 'begins' with начнёт).

390. Instances of metatony, determined as before by the adverbialization of phrases and conditioned by the immediate juxtaposition of proclitic and stressed syllables, are fairly numerous
(e.g. *O kniž. per.*, 16th cent.: на́ гла́дко 'smoothly', на́ туго
'tightly', на́ чисто 'cleanly'; *Ulož.*, 1649: не́ было 'there was
not', до́ пряма 'straight', за́ очи 'in absence', на́ поле 'in the
open'). Contrast with these the stressing of such phrases as
отруки́ 'from the hand', нестыдя́ся 'unashamed', насебя́ 'for
oneself', found in Tsar Alexis's 'Code', where the already specified conditions do not obtain. It will be observed, moreover,
that the phrases in question are written together. This also
applies to other groupings which, although syntagmatic and
therefore, as it were, uttered 'in one breath', are not adverbialized (e.g. *Ulož.*, 1649: произмѣну 'about treachery' for про
измѣну, исполко́въ 'from the regiments' for изъ полко́въ,
придержа́вѣ 'under the rule' for при держа́вѣ, and many similar 'compounds'). The unseparated words, which are common
enough at this time, serve indirectly as an indication of the
position of the stress (e.g. *Istorija o Petre zlatych ključej*, early
18th cent.: усебя́ 'at home', where there can be no metatony,
because the normal conditions for it are not satisfied).

391. The evidence for eighteenth-century Russian stress is, as
we have seen, very diverse. The stressed texts are sufficiently
numerous to give a fairly accurate picture of it and consequently
of the difference between it and modern Russian stress. The
following have been gathered from Magnickij and Polikarpov-
Orlov respectively (cf. *Arif.*, 1703: цвѣты́ 'flowers' with цветы́,
предложе́но 'suggested' with предло́жено, у́зриши 'thou wilt
see' with узри́шь; *Leks. trej.*, 1704: собра́ное 'collected' with
со́браное, разположе́ное 'arranged' with распо́ложеное, dat.
pl. язы́камъ 'to languages' with языка́м). The discrepancies

between the stressing of early eighteenth-century words, even though these are 'high-style' and therefore Church Slavonic in the main rather than Russian, and the corresponding words in present-day Russian, have become fewer since the seventeenth century, and we are approaching a period—the latter part of the eighteenth century—when they will have become almost negligible.

392. We have drawn attention to differences between Church Slavonic and Russian stressing in the early eighteenth century, and it is necessary to bear this in mind as a stylistic discrimination which also points to a difference between two historical periods, viz. the early and the modern; for the Church Slavonic pronunciation is undoubtedly archaic. The comparisons we have made so far have shown what the differences between the old and the new consist in. Admiral A. S. Šiškov[1] penalized as 'vulgar' the pronunciation, say, хитио́ръ 'cunning' as against Church Slavonic хитеръ, but these are not distinguished by the position of the stress. On the other hand, Sumarokov[2] attacked Lomonosov for following Russian provincial usage in his verse, as disclosed by the latter's rhythms (e.g. nom. pl. лета́ 'years' for ле́та, gen. pl. градо́въ 'of towns' for гра́довъ), and Trediakovskij in his turn points out deficiencies in Sumarokov's stressing (e.g. врѣднѣйший 'most injurious' for врѣдне́йший, разру́шилъ 'he destroyed' for разруши́лъ, кро́мѣ 'besides' for кромѣ́). At the beginning of the nineteenth century A. A. Prokopovič-Antonskij[3] drew up a list of words differentiating stress in Church Slavonic ('high style') and Russian ('colloquial style'). Some of these are reproduced here, viz.

Church Slavonic		*Russian*
высо́ко (adv.)	'high'	высоко́
да́ры	'gift"	дары́
жесто́къ	'harsh'	жесто́къ
защи́тить	'to defend'	защити́ть
крамола́	'feud'	крамо́ла
преда́нный	'devoted'	пре́данный
принесе́но	'brought'	принесено́

---

[1] *Sobranije sočinenij i perevodov*, iii, St Petersburg, 1818, pp. 31–40.
[2] *Sočinenija*, x, St Petersburg, p. 7.
[3] Cf. *Trudy Obščestva ljubitelej rossijskoj slovesnosti*, iv, Moscow, 1812, pp. 71–77.

Church Slavonic		Russian
сумрáкъ	'darkness'	сýмракъ
терпи́т'ь	'he suffers'	тéрпитъ
ц'ѣна	'price'	цѣнá

393. The verse of the early nineteenth century is in some respects a guide to the contemporary stressing of Russian words. The availability of Church Slavonic variants considerably eased the task of the poet in both rhyme and rhythm: thus Puškin in *Vospominanija o Carskom Sele* (1814) rhymes нóщи (cf. R. нóчи) with рóщи, and Krylov in *Dub i trost'* (1816) writes бушýетъ вѣтръ (cf. R. вéтеръ), удвóилъ си́лы онъ 'the wind rages, redoubles its force'.

394. The development of linguistic study in the nineteenth century led to the accumulation of a considerable body of material on Russian stress. V. I. Dal's *Tolkovyj slovar' živogo velikorusskogo jazyka*, i–iv (Moscow, 1863–6) and the researches of Grot (cf. *Filologičeskije razyskanija*[3], St Petersburg, 1885), for instance, provide the investigator with valuable, though not exhaustive, data. Furthermore, we have the evidence of metre, as before, and towards the end of the century the first phonetic transcriptions with indications of stress.

395. As in previous centuries, there have been hesitations in stressing, and two variants in some words have been admitted (e.g. глубóкó 'deep'). This is paralleled in the present state of 'standard' (literary) English. The guidance of metre may, indeed, be sought; but poetic licence in verse-writing has a tradition in Russia as it has in England, so that the evidence of metre must be collated with the data furnished by lexicographers and grammarians. Late nineteenth-century Russian stressing is inevitably little different from that of the modern language, especially as the speech of the aristocracy and *bourgeoisie* was being gradually modified by that of the many *raznočincy* like V. G. Belinskij and others in the 1840's.

396. For the study of contemporary Russian stress we were able till very recently to use only the material provided by the two large Soviet dictionaries of Ušakov and Ožegov,[1] neither of which adheres to the phonetic principle. Moreover, there was

---

[1] *Slovar' russkogo jazyka*[2], Moscow, 1952.

no counterpart in Russian to Daniel Jones's *English Pronouncing Dictionary*, which had appeared as long ago as 1917. But in 1955 the promised and long-awaited 'orthoepic' or normative Russian dictionary finally came out as an explicitly tentative compilation of R. I. Avanesov and S. I. Ožegov, a phonetician and a lexicographer. *Russkoje literaturnoje udarenije i proiznošenije*, unlike Jones's work, lays emphasis on stress rather than on the phonetic features of the units which it organizes. From our immediate point of view such emphasis is welcome, but for the exhaustive study of Russian pronunciation a full phonetic transcription of each item in the dictionary would obviously seem preferable to the partial indications to which the two authors have limited themselves.

397. Variation in the incidence of stress in modern literary Russian goes back in part to the destruction of the old social order which followed the revolution of 1917 and exposed the language to influences from 'below'. The main factors here were 'vulgarisms' (*prostorečije*), slang, and dialect, whose intersection and interaction have produced an involute design of stress-usage, to which hesitations in the pronunciation of foreign loanwords have added their own complications. Thus 'vulgar' pronunciation has contributed such forms as красивée 'more beautiful', for красивее, звóнишь 'thou ringest' for звонишь, вы правы́ 'you are right' for вы пра́вы, библиотéка 'library' for библиотéка; slang offers дóбыча 'gain' for добы́ча, кварта́л 'quarter' for кварта́л, рóман 'novel' for рома́н, доцéнт 'university reader' for доцéнт, клима́т 'climate' for кли́мат, мóлодежь 'youth' for молодёжь; and dialect is responsible for such stressing as that of полóжил 'he put down' for положи́л and облéгчить 'to relieve' for облегчи́ть.

398. As the bias of the literary language is to avoid variation in stressing one and the same word so far as this is possible, it naturally regards one of the two modes of stressing such words as 'acceptable' and the other as 'unacceptable'. The latter, accordingly, tends to be eliminated, unless it lends itself to semantic differentiation. For instance, the till recently 'vulgar' pronunciation of кварта́л as ква́ртал is acquiring the meaning 'quarter of the year' in the literary language. Further example of semantic differentiation are offered by such alternativel stressed words as широкӣ 'wide', мáлó 'little', высóкó 'high', мóлодéц 'fine fellow', нáчáтый 'begun', fem. sg. великá 'great'. The first three of these are differentiated grammatically, the next two stylistically, and the last purely semantically. As adverbs широко and высоко show final and мало penultimate stress; as predicative adjectives they take either stress (cf. это мáлó 'this is little' with он мáло говорит 'he talks little'). In other instances we find stylistic variants (cf. the 'neutral' молодéц 'fine fellow' with the poetic мóлодец, or the modern нáчатый with the archaic начáтый) and semantic differentiation (cf. великá 'great' with великá 'big'). In other instances still both modes of stressing are neutral and recognized (e.g. возбýдишь 'thou wilt arouse', собрáлся 'he intended', pl. нýжны́ 'needed', твóрóг 'curds', инáче 'otherwise', óбýх 'butt'). An instance of triple stressing is seen in кóрóткó 'short'. And metatony is illustrated by one of the stresses in нá гóд 'for a year' and нá стéнý 'on to the wall', where both metatonic forms have become adverbialized.

399. Variation of stress in the paradigm in contemporary Russian is one of the real difficulties of the language, because it functions as a grammatical device and penetrates into all the major parts of speech and their diverse forms (e.g. neut. nom. sg. пóле 'field', nom. pl. поля́, masc. nom. pl. лéбеди 'swans', gen. pl. лебедéй, fem. nom. sg. рукá 'hand', acc. sg. рýку; 1st sg. pres. ind. люблю́ 'I love', 2nd sg. лю́бишь; 3rd sg. past ind. neut. брáло 'took', fem. бралá; past part. pass. masc. прóдан 'sold', fem. проданá).

400. The greatest difficulty, however, in Russian stressing for natives as well as for foreigners resides in the disparity between grammatical form and stress. Thus we find such formally identical verbs as печь 'to bake' and сечь 'to beat', which nevertheless are different in the stressing of their past tense (cf. пёк–пеклó–пеклá with сек–сéкло–сéкла). The interaction of the two has led to the emergence of 'incorrectly' stressed forms (e.g. она пересеклá улицу 'she crossed the road'), and such forms tend to be numerous and on the increase.

IX

MORPHOLOGICAL CHANGES

401. General. In studying morphological change it will be more convenient to discuss phenomena of declension and conjugation under the appropriate rubrics in historical perspective. This will entail examination of changes in the nominal categories under the headings of declensional types, case, number, gender, comparison, numerals, and pronouns, and the changes in the verb under the headings of tense, aspect, mood, voice, person, participles in transition to gerunds and the invariable infinitive and supine. As the adverbs and particles are formally connected with both noun and verb they will be treated in a separate paragraph, preceding the concluding section on word-formation.

I. NOMINALIA

402. As early as the eleventh century we have observed, for instance in the 'Svjatoslav Miscellany' (1073), 'irregular' forms like gen. pl. грѣховъ 'of sins' for грѣхъ and dat. sg. тѣлу 'to the body' for тѣлеси. This intersection and mutual influence of the *o*-stems and *u*-stems on the one hand and of the *o*-stems and consonantal stems on the other are a vivid reminder of the confusion and progressive levelling of declensional types which must have been active before the recorded period. Other instances of interaction will also be found, and we shall study them all in the order in which we have already dealt with the paradigms to which they belong in Part I.

403. Declensional types. The interaction of the *o*- and *jo*-stems is limited to the locative singular and plural. Here the *jo*-stem forms -и, -ихъ were replaced by the corresponding *o*-stem forms -ѣ, -ѣхъ (Mod. R. -e, -ях). The earliest instances occur at the end of the eleventh century (e.g. loc. sg. *Nov. min.*, 1095: въ человѣчѣ образѣ 'in the image of men' for въ человѣчи образѣ; *Nov. korm.*, *c.* 1282: в Ярославлѣ 'in Jaroslavl'' for въ Ярославли; *Lavr.*, 1377: въ огнѣ 'in the fire' for въ огни; loc. pl. въ манастырѣхъ 'in monasteries' for въ монастырихъ; *Pskov Apostol*, 1307: при князѣхъ 'under princes' for при князихъ`

The preponderance of o-stem types is noteworthy in the sixteenth century. The ending -и in the loc. sg. survives in some forms of South Russian today, but the corresponding plural forms would appear to be obsolete.

404. The contrary influence of soft on hard stems in this declensional group may be seen sporadically from the thirteenth century in the nom. pl. (*Nov. prol.*, 1262: приятѣ быша 'were received' for прияти; *Nov. jev.*, *c.* 1362: народѣ угнѣтають тя 'the peoples oppress you' for народи). The latter feature seems to be confined to the Novgorod dialect and is common there even in some fifteenth-century manuscripts (e.g. *Apostol*, 1495).

405. Confusion of the masculine o-stems with the u-stems is recorded as early as the late eleventh century. The cases affected are the gen., dat., and loc. sg. and the nom. and gen. pl. The first three are illustrated by the following examples, viz. gen. sg.—*Svjat.*, 1073: отъ льну 'of flax' for отъ льна; *Nov. korm.*, *c.* 1282: солоду 'of malt' for солода; *Lavr.*, 1377: роду 'of the clan' for рода; *Kol. pal.*, 1406: съ холму 'from the mound' for съ холма; dat. sg.—*Mst.*, *c.* 1130: Георгиеви 'to St George' for Георгию; *1 Nov. let.*, 13–14th c.: отцеви 'to (his) father' for отьцу; loc. sg—*Nov. korm.*, *c.* 1282: на търгу 'in the market-place' for на тързѣ;[1] *Pskov. paraklitik*, 1369: при князи при Борису 'under Prince Boris' for при Борисѣ. And throughout the period between the fifteenth and the seventeenth centuries such u-declension forms are not uncommon in the gen. and loc. cases of the singular (e.g. *Mos. gramoty*, 16th–17th cent., въ Смоленску 'in Smolensk' for въ Смоленскѣ).

406. The gen. sg. of the u-stem declension has provided Russian masculine substantives denoting materials with a variant in -y which in course of time has acquired a partitive meaning (e.g. *Dom.*, 16th cent.: борщу 'of borshch', солоду 'of malt'; cf. Mod. R. чаю, сахару 'some tea, sugar').

407. The ending -y in the loc. sg. is very common in the sixteenth and seventeenth centuries, but has now been reduced to a relatively restricted number of forms (e.g. *PDSK*[2], 1516: на

---

[1] Note, however, the corresponding Lith. form *turgùs* which belongs to the u-declension in that language.

[2] G. F. Karpov, *Pamjatniki diplomatičeskich snošenij s Krymskoju i Nagajskoju ordami i s Turcijeju*, St Petersburg, 1884–95 (abbrev. PDSK above).

другомъ молоду 'at the next new moon' for на другомъ молодѣ; *Dom.*, 16th cent.: въ миру 'in the world'; cf. Mod. R. в саду 'in the garden', на мосту 'on the bridge', в этом году 'this year').

408. The nom. pl. in -еве/-ове is found from the fourteenth to the sixteenth century, but tends to disappear later (e.g. *Nov. gram.*, *c.* 1300: пословѣ 'ambassadors' for посъли; *Lavr.*, 1377: воробьеве 'sparrows' for воробьи; *PDSK*, 1474: фрязове 'Franks' for фрязи).

409. Gen. pl. forms of the *u*-stem declension in -евъ/овъ are found from the late eleventh century (e.g. *Svjat.*, 1073: грѣховъ 'of sins' for грѣхъ; *Svjat.*, 1076: вождевъ 'of leaders' for вождь; *Žitije Jepifanija Kiprskogo*, 12th cent.: бѣсовъ 'of devils' for бѣсъ; *Pand. Nik. Čern.*, 1296: трудовъ 'of labours' for трудъ; *Kal.*, 1327–8: поясовъ 'of girdles' for поясъ). By the sixteenth century the masculine *u*-stem forms had prevailed, as they help to differentiate the original gen. pl. from the original nom. sg.; but in the corresponding neuter plural the *o*-stem forms remained undisturbed, because there was a clear-cut formal difference between the nom.–acc. sg. and the gen. pl. (cf. nom.–acc. sg. село 'village' with gen. pl. селъ).

410. In the paradigm of the *a*- and *ja*-stems the interaction of the hard and the soft declensional types has resulted in the latter adopting the endings of the former in the gen., dat., and loc. cases of the singular, in the nom. and acc. of the dual, and in the nom. and acc. of the plural. Here follow some examples with -и as the soft correlate of -ы, from manuscripts dated from the eleventh to the thirteenth century (e.g. gen. sg.—*Nov. min.*, 1095: изъ отроковичи[1] 'of the maiden' for изъ отроковицѣ; *Mil. jev.*, 1215: милостыни 'of grace' for милостынѣ; *Rjaz. korm.*, 1284: княгини 'of the princess' for кънягынѣ; dat. sg.— *Nov. min.*, 1095: госпожѣ 'to the lady' for госпожи; loc. sg.—*Pant. jev.*, 12th cent.: в тьмьницѣ 'in the cell' for в тьмьници). By the sixteenth century the hard type of ending would appear to have become predominant in these case-forms.

411. The nom.–acc. dual of *ja*-stems is rarely replaced by the corresponding *a*-stem form up to the fourteenth century (e.g. *Pant. jev.*, 12th cent.: дъвѣ пътицѣ 'two birds' for дъвѣ пътици;

---

[1] Also an illustration of *cokan'je*.

Pogodinskij prolog, 14th cent.: дъвѣ свѣщѣ 'two candles' for
дъвѣ свѣщи; cf. OR свѣчи). These dual forms disappeared with
loss of the dual number.

412. The opposite influence of the *ja*-stems on the *a*-stems also
occurs in the eleventh century. It affects the gen. sg. and the
nom.–acc. pl. and results in the replacement of hard -ы by soft
-ѣ (e.g. gen. sg.—*Nov. min.*, 1096: съ высотѣ 'from on high' for
съ высоты; *Nov. korm.*, *c*. 1282: полъ гривне 'half a mark' for
гривьны; *Izmaragd*, 14th cent.: нищетѣ ради 'for poverty's
sake' for нищеты ради; *Ipat.*, *c*. 1425: до Москвѣ 'as far as
Moscow' for до Москвы; nom.–acc. pl.—*Nov. gram.*, 1314:
Андрѣевѣ дѣти 'Andrej's children' for Андрѣювы дѣти). The
reverse tendency survives in a petrified proverbial expression,
viz. у голодной куме (for кумы) всё хлеб на уме 'hunger is the
best cook'.

413. The considerable influence of the *a/ja*-stems on all the
other stems has turned the plural paradigm into almost a uniform type, with the *a/ja*-stems accounting for half of it, viz. the
dat., instr., and loc. cases. Their influence made itself felt in the
thirteenth century (e.g. dat. pl.—*Rjaz. korm.*, 1284: къ лати-
намъ 'to the Latins' for къ латиномъ; instr. pl.—*Nov. parimej-
nik*, 1271: съ клобуками 'with hats' for съ клобукы; loc. pl.—
Mos. jev., 1339: на сборищахъ 'in assemblies' for на сбори-
щихъ). But the process is still incomplete owing to the
resistance of end-stressed *i*-stems (e.g. instr. pl. лошадьми 'with
horses').

414. The interaction of substantival declensions has, among
much else, led to the elimination of the velar-sibilant correlations. The alternation of к/ч, г/ж, and х/ш lapsed with the disuse
of the vocative case, which began to be gradually replaced by
the nominative from the eleventh century (e.g. the first instances
occur in *Ost.*, 1056–7) and finally petered out during the eighteenth. The к/ц, г/з, and х/с correlations also began to disintegrate at that time as the result of a different influence, viz.
paradigmatic pressure (e.g. dat. sg.—*Nov. min.*, 1095–7: Дъмькѣ
'to Dŭmka' for Дъмъцѣ; loc. sg.—*Lěstvica*, 12th cent.: дъскѣ
'on the board' for дъсцѣ). The commonest early examples here
are short adjectives rather than substantives. The correlations

survive, however, into the sixteenth and seventeenth centuries (e.g. *Ulož.*, 1649: во дьяцѣхъ 'among clerks').

415. The forms of the binary declension of the short or indefinite adjective, which occur now and then in eleventh- and twelfth-century manuscripts (e.g. *Ost.*, 1056–7: dat. pl. крьстияньскамъ 'to Christian'; *Nov. min.*, 1096: acc. pl. на мънога лѣта 'for many years'; *Mst., c.* 1130: acc. sg. блюдо серебрьно 'silver dish'), are rarely met with later in the oblique case-forms and we are therefore warranted in assuming that they soon became obsolete. The 'Novgorod Birch-bark Writ No. 9' already uses the long or definite form at the turn of the eleventh century (e.g. водя новую жену 'marrying a new wife'), and since then the use of the long forms of the adjective has been encroaching on the short forms in attributive function. These have survived to this day only in predicative usage, in which, moreover, the long forms compete with them in some syntagmata (e.g. Mod. R. он болен/больной 'he is ill'). Between medieval times and the eighteenth century the short form appears to have existed in folk-songs. These, however, were set down for the first time only in the early seventeenth century[1] and accordingly use the short adjectives as little more than clichés (e.g. бѣлъ–горючъ–камень 'white burning stone', ворота тесовы 'deal gates'); and this use survives today in set phrases (e.g. от мала до велика 'great and small'). The use of the short adjectives in the eighteenth and nineteenth centuries arose out of this influence and became a form of poetic licence (e.g. Lomonosov, *Večerneje razmyšlenije o božiem veličestve*, 1743: какъ мала искра въ вѣчномъ льдѣ 'like a small spark in eternal ice'; Puškin, *Car' Saltan*, 1831: на добра коня садясь 'mounting his good horse').

416. Somewhat exceptional among these adjectives are the possessives which we find in the twelfth century (e.g. *Mstislavovo jev.*, 1117: Яковль 'James's'; *Mst., c.* 1130: Володимирь сынъ 'Volodimir's son') and in much later centuries (e.g. *Ulož.*, 1649: masc. патриаршь 'patriarchal', neut. епископле 'episcopal'), and survive to this day in such expressions as сестрин муж 'sister's husband', Ноев ковчег 'Noah's ark' and in such proper

---

[1] e.g. the 'historical songs' found among the papers of R. James. Those items appear to have been written down for him in 1619–20. Cf. P. K. Simoni, *Pesni zapisannyje dlja Ričarda Džemsa*, St Petersburg, 1907.

names as Ярославль 'Jaroslavl'', i.e. Jaroslav's (city). These adjectives are now of limited use and their paradigms of declension incomplete.

417. Confusion of the binary *o*-stems (in the *jo*-form) and the unitary *i*-stems is attested by the earlier Russian monuments. It is the *jo*-stems which have modified the masculine *i*-stems (e.g. *Rjaz. korm.*, 1284: отъ путя 'from the road' for отъ пути); in the gen. pl., however, *i*-forms have become exclusive in the binary declension (e.g. ibid., мужий 'of men' for мужь; *Lavr.*, 1377: князий 'of princes' for князь; *Ipat., c.* 1425: мѣсяций 'of months' for мѣсяць).

418. The masculine *i*-declension was bolstered up for some time by intersection with the masculine *n*-stems. In the fourteenth and fifteenth centuries we find the consonantal stems камень (acc. for nom. form) 'stone' and дьнь 'day' with gen. and loc. forms in -и instead of -e. But here probably the added influence of the dat. ending -и must also be taken into account (e.g. *Gram.*, 1482: отъ камени 'of stone' for отъ камене; *PDSK*, 1516: день отъ дни 'day by day' for день отъ дьне). The gen.–loc. forms камени and дни survive into the eighteenth and even the nineteenth century (e.g. *Vedomosti*, 1706: изъ камени 'of stone', Lermontov, *Strannyj čelovek*, 1831: къ вечеру того же дни 'towards the evening of the same day').

419. The feminine *i*-stems show confusion with the *r*-stems and *ū*-stems, so that from early times we find alternative forms in -и in the gen. and loc. sg. and in the nom. and gen. pl. of the last two declensional types. By the sixteenth century these are seen to have been adapted to the predominant *i*-type (e.g. gen.–loc. sg. матери < мать 'mother', церкви < церковь 'church').

420. The binary composite declension of adjectives, both positive and comparative, and of participles shows a parallelism in contracted and uncontracted forms in the ecclesiastical monuments of the eleventh century (cf. *Svjat.*, 1076: gen. sg. грѣшьнааго 'of the sinful'; *Nov. min.*, 1097: instr. pl. вѣрныими 'with the faithful', противьныими 'by the hostile' with *Nov. min.*, 1096: gen. sg. грѣшьнаго; *Svjat.*, 1073: съ вьсякого 'from each'; *Var., c.* 1092: instr. pl. злыми 'by evil'). The presence of the uncontracted form is still found in the twelfth century (e.g.

Mstislavovo jev., 1117: dat. sg. благовѣрьнуому 'to the devout', новъгородьскуому 'to the Novgorodian'), but these appear to be 'reminiscences' of the Old Church Slavonic manner of writing and are therefore archaic and artificial. The purely Russian gen. sg. forms -ого/-его (e.g. *Nif.*, 1219: gen. sg. грѣшного 'of the sinful') occur side by side with the contracted Church Slavonic types (e.g. *Nov. min.*, 1095: gen. sg. убогаго, унылаго, недостоинаго 'of the poor, miserable, unworthy'), but they are at first rarer than the latter, even in secular material (e.g. *Nov. gram.*, 1262–3: gen. sg. вѣснаго 'ponderable'; *Nov. gram.*, 1264–5: тысяцькаго 'of the prefect'). But by the thirteenth century they prevail in the secular documents, and the Church Slavonic forms are confined to ecclesiastical writing, from which they find their way into the monastic chronicles (e.g. *Lavr.*, 1377: gen. sg. старѣшаго 'of the eldest', рускаго 'of the Russian', ненавидящаго 'of the hating'). The influence of the Church Slavonic gen. sg. forms -аго/-яго began to predominate, especially in ecclesiastical writing, from the fourteenth century onwards owing to the conservative practice of the South Slavonic scholars, and their use was confirmed in the eighteenth century and survived till the spelling reform of 1918, when their Russian counterparts were officially restored. Outside this reactionary influence, Old Russian usage was steadily maintained in individual manuscripts (e.g. gen. sg.—*Af. Nik.*, 16th cent.: великого 'of the great'; *Stoglav*, 16th cent.: ручного 'manual'; *Ulož.*, 1649: из московского 'from the Muscovite'; *Kot.*, *c.* 1664: Российского 'of the Russian').

421. The binary pronominal declension reveals the interaction of the hard and the soft stems in manuscripts dating from the thirteenth century (e.g. gen. pl.—*Rjaz. korm.*, 1284: всихъ 'of all' for вьсѣхъ, тихъ 'of those' for тѣхъ; *Pand. Nik. Čern.*, 1296: сѣхъ 'of these' for сихъ).

422. Case. Having considered the interaction of declensional types we can now study the vicissitudes of the cases themselves.

423. The vocative case, as we have seen, had distinctive forms only for the substantive and that only in the singular. Mostly its function was fulfilled by a form which was indistinguishable from the nominative. This naturally led at first to such sporadic substitutions as the vocatives Варламе (*Var.*, *c.* 1092) and Михаиле (*Nov. min.*, 1097) for the nominatives Варламъ and Михаилъ, as well as the use of nominative for vocative (e.g. *Nov. min.*, 1095: Захария свящєньниче 'O priest Zachariah' for Захарие; *Nov. jev.*, 1270: врачь исцѣлися самъ 'physician, heal thyself' for враче; *Lavr.*, 1377: потянѣте по князѣ, дружина 'follow the prince, men' for дружино). Such confusion is found occasionally in later times (e.g. *Dvinskaja kupčaja*, 15th cent.: купи Игнате 'Ignat bought' for Игнатъ; *Mos. gramoty*, 16th–17th cent.: Юрье 'George' for Юрий), and has survived in the language of folk-songs (e.g. Петре, Садке, воронке for Петръ, Садко, воронко 'raven horse').

424. Confusion of nominative and accusative is found in the masculine *o-*, *u-*, and *i-*stems (e.g. nom. for acc.—*Svjat.*, 1073: три друзи 'three friends' for трие; *Nif.*, 1219: князи имамъ 'we have princes' for князѣ; *Lavr.*, 1377: нача вои совокупляти 'he began to gather warriors' for воѣ).

425. Nominative forms showing the presence of sibilants were evidently still used in the sixteenth century (e.g. *Sudebnik*, 1550: послуси 'witnesses'; *Mos. gram.*, 16th cent.: недрузи 'enemies'), and these appear also as accusative forms. But the accusatives have finally prevailed over the nominatives in the masculine *o-* and *i-*stem declensions, for today we have only волки 'wolves', пути 'ways' for Old Russian nom. pl. вълци, путие and acc. pl. вълкы, пути.

426. Nominative for accusative in feminine *a-*stems is found in a special construction with the infinitive to which the substantive stands in the relation of object (e.g. *Mil. jev.*, 1215: жена пустити 'to divorce a wife' for жену; *Nov. gram.*, 1270: та грамота дати назадъ 'that writ to be returned' for ту грамоту; *Dom.*, 16th cent.: солома переняти грязная 'to change dirty straw' for солому... грязную; *Ulož.*, 1649: земля отдати 'to give back the land' for землю). This construction survives in the North Russian dialect today (e.g. надо корова купить 'it is necessary to buy a cow') and is regular in West Finnic (e.g. Est. *lehm tarvis osta*).

427. Russian, like other Slavonic languages, generally uses genitive for accusative in the direct object of negative verbs and occasionally in the direct object, whether animate or inanimate, of verbs which are not negative (e.g. *Ost.*, 1056–7: чьтж отьца своего 'I honour my father', живота вѣчьнааго имате 'ye have everlasting life'; *Zlatostruj*, 12th cent.: въсташа языкъ на языка 'nation rose against nation'; *Nov. gram.*, 1195: потвердихомъ мира старого 'we confirmed the former treaty'). The practice of using this case as that of an animate or inanimate substantival object may perhaps be connected with the example of the personal and interrogative pronouns, which had identical forms in the accusative and genitive (e.g. мене '(of) me', кого '(of) whom', васъ '(of) you'). As a result of this identity of case-form in singular and plural, we also find the genitive used for the accusative in the dual (e.g. *Putjatina mineja*, 11th cent.: ваю хвалимъ 'we praise you both' for ва; *Lavr.*, 1377: наю пустити 'to let us both go' for вѣ; *Tolstovskij sbornik*, 13th cent.: Господь крьсти обою 'the Lord baptized both' for оба). The oldest example of the use of genitive for accusative with a verb without negation goes back to the fourteenth century (e.g. *Kal.*, 1327–8: acc. pl.—сокольниковъ 'falconers' for сокольникы; *Čud.*, 14th cent.: на всѣхъ ихъ 'on all of them' for на вьси ѣ). Since then the practice spread rapidly, especially where substantives were qualified by adjectives. Presentɩ usage normally invests with the genitive-type accusative form a direct object whenever the verb is negative,[1] an animate masculine substantive in the singular when the verb is not negative, and both masculine and feminine animate substantives in the plural with non-negative verbs (e.g. я не заметил собаки 'I did not notice the dog', конюх оседлал коня 'the groom saddled the horse', мы встречали и мужчин и женщин 'we would meet both men and women').

428. Confusion of genitive with dative–locative forms occurs in the singular of feminine substantives in early Novgorod manuscripts (e.g. *Nov. stich.*, 1157: в руцѣ своего сына и владыцѣ 'in the hands of his son and bishop' for владыкы; *Ipat.*, c. 1425: нашему старѣйшины 'to our elder' for старѣйшинѣ). The same feature may be found in the long or definite adjective (e.g. *Nov. gram.*, 13th cent.: в иное земли 'in another land' for инои).

---

[1] But see Zinaida Uglitsky, 'Accusative and Genitive with Transitive Verbs preceded by Negative in Contemporary Russian' (*SEER*, xxxiv. 83, pp. 377–87).

429. Dative and instrumental case are found intermixed occasionally in the plural paradigm in the fourteenth and fifteenth centuries (e.g. *Nov. službenik*, 1400: даруи Боже молящимися 'give, O God, to those that pray' for молящимся; *Ipat., c.* 1425: како будеть объими нами годно 'as it will befit us both' for объимъ намъ).

430. The interaction of dative and locative in certain case-forms, which have alternate velar and sibilant, is found as early as the eleventh century (e.g. *Svjat.*, 1076: въ добротѣ женьскѣи 'in a woman's goodness' for женьстѣ (< женьсцѣ); *Žitije Feodosija Pečerskogo*, 12th cent.: въ селѣ манастырьскѣ 'in the monastic settlement' for монастырьстѣ (< монастырьсцѣ)). As we have already seen, in another connexion (§ 414), the velars gradually extended their domain and ousted the older sibilants in the interests of paradigmatic uniformity.

431. Confusion of instrumental and locative is met with in the singular of masculine and neuter substantives in some of the older manuscripts (e.g. *Lěstvicu*, 12th cent.: о вседьневнымь крещении 'of daily baptism' for вьседьневномь; *Nov. jev., c.* 1362: о глаголѣ глаголанымь 'of the spoken word' for глаголаномь).

432. Number. The three numbers of Old Russian were gradually reduced to two by the loss of the dual, which was originally used with дъва/дъвѣ 'two' and оба/объ 'both', with naturally paired objects (e.g. руцѣ 'both hands'), and with enumerated couplings (e.g. коня 'two horses'). This usage lasted to the end of the fourteenth century (e.g. *Nif.*, 1219: изуваше сапога своя 'they took off their boots'; *Nov. korm., c.* 1282: за мѣхъ двѣ ногатѣ 'two pence for the fur'; *Lavr.*, 1377: къ тѣма мученикома 'to those [two] martyrs', лось рогома болъ 'the elk butted with its horns').

433. Confusion of the dual with the singular and the plural begins in the thirteenth century (e.g. *Nif.*, 1219: помози рабомъ своимъ Ивану и Олексию 'help thy servants Ivan and Aleksij' for рабома своима; *1 Nov. let.*, 13–14th c.: перенесена быста Бориса и Глѣба 'Boris and Gleb were translated' for Борисъ и Глѣбъ). The many examples of the substitution of dual for singular number, as in our specimen from the

'Novgorod Chronicles' referred to above, are obviously mecha-
nical slips and not due to grammatical changes in the language,
but the substitution of plural for dual seems to be in accordance
with normal linguistic development (e.g. the specimen from
Nif. above, also *Duch. kn. Dmitrija Donskogo*, 14th cent.: мои
два жеребья 'my two colts' for моя; *Čud.*, 14th cent.: быста
друзи 'they were friends' for друга). Gradually the dual form,
except in the nominative and accusative, was replaced by the
plural. As the masculine and feminine nom.–acc. dual forms in
-a and in -и respectively coincided in general with the gen. sg.
forms, these served as models for the formation of new 'duals',
which came to be interpreted later as singular oblique forms
(e.g. *Kal., c.* 1327–8: двѣ чары 'two cups' for чарѣ; *Ipat., c.* 1425:
двѣ жены 'two women' for женѣ). The neuter dual forms
adapted themselves to the masculine types, because of the close
formal links between these two genders, and the new neuter
ending became -a instead of -ѣ (e.g. *Duch. Klim.*, 13th cent.:
даю два села 'I bequeath two villages' for дъвѣ селѣ; *1 Nov. let.*
13–14th c.: два лѣта 'two years' for дъвѣ лѣтѣ).

434. The predominance of the notion of plurality, which ultimately ousted that of the dual, except in combinations of substantives with дъва/дъвѣ and оба/обѣ, appears to have been
influenced by the formal expression of the notion of collectivity,
as in the feminine substantives in -a (e.g. *1 Nov. let.*, 13–14th c.:
свея 'Swedes'; *Lavr.*, 1377: латина 'Latins', зимигола 'Zem-
galians', литъва 'Lithuanians' and others of similar meaning).
Such substantives are found early with the associated verb in the
plural (e.g. *Ost.*, 1056–7: народъ глаголаху 'the people spoke';
Skaz. B. G., 12th cent.: приобрѣтоша братия 'the brethren
acquired'; *Lavr.*, 1377: дружина рекоша 'the retinue said',
приѣхаша ростовьская земля 'the people of the land of Rostov
arrived'; *Čud.*, 14th cent.: сущии со мною вси братья 'all the
brethren with me'). In due course the -a/-я collectives, conceived now as plurals, added a new group to the masculine
plural substantives (e.g. братья 'brothers', князья 'princes').
These were increased by two other groups of substantives, i.e.
the remnants of the dual in -a (e.g. берега 'banks', бока 'sides',
края 'edges, countries', рога 'horns') and neuter collectives in
-ие, which in some instances adopted the ending -ья (e.g. *Lavr.*,

1377: столпья, колья 'palings'; *Nov. par.*, 1378: каменья 'stones'). Furthermore, between the fourteenth and seventeenth centuries we encounter the now obsolete 'collectivized' forms дворяня 'gentry' for дворяне and бояря 'boyars' for бояре.

435. Gender. Confusion in gender penetrated chiefly into the domains of adjective, participle, and pronoun. It led eventually to the levelling of the plural forms of the nominative and accusative cases (e.g. *Nif.*, 1219: хвалы всякоя чистоты исполнені 'praises full of all manner of purity' for испълнены; *Rjaz. korm.*, 1284: книгы трои 'three books' for троѣ; *Mos. jev.*, 1358: дѣла зли суть 'they are evil works' for зъла). By the seventeenth century the plural forms had become uniform, although the old orthography of the eighteenth century, which survived till 1918, artificially discriminated between masculine plurals in -е and feminine and neuter plurals in -я in adjective, participle, and pronoun (e.g. добрые–добрыя 'good'). Today there is only one written form here (e.g. добрые, знающие 'knowledgeable', все 'all').

436. Moreover, all substantives without a singular number, the so-called *pluralia tantum*, are on that account to be regarded as genderless (e.g. щи 'sour-cabbage soup', кудри 'curls').

437. Comparison. Of the two kinds of comparative adjectives in Old Russian, the short or indefinite gradually lost its declinability and entered the category of the adverb (e.g. *Zlatostruj*, 12th cent.: не юси богатѣе Давида 'thou art not richer than David'). In doing so they generally adopted the neuter nom.–acc. forms -ѣе (e.g. добрѣе 'kinder'), -е (e.g. выше 'higher'), and -ше (e.g. старше 'older'). In the seventeenth century we also come across the form -яе/-яй in the Moscow area (e.g. B. Morozov, *Pis'mo*, 1660: чтоб поскоряе отказали 'that they might refuse the sooner'). This is the immediate source of the widespread eighteenth-century usage (e.g. Sumarokov, *Pritči*, 1765: такъ стала кошка посмирняе 'so, the cat became better behaved'), which did not entirely receive Lomonosov's approval in his 'Grammar'. Today these forms are obsolete.

438. The endings of the long or definite adjective -ѣйший/-айший lost their original comparative value and acquired a superlative sense, although in the nineteenth century we still sometimes find them treated as comparatives (e.g. Žukovskij, *Odisseja*, 1842–9: впятеро тяжелѣйший 'five times heavier'; Dostojevskij, *Zapiski iz mjortvogo doma*, 1861–2: въ еще сильнѣйшемъ испугѣ 'in even greater fright').

439. Numerals. The Old Russian numerals have undergone considerable change of form, and their system of declension has been impoverished. The cardinal numeral одинъ 'one', declined in all genders and numbers, has, like the ordinals, adjectives, and participles, lost its dual and levelled its genders in the plural. Дъва/дъвѣ developed a gen.–loc. form дъву for дъвою (e.g. *Nov. korm., c.* 1282: на дву коню 'on two horses'), and the alternative forms are now used, along with a third, viz. двухъ, in word-formation (e.g. двоюродный 'in the relationship of a cousin', двусмысленный 'ambiguous', двухэтажный 'two-storied'). The influence of the concept of plurality led to the change of the declension of дъва/дъвѣ into a plural system (e.g. gen.–loc. двухъ, dat. двумъ, instr. двумя). The declension of дъва/дъвѣ was naturally influenced by those of трие/три and четыре/четыри, both of which, like дъва/дъвѣ, had two generic forms. In their turn these higher numerals began to combine not with plural but with dual forms, which in Modern Russian, as we know, are interpreted as forms of the genitive singular (e.g. Mod. R. два, три, четыре часа 'two, three, four o'clock', literally 'of the hour').

440. In Old Russian numerals of the second decade (11–19) and the higher decades (20–90), only the first part of the syntagma was declined (e.g. дъва на десяте 'twelve', пять десятъ 'fifty'): thus in the 'Svjatoslav Miscellany' (1073) we read съта и шести десятъ и пяти отьць 'of a hundred and sixty-five monks', and in the Laurentian MS (1377): семью десятъ жерелъ 'by seventy mouths'. In due course, from the eleventh to the fourteenth century, the second element of the decade took the cardinal form десять (e.g. *Arch. jev.*, 1092: седмь десять 'seventy' for десятъ; *Rjaz. korm.* 1284: треми десять 'by thirty') until the two elements were completely fused as they are today (cf. *Čud.*, 14th cent.: тридесяти и пяти лѣтъ 'of thirty-five years' and Mod. R. тридцати пяти лет). Other changes have been the substitution of сорокъ, originally meaning a bag (cf. Scots *sark* 'shirt') to contain forty pelts, for четыре десяте, and of девяносто 'ninety', an assimilation to съто,[1] for девять десятъ. Both new forms emerge in the fourteenth century, сорокъ in *Russkaja pravda* (*c.* 1282).

441. The modern collectives двое, трое, четверо, &c., go back to a more developed system, which was declined in the singular as well as the plural as a mixed nominal–pronominal type (e.g. *Svjat.*, 1073: четворѣх 'in the fourfold'; *Nov. min.*, 1096: троего 'of a threefold').

442. Pronouns. The declension of personal pronouns shows some signs of adaptation to the nominal type. The Old Russian accusative and genitive forms of the 1st and 2nd persons singular developed new forms in the course of the fourteenth century (e.g. *Mos. gram.*, 1389: чимъ благословилъ тобя отецъ твои 'what thy father blessed thee with' for тебе; *Mos. gram.*, 1397: съ себя 'from oneself' for себе). Earlier still the spellings менѣ, тебѣ, себѣ occur as alternatives to мене, тебе, себе in the accusative and genitive (*Ost.*, 1056–7: възмѣте иго мое на себе 'take my yoke on yourselves'; *Arch. jev.*, 1092: не посѣтихомъ тебѣ 'we did not visit thee'; *Nov. min.*, 1095: ис тебѣ 'out of thee'). No doubt, this mode of spelling arises out of the eleventh-century confusion in the use of Old Church Slavonic e and ѣ in Old Russian and possibly as a result of the influence of the dative forms. The original Old Russian accusative and genitive forms are still used in South Russian (e.g. у тебе 'thou hast' for Lit. R. у тебя). The forms of the 2nd singular with root vowel o also appear in the fourteenth century (e.g. *Mos. gram.*, 1367: межь собя 'among themselves'; *Lavr.*, 1377: у тобе 'thou hast').

443. The interrogative pronouns illustrate the beginnings of change and mutual influence also in the fourteenth century: thus the instr. sg. цѣмь of къто 'who' develops the 'regularized' form кѣмь through pressure of the rest of the paradigm, and we find the analogical чѣмь for чимь as the instr. of чьто 'what'. Both new forms figure in the 'Čudovo New Testament'. Moreover, чьто began to use the new form чего, modelled on кого,

---

[1] Cf. Gk ἐνενήκοντα < *neụenē-konta. Parallel to this F. Prusík (cf. L. A. Bulachovskij, *Kommentarij k literaturnomu russkomu jazyku*, Char'kov–Kiev, 1937, pp. 139–40) derives девяносто from *neụeno(d) kŋto.

for historical чьсо/чесо. This appears in the twelfth century (e.g. in *Zlatostruj*).

444. The remaining pronominal forms had, as we already know, a binary type of declension, represented by, say, тъ 'that' and и 'he', and a type showing interaction between the two (e.g. вьсь 'all'). The existence of such a type probably occasioned further changes and simplifications in the parallel paradigms. Thus we find pronouns of the hard and the mixed declension (e.g. тъ, онъ, вьсь) generalizing the feminine nominative ending -ѣ in the plural (e.g. *Nov. korm.*, *c.* 1282: тѣ цари́е 'those kings'; *Nov. prol.*, 1356: онѣ (бѣси) хотяху 'those (devils) wanted'). There was also confusion between the hard and the mixed types of declension inside the paradigm (e.g. *Duch. Klim.*, 1270: instr. sg. всимь 'by all' for вьсѣмь; *Rjaz. korm.*, 1284: gen. pl. всихъ 'of all' for вьсѣхъ).

445. The ancient parallelism of the demonstratives и–е–я and онъ–оно–она led ultimately to the substitution of the latter set for the former as personal pronouns in the nominative case, and the former set with the addition of the particle -же (i.e. иже-еже-яже) retained the value of relatives. But и–е–я continued to provide the oblique cases of the paradigm. These in conjunction with the prepositions generalized the infix н, which led to a variant duplication of the entire set of forms (e.g. masc. and neut. gen. sg. его/него, fem. sg. её/неё). The infix was the result of original metanalysis of syntagmata with prepositions ending in н (e.g. съ(н)- 'with', въ(н)- 'in(to)', къ(н)- 'to', with which cf. Gk ξυν-/συν-, ἐν-, Skt *kam*- respectively). The 'metanalysed' forms are found in the eleventh century (e.g. *Ost.*, 1056–7: къ нему 'to him'; *Var.*, *c.* 1092: в немь 'in it'). In course of time the use of 'metanalytical' н spread to all other prepositional syntagmata containing the personal pronoun (e.g. *Nif.*, 1219: на нь < на (н)и 'on him'), and to the verbal prefixes other than съ- and въ- combined with -яти 'to take' (cf. отъ-няти 'to take away' with сън-яти 'to take down').

446. Of the earlier demonstratives сь–се–ся 'this' and тъ–то–та 'that' represent the first and second degrees of relative distance and онъ–оно–она represents the third (cf. E. *this–that–yon*). The pronominal set сь–се–ся has been replaced by этот–это–эта, found in the seventeenth century as етотъ–ето–ета, which are also Lomonosov's forms in 1755; and тъ has been reduplicated into тътъ, which has given the modern тот. The element e (later written э) is interjectional.

II. VERBALIA

447. In Old Russian the abundance of tenses was complicated by the presence of aspect, which gave it the semblance of the now familiar dichotomy of imperfective and perfective. The more articulated tense system, however, endowed the older language with a different character from that of its modern counterpart. But in process of time the system of tenses began to disintegrate, and the system of aspect was developed to meet the new demands.

448. Tense. Confining ourselves to the indicative mood first, we shall note the changes that have taken place in the present tense of athematic verbs. The preponderance of the thematic type led to the accommodation of the athematic to the thematic (e.g. *Psalt.*, 14th cent.: до избытка ѣши 'thou eatest to satiety' for ѣси; *1 Nov. let.*, 13–14th c.: или не выдадите 'if you do not give' for выдасте; *Ipat.*, *c.* 1425: оже мы дадимъ симъ животъ 'if we spare these' for дамъ).

449. The verb быти 'to be', which belongs to the athematic group, was used not only as an auxiliary of the perfect tenses (§§ 457, 459–60), but independently either as a copulative or as a verb meaning 'to exist'. The copulative was sometimes omitted (e.g. *Svjat.*, 1076: идеже криво 'where it is wrong'; *Lavr.*, 1377: бѣда ако въ роднѣ 'trouble is as one of the family'; *Molenije Daniila Zatočnika*, 16th cent.: орелъ царь надъ птицами 'the eagle is the king of birds'); but there are also many instances of its use (e.g. *Lavr.*, 1377: есть веселье пити 'there is pleasure in drinking'; *Mol.*, 16th cent.: умный дорогъ есть 'a wise man is precious'; *Jevangelije Tjapinskogo*, 16th cent.: береме мое легко есть 'my burden is light').

450. The gradual disappearance of есть 'is' and the rarer суть 'are' led also to the loss of the other persons of the present tense of быти beginning with the fourteenth century (e.g. *Lavr.*, 1377: азъ имъ противенъ 'I am their enemy', ты господинъ 'thou art master'). Some of these forms are still found in the seventeenth century, for instance in the Moscow writs of that time.

451. The negative forms нѣсмь, нѣси, нѣсть (also нѣ) were apparently obsolete by the fourteenth century (e.g. *Lavr.*, 1377: нѣ есмы 'we are not' for нѣсмъ/нѣсмы).

452. The interaction of the unitary conjugation (люблю-type) with the binary (несу-type) resulted in certain changes of form. Thus the verb дышати 'to breathe' would seem to have been originally a mixed verb, i.e. to have belonged simultaneously to the unitary and the binary conjugational type, as both дышить and дышеть 'he breathes' are found in the thirteenth century. The unitary type дышит survives to this day.

453. Both conjugations participate in the results of the hardening or velarization of the end-consonant, notably in the 3rd sg. and pl. of the present tense. This hardening process appears to go back to the fourteenth century in the Moscow area (e.g. *Duch. kn. Dmitrija Donskogo*, 14th cent.: вѣдаетъ свою треть 'cares for his own third', Володимеръ дастъ 'Volodimer will give'). The Old Russian present-tense ending -тъ was also, no doubt, influenced by a similar phonetic tendency prevailing in the north-west (e.g. *Pskov. gram.*, 1483: а проѣзду не дадутъ 'they will not give us right of way'). This tendency appears to have been due to an attempt to avoid homophony when most infinitive forms shed their final syllable and the preceding consonant became palatalized (e.g. любити > любить).

454. The present tense in Old Russian had sometimes future meaning in accordance with the aspect of the particular verb. If the verb was perfective, the future meaning of its present tense was a corollary (e.g. *Nov. ber. gram.*, No. 9: а мънѣ не въдасть ничьто же 'and he will give me nothing'); but sometimes even an imperfective verb could function as a future tense (e.g. *Ost.*, 1056–7: слъньце мрькнеть и луна не дасть свѣта 'the sun shall be darkened and the moon shall give no light' for помьркнеть). The only simple verb in Old Russian, however, which has an exclusively future meaning is буду 'I shall be' (e.g. *Nif.*, 1219: нъ не побѣженъ будеши 'but thou shalt not be defeated'). The lack of a formal future tense, in the absence of the ascendancy of aspect, led to the formation of a compound future tense with the aid of certain full verbs functioning as partial auxiliaries. Буду was generally not one of these. The verbs mostly used here were, as we know, начяти, почяти, учяти 'to begin', стати 'to become', хотѣти 'to wish', and имѣти 'to have' (e.g. *Mst.*, *c.* 1130: который князь почьнеть хотѣти...отъяти 'whatever prince . . . shall wish to take away'; *Lavr.*, 1377: Христосъ имать сохранити тя 'Christ shall preserve thee', то ли не будеть межю нами мира, елико камень начьнеть плавати 'there shall be no peace between us until the stone shall float', но хочю вѣ почтити наутрия 'but I shall honour you tomorrow'). Хотѣти is particularly common in the Laurentian MS of the 'Primary Chronicle'. One or other of these 'auxiliaries' continues to be used down to the sixteenth century, when the -чяти group of verbs was mostly in use (e.g. *Dom.*, 16th cent.: а о комъ учнутъ печаловатися 'and whomever they shall take care of'). The verb буду, however, now begins to appear in this function (e.g. *Pskov. gram.*, 1588: я о том буду писать 'I shall write about it'; *Dom.*, 16th cent.: ино уже вдвое будеть платити 'then he shall pay double'), especially in the writings of Ivan Peresvetov (e.g. his *Skazanije o Magmete saltane*, 16th cent.: намъ будеть отъ него суетное житье 'we shall experience much trouble through him'). This usage became common in the following century and would seem to have emerged under Polish influence.

455. Of the two past tenses in Old Russian, the imperfect seems to have been the first to decay. This tense is comparatively rare in ecclesiastical works of the early centuries and is not found in the rather limited secular literature represented by the writs and legal code. It may be assumed therefore that in the thirteenth century, with which we begin our history of changes, it was hardly used in colloquial speech. The aorist on the contrary is very frequent in ecclesiastical writings and in the annals, but not in the writs (e.g. *Nov. gram.*, 1262–3: отложихомъ 'we set aside'; *Nov. korm.*, *c.* 1282: уставиша 'they established'; *Klim.*, 13th cent.: написах 'I wrote'; *Dvin. gram.*, 14th–15th cent.: купи 'he bought'). Apparently, the aorist forms began to disappear in the course of the fifteenth century, for they are rather less common in the Novgorod and Pskov writs of that time (e.g. *Nov. gram.*, 1456: велѣхомъ 'we ordered'; *Nov. gram.*, 1459: биша 'they beat'; *Nov. gram.*, 1471: приѣхаша 'they arrived'; *Pskov. gram.*, 1483: дахомъ 'we gave').

456. Confusion of imperfect and aorist is occasionally observed in the period between the thirteenth and fifteenth centuries (e.g. *Mil. jev.*, 1215: птица небесьныя позобаше е 'the birds of heaven ate it up' for позобаша; *Nov. jev.*, 1339: приведоху 'they brought' for приведоша; *Nov. gram.*, 1372: повелѣше 'they ordered' for повелѣша; *Lavr.*, 1377: стояше 'they stood' for стояша; *Pskov. Lukino jev.*, 1409: придоху 'they came' for придоша). In later manuscripts we find a completely inaccurate use of the two tense-forms, i.e. without regard for the requirements of grammatical person and number (e.g. *2 Nov. let.*, 17th cent.: садъ весь изгорѣша 'the entire garden was burnt up' for изгорѣ, иные въ воде потопаше 'some were drowned in the water' for потопаша; *Kot.*, *c.* 1664: Иванъ Грозный сына своего смири на оный свѣтъ, пробиша его осномъ своимъ 'Ivan the Terrible despatched his son to the other world, transfixed him with his stick' for проби). Those with better knowledge of Church Slavonic usage like the Archpriest Avvakum do not commit such errors, but it would appear nevertheless that the aorist in the seventeenth century was an archaism. It was replaced by the perfect.

457. We find the perfect tense in use in the eleventh century, even without the supporting auxiliary быти 'to be' in the 3rd person (e.g. *Tmut.*, 1068: Глѣбъ князь мѣрилъ мо(ре) 'Prince Gleb measured the sea' for мѣрилъ есть; *Nov. b. gram.*, No. 9, 11th cent.: еже отьць даялъ и роди съдаяли 'what my father bequeathed and my relatives bequeathed' for даялъ есть and съдаяли суть; *Mst.*, *c.* 1130: азъ... повелѣлъ есмь 'I . . . have ordered', я Всеволодъ далъ есмь 'I, Vsevolod, have given', язъ далъ 'I have given'). The old use of the auxiliary, to judge by most of these examples, was mainly determined by the absence of an expressed subject, whether substantive or pronoun, immediately before the *l*-participle. In the *Russkaja pravda* (*c.* 1282) the numerous past-tense forms, with negligible exceptions, are perfects, not aorists. It is curious too to find, in this connexion, the perfect and aorist included in the same syntagma. The Laurentian MS (1377), for instance, contains such a confused sentence as this: рекоша, яко Кий есть перевозникъ бысть 'they said that Kij was a ferryman' (for былъ), and the Hypatian MS (*c.* 1425) goes so far as to use the following construction: б възложи 'he placed on' (for възложилъ). Here we have a glut of incompetently handled archaisms. It may be observed, in this connexion, that the past-tense meaning does not appear to be cancelled out but rather to be reinforced by the competing forms.

458. The absence of the auxiliary in combination with the *l*-participle, which we have observed in the eleventh and twelfth centuries, becomes more conspicuous in the ensuing period (e.g. *Jur. jev.*, 1120: Угриньць псалъ 'the Hungarian has written'; *Nov. gram.*, 1262–3: что ся учинило тяже 'as for litigation having arisen'; *Lavr.*, 1377: въ се же лѣто Всеславъ рать почалъ 'this year Vseslav has started a war'). In these examples it will be remarked that the verb is associated with a subject in the 3rd person. When the subject is either in the 1st or in the 2nd person (cf. our earlier examples Глѣбъ князь мѣрилъ мо(ре) and азъ . . . повелѣлъ есмь), the auxiliary, it would seem, has a better chance of survival (e.g. *Klim.*, 13th cent.: взялѣ есмь 'I have taken'; *Nov. gram.*, 1294: есте прислали 'you have sent'; but князь великий послалъ к вамъ сына 'the grand prince has sent you his son'). Examination of Old Russian literature, both ecclesiastical and secular, in the eleventh and twelfth centuries, however, shows that personal pronouns are rarely used with verbs, and the same holds good for the most part of the secular manuscripts of the period between the twelfth and the fourteenth centuries. Wherever these pronouns are used, their purpose seems to be to emphasize (e.g. *Mst.*, *c.* 1130: азъ Мстиславъ Володимирь сынъ 'I, Mstislav, son of Volodimir; *Nov. korm.*, *c.* 1282: оже кто възищеть кунъ на друзѣ, а онъ ся начьнеть запирати 'if anyone should demand money of another and that other should refuse'; *Lavr.*, 1377: азъ Бога познахъ и радуюся, аще ты познаеши и радоватися почнешь 'I have found God and rejoice that thou wilt find (him) and rejoice'). This usage helped to detach the auxiliary from the composite form of the perfect, for the pronominal subject was felt to be in some sort a compensation for it. Nevertheless, the occasional use of the auxiliary continues in the sixteenth and seventeenth centuries (e.g. *Nov. gram.*, 1577: дали есме 'we have given'; *Dom.*, 16th cent.: ночевала есмь 'I (fem.) spent the night'). In the modern dialects there are still traces of the auxiliary but none in the literary language.

459. Whereas буду developed late as a simple future, it had been used in medieval times as a component of the future perfect (e.g. *Lavr.*, 1377: отци и братия, оже ся гдѣ буду описалъ или переписалъ или не дописалъ, чтите исправливая, Бога дѣля 'fathers and brethren, if I shall have blundered, or added, or omitted (anything), read on, after having emended (it), for God's sake'). This form began to disappear from the spoken language in the sixteenth century, although there are examples of its use in the seventeenth. In a sixteenth-century writ we may read such a clause as: а чего будетъ (for буду) забылъ написать 'and what I shall have forgotten to write'. The solecism будетъ has survived as the particle буде (e.g. I. Gončarov, *Oblomov*, 1855: буде же я, Обломовъ, пожелаю прежде времени съѣхать съ квартиры 'if, I, Oblomov, shall wish to leave the flat before the time is up').

460. The pluperfect, which was formed in Old Russian with the imperfect of быти 'to be' (viz. бяхъ 'I was') and even with the Old Church Slavonic form бѣхъ 'id.' as auxiliary, also made use of the composite былъ есмь 'I have been' in the same capacity. The formations with бяхъ and the Old Church Slavonic бѣхъ disappeared along with the imperfect and aorist, but the expanded secondary formation survived into the modern period and has left a reminder of itself in the invariable form было (e.g. Mod. R. он было ушёл 'he nearly went off'). The period between the fifteenth and seventeenth centuries furnishes many examples (e.g. *Mos. gram.*, c. 1455: язъ велѣлъ былъ ихъ судити 'I had ordered them to be judged'; *Gramota archijepiskopa Gennadija*, 1490: которые еретики были покаялися 'the heretics who had recanted'; A. M. Kurbskij, *Istorija o velikom knjaze Moskovskom*, 16th cent.: что ихъ было осталося 'whatever had remained of them'; *Učenije i chitrost' ratnogo strojenija pechotnych ljudej*, 1647: ему же не довелося было 'he had not succeeded').

461. Aspect. The function and static morphology of aspect have been referred to already (§§ 119, 226). Here we shall try to see it in historical perspective. Till the disappearance of the imperfect and the aorist it existed, as it were, in a latent condition. The modification of verbs by prefixes inevitably gave them a perfective meaning (e.g. *Lavr.*, 1377: поищемъ собѣ князя 'let us seek a prince for ourselves', и поидоста по Днѣпру 'and the two followed the Dnieper'), and some verbs could be perfective even without a prefix (e.g. *Ost.*, 1056–7: иду по тебѣ 'I shall follow thee', еже, аще рекуть ч(е)л(овѣ)ци 'which if men shall say'). Apart from prefixes to form its perfective aspect, we find that Old Russian uses suffixes (e.g. -ива-/-ыва-) to obtain an imperfective meaning (e.g. *Nov. gram.*, 1264–5: а грамоты ти кн(я)же не посуживати 'and thou shalt not change this writ, O Prince; *Lavr.*, 1377: но умыкиваху у воды д(е)в(и)ця 'but they carried off maidens by the river'). In later Novgorod writs we find other formations of this kind (e.g. приставливати 'to keep setting'), and the sixteenth and seventeenth centuries provide us with numerous examples of them (e.g. *Dom.*, 16th cent.: лугъ кашивалъ 'kept mowing the meadow'; *Kot.*, *c.* 1664: не посылывали 'they did not keep sending'). Ever since then such frequentative-iterative verbs have been very productive in Russian (e.g. Puškin, *Jevgenij Onegin*, 1823–31: здѣсь съ нимъ обѣдывалъ зимою 'here he would dine with him in winter'). In 1522, incidentally, these forms had been recorded by Dmitrij Gerasimov (known as Dmitrij Tolmač), the translator to Tsar Vasilij III, in his adaptation of Donatus's Grammar (e.g. любливахъ 'I had kept on loving', учивахъ 'I had kept on teaching'). Even in the middle of the eighteenth century Lomonosov reproduced them in his *Rossijskaja grammatika* (§ 268). The nineteenth-century and modern view is that they belong to the imperfective aspect, for by the seventeenth the system of aspect had already succeeded to that of tense.

462. Mood. The imperative mood, actually the optative in origin, combined the meaning of these two moods in Old Russian as well as, to some extent, that of the subjunctive or conditional. The 1st person singular disappeared early, and there are only rare instances of its use (e.g. *Tolstovskij psaltyr'*, 12th cent.: будѣмь 'may I be'). The 3rd pl. is not known even fragmentarily. This leaves us with the 2nd and 3rd sg. and the 1st and 2nd du. and pl. Forms of the athematic verbs like дажь 'give' were already obsolete in the fourteenth century (e.g. *Polikarpovo jev.*, 1307: хлѣбъ нашь даи же намъ днесь 'give us this day our bread').

463. Various forms of the imperative influenced one another, thus creating new forms: those of the 2nd and 3rd sg. in -жь influenced the 2nd pl. (e.g. *Korm.*, 13th–14th cent.: 2nd sg. вижь 'see' gave 2nd pl. вижьте for видите; *Lavr.*, 1377: повѣжьте 'tell ye'). Forms of the 1st and 2nd du. and pl. in -ѣвѣ, -ѣта, -ѣмъ, -ѣте (e.g. ведѣмъ 'let us lead') and -ивѣ, -ита, -имъ, -ите (e.g. ходимъ 'let us walk') also influenced one other (e.g. *Ost.*, 1056–7: приведите 'bring ye' for приведѣте; *Arch. jev.*, 1092: метимъ 'let us cast' for метѣмъ). The thirteenth and fourteenth centuries witnessed the emergence of a great many similar mixed forms (e.g. *Nif.*, 1219: поидивѣ 'let us two go' for поидѣвѣ; *Nov. korm.*, *c.* 1282: съведитеся 'assemble ye' for съведѣтеся; *Nov. jev.*, 1355: идите 'go ye' for идѣте). But there was also confusion of imperative and indicative forms, as these in many instances differed only in spelling (e.g. *Nov. Prol.*, 1262: подражаемъ 'let us imitate' for подражаимъ; *Lavr.*, 1377: поидемъ 'let us go' for поидѣмъ). The interaction of imperative and indicative is best seen where the former had stems in hiss-sibilants instead of the velars, which were to replace these later (e.g. *Lavr.*, 1377: 2nd sg. рьчи 'speak' for рьци; *Ipat.*, *c.* 1425: 2nd sg. стережи 'guard' for стерези).

464. The subjunctive or conditional function of the imperative occurs in Church Slavonic texts copied by Russian scribes and it is found also in purely Russian monuments (e.g. *Nov. korm.*, *c.* 1282: хотя си буди холопъ или раба 'though it be a bondman or bondwoman'; аще и мьртвыя воскрешаи 'even if thou raise the dead'). The use of the imperative form with conditional force is a common modern innovation in Russian (e.g. скажи я ему, он всё сделает 'if I give the word, he will do everything'). Another, later, use of it is the expression of a sudden action (e.g. он ей и скажи 'he went and told her').

465. The conditional is represented in Old Russian by a combination of the *l*-participle with the Russian-type aorist быхъ 'I was'. The common 2nd- and 3rd-person form бы began to be used sometime in the thirteenth century as an invariable particle (e.g. *Mil. jev.*, 1215: аще бы в Турѣ быша силы были 'if there had been forces in Tur (Tyre)'; *Mos. jev.*, 1339: аще бы мене бысте вѣдали 'if you had known me'; *Lavr.*, 1377: въ дне бы есте пришли 'you might have come by day'; *Ipat.*, *c.* 1425: вы бы есте повѣдалѣ 'you might have told'). Our examples show a ponderous construction in which the full compound past tense (perfect or pluperfect) is associated with бы. Other constructions, especially later ones, reveal the absence of this originally redundant particle. Nevertheless, by the fourteenth century it had established itself and is seen combined with other particles, for instance абы, штобы (чьтобы), дабы 'so that' (e.g. *Povest' ob Akire*, 15th cent.: уне есть женѣ дабы свой сынъ умерлъ бы 'it is better for the woman that her son should die').

466. Voice. The equivalent of voice, both middle and passive, was expressed in Old Russian by using the unstressed reflexive pronoun ся (acc.) and its variant си (dat.). They appear at first indifferently as proclitics and enclitics (cf. *Svjat.*, 1076: коньчашя ся книги сия 'this book was finished' with *Mst.*, c. 1130: донелѣ же ся миръ състоить 'while the world lasts'). On occasion we also find two instances of one and the same particle in monuments of the period between the fifteenth and the seventeenth centuries (e.g. *Ipat.*, c. 1425: а не можемъ ся вмѣститися в печерѣ 'and we cannot fit in the cave'). We may note here too that post-positive -ся evolved the shortened form -сь in the fourteenth century (e.g. *Nov. gram.*, 1373: учинилось 'it happened'). The particle си is found with verbs governing the dative case (e.g. *Jur. jev.*, 1120: судити си 'to be judged'; *Lavr.*, 1377: сотснити си 'to join together'), and its area was extended by trespass on that of -ся (e.g. *Lavr.*, 1377: възвратити си 'to return'). The use of -ся, however, prevailed in the course of the sixteenth and seventeenth centuries (*Mos. sudebnik*, 1550: чей ся жребій выиметъ 'whoever shall draw the lot'; *Af. Nik.*, 16th cent.: судно ся розбило под Тархи 'my ship was wrecked near Tarchi'; *Učen.*, 1647: о силѣ, которой они ся предають 'concerning the power to which they submit'). It will be remarked here that the reflexive particle figures as a proclitic, and this practice survives in the folk-lore which was set down in the eighteenth century (e.g. куда ся не кинуть, такъ по уши въ смолу 'wherever one throws oneself one is up to the ears in pitch'). By the beginning of that century the particle in the literary language had become not only post-positive but attached to the verb.

467. Person. The personal endings of the verb have shown changes since the eleventh and twelfth centuries. These changes have been: (*a*) depalatalization of the endings of the 2nd sg. and 3rd sg. and pl. of the present indicative, (*b*) disappearance of the dual forms, and (*c*) the interaction of the endings of indicative and imperative, which have already been examined under Mood (§§ 462–5).

468. The ending of the 2nd sg. -ши, which replaced -си of the athematic verbs from the fourteenth century, appears to have begun to harden after the loss of the ending, i.e. after becoming -шь, in secular literature in the thirteenth century. The results of hardening are already apparent in the sixteenth.

469. The ending of the 3rd person, both singular and plural, shows the earliest sporadic signs of hardening in the thirteenth century (e.g. *Nov. korm.*, *c.* 1282: познает ли 'if he recognizes'), but continues to be written -ть even in the sixteenth century, especially in ecclesiastical manuscripts (e.g. *Chronologija Kirika*, 16th cent.: на четвертое лѣто приходить д(е)нь единъ 'to the fourth year a day is added'), although in combination with the reflexive pronoun it was often not written (e.g. *Kir.*, 16th cent.: исправится 'is corrected'). In fact, the hard ending under these circumstances was anticipated two centuries before (e.g. Kiril Turovskij, *Slovo na antipaschu*, 14th cent.: не нарекутся 'shall not be called'). Most secular manuscripts have the hard ending in the sixteenth century (e.g. *Stoglav*, 16th cent.: даютъ 'they give'). By the seventeenth the hard ending was general (e.g. *Ulož.*, 1649: кто возложитъ хулу 'whoever shall lay a curse').

470. The hardening process was not only phonological but morphological, as it concerned specific categories of words both nominal and verbal (cf., in illustration of the hardening of final labials, instr. sg. волкомъ 'by the wolf' and дамъ 'I shall give' with the original вълкъмь, дамь). The hardening appears, as we have observed, to have started in the northern (e.g. Novgorod) area and did not affect the southern, where soft forms survive in dialect to this day.

471. The disappearance of the dual number in conjugation as in declension was a gradual process and took place at different rates in different categories of words. It would seem that verb and adjective show loss of dual forms earlier than the substantive, whose dual was protected by association with the numerals дъва/дъвѣ and оба/обѣ (e.g. *Lavr.*, 1377: два братеника бесерменина утекла 'two infidel brothers escaped'; *Ipat.*, *c*. 1425: взя два города Галичьскыи 'he captured two Galician towns'). In the last example it will be noted that the adjective stands in the plural while the substantive is in the dual. The process of the disintegration of the dual accordingly is observable in the fourteenth century, and by the fifteenth it was already complete, although there are later sporadic survivals.

472. Participles. The active participle in -a/-я belonged at first only to the present tense (e.g. *Ost.*, 1056–7: прохождааше исцѣля вьсякъ недугъ 'he went about healing every sickness'; *Skaz. B. G.*, 13th cent.: рака ста не поступячи 'the coffin remained immobile'), but in due course it began to function as a past participle. We find this usage in the thirteenth and fourteenth centuries supplementing the past-tense forms in -ъ/-въ (e.g. *Nov. Prol.*, 1262: мощи ея възмя Акакий и погрѣбѣ 'Akakij took her remains and buried them'; *Lavr.*, 1377: пожга городъ възвратишася 'having burnt the town, they returned'). Modern literary Russian knows only the -a/-я forms in this function, but in the seventeenth century the plural forms in -че/-чи were also in use (e.g. *Kot.*, 17th cent.: поидучи въ походъ 'having gone campaigning'). The form in -чи was feminine singular in origin, but appears to have been reinterpreted as a plural.

473. The past participle proper sometimes had the stem-ending -м or -н (e.g. възьмъ < възяти 'to take', начьнъ < начяти 'to begin'), and these forms, which figure in the older language, survive in dialect at the present time (e.g. вземши 'having taken' for взявши), whereas those in -въ/-въши belong to the literary language and have superseded the old forms with dental and nasal stems (e.g. OR ѣдъ 'having eaten' > ѣвъ > Mod.R. ев(ши), OR начьнъ 'having begun' > начявъ > Mod.R. начав(ши)).

474. Both these participial forms lost their attributive force by becoming invariable and began to be used as what Russian grammar loosely calls 'gerunds', i.e. participles in an adverbial function.

475. Infinitive. Of the other nominal forms of the verb the infinitive and supine were invariable, being familiar case-forms, the first dative and the second accusative. The morphological varieties of the infinitive are the predominant -ти and the rare variant -чи (cf. печи 'to bake' < *pek-ti*, беречи 'to look after' < *bereg-ti* with нести 'to carry', любити 'to love'). The ending -ти occurs in some thirteenth-century manuscripts. By the seventeenth we observe a hesitation between -ти and the curtailed form -ть (e.g. *Ulož.*, 1649: рать збирать 'to gather troops', доводить государево дѣло 'to prosecute for the crown', кому насильство чинити 'to assault someone', рыбы никому на себя не ловити 'none is to catch fish for himself', учнетъ тѣ печати прикладывать 'shall begin to affix those seals'). In the eighteenth century the full form of the infinitive is still found, but only in the 'higher' genres (e.g. Radiščev, *Putešestvije iz Peterburga v Moskvu*, 1790: отъяти жизнь 'to deprive of life'). In modern times only the end-stressed forms of the full infinitive survive (e.g. нести 'to carry', найти 'to find').

476. Supine. The ending of the supine -тъ lasts into the fourteenth century and may be found in the chronicles (e.g. *1 Nov. let.*, 13–14th c.: идоша блюстъ Торжку 'they went to keep order in Toržok'; *Lavr.*, 1377: идетъ рыбъ ловитъ 'goes to catch fish', посла Ярополкъ искатъ брата 'Jaropolk sent to look for his brother'; *Šestodnev*, 1374: поехати питъ въ Зряковици 'to go for a drink in Zrjakovica'; *Ipat.*, c. 1425: их же бяхуть послалѣ языка ловитъ 'whom they had sent out to get information'). By the fifteenth century the form had been replaced by the infinitive.

477. Adverbs and Particles. These are a complex and miscellaneous group and have grown historically at the expense of other, more homogeneous parts of speech, both nominal and verbal.

478. Substantives have contributed oblique cases to the adverbial category, for instance, modern домой 'homewards' < dat. sg. домови, which was used allatively (cf. *Lavr.*, 1377: идѣте съ данью домови 'go ye home with the tribute'; *1 Nov. let.*, 13–14th c.: понесеть его домовь 'will take it home'; even *Ulož.*, 1649: збѣжитъ къ себѣ домовь 'runs to his home'), or syntagmatic units consisting of a preposition governing a substantive (e.g. Mod.R. назад 'back' < на 'on'+задъ 'back').

479. Some of these adverbs derive from adjectives consolidated with a preposition (e.g. Mod.R. слева 'from the left' < съ+

лѣв-а, вдалеке 'in the distance' < въ+далек-ѣ, вкратце 'in brief' < въ+кратъц-ѣ, по-русски 'in Russian' < по+русь-скы,[1] теперь 'now' < то+пьрво); others are the outcome of loss of flexion by mainly neuter forms of the comparative adjective (§ 437), for instance, modern лишь 'only' < лише < лихъ 'additional' (cf. Avvakum, *Žitije*, 1672–3: а онъ лишо излаялъ мене 'but he only cursed me'). Still others are of pronominal origin, with a specifically adverbial particle attached (e.g. Mod.R. где 'where' < къ-де, здесь 'here' < сь-де-сь).

480. Verbal roots have contributed, among others, such forms as де, мол, and чай to this group. These are strictly 'modal' particles, showing the presence of the speaker's interest or attitude in the enunciation. They derive from Old Russian дѣеть 'does', молвить 'says', and чаяти 'to expect' respectively. The particles де and мол would mean much the same as the expletive 'says' in English, and чай is approximately 'I expect'.

481. Other particles are traditionally classified as prepositions, conjunctions, and interjections. These also sometimes have an origin which is more or less transparent. The preposition межь 'between', for instance, is the petrified relic of a substantive in the locative case, viz. межи < межа 'border' (cf. между < OCS междд 'id.'), the conjunction если 'if', a late development in Russian, is derived from есть ли 'is it' (cf. E. originally concessive *if* < OE *gif* < *giefan* 'to give'), and the interjection used by Puškin in the lyric Ночной зефир, 1824, viz. чу . . . гитары звон 'hark, . . . the twang of a guitar', goes back to Old Russian чути 'to be aware'.

482. Word-formation. The history of Russian word-formation, as distinct from the absorption of loan-words by the language, is part of the domain of morphology; and we shall consider here some of the changes and developments in this sector under the familiar word-categories—nominals and verbals. We shall observe throughout our survey the gradual obsolescence of some modes of derivation and the emergence of others to replace them; for, as we have learnt already, word-formation is a perpetual process of transformation.

483. The substantival formants such as -ие, which is Old

---

[1] This type of adverb was used in OR without the incongruent preposition (cf. *Ost.*, 1056–7: мирьскы 'in the world').

Church Slavonic in origin, sometimes show a tendency to contract (e.g. *Lavr.*, 1377: поученье 'admonition', cf. OCS пооученнѥ); but the full form is later restored under ecclesiastical influence and has survived to this day in the literary language. Further, the singulative suffix -инъ, which is attached to animate substantives in -ане/-яне/-ѣне, shows itself to be very productive in the Old Russian period (e.g. *Pskov. let.*, 14th cent.: от псковитина 'from a burgher of Pskov'). The corresponding suffix for inanimates was -ина (e.g. горошина 'a pea' < горохъ 'pease'). But this attracted animates, e.g. людина 'man' < людие 'people' (cf. *Svjat.*, 1073: людинъ 'human being'); and людина and cognate derivatives have assumed the sense of 'bigness' (e.g. купчина 'big merchant'). The singulative -инъ, moreover, was attached to such collectives as Русь 'Russians', мордва 'Mordovians', челядь 'domestics', господа 'gentry', giving the forms русинъ (found in 13th-cent. writs), мордвинъ, челядинъ, господинъ. In modern times the suffix has ceased to be productive. This also holds good mostly of masculine diminutive formants like -енъкъ and -ьць. The first of these derives from neuter stems in *nt* (e.g. теля 'calf' < *tel-ent-*, козля 'kid' < *kozьl-ent-*, утя 'duckling' < *ǫt-ent*) and provides a masculine singular to a neuter plural (e.g. Mod.R. телёнок/телята). The suffix -ьць has had a numerous progeny (e.g. пѣхота 'infantry' which has given пѣхотинецъ) and is still occasionally resorted to as a hypocoristic (e.g. капиталецъ 'a little capital'). Pejorative diminutives figured in the speech of Muscovy, as they do in present-day Russia, and one of the commonest of them -ка is still productive. In Muscovy it was reserved for the common man (e.g. Микит-ка Плещеевъ), whereas the eminent were provided with a patronymic (e.g. князь Никита Ивановичъ Одоевский or the falconer Петръ Семеновичъ Хомяковъ). In our times the patronymic is an essential part of the name of every Russian, man or woman (cf. the adult names of a brother and sister—Алексей Петрович Ильин and Анна Петровна Ильина).

484. Among adjectives certain types command preference, especially those with the suffix -ьск-, which are still productive, while others like those with a palatalized final consonant (e.g княжь 'princely' < князь) have become obsolete.

485. The numerals, as we have seen, converted Old Russian syntagmata like одинъ на десяте 'eleven' into compounds of the type одиннадцать, and these composite forms restricted declinability to their final element (cf. *Rjaz. korm.*, 1284: въ четвертѣмь и осмьдесятнѣмь правилѣ 'in rule eighty-four' with Mod.R. в восемдесят четвёртом правиле).

486. Pronouns show a special development of indefinite types with the aid of such formants as the vaguely selective -либо (e.g. Mod.R. кто-либо 'whoever' < любо 'it pleases'; cf. *Nov. korm., c.* 1282: мьстити брату брата любо отьцю любо сыну 'brother must avenge brother or else father or son (must avenge)'). Alternatives to -либо are the equally unspecific -нибудь (e.g. Mod.R. кто-нибудь 'whoever' < ни буди 'it may be') and the more definite -то (e.g. Mod.R. кто-то 'whoever'). In что это за человек! it is hard not to see a calque of German *was für ein Mensch* which is found also in other neighbouring languages, for instance in Czech (*co je to za človĕka!*) and Latvian (*kas tas par cilvēku*).

487. Changes in the formation of verbs have been comparatively late, for the prefixes and suffixes which are mostly instrumental in the function of differentiating aspect were on hand in Old Russian. Some suffixes received considerable extension, for instance -ева/-ова in the seventeenth and early eighteenth century. These were used in the formation of new verbs from West European roots (e.g. танцевать/танцовать 'to dance', командовать 'to command'). In the nineteenth century the German suffixes -*ieren*, -*isieren* gave rise to many more (e.g. абонировать 'to subscribe', музицировать 'to make music'). In still later times we find hybrid types such as локализовать 'to localize' for локализировать. And the simultaneous use of prefix and suffix occurs in the formation of some modern verbs as it did in the earlier language (e.g. о-без-кров-еть 'to become anaemic', where, incidentally, we note a double prefix).

488. The process of adverbialization by the methods we have already examined may be seen in a series of later forms of different types of adverbs (e.g. залпом 'at one gulp', исподтишка 'on the quiet', навсегда 'for good', нехотя 'unwillingly', поскольку 'inasmuch').

X

SYNTACTIC CHANGES

489. General. The contrast between Old Russian and Old Church Slavonic existed from the beginning, but the contrast was not absolute. From the first, Old Church Slavonic in the East European area had assumed a Russian or rather an East Slavonic face; for this language, as we know, was an artificial literary language which had been taken over bodily with a set of Scriptural texts and a chanted liturgy. No doubt, at first, the Bulgarian form had been imitated by the Russian priests; but the pronunciation of the language must have been imperfect as the copyists' errors in the 'Ostromir Gospels', for instance, clearly show. By the second half of the eleventh century, two generations after the official christianization, the spoken form of Old Church Slavonic (actually Old Bulgarian) in Rus' had been substantially russianized. This had affected the morphology too, and colloquial speech had exerted an influence on the written language, especially in the secular sphere. As we have seen, all extant eleventh-century monuments, even those copied from Old Church Slavonic originals, illustrate the syntax of what may be called an early form of the Russian literary language. The two elements, native and alien, were both represented, the first of them, especially, in the simple sentences of secular writing (e.g. writs, correspondence, legal documents) and the second in the more complex sentences of ecclesiastical writing. We have already observed the syntactic features of the older language in the eleventh and twelfth centuries (§§ 236–51), and it now remains for us to trace its development during the next eight.

I

490. The Simple Sentence. This receives ample illustration in the writs and legal code (*Russkaja pravda*) of the thirteenth century; but the influence of ecclesiastical syntax gradually introduces complexity into secular literary writing, of which the earliest specimens are hagiographies represented, for instance by the late twelfth-century 'Legend of Boris and Gleb', and the chronicles, of which the oldest, palaeographically, is the 'First Novgorod Chronicle' of the thirteenth-fourteenth century.

491. Most writs illustrate the presence of simple statements like the sequence of them at the end of the treaty concluded by Prince Aleksandr Jaroslavič of the Neva and the Novgorodians with the Germans and Swedes in 1262–3, viz. а гдѣ ся тяжя родить, ту ю кончати, а иноѥ грамоты у насъ нѣтуть, ни потаили ѥсмы, ни вѣдаѥмъ, на томь кр(ь)стъ цѣлуѥмъ 'where a litigation shall arise there it must be ended; we have no other writ, neither have we concealed (it) nor know (about one); we give our oath on that.' The staccato effect here results from a breathless succession of short sentences, yet they are closely bound together semantically and even formally (cf. гдѣ . . . ту 'where . . . there'). This has a parallel in *Russkaja pravda* (e.g. аже кто не вложить ся въ дикую виру, тому людьѥ не помагають 'whoever does not contribute to the collective fine will not be helped by people', where the link is furnished by the correlation of аще (аже, оже, аче) 'if' and the inverted dative pronoun тому 'to that one'). The 'First Novgorod Chronicle' again is remarkable for its reliance on the unit of the simple sentence and frequently combines several of these by using the copulative conjunction и 'and' as may be seen in the following extract, viz. въ лѣт(о) 6651 (1143) стояше вся осенина дъждева, от(ъ) г(оспо)жина д(ь)ни до корочюна, тепло дъжгъ, и бы вода велика вельми въ Волхове и всюде, сено и дръва разнесе, озеро морози въ нощь, и растьрза вѣтръ, и вънесе в Волхово и поломи мостъ 4 городнѣ, отинудь бе знатбе[1] занесе 'in the year 1143 all the autumn was rainy from the Assumption till Christmas; it was warm rain; and the water stood very high in the Volchov and everywhere; it carried away hay and timber; the lake (sc. Ilmen') froze in the night; and the wind broke up (the ice) and carried it into the Volchov, and broke the bridge, four spans (of it), carrying the timbers completely away, beyond ken'. The linking of this series of statements is of the simplest.

492. As simple, or even simpler if possible, are the Pskov writs, for instance the Burgomaster Sidor's extradition writ to Riga in

---

[1] Dialectal for безъ знатьбы. Note also тепло, Волхово for теплъ, Волховъ.

the fourteenth century, part of which reads as follows: а Ивана Головачка нашего въвелъ въ поруку, а Ивапъ въ Новъгородъ, и онъ побѣжалъ къ вамъ, и нынѣ учините правду, выдадите Нездильца поручнику, здѣ ваша братия и дѣти ваши торгуютъ и въводятъ люди добры въ поруку, и мы за виноватымь не стоимъ, или не выдадите Нездильца поручнику, то мы исправимъ въ Пльскове на вашеи братии а вамъ повѣдаюмъ 'and he (Nezdilec) involved our Ivan Golovaček in giving a guarantee, and Ivan has gone to Novgorod, and he (Nezdilec) has fled to you; and now see to it that justice is done, deliver Nezdilec to the guarantor; (for) your colleagues and offspring trade here and involve good folk in giving guarantees, and we do not uphold the guilty; if you do not deliver Nezdilec to the guarantor, we shall set the matter right with your colleagues in Pskov and inform you (about it).' The second sentence here is remarkable for its apparent 'modernity': it secures its pace by the omission of the verb. And again we observe a rapid sequence of short 'breath groups' with elementary connectives.

493. Apt examples of successions of simple sentences will be found in sixteenth-century manuscripts, especially in Afanasij Nikitin's 'Journey beyond Three Seas', which was written about 1472. Here, for instance, we come across the following: и язъ грѣшный привезлъ жеребца в ындѣйскую землю и дошелъ есми до Чюнеря, Б(о)гъ далъ поздорову все, а стал ми во сто рублев, зима же у них стала с троицына д(ь)ни, а зимовали есмя в Чюнерѣ, жили есмя два м(ѣ)с(я)ца, ежед(ь)нь и нощь 4 м(ѣ)с(я)цы, всюда вода да гряз 'and I, a sinner, brought my stallion to the land of India, and I reached Čjuner' (Junnar); God prospered me in all things, and I made a hundred roubles; the winter (sc. rainy season) began here at Whitsuntide: we spent the winter (sc. rainy season) in Čjuner, we lived (here) two months; (it rains) day and night for four months, there is water and mud everywhere.' The transitions are sudden throughout, especially between the fourth and fifth sentences, and the pace is consequently rapid.

494. This kind of language, compacted of many simple sentences, occurs in a more developed form in some of the simpler kinds of seventeenth-century narrative prose like, say, the anonymous 'Story of the Byzantine Emperor Michael' (*Povest*

o vizantijskom care Michaile).[1] An extract from this will make its
characteristics plain: бысть в Цареграде царь Михаилъ благо-
честивъ и славенъ зело во всѣхъ странахъ. И родился у него
конь велми чюденъ и грозенъ, и нихто на него не смѣяша
сесть, царь на нем не ѣздиша, в желѣзнои конюшне стояше,
повинныхъ к нему меташе 'there lived in Constantinople the
Emperor Michael, (who was) devout and famous in all countries. And a horse was born to him, very marvellous and terrible,
and none dared to mount him; the Emperor did not ride him;
he stood in an iron stable, (and) wrongdoers were thrown to
him.' Other examples, notably the satirical stories *Jorš Jeršovič*
and 'Šemjaka's Case' (*Šemjakin sud*), possess the simple force
and flair of folk-lore. Here is a fragment from the former: а у
суднаго дѣла сидѣли всѣ добрыя люди; дьякъ былъ сомъ з
большимъ усомъ, суднои списокъ писалъ вьюнъ, а доброи
человѣкъ былъ карась, а печаталъ ракъ-глазунъ лѣвою
клещею, и у печати сидѣлъ вьюнъ переславскои да сигъ
ростовскои, а справилъ стер(ля)дь своимъ долгимъ носомъ.
Судному дѣлу конецъ 'and all good folk took part in the case;
the sheathfish with its long moustaches was the clerk, the records
were kept by the loach, and good man carp was there, and the
goggle-eyed lobster sealed with his left claw, and the loach from
Perajaslavl' sat by the seal along with the lavaret from Rostov,
and the sturgeon signed it with its long nose. This is the conclusion of the case.'

495. We have here the brevity of the 'Alphabetic Saws and Proverbs' (*Povesti ili poslovicy vsenarodnejšije po alfavitu*), for instance,
Анна не всякому манна 'Anna is not manna to everyone'; гдѣ
насъ нѣтъ тамъ по двѣ милостыни даютъ 'alms are given twice
where we are not present'; дуракъ стыда не знаетъ 'a fool does
not know shame'; искра мала великъ родитъ пламень 'a little
spark makes a big fire'; медъ сладко а муха падко 'where there
is honey there are flies'; на чюжои ротъ не пугвица нашить[2]
'you cannot sew a button on another's mouth.' Such brevity
pertains especially to the collection of folk-tales (*Narodnyje
russkije skazki*) which was published by A. N. Afanas'jev in 1855
and to the brilliant subjective stylization of Russian folk-lore

---

[1] The relative simplicity of this manuscript is no doubt partly due to its much
earlier origin.
[2] An illustration of the nominative as object of the infinitive.

material by both Aleksej Tolstoj and Aleksej Remizov under the title *Skazki russkogo naroda*.[1] This direct language, indeed, is in ever-present antithesis to the more involved constructions and a happy solvent to complexity.

II

496. The Complex Sentence. The history of the complex sentence in Old Russian may be equated with the penetration of ready-made Church Slavonic constructions into the simplicity of a vernacular that had become literate by imitating them. The simple sentence, even in its expanded form (e.g. *1 Nov. let.*, 13–14th c.: и пріде съ поклономъ съ князи половецькыми къ зяти въ Галичь к Мьстиславу и къ всемъ кн(я)земъ русьскымъ 'and he came to Galič with Polovecian princes to greet his son-in-law Mstislav and all the princes of Rus''), uses very rudimentary devices like the copulative verb and prepositional syntagmata to effect linking of the sentence constituents. In contrast to these we have an elaborate set of connectives to establish the relationship not only of co-ordination but of subordination.

497. Apart from the co-ordinative conjunctions, viz. и, а, да 'and', (и)ли 'or', which loosely knit together the simpler narratives (e.g. A. Nikitin's 'Journey beyond Three Seas'), we find яко, чьто 'that', како 'how', коли 'when', аче/аще (OCS аще), аже/оже 'if', зане 'because', донелѣже, доньдеже 'while', and (и)бо 'for'. But the use of all these and of other conjunctions is restricted by sense and style, and their variety and frequency increase the nearer we draw to the artifice of ecclesiastical writing. Secular prose, on the contrary, contents itself mostly with a small number of them, e.g. яко, which has many meanings (e.g. *1 Nov. let.*, 13–14th c.: и услыша Новѣгородѣ, яко Святопълкъ идеть къ нимъ 'and they heard in Novgorod that Svjatopolk was coming against them'; и присла въ Новгородъ, яко не хоцю у васъ княжити 'and he sent to Novgorod to say, I do not wish to rule you'; толми бяше лютъ пожаръ, яко по водѣ огнь горяше 'so hot was the conflagration that fire burnt on the water'; и отыниша тыномь всь около, яко же инии гради имаху 'and they fenced the village all about with a fence

---

[1] Cf. Walter de la Mare, *Told Again*, London, 1927, in which English fairy-tales are treated in the same way.

such as other towns have'; яко да отмьстять крървь крестьянську 'in order to avenge Christian blood'; и яко быша на озѣре Серегери преставися ... Мартурий 'and when they were on Lake Seliger ... Marturij died'). Here in an incomplete set of examples we find яко used to introduce a clause, to indicate direct speech, and to express consequence, comparison, purpose, and time respectively. In all these cases we have a principal clause, although this is not always cited in our examples.

498. Another conjunction of frequent recurrence in subordinative sentences is the conjunction a, which is in origin a co-ordinative conjunction of adversative type. It often figures in writs of the period between the twelfth and fourteenth centuries either alone or reinforced by the particle же (жь). In this form it is sometimes reduplicated by оже, apparently the Russian variant of Old Church Slavonic ѥже (e.g. *Nov. gram.*, 1301: аже будеть тягота мнѣ от Андрея ... вамъ потянути со мною 'if I have trouble with Andrej ... you must side with me'; оже будеть не чистъ путь въ рѣчкахъ, князь велить ... проводити сий гость 'if the tributaries are infested (sc. with robbers), the prince orders ... safe conduct to be given to this merchant'). The manuscript of *Russkaja pravda* (*c.* 1282) sporadically uses Old Russian аче for the conditional conjunction in the writs (e.g. аче ли будеть русинъ ... любо словенинъ ... то 40 гривьнъ 'if it is a Varangian ... or a Slav ... (he is to pay) forty marks'). But in nearly every instance, whatever the conditional conjunction may be, the correlative то (тъ) also appears (cf. the preceding example). As an alternative to these correlatives we find the literary аще ... то. And the sixteenth-century manuscript of the 'Pskov Legal Writ' (*Pskovskaja sudnaja gramota*) consistently uses а ... ино (e.g. а которому посаднику сѣсти на посадниство, ино тому посаднику кр(е)стъ цѣловати на томъ, что ему судитъ[1] право по крес(тн)ому цѣлованію 'whichever burgomaster is to take up the burgomastership, he must take oath that he will give fair judgement according to his oath').

499. By the time we come to the turn of the sixteenth century and reach the seventeenth, the Old Russian conditional conjunctions, which were still known in Muscovy in the preceding

---

[1] For судить. The hard ending is typical of this document.

century, have lapsed, and their place is taken by буде(ть), which had entered official Muscovite usage in the fifteenth century[1] (e.g. *Pis'mo Ivana IV dumnomu dvorjaninu V.G. Grjaznomu-Il'inu*, 1574: а будеть станишь за гордость на крестьянство, ино Христосъ тебѣ противникъ 'and if in your pride you should go against Christianity, then may Christ be against you'; *Ulož.*, 1649: а будеть кто на кого похвалится лихим дѣлом 'if anyone should boast to another of a wicked deed'). It is also at this time that есть ли (> если) and ежели 'if' (cf. оже ли in *Russkaja pravda*) appear (e.g. *Pis'mo Petra Velikogo F. M. Apraksinu*, 3. i. 1707: ежели неприятель похочеть 'if the enemy should desire'). By the nineteenth century если prevails as it does today.

500. This record of vicissitudes in the use of a subordinative conjunction from the eleventh to the present century is intended here to illustrate the gradual changes in the 'symbolization' of a semantic category. Other conjunctions, for instance донелѣ же 'while', яко 'that', коли 'when', illustrate the same tendency, for all three had become obsolete by the seventeenth century, when they were replaced by пока (< покамѣста), что, and когда respectively.

501. Another set of subordinative words is constituted by the relative or anaphoric pronouns иже–юже–яже 'who, which', that figure in the early ecclesiastical writings and are gradually confused without evolving a common invariable form in compensation (e.g. *Chronika Georgija Amartola*, 13th–14th cent.: тѣмь и диктатор нарицаються юже юсть сказаюмо юдино-властитель 'therefore he is called dictator, which means autocrat';[2] *i Nov. let.*, 13–14th с.: языци незнаюмі их же добрѣ никто же не вѣсть 'unknown peoples about whom no one knows anything precisely'; *Kir. Tur., Slovo na antipaschu*, 14th cent.: образъ имуще ветхаго закона, иже завѣща б(о)гъ въ Югуптѣ Моисѣюви 'having the likeness of the Old Testament which God bequeathed to Moses in Egypt').

502. Parallel to the ecclesiastical иже–юже–яже we have the native Russian use of the interrogatives кто 'who', чьто 'what' as anaphoric relatives. Examples of this use go back to the

---

thirteenth century, but they are then sporadic like the anaphoric use of который 'which of two' (e.g. *Nov. gram.*, 1264–5: а что княже брат твои ... дѣялъ насилиɪє на Новѣгородѣ 'and the wrong that your brother, O Prince, did to Novgorod'). The relative use of all three is the origin of their subsequent anaphoric usage. Кто and который have survived to this day as anaphoric relatives. Что was lost in official prose (R. *delovoj jazyk*) in the seventeenth century after который had prevailed over the short-lived кой (cf. *Sudebnik*, 1589).

503. But from the beginning the use of the anaphoric relative pronoun as a declinable form had a rival in the use of the declinable participles which entered Old Russian along with it. We have already seen the use of participles as relatives in previous illustrations and shall limit ourselves here to a quotation from the *Žitije Nifonta* (1219), viz. и на пути томь стояху мужи чьрни велици въоружени, копия дьржаще в руку и стрѣжаху путь тъ, не дадуще никому же миновати 'and beside that road stood huge black men armed, holding spears in their hands and guarding that road (and) not allowing (lit. giving to) anyone to pass by'. Here the participles дьржаще 'holding' and дадуще 'giving' function as иже дьржатъ 'who hold' and иже дадутъ 'who give' respectively. The preference for participial constructions ultimately led to the obsolescence of the old borrowed anaphoric pronouns, for which we find the modern paradigm of который in the seventeenth century (e.g. *Ulož.*, 1649: о измѣнничьихъ дѣтехъ, которые жили отъ измѣнника въ роздѣле 'concerning the children of traitors who have lived apart from the traitor').

504. Besides participles and the anaphoric relative pronoun the old language made use of appositions (e.g. *1 Nov. let.*, 13–14th c.: выведе княгыню свою к себе дъчерь Мьстиславлю 'he had his princess, the daughter of Mstislav, brought in'; *Ipat., c.* 1425: в то же время С(вя)тославичь Игорь, внукъ Олговъ поѣха из Новагорода 'at the time Igor' Svjatoslavič, grandson of Oleg, rode out of Novgorod'; Ilarion, *Slovo o zakone i blagodati*, 16th cent.: благословенъ господь богъ Іизраилевъ, богъ христіанескъ 'blessed be the Lord God of Israel, the Christian God'). This device was carried to excess in the royal documents of the Muscovite period, for instance, in the correspondence between

Ivan IV and Kurbskij, and in the later imperial decrees of the eighteenth and nineteenth centuries. In moderation it still occurs as a syntactic feature of imaginative works.

505. Parallel to this device is parataxis, which may be illustrated in the older language by и поидемъ поищемъ мужь своихъ (*1 Nov. let.*, 13–14th c.) 'let us go (and) look for our husbands', and пророци, патриарси трудившеся, в раистѣи почиваютъ жизни (*Kir. Tur.*, *Slovo na antipaschu*, 14th cent.) 'prophets (and) patriarchs rest in paradise after their labours'. At a later stage the absence of a connective, whether between subjects or between verbs, is made into a stylistic device especially in the nineteenth and in the present century: parataxis is now no longer a mark of primitiveness but of cultivation (e.g. Puškin, *Brat'ja razbojniki*, 1822: Душа рвалась къ лѣсамъ и волѣ, / Алкала воздуха полей 'My soul longed for the woods and freedom, / Thirsted for the air of the fields'; M. Bulgakov, *Belaja gvardija*, 1927: тревожно в городе, туманно, плохо 'it is disturbing in the town, foggy, bad'; Ju. Galič, *Zolotyje korabli*, 1927: на пристани . . . шумит, галдит, переливается толпа 'at the landing place the crowd is noisy, boisterous, moving to and fro').

506. We shall now examine specific features of Russian syntax, and then some which we have already considered synchronically (§§ 236–51). The appositional nominative case and the appositional accusative occur in the literature of fourteenth- and fifteenth-century Russian (e.g. nom.—*Duchovnaja kn. Ivana Kality*, 1327–8: ты имъ будешь печалникъ 'thou shalt be their custodian'; *Lavr.*, 1377: я живъ не иду из своеѣ волости 'I will not leave my country alive'; а вѣ ему будевѣ местники 'and we two will be his avengers'; acc.—*Lavr.*, 1377: тебе бо имуще помощницю 'because of having thee as helper (fem.)'; не лѣнива бо мя богъ сотворилъ 'for God had not made me idle'; *Ilar.*, 16th cent.: сынъ твой Георгий егоже створи господь намѣстника по тебѣ 'thy son, Georgij, whom the Lord made thy successor after thee').

507. This construction had a potent rival in the predicative instrumental, which was used at first, however, in the pluperfect tense (e.g. *1 Nov. let.*, 15th cent.: бѣ бо у Ярополка жена Грикинѣ, бяше была прежде черницею 'for Jaropolk had a Greek wife who was formerly a nun'), but was subsequently extended to the other tenses (e.g. ibid.: и самъ царемъ ста 'and became tsar himself'). In the sixteenth and seventeenth centuries the predicative instrumental displaced not only the nominative but the accusative in appositional use. In the eighteenth century the extension of this construction was aided by the influence of Ukrainian and Polish practice. In Lomonosov's time it was considered to be obligatory with быть 'to be' (e.g. D. I. Fonvizin: я теперь былъ свидѣтелемъ пресмѣшныя сцены 'I was just now witness of a very funny episode'). The preference of the instrumental to the nominative predicate was partly due to a desire to avoid formal coincidence.

508. The nominative as object of an infinitive, which is characteristic of some north Russian dialects today (e.g. земля пахать 'to plough the ground', печка истопить 'to heat the stove', живая вода достать 'to get living water'), is a construction with a long history. It is found, for instance, in *Russkaja pravda* (*c.* 1282) (e.g. уставиша . . . взяти гривна кунъ 'they fixed . . . the fine at one mark in money'; даи богъ исправити правда новгородская 'may God (help us) to carry out the law of Novgorod') as well as in some writs of earlier date (e.g. *Nov. gram.*, 1270: а та грамота княже дати ти назадъ 'and this writ, O Prince, thou art to return'). This construction continued to be used down to the seventeenth century (e.g. *Mos. gram.*, 1601: и наша царская жалованная грамота велѣти имъ дати 'and it has been ordered to give them our imperial charter'; *Učen.*, 1647: торговля ему . . . надобно вѣдати 'he ought to know . . . about trade'; *Ulož.*, 1649: и ему та мельница строити волно 'and he is free to build that mill'). By the eighteenth it had become obsolete in the literary language.

509. Allative force is conveyed in Old Russian by a verb of motion combined with the accusative or the dative without a preposition (cf. *Lavr.*, 1377: поиде ко тьсту своему Киевъ 'he went to Kiev to his father-in-law'; и приде Холмъ 'and came to Cholm'; Глѣбъ же вниде Черниговъ 'Gleb, however, entered Černigov' with си же Ольга приде Киеву 'the same Olga, however, came to Kiev'; но пришедъ Смолинску и поимъ вои 'but coming to Smolensk and collecting troops'). Other constructions of this kind are found with prepositions, the accusative with въ 'into' and the dative with къ 'to' (e.g. *Lavr.*, 1377:

Володимеръ вниде в Киев 'Volodimer entered Kiev'; поиде к Мурому 'went to Murom'). There would appear to have been some difference between the two varieties of dative usage, as they occur side by side in the *Povest' vremennych let* (Laur. MS, 1377) and especially in the 'First Novgorod Chronicle', whose manuscript, as we know, is of a much earlier date. Study of them enables us to conclude that the pure dative construction was illative, i.e. it was used to mean 'into a place', whereas the prepositional dative was allative and meant 'into the neighbourhood of'.

510. The genitive object, a well-known feature of Slavonic syntax, is found in eleventh- and twelfth-century Russian texts and continues to be used down to the present time. It is illustrated by several examples in *Russkaja pravda* (e.g. а головника не ищють 'and they do not seek the murderer') and in the Laurentian MS of the *Povest' vremennych let* (e.g. и не бѣ двора идеже не горяще 'and there was not a house that was not burning'). A relaxation of this usage occurs in the seventeenth century in which we find the genitive and negative coexisting with nominative and infinitive (cf. *Р.Р.А.*, блинъ не клинъ, брюха не росколеть 'a pancake is not a wedge and will not split the paunch' with ibid., на чюжои ротъ не пугвица нашить 'you cannot sew a button on another's mouth'). Instances of the use of the accusative as the object of a negated infinitive as well as of a negative finite verb are frequently met with in the late nineteenth and especially in the present century.[1]

511. The instrumental, as in Modern Russian, could express the local meaning of 'by way of' or 'through' (cf. *1 Nov. let.*, 13–14th c.: Мьстиславъ же поиде Серегеремъ 'Mstislav, however, went by way of Lake Seliger' with the modern idiom итти лесом 'to go through the woods'). Between the thirteenth century and modern times we find this construction often used in folk-songs (cf. A. F. Gil'ferding, *Onežskije byliny*, 1873: скакалъ его добрый конь стѣною городскою 'his good horse galloped through the town walls' with the variant скакали кони богатырскіе/черезъ стѣну городовую 'the heroic steeds galloped over the town walls').

[1] Cf. Z. Uglitsky, 'Accusative and Genitive with Transitive Verbs preceded by a Negative in Contemporary Russian' (*SEER* xxxiv. 83, London, 1956, pp. 377–87).

512. The pure locative, which has become the later, exclusively prepositional case, is a characteristic of Russian in the eleventh and twelfth centuries. In the fourteenth-century Laurentian MS this locative is quite common in indicating place (e.g. Бѣлгородѣ затворися Мстиславъ Романович 'Mstislav Romanovič shut himself up in Belgorod'; поиди сяди Кыевѣ 'go take the throne in Kiev'; бысть пожаръ великъ Кыевѣ городѣ 'there was a great fire in Kiev town'; (цьрковь) иже стоить до сего дне Тмутороканѣ '(the church) which stands to this day in Tmutorokan''), and its 'transferred' temporal use is even more frequent (e.g. ibid.: томь же лѣтѣ приде Мстиславъ 'Mstislav came the same year'; идоша веснѣ на половцѣ 'they set out against the Polovecians in the spring'). In course of time prepositional constructions began to compete with these and finally ousted them (e.g. *Pskov. sud. gram.*, 16th cent.: а кто с кимъ побьется во Псковѣ 'whoever shall fight with another in Pskov'; *Af. Nik.*, 16th cent.: в Бедере ж торгъ на кони 'there (is) a horse-market in Beder' (Bidar)'; *Kot., c.* 1664: покупалі мѣдь на Москвѣ 'they would buy copper in Moscow'; учинить в Москвѣ смуту 'to foment trouble in Moscow').

513. The repetition of prepositions with governed words was, as we have remarked, an idiosyncrasy of Old Russian. This practice continued throughout the Middle Ages (e.g. *Nov. korm.*, *c.* 1282: а за тиунъ за огнищный 'and for a house steward'; *Nov. gram.*, 1301: поклон от князя от Михаила к отьцю ко вл(ады)це 'greetings from Prince Michail to my father the bishop'; *Kal.*, 1327–8: а чт(о) остало из моихъ судовъ из серебрьныхъ 'and what is left of my silver plate'). In the seventeenth century we have found examples in the 'Legal Code' (1649) of Tsar Alexis (e.g. с литовскими и с немецкими с порубежными людями живутъ смежно 'they live side by side with the Lithuanian and the German frontier folk'; *Avv.*, 1672–3: скаску имъ тутъ з бранью з большою написалъ 'here I wrote for them a report with much cursing'). By the early nineteenth century we meet with only literary imitations of the construction (e.g. Puškin, *Skazka o medvedice*, 1831: что изъ лѣсу, изъ лѣсу изъ дремучаго 'out of the forest, out of the forest, out of the dark forest').

514. The usage seems to have been emphatic rather than

pleonastic, and it is paralleled by the repetition of conjunctions (e.g. *Nov. gram.*, 1264–5: на цѣмь то цѣлова и дѣди и о(ть)ци и от(ь)ць твои Ярославъ 'our grandfathers and fathers and thy father, Jaroslav, took the oath on this (cross)'). Both features are combined in such an example as учнутъ въ золото или въ серебро мѣшати мѣдь и олово и свинецъ 'will begin to mix copper, tin, and lead with gold and silver' (*Ulož.*, 1649). After the seventeenth century these redundancies became obsolete, and they do not occur even in the modern dialects.

515. The post-position of the attribute or epithet, which we have noted in the eleventh century as a feature of Old Church Slavonic, was resorted to occasionally under the influence of that language in Russian secular documents, especially those with an ecclesiastical colouring, for instance in the 'Mstislav-Vsevolod Writ' of *c.* 1130. From the thirteenth century we find this influence present down to the end of the eighteenth, when Karamzin and his school established the modern usage of pre-position.

516. The use of pre-positive adjectives begins early, indeed it is obligatory with some adjectives at the very outset (e.g. три гривьнѣ 'three marks', великый къназь 'grand prince', старая правьда 'old law', грѣшьный рабъ 'sinful servant', вѣсьный товаръ 'heavy goods', дикая вира 'community fine', вьси новьгородьци 'all Novgorodians'), but the Graeco-Bulgarian practice of placing the possessive adjectives after their substantives seems to have taken a stylistic hold (e.g. *Lavr.*, 1377: пусти дружину свою домови 'sent his retinue home'; *Pskov. sud. gram.*, 16th cent.: ино мужу ея владѣти тою отчиною 'then her husband shall have that patrimony'). Already in the sixteenth century we find pre-position of the possessive adjective (e.g. *Pskov. sud. gram.*, 16th cent.: до своего живота только 'only while he lives'; *Af. Nik.*, 16th cent.: на свой ч(е)стный празд-никъ 'on his holy day'; *Ulož.*, 1649: сверхъ своих запасовъ 'in addition to their supplies'), and during the seventeenth century only authors like the archpriest Avvakum use the post-positive attribute occasionally, whereas secular writers like Kotošichin normally prefer pre-positive usage (cf. *Avv.*, 1672–3: по сем мати моя отъиде к богу в подвизѣ велицѣ 'after that my mother passed away to God in great devotion' with *Kot.*, *c.* 1664:

думныхъ и у ближнихъ людей и у иныхъ чиновъ . . . обычай
таковъ 'this is the manner . . . of counsellors and of confidants
and of other ranks').

517. The structure of the definite adjectives has been considered
elsewhere (§ 209), and their presence in Old Russian made for
specialization of the short and the long sets of adjectives. The
original use of the long or definite types, which today are paralleled in form and origin by Baltic—Lithuanian and Latvian—
counterparts of similar structure (cf. OR добръ-и 'the good'
with Lith. *geràs-is*, Latv. *laba-is*—'id.'), may be divined from
present-day Baltic practice as that of determination or 'articulation', i.e. the use of these adjectives as adjectives with an article.
This usage may be seen in Old Russian, for instance in the
colophon to the 'Ostromir Gospels' (1057), where the indefinite
adjective is contrasted with the definite (e.g. мънога же лѣта
даруи б(о)гъ сътяжавъшуму Е(ван)г(е)лие се на утѣшение
мъногамъ д(у)шамъ кр(ь)стианьскамъ 'may God grant many
years to the one who commissioned these Gospels for the comfort of many Christian souls'). Here the definite adjective
сътяжавъшуму 'to the one who commissioned' singles out the
person who ordered the copying of the *evangeliarium* (Gospel
readings), whereas the indefinites мънога 'many' and мъногамъ...кр(ь)стианьскамъ 'many Christian' have a general significance. Again in the 'Svjatoslav Miscellany' (1073) we read
in the colophon великый въ князьхъ князь Святославъ 'the
great prince among princes, Prince Svjatoslav', which isolates
Prince Svjatoslav from among others and gives him 'definiteness'. And again in the marginalia to the 'Novgorod Menaeum
for September' (1095) Dŭmka refers to himself as азъ грѣшьный
рабъ б(о)жий, недостойный 'I, the sinful and unworthy servant
of God', i.e. by the same morphological process of 'definition' or
'determination'. The use of the definite forms was rapidly and
steadily extended, so that we find them competing with the
indefinite forms on their own ground, viz. in attributive function, especially in proper adjectives, which by their character
are definite (cf. *Mst.*, *c.* 1130: русьску землю 'land of Rus'' with
Mst. jev., *c.* 1117: князю новъгородьскуому 'to the prince of
Novgorod' or again Новъгородъ 'Novgorod' (New-castle) with
Новый Тържькъ 'Novyj Toržok' (New-market), where the

first of the two sets of adjectives represents the original function of the adjective in its short or simple form, and the second of the two the 'improper' use of a long or formally composite adjective in the function of the short one.

518. The formal differentiation, which appears to have been intended to express or symbolize the semantic difference between the concepts of definiteness and indefiniteness, or between anaphoric and non-anaphoric usage, was later reinterpreted as the contrast of attributive and predicative relations, and the predicative adjective finally lost its declinability and began to approach the status of adverb (cf. the earlier practice in *Lavr.*, 1377: и плака ся по неи сынъ ея плачемъ великимь 'and her son bewailed her with great wailing'; *1 Nov. let.*, 13th–14th c.: великъ страхъ и тьма бысть 'there was great fear and darkness'; ibid.: на западѣ явися звѣзда велика 'a great star appeared in the west' with the later practice in *Aleksandrija*, 15th cent.: створшему Македоніи великую свободу '(to thee) who gavest Macedonia great freedom'; ibid.: и абіе успе Александръ вѣчнымъ сномъ 'and then Alexander fell into eternal sleep'; *Ilar.*, 16th cent.: хвалитъ же похвальными гласы Римъскаа страна Петра и Павла 'and the land of Rome praises St Peter and St Paul with voice of praise'). By the sixteenth century the definite adjective was mostly in evidence as an epithet (e.g. *Dom.*, 16th cent.: а рыбу всякую, и свѣжую и длинную осетрину 'and all sorts of fish and the fresh and long sturgeon'; *Peresv.*, 16th cent.: Магмет салтанъ самъ былъ философъ[1] мудрый 'Sultan Mahomet himself was a wise philosopher').

519. The modern use of the definite form was due to morphological as well as to semantic considerations; for both the possessive and the superlative adjectives were definite: moreover the presence of -мь in the nominal declension lent itself to confusion with the short indefinite form (cf. indef. instr. sg. добрѣмь < добръ 'good' with def. добры(и)мь 'with the good'). In the sixteenth and seventeenth centuries the modern Russian usage already prevailed, although even in the eighteenth century poets still freely use the indefinite forms as definites. Some adverbialized syntagmata with indefinite or short forms of the

---

[1] This anticipates an orthographic vagary of Peter the Great.

adjectival epithet still survive (e.g. среди бела дня 'in broad day-light', от мала до велика 'great and small'). But the specialization of the indefinite adjective in predicative function is not absolute, because we find modern syntagmata such as стол белый (деревянный) 'the table is white (wooden)' for бел (деревянен) where the adjectives are qualitative. Definite par-ticiples, moreover, are also used predicatively rather than the corresponding indefinites, although these, as we have found, could be used even as epithets in the eighteenth century (cf. *Sum.*, 18th cent.: и ломитъ такъ какъ вѣтеръ бунтующъ многи дни 'and breaks like the blustering wind for many days' with Mod.R. та не танцующая 'she over there does not dance').

520. The Old Church Slavonic dative absolute construction, which has parallels in both modern Baltic languages, was a literary device in Old Russian which has not survived to modern times. The essence of the construction is an elliptical use of a substantive and an active participle in concord in the dative case to express the sense of a temporal or causal clause. The choice of the dative rather than of the genitive as in Greek in this absolute construction and the presence of a dative absolute in Baltic might suggest a native origin; but this granted, the use of the construction in Old Church Slavonic was obviously of Greek inspiration, and its employment in Old Russian was the outcome of borrowing. Eleventh-century Russian monuments from the 'Ostromir Gospels' onwards illustrate it (e.g. *Ost.*, 1057: Изяславу же князу тогда прѣдрьжящу обѣ власти 'Prince Izjaslav then ruling both principalities'). Later manu-scripts down to the nineteenth century provide further illustra-tions. Up to the fourteenth century the construction is generally used correctly, but manuscripts from that time indicate that it has become archaic by distorting it or introducing irrelevant elements into it (cf. *Lavr.*, 1377: Аньдрѣеви же немогущу супро-тивити имъ 'as Andrej could not resist them' with ibid.: идучи ми сѣмо 'as I was on my way here', where the participle is in the nominative instead of being in the dative case, and with F. Gribojedov, *Stepennaja kniga*, 17th cent.: а егда же сему . . . великому князю . . . преставльшуся 'and when this . . . grand prince . . . died', where егда 'when' is redundant). Lomonosov was willing to accept certain remnants of this now obsolete construction and to use them judiciously in 'elevated verse' (*vysokije stichi*), and we find it used by Radiščev (e.g. *Put.*, 1790: еѣдущу мнѣ изъ Едрова 'as I was on my way from Jedrovo') and even by Žukovskij (e.g. *Ceiks i Gal'ciona*, 1819: кругомъ взгроможденному морю 'the sea being piled up around').

521. Another feature of Russian syntax involving the presence of participles, this time the passive varieties, survives in the northern dialect as well as in Ukrainian.[1] This is the use of the neuter passive participles with either a nominative or an accusative complement. The prototypes of the construction occur in the eleventh century (e.g. *Svjat.*, 1073: медъ дано бысть богомь 'honey it was given by God'; *Nov. gram.*, 1314: а что головы поимано по всеи волости новъгородьской, lit. 'and that persons it was apprehended over the entire territory of Novgorod'). The construction appears to have been known in the sixteenth century (e.g. *Dom.*, 16th cent.: не богатествомъ жито з добрыми людьми, lit. 'not through riches it is lived with good people'; а остатки сверчено и связано, lit. 'and the remnants it was twisted and bound'). In our last example here we find the nominative or accusative case with an incongruent passive participle. This tallies with our eleventh-century example медъ (nom.) дано бысть богомь 'honey was given by God' and our fourteenth-century one а что головы (acc.) поимано по всеи волости новгородьскои 'and that persons were apprehended over the entire territory of Novgorod'. It is difficult on purely formal grounds to decide here which case is intended. Comparison with the nominative-with-infinitive construction may lead us to favour the interpretation of the nominal complement as nominative. But let us examine some later developments of the construction. In Kurbskij's story of the capture of Kazan (in *Istorija o velikom knjaze Moskovskom*), written in the late sixteenth century, we read: половину войска пѣшого штурму послано 'half the infantry were ordered to storm' and подкопомъ воду отнято 'and the water was removed by sapping', in which an obviously accusative 'object' seems to depend on the semantics of the neuter passive participle. This construction also occurs in Kotošichin's 'Russia under Tsar Alexis' (*O Rossiji v carstvovanije*

---

[1] For a detailed discussion of this construction see W. K. Matthews, 'Lithuanian Constructions with Neuter Passive Participles' (*SEER*, xxxi. 81, London, 1955, pp. 350–71).

Alekseja Michajloviča, c. 1664); for instance: а для нынешние Полские и Свейские войны збирано ... дватцатую деньгу 'in the present Polish and Swedish wars ... the twentieth part was collected'. The use of accusative with neuter passive participles appears only in writers who had western 'affiliations', as the construction is known in Polish, Ukrainian, and Lithuanian. Nevertheless, present-day north Russian dialects also show a characteristic use of it even with intransitive verbs (e.g. у него уехано 'he went away', жененосъ то было 'he had married'), and this use seems to derive from the seventeenth century (e.g. *Pamjatniki smutnogo vremeni*[1]: а у меня де уже говорено з Григорием з Микулиным 'and I, he says, have already spoken with Grigorij Mikulin'; *Gramoty Stepana Razina*, 17th cent.[2]: а съ калмыками де у нихъ помиреносъ же 'and it seems they have already made it up with the Kalmyks').

522. In the domain of the finite verb we have already examined the various devices by which Old Russian expresses future time (§ 454) and have now to trace their development. We have the auxiliary verb бѫдѫ in Old Church Slavonic; but Old Russian, as we know, did not favour this and normally preferred a selection of verbs of full meaning with auxiliary function, viz. хотѣти, имѣти, three compounds of -чяти, and стати. Alongside the use of these auxiliaries we have the present tense used as a future (§ 454), and this is found as late as the fourteenth century (e.g. *Lavr.*, 1377: что ради губивѣ дружину межи собою 'why should we destroy each other's forces?'). Parallel to such usage we have the use of the future auxiliaries (e.g. *Lavr.*, 1377: аще не идеши, то же имуть створити намъ 'if thou dost not go, they will do likewise to us'; аще ли не хощеши створити 'if thou wilt not do this'; *Ipat.*, *c.* 1425: како я хочю молвити 'as I shall tell'). These could combine also with prefixated verbs (e.g. *Lavr.*, 1377: Но хочю вы почтити наутрия предъ людьми своими 'but I will honour you tomorrow before my people'). The auxiliaries of the future tense for their part naturally had the force of verbs of full meaning when they were used independently. In due course a third mode of expressing future time stood revealed in the presence of prefixated verbs

---

[1] Cf. *Pamjatniki drevnej russkoj pis'mennosti, otnosjaščijesja k Smutnomu vremeni*[2], St Petersburg, 1909.

[2] Cf. A. Popov, *Materialy dlja istorii vozmuščenija Stepana Razina*, Moscow, 1857.

without the aid of auxiliaries (e.g. *Lavr.*, 1377: да аще одолѣеши ты, то возмеши имѣнье мое 'and if thou winnest thou shalt take my possessions'). Later development shows that as the aspectual force of prefixes became more apparent with loss of the simple past tenses, the perfective present became the new future tense. Along with this the future auxiliary буду came into use, probably through the influence of Polish and White Russian. It is found sporadically in the sixteenth century (e.g. *Dom.*: ино уже вдвое будеши платити 'then thou wilt have to pay double'; *Peresv.*: крѣпко будет за вѣру христианскую стояти 'shall stand firmly for the Christian faith') and becomes common in the seventeenth and the eighteenth. We find it particularly in the works of Russians who had had contacts with the West (cf. P. I. Potjomkin, *Statejnyj spisok*, 1667: а указу имъ королевского ожидать будетъ много время 'but they will have to wait a long time for the royal decree'; F. Prokopovič, *Slovo pochval'noje o flote rossijskom*, 1720: долженъ будетъ славити 'shall have to praise' with *Ulož.*, 1649: кто . . . учнетъ мыслити на государьское здоровье злое дѣло 'whoever shall conspire to do an evil deed against the sovereign's well-being'; Avv., *Kniga besed*, 17th cent.: иконники учнуть Христа в Рожествѣ з бородою писать 'icon-painters will begin to paint Christ at Christmas with a beard'). The modern auxiliary of the future tense is буду, but the competition of aspect as well as of other auxiliaries (e.g. стать 'to become') restricts its use (e.g. M. Lermontov, *Kazač'ja kolybel'naja pesnja*, 1840: стану я тоской томиться 'I shall fret with grief').

523. The obsolescence of the imperfect and the aorist was a gradual process which began in the twelfth century with the competitive development of the perfect tense and the inroads of aspect. We recollect the use of the perfect without the copula in the 'Tmutorokan' Inscription' of 1068, viz. Глѣбъ князь мѣрилъ мо(ре) по леду 'Prince Gleb measured the sea on ice', and the same syntagma, docked in the same way, in the 'Mstislav-Vsevolod Writ' of *c.* 1130, viz. а язъ далъ рукою своюю 'and I have given with my own hand'. The first of these is tied to a date and functions as an aorist; the second has as obviously the sense of a perfect. In the thirteenth and fourteenth centuries we find imperfects and especially aorists in plenty in the chronicles (e.g. *Lavr.*, 1377: собралися лучшие мужи, иже дерьжаху Деревьску землю 'the leading men gathered who enjoyed authority in the land of the Derevljane'), and sometimes aorist and perfect occur side by side (e.g. ibid.: кто въ Киевѣ нача первѣе княжити и откуду руская земля стала есть 'who began first to rule in Kiev and how the land of Rus' came into being'). The contrast between the 'pastness' of the aorist and the links of the perfect tense with the present comes out clearly in the above examples, which may be supplemented by the following: в се же лѣт(о) рекоша дружина Игореви: отроци Свѣньлжи изодѣли ся суть оружьемъ и порты, а мы нази 'in this year the young men said to Igor': Sveinald's men have arrayed themselves in armour and clothing, but we are naked'. The comparatively tenacious aorist is found even in reported dialogue, which would seem to lend support to the assumption that it was also familiar to the spoken language. We find it in the thirteenth and fourteenth centuries in monuments written outside the pale of Church Slavonic influence such as the 'Legal Code' (*Russkaja pravda*) and the writs. These in their extant form all originate in Novgorod, whose conservative tradition is found even in writs of the North Dvina region (*Dvinskaja zemlja*); for instance: се купи игуменъ Василеи 'the abbot Vasilij bought this' (*Dvinskaja gram.*, 15th cent.).[1] Nevertheless, it would seem that the aorist, not to say the less robust imperfect, had become an archaism by the fourteenth century, as is shown by the confusion of the two tenses (e.g. *Nov. gram.*, 1372: а на семъ повелѣше весь Новъгородъ Юрью и Якиму миръ взяти съ кн(я)з(е)мь с Михаиломъ 'and hereby all Novgorod ordered Jurij and Jakim to make peace with Prince Michail', where повелѣша seems to have been intended) and the competition of the perfect (e.g. *Lavr.*, 1377: лютый звѣрь скочилъ ко мнѣ на бедры и конь со мною поверже и б(ог)ъ неврежена мя съблюде 'a wild beast (panther) sprang on to my hips and threw me down with my horse, and God preserved me uninjured'). The survival of these archaic tenses, especially of the aorist in one form or another, is attested not only by the correspondence between Ivan IV and Kurbskij in the late sixteenth century but by the private papers of Peter the Great at

[1] S. N. Valk (ed.), *Gramoty Velikogo Novgoroda i Pskova*, Moscow–Leningrad, 1949, p. 201.

the turn of the seventeenth, and possibly by the 'interjectional' verbs of later times. The Onega ballads (*byliny* or *stariny*),[1] among others, use the aorist on occasion (e.g. in the pluperfect construction быстъ князь велѣлъ 'the prince had ordered it'), and the modern employment of the 'imperative' as a past tense (e.g. I. Turgenev, *Smert'*, 1851: а онъ возьми да прямо побѣги 'and he went and ran for it') has been interpreted by grammarians like Šachmatov as a fossilized aorist. Šachmatov also presumes that the 'interjectional' verbs of the type of хвать 'grab', глядь 'see' (e.g. A. Puškin, *Skazka o mjortvoj carevne*, 1833: но царевна въ обѣ руки | Хвать поймала 'but the princess caught (the apple) with both hands') are closely connected with the old aorist, although it would seem that the interjectional origin of these verbs is not precluded.

524. The perfect tense, first recorded in the eleventh century, is today the only past tense in Russian. Its participial origin has endowed it with the ability to express gender, and loss of its auxiliary verb, which we noticed in the 'Tmutorokan' Inscription' (1068), has necessitated the use of personal pronouns in the absence of a substantival subject. The original present-tense affiliations of the perfect had given it a semantic bias which was not lost in the sixteenth and seventeenth centuries (e.g. *Kniga Bol'šoj čertež*, 1626: а по сторонамъ того рва обойти нельзя ... пришли лѣса и болота 'it is impossible to skirt that trench ... woods and swamps lie beyond'; ibid., а отъ усть рѣки Пантины, близко отъ Дона, вытекла рѣка Царица и потекла къ рѣкѣ Волгѣ, пала въ Волгу противъ Царицына острова 'and from the mouth of the river Pantina, near the Don, the river Carica issues and flows to the Volga, falling into the Volga opposite Carica island'). Such usage survives in north Russian dialects of the Olonec type and is sometimes found in literature (e.g. Lermontov, *Geroj našego vremeni*, 1839–40: сижу у окна; сѣрыя тучи закрывали горы до подошвы; солнце сквозь туманъ кажется жёлтымъ пятномъ 'I am alone at the window; gray clouds cover the hills to their foot; the sun seems a yellow spot through the mist').

525. After the decline of the simple past tenses in Old Russian

---

[1] *Bylina* is the current literary term; *starina* was used by the ballad-singers. The first in the sense of 'tradition' figures in the 'Lay of Igor'".

the evolution of the composite tenses resulted in the emergence of a double pluperfect of the type есмь былъ пришелъ 'I had come' (lit. 'I have been come') in narrative *passus* in the thirteenth century (e.g. *Lavr.*, 1377: не лѣнива мя былъ створилъ 'he had not made me idle'. This new form had a long spell of use and occurs in the seventeenth century, although curtailed of its auxiliary (e.g. Ivan IV, *Poslanije ko kn. Andreju Kurbskomu*, 1564: а онъ былъ отъ того и отошелъ 'and he had already forsaken that'). In the eighteenth century there is no trace of the construction, except in the formula жилъ-былъ, which is a favourite beginning of folk-tales as 'once upon a time' is of our fairy-tales, and in the 'approximate' particle было 'to be about' (e.g. ibid.; и съ тѣми измѣнники пошелъ было къ Новугороду 'and with these traitors was about to go to Novgorod'; Avv. *Žitije*, 1672–3: на колъ было посадилъ 'he all but planted me on a stake'; I. Turgenev, *Nov'*, 1870: онъ хотѣлъ было пройти мимо 'he was about to go past').

526. Of the three moods of Old Russian the imperative could be expressed as it is today, not only by its specific paradigm but by the use of the infinitive (e.g. *Nov. gram.*, 1262–3: а нѣмцьмъ и г(о)тъмъ гостити в Новѣгородѣ бес пакости 'and the Germans and Gothlanders are to trade in Novgorod without offence'; *Nov. korm.*, c. 1282: а сему платити что у него погыбло 'and this (man) to be recompensed for his loss'). This use is found in Muscovite times (e.g. *Kot.*, c. 1667: и соболей своихъ худыхъ и иные мягкие рухляди в казну не приносить и не обменивать 'and they are not to bring their poor sables and other furs to the treasury for exchange'). It also seems to have 'necessitative' future sense in the older Russian (e.g. *Delo o patriarche Nikone*, 17th cent.: не быти мнѣ слыти патриархомъ московскимъ 'I shall not be known as the patriarch of Moscow'). Even Lomonosov in his grammar (§ 530) considers быть писать 'to have to write' to be a legitimate construction of the literary language. Probably it was an archaism or provincialism in his time. It is found in contemporary proverbs (e.g. сколько ни плакать, а быть перестать 'however much you may weep, you have to stop some time'); and Radiščev, with his literary conservatism, makes use of it in the 'Journey from St Petersburg to Moscow' (1790) by putting it in the mouth of a peasant, viz.

грустно мнѣ будетъ, а быть терпѣть 'I shall be sad, but I shall have to bear it.'

527. The conditional mood in Russian has undergone most change by reducing its auxiliary verb to a particle. This auxiliary, as we have seen (§ 465), was an aorist in form (e.g. быхъ неслъ 'I should have carried'). By the thirteenth century this aorist is sometimes employed tautologically in the composite tenses (e.g. *Mil. jev.*, 1215: аще бы въ Турѣ быша силы были 'if there had been forces in Tur (Tyre)'), and by the fourteenth, with decay of the aorist, we find this form combining with the perfect as a conditional particle (e.g. *Mos. jev.*, 1339: аще бы слѣпи были 'if they had been blind'). This is the modern usage; but it is not general at that time, for we still come across hesitant constructions (e.g. *Duch. kn. Simeona Gordogo*, 1353: а лихихъ бы есте людии не слышали 'and that you might not listen to evil people'). But by the sixteenth century modern usage was firmly established (e.g. *Dom.*, 16th cent.: а въ огородѣ колодязь бы былъ 'and that there should be a well in the orchard'). In the same century, moreover, the particle бы could be used with passive participles and without the copula (e.g. ibid.: и питье бы всякое часто въ ситцѣ бы цѣжено 'and all sorts of drinks should be often strained through muslin'). This device is found later in proverbs (e.g. овцы бы цѣлы, а волки бы сыты 'may the sheep be alive and the wolves unfamished') and in such modern colloquial usage as радъ бы это сдѣлать 'I should be pleased to do this'.

528. The contacts of tense and aspect preceded the recorded annals of Russian, and their interaction may be studied in the course of these. With the disintegration of the past tenses, aspect, 'latent' till then, came into its own in the language and divided verbs into new formal and semantic categories (§ 461). There was and still is disparity between tense and aspect, as they represent different points of view. We have already dealt with the formal side in Chapter VI (§ 226). Here we shall confine ourselves to the semantic.

529. The perfective aspect, generally speaking, is marginal, the imperfective intermarginal; the former draws lines of initiation and completion in an action or process, the latter expresses its duration or continuity. These by right were the respective functions of the twin past tenses, the imperfect being progressive and aorist 'punctual'. But formally, as we have seen, the two tenses did not coincide with the two aspects. These were formally defined mainly by prefixes and occasionally by suffixes, whereas the tenses were primarily formed by suffixes, and the presence of prefixes here was always semantically secondary. The independence of tense and aspect and the priority of tense in Old Russian may be seen in thirteenth- and fourteenth-century manuscripts of the chronicles (cf. impf.—*Lavr.*, 1377: и бяху ловяща звѣрь, бяху мужи мудри и смыслени, нарицаху ся поляне 'and they would hunt wild beasts (and) were wise and sensible men (and) were called Poljane'; with aor.—*1 Nov. let.*, 13–14th c.: тои же осени много зла ся створи, поби мразъ обилье по волости 'that autumn much damage was done, frost destroyed grain all over the country'). Collation of the use of the imperfect and the aorist will show that the imperfect is formed mainly from imperfective verbs and the aorist from the perfective. There are, of course, exceptions to such a generalization (e.g. *1 Nov. let.*, 13–14th c.: а бояре его ѣхаша въ Тферь 'and his boyars rode to Tver'; *Lavr.*, 1377: и по семь собравше кости вложаху въ судину малу и поставяху на путехъ 'and after that, having gathered the bones, they put them in a small vessel and set it by the wayside'), but for the most part the formal connexion between tense and aspect is unmistakable. It may be interesting here to note some of the later changes in the text of the chronicles: the Radziwiłł and Academy manuscripts of the fifteenth century, for instance, replace the word вложаху 'they put' of the Laurentian MS with влачаху 'they dragged' in accordance with the emergent 'rule' that an imperfect tense derives from an imperfective verb. Still later practice shows that the semantic difference of aspect as we have it now took time to evolve. In the sixteenth-century manuscripts we have the use of perfective forms where the imperfective, as we know it, would have been in place (e.g. *Af. Nik.*, 16th cent.: а кто ея хочеть убити, ино у нея изо рта огонь выидеть 'when anyone wishes to kill it, fire issues from its beak'; *Kot., c.* 1667: а доходовъ въ тотъ приказъ ... соберется въ годъ мало болши 1000 рублевъ 'and the revenues of that ministry amount to rather over a thousand roubles a year').

530. The passive voice in Old Russian, as today, utilizes two different modes of expression, viz. the passive participle, which we have considered elsewhere (§ 521), and the reflexive verb (cf. also § 466). This uses the reflexive pronoun ся which was proclitic as well as enclitic in the older language and could occasionally be replaced by the use of the dative form си. The detached use of the reflexive pronoun continues into the seventeenth century (e.g. *Mos. gram.*, 1615: съ воры ся ему не видити 'he must not associate with thieves'). And the alternative dative form of the pronoun is still found in some modern dialects (e.g. садилси 'he sat down' for Lit.R. садился).

531. Old Russian preferred to report direct speech unmodified, and this habit persists down to the middle of the eighteenth century. The chronicles from the thirteenth to the fifteenth century illustrate the usage (e.g. *Lavr.*, 1377: они же рѣша, не едемъ на конихъ ни на возѣхъ 'but they said: we will not go on horseback or in carts'). In the seventeenth century it was still common (e.g. *Delo o patriarche Nikone*, 17th cent.: и противъ той моей отписки писалъ патриархъ съ Микитою, что буду въ Москвѣ 'and in reply to my letter the Patriarch wrote through Mikita that he would be in Moscow'). Western practice, as illustrated by Latin and German in the eighteenth century, introduced oblique speech.

532. Word-order in Old Russian, as in Old Church Slavonic, exhibits considerable freedom. This was partly due to the impingement of various alien influences, notably Greek, as reflected for the most part in Old Church Slavonic, and possibly in Germanic, viz. Scandinavian[1] and Low German. From the sixteenth century we find Russian word-order exposed to Latin and Polish example, then Latin is reinforced by German influence in the late seventeenth and the early eighteenth, and these prevail until the influence of French syntax becomes paramount and decisive in the late eighteenth and the early nineteenth century. Since then a more regulated, but still rather flexible word-order has been used.

533. In the Old Russian simple sentence, as illustrated in eleventh- and twelfth-century manuscripts, the subject precedes the predicate, but this order can be reversed at will (cf. *Nov. min.*, 1095: недостоиныи Дъмъка написахъ кънигы сия 'the

---

[1] Ad. Stender-Petersen and S. Congrat-Butlar, *Anthology of Old Russian Literature*, New York, 1954, p. ix.

unworthy Dŭmka wrote this book' with *Svjat.*, 1076: коньчяшя ся книгы сия рукою грѣшьнааго Иоана 'this book was finished by the hand of sinful Ioan').

534. Epithets precede the qualified word as a rule, but postposition occurs for emphasis (cf. *Lavr.*, 1377: брань славна луче есть мира студна 'a glorious war is better than a shameful peace' with *Chronika Georgija Amartola*, 13th cent.: не дажь бестудному волку хыщьнику внити въ с(вя)тую ц(е)рковь 'do not let the abominable predatory wolf enter thy holy church'). Even the genitive case as a qualifier could precede (e.g. *Ipat.*, *c.* 1425: сбирашеть отъ вѣрхънихъ земль вои 'he was levying troops up country'; *Dom.*, 16th cent.: или которой хоромины кровля гнила или обветшала 'and whichever dwelling has a rotten or weathered roof'). This usage is found in the eighteenth century (e.g. A. A. Matvejev, *Zapisnaja kniga*, 1700–2: всеи Франции высокихъ фамилий дѣти 'the children of aristocratic families in France').

535. At the turn of the seventeenth century the Latin and German habit of placing the verb last in the sentence in accordance with specific rules appears, for instance, in Peter the Great's letter to A. D. Menšikov (1710): в заплату трудовъ своихъ с нами купно причастникомъ былъ 'that you might be a sharer together with us as a reward for your services'; but this construction, though common in Lomonosov, is now foreign to Russian literary practice.

536. Complements normally follow the verb (e.g. *Ipat.*, *c.* 1425: тако нынѣ жалую болши по Игорѣ братѣ моемь 'thus I am now more grieved for my brother Igor''), but here again inversion is possible for emphasis (e.g. Sofonij Rjazanec, *Zadonščina*, 15th cent.: уже погании татарове на поля на наши наступають а вотчину нашю у насъ отнимають 'already the heathen Tartars are overrunning our fields and taking away our patrimony from us').

537. Adverbs normally have great mobility in the sentence, although the qualitative often tend to follow the verb (e.g. *Ipat.*, *c.* 1425: и тако бишася крѣпко 'and so they fought strongly').

538. In the composite and complex sentence the subordinate clause may precede or follow the principal according to the degree of stress placed upon it and according to its situation in the sentence (e.g. *Lavr.*, 1377: идущю же ему опять, приде къ Дунаеви, възлюби мѣсто и сруби градокъ малъ 'while on his way back he reached the Danube, took a fancy to the place, and built a small town'; kn. Andrej Kurbskij, *Epistolija pervaja k carju moskovskomu*, 1563: писано Волмере, граде государя моего, Августа Жигиманта короля, отъ него же надѣюся много пожалованъ и утѣшенъ быти ото всѣхъ скорбеи моихъ, милостію его государскою, паче же богу ми помогающю 'written in Volmer (Latv. Valmiera), in the town of my lord, King August Zygmunt, from whom I hope to receive much favour and comfort for all my sorrows, by his royal grace, and especially God helping me'; M. Lomonosov, *O pol'ze knig cer'kovnych v rossijskom jazyke*, 1757: въ древнія времена, когда Славенскій народъ не зналъ употребленія письменно изображать свои мысли, которыя тогда были тѣсно ограничены, для невѣдѣнія многихъ вещей и дѣйствій, ученымъ народамъ извѣстныхъ; тогда и языкъ его не могъ изобиловать такимъ множествомъ реченій и выраженій разума, какъ нынѣ читаемъ 'in ancient times, when the Slavonic people had no knowledge of writing down their thoughts, which were then strictly confined, because of ignorance of many things and processes known to cultivated peoples, their language could not possess such a multitude of intellectual locutions and expressions as we now have').

XI

LEXICAL CHANGES

539. General. In studying changes of vocabulary in Russian
we may reasonably adopt the two points of view offered to us by
lexical categories and loan-words. These naturally overlap; but
by selection of material we can avoid repetition of examples.
The lexical categories will also have to be selective. This, however, should not make them any the less representative. They
will, moreover, include chiefly vernacular material, although
the presence of loan-words will have to be admitted and even
indicated. The classes of loan-words will be made comprehensive, at least in the enumeration of sources, and the historical
element will accordingly be seen in clearer perspective. Finally,
consideration of the selected material from two points of view
in inevitable sequence should enable us to form a fuller, if more
complex conception of the history of the Russian vocabulary.

I

540. Lexical Categories. The Russian vocabulary of the
eleventh and twelfth centuries was, as we have already indicated (§§ 252–9), a complex of mainly Slavonic elements and
a relatively small proportion of discernible borrowings from
Greek, Germanic (Swedish and German), and Turkic. But the
Slavonic element was by no means uniform, as it included large
numbers of Old Church Slavonic terms, many of them calques
from Byzantine Greek. These, moreover, are recognizable for
the most part by their phonetic features, viz. the presence of
nasal vowels (alien to Old Russian), the groups шт/жд, and
non-pleophonic forms such as лѣ/рѣ, ла/ра for Old Russian
ело/ере, оло/оро. This mixed vocabulary, which may be compared to that of Old French with its Romance basis, Latin and
German loans, and small Celtic deposit, is seen in steady development, but at a slow rate, in the thirteenth century, when
it was in contact with Low German, Medieval Latin, Byzantine
Greek, and forms of Turkic. These linguistic influences affected

it little, because it was engaged in digesting the Church Slavonic element which had disturbed its equilibrium in the tenth and eleventh centuries.

541. The christianization of the country, officially achieved in 988 according to the annalists, had led to the gradual replacement of the pagan terminology, which the chronicles still remembered as archaisms, in the period between the thirteenth and fifteenth centuries (e.g. капище 'heathen temple' < капь 'image', вълхвъ 'sorcerer', pl. чары 'spells', трѣбище 'altar', Перунъ 'god of thunder', Дажьбогъ or Хърсъ 'sun-god', Стрибогъ 'god of winds', Велесъ/Волосъ 'god of cattle'). The Christian terminology, as might be expected, was mainly Greek and introduced words like цьркы (through Germanic) 'church' (cf. OR божьница > Latv. *baznīca*), епископъ 'bishop' (cf. also obsolete бискупъ/пискупъ), иерей 'priest', игуменъ 'abbot', диаконъ 'deacon', евангелие 'Gospels', ересь 'heresy', and many more recognizable ecclesiastical terms which still survive. Other terms, especially of vernacular origin (e.g. божьница 'church', чьрньць 'monk'), have become obsolete.

542. The semi-feudal order of princely Rus', which had replaced a tribal community, began to change with the decay of Kiev, and the earlier social terminology was inevitably modified: бояре/боляре 'boyars' was substituted for the earlier къняжи мужи 'the prince's men', дѣти боярьстии 'younger nobility' or дворяне 'gentry' for дружина 'retinue', отроци or дѣтьскыи 'young men' (also 'court officers') for гридь 'men-at-arms'. According to the *Povest' vremennych let* (cf. Laurentian MS, 1377) the бояре were contrasted with людие 'commoners'. These 'commoners' comprised the горожане 'townsfolk', смьрди 'freemen' and челядь, холопи, or обели[1] (fem. робы) 'serfs', as well as the half-free закупи and наимити. The смьрди were organized in village communities known as вьрви 'communes', which were later called миръ, and they were sometimes collectively responsible for the misdemeanours of a member (e.g. вира дикая, lit. 'alien fine', was a fine paid by the commune for murder committed on its territory). Such a member, known as

---

[1] обель derives from обьлъ 'round'. Cf. Lith. *apvalùs*, Latv. *apaļš* 'id.' The Russian expression обельное холопство 'complete servitude' may be likened to круглый сирота 'complete orphan'.

людинъ, could be an изгои 'outlaw', i.e. one who was outside the 'peace' (гои, миръ) or commune. By the end of the fourteenth century the term смърдъ 'freeman' was replaced by крестьянинъ, an earlier variant of христианинъ 'Christian', to distinguish the Russian peasant from the 'infidels' (cf. Sp. *cristiano* 'Christian', which the Argentinian gaucho had adopted to distinguish himself from the native Indians—*los indios*).[1] In Muscovy at this time the term сельчанинъ 'villager', which goes back to the fourteenth century, was also in local use. By the fifteenth and sixteenth centuries the ascendancy of Moscow led to considerable social and administrative changes, which made names like биричь 'herald', тиунъ 'steward', огнищанинъ 'householder', посадьникъ 'burgomaster', тысячьскыи[2] 'prefect', ябетьникъ 'official', obsolete, and these were recorded in a new terminology. Царь (< цьсарь < Caesar) 'tsar' came into use as an additional title of the Grand Prince of Muscovy, who claimed to be heir to the Byzantine emperors. And his administrative system may be selectively defined by the terms боярская дума 'council of boyars', приказъ 'ministry', дьякъ 'civil servant', работные люди 'artisans', стрѣльцы 'bodyguard'.

543. By this time, too, changes had taken place in the sphere of trade. Not all the old units of currency survived, even with changed values: the гривьна 'mark' and its subdivisions ногата, куна, рѣзана, веверица, which figure in the medieval writs, were replaced in Muscovy by рубль 'rouble' and its subdivisions полтина 'half-rouble' and копейка 'copeck', both of which go back to earlier times. The words гривьна 'necklet, bangle' (< грива 'mane; cf. Skt *grivá* 'neck'), рѣзана (< рѣзати 'to cut, pare'), and рубль (< рубити 'to chop, cleave') imply the existence of a metal coinage, whereas such words as куна, 'marten, marten-pelt', веверица 'squirrel' (cf. Latv. *vāvere*), вѣкъша 'squirrel, squirrel-pelt', and бѣла 'squirrel-pelt', which figures in the 'Lay of Igor'', point to a currency based on furs (OR скора). Although this terminology, as we have learnt, was already archaic in Muscovy, the two bases of the currency— precious metal and fur—had their counterparts there, for beside the metal unit рубль we have the fur unit мордъка 'fur with

[1] Cf. W. H. Hudson, *The Purple Land*, London, 1885.
[2] By *cokan'je* we have the Novgorodian form тысяцькыıй.

head attached', the latter going back to the fourteenth century
(e.g. *Mos. gram.*, 1396: с воза по мордъкѣ 'a mordka from each
wain'). In the sixteenth century грошъ, which is from German
Groschen (cf. E. *groat*), is introduced in a Polish form (viz.
grosz), and копейка, which belongs to the same period, is thought to be
a vernacular diminutive formation from the word копье 'lance',
i.e. the 'lance-coin', because St George with lance in hand was
represented on the coin. The sixteenth-century полушка 'half-
copeck' is also of native origin (< полъ 'half') and represented
the smallest item in the pre-revolutionary coinage. Such a coin
in the thirteenth century was called вѣкъша (e.g. *Nov. prol.*: ни
вѣкоши имуть въ кельѣ 'they have not a farthing in the cell').
Деньги, still the word for 'money', is the plural of деньга 'half-
copeck', a metal coin current in medieval Russia and apparently,
like алтынъ '3 copecks', of Oriental provenance.

544. Like the coinage, the system of weights and measures
suffered some change in process of time. The units of weight
which were used till the revolution have been replaced by the
French metric system. This was a radical change of the sort that
normally takes place in the wake of a political upheaval; but
there were other, much earlier changes which resulted in the
main from gradual development. Пудъ 'pood' (40 Russian lb.)
is recorded in the twelfth century and appears to be of Germanic–Latin origin (cf. L. *pondo* > LG *pund*, cf. E. *pound*). The
High German equivalent of *pund*, viz. *pfunt*, is the source of the
later loan-word фунтъ, which is recorded in the fourteenth
century and may have reached Russian through a Polish source,
if not directly. The Old Russian substantivized adjective
бьрковьскъ (Mod.R. берковец), a weight of ten poods (400
Russian lbs.), has also a Germanic source, viz. the Swedish
place-name Björkö (< OSw. *Biærkö*; cf. § 257).

545. The more tenacious linear measures in the language, all
of them made obsolete by the recent introduction of the metric
system, are, in contrast to the weights, of Slavonic origin. They
include вьрста 'verst' (cf. OCS врьста 'stadium'), originally a
field-measure (cf. L. *vorsus/versus* < *vertere* 'to turn'), and сажень
(cf. OCS сѧжень) 'fathom', which is mentioned in the 'Tmutorokan' Inscription' (1068) and is historically the older of the
two. Сажень/сяжень, it would seem, meant the reach of the

outstretched arms (cf. OR сягати 'to reach') like its English
equivalent (< OE *fæþm* 'embrace'). In the modern language
it represents seven feet and not six like the English fathom. It is
subdivided into three 'ells' (OR локъть, cf. Lith. *uolektìs*), and
the локъть, in its turn, was made up of two 'spans' (OR пядь).
Another subdivision of the сажень was поясъ 'girth', which
measured half a fathom. In modern times these measures of
length were replaced by others. Аршинъ, the third part of a
сажень, appears to have been in common use in the sixteenth
century like the Slavonic вершокъ, one sixteenth of an аршинъ
or approximately two inches. Both of them are found in
Domostroj. The later words футъ 'foot' and дюймъ 'inch' are
eighteenth-century loans from the Dutch, viz. *voet* 'foot' and
duim 'thumb'.

546. The administration of justice in medieval Rus' entailed
the growth of a legal terminology which started from the vocabulary of the civil and criminal code as contained in twelfth-
century writs and the *Russkaja pravda* (*c.* 1282). As time went on
this was amplified by the provisions of the 'law books' from the
manuscript *Sudebnik* of Ivan III (1497) to the printed *Uloženije*
of Tsar Alexis (1649). In the space of several centuries the legal
terminology would naturally undergo changes reflecting modifications in the political and social order. For instance, under
Ivan III the criminal code no longer used вира (cf. OE *wergeld*
'capitis aestimatio'), or урокъ for 'regulation', or соромъ for
'insult'—terms which were current at the turn of the thirteenth
century. And witnesses (OR послуси and видоци) in a litigation (OR тяжа) no longer went ротѣ or на роту to take 'oath'
(OR рота)[1], although послухъ was still used in the fifteenth
century. The word продажа 'fine' retained its original meaning
in the *Sudebnik* of Ivan III and was contrasted with противень
and пошлина 'court fee', while пеня and боранъ came into use
for 'fine'.

Native roots and prototypes were mostly the ground of
later changes in the legal vocabulary: thus свидѣтель 'witness' has a prototype in fourteenth-century свѣдокъ/свѣдьць.[2]

---

[1] Клятва 'oath' figures in the historically tenth-century treaties concluded by
Oleg with the Greeks.
[2] The change of ѣ into и is due to contamination with видѣти 'to see' (cf. OR
зидокъ 'witness').

Much more of this earlier terminology (e.g. воля 'decree', вѣно 'dowry', головьникъ 'murderer', задьница 'inheritance', изводъ 'testimony', мечьникъ 'court officer' (lit. 'sword-bearer'), орудие or съвада 'litigation', поконъ 'statute, law', потокъ 'exile', проказа 'crime', рѣзъ 'interest', рядъ 'contract') had become archaic by the seventeenth century and is meaningless today. But the general terms законъ 'law' (originally 'custom'), судъ 'trial', уставъ 'statute', истьцъ, now only 'plaintiff', and отвѣтьчикъ 'defendant' remain as links with the past, and the wider правьда has become the narrower право, which came in with Polish influence (cf. G. *Recht*).

547. The terminology of trade, already touched on here in connexion with the discussion of weights and measures (§ 544), has a legal aspect, and we shall meet with such early Russian words as гость, варягъ (cf. ON *væringr* 'bodyguard'), and кълбягъ (cf. ON *kylfingr*) 'merchant'(p. 287), the last two showing contacts between ancient Rus′ and Scandinavia. Later купьць 'trader, tradesman' came into use and still survives. Buying and selling took place in the тържъ 'market-place', and this word also meant 'trade' and 'market-dues' and gave rise to a verb тържовати 'to trade'. The result of trading might well be and often was добытъкъ 'profit, estate' or дългъ 'debt'. Товаръ still survives for 'merchandise', but there were other expressions for this, like исто, which have become obsolete.

548. The vocabulary of war, which is closely connected with that of trade, has varied greatly since the earliest words recorded in Old Russian for this institution and its instruments. Рать[1] was the old word for 'war', which occurred at that time mostly as a result of котора or коромола 'feud' (cf. OCS крамола); it had a wider semantic scope than война, the modern word for 'war', as it could also mean 'army' and 'enemy' (OR ворогъ, Mod.R. враг < OCS врагъ; cf. the Germanic пълкъ 'host, campaign'; cf. OHG *folc*). Old Russian пълкъ is still in use today as полк 'regiment' and has therefore narrowed its application. Воинъ 'warrior', the singulative of the ancient plural вои 'host', belongs now to the poetical vocabulary, and воевода 'military leader' has been ousted by titles taken from Western languages.

---

[1] Cf. also боронь (OCS брань) as used in the 'Lay of Igor″.

549. The weapons of war have, as might have been expected, varied a great deal with the inventions and refinements of the centuries, and the words by which they are indicated have either completely disappeared or survive in a semantically different form: an ancient сѣкира 'axe' was replaced by топоръ, an Iranian loan-word apparently, which is still in use for a domestic implement; and щитъ 'shield', бръня 'mail', лукъ 'bow', стрѣла 'arrow', копие/копье 'spear, lance' survived until the wider use of fire-arms in the seventeenth century, when пищаль 'musket' and пушка 'gun' became common currency. The former was replaced by ружьё 'rifle' (cf. OR оружье 'arms'), and the latter widened its meaning to 'cannon'. It is curious, however, that the earlier стрѣляти 'to shoot' (cf. стрѣла 'arrow') has ousted the later палити 'to fire', although this is still used in commands (e.g. пали! 'fire!').

550. Words of material culture have kept pace with time and the evolution of Russian society. Old Russian uses the ancient and tenacious домъ 'house' as well as хоромъ, since obsolete, and дворъ, which had also the sense of 'homestead' and is sometimes qualified by княжь, viz. княжь дворъ 'palace'. This had the synonym теремъ (< Gk τέρεμνον), which was lost in due course and replaced by the derivative дворьць (< дворъ). Subdivisions of the house were клѣти 'rooms', which were called истьбы (cf. OHG stuba, OE stofa 'stove') in the sixteenth century and after that комнаты (< cf. MHG kemenete < Med.L. caminata).

551. Those engaged in husbandry were acquainted with such terms as роля 'field', огородъ 'paddock', рало 'plough', бърть 'bee-hive'. Some of these have become obsolete—роля is now пашня, рало has been replaced by плугъ, бърть may be glossed as пасѣка or пчельникъ, but огородъ is still the modern term for 'orchard'. Animals were kept in хлѣви 'shippons' (cf. Mod.R. pl. хлева). Food for both man and beast was кърмъ, and this word is still used to designate provender for animals. For human food борошьно (cf. OCS крашьно) was also used in Old Russian, but today human food is пища. Clothing was пърты, a plural form which was later to be replaced by the Church Slavonic одежда (cf. R.dial. одёжа).

552. With the advance of material culture new words gradually came into use with the things they represented. These were very often loan-words from other languages, and we have noted some of them already. Here we shall deal with them exclusively as representative of the stages of historical development.

II

553. Loan-words. The growth of civilization in the East Slavonic area is intimately connected with the external relations of its polity, and these are more or less clearly mirrored in the language. At the beginning of the historical period, as we have seen (§§ 253–8), the fundamental vocabulary of Slavonic and Indo-European origin was supplemented by three sets of loan-words—Greek, Germanic, and Turkic; and these sets of loan-words, each of different age and background, represented in eleventh-century Rus' the intersection of the three dominant foci of influence (§ 253).

554. Greek influence, represented by direct loans as well as by numerous calques of Bulgarian origin, prevailed till the early thirteenth century, when Kiev was destroyed by the Tartars (Mongols) and direct contacts with Byzantium were interrupted. Nevertheless, the influx of Balkan Slavs from the fourteenth century onwards reinforced this influence, although its main contribution to the Russian vocabulary had already been made in the tenth and eleventh centuries, at the time when Greek religious culture in a Bulgarian form had been taken over in substance and spirit. The Greek vocabulary included personal names as well as the terminology of the Church and some words of secular culture, among them borrowings from Latin. The Russian vernacular tendency was to substitute initial o for Greek εὐ- (e.g. Овдотья < Εὐδοκία, Остапъ < Εὐστάθις) as well as for ἐ-/έ- (e.g. Олена < Ἑλένη) and ἀ- (e.g. Олександръ < Ἀλέξανδρος), but later 'emendations' established the modern forms Евдокия, Евстафий, Елена, and Александръ. As similar changes are found in Modern Greek dialects (e.g. Ὀλέφθερος < Ἐλεύθερος) it has been argued[1] that they may have influenced the Russian forms; but the supposition is unhistorical, as it is based on late evidence. Greek words with masculine or neuter endings were normally docked (e.g. епископъ

---

[1] A. I. Sobolevskij, *Lekcii po istorii russkogo jazyka*[4], Moscow, 1907, p. 33.

'bishop' < ἐπίσκοπος, ладанъ 'incense' < λάδανον; but cf. nom. Христосъ 'Christ', gen. Христа) in contrast to feminine loan-words (e.g. просфора 'wafer' <. προσφορά, скиния 'tabernacle' < σκηνή). Our last example here shows an 'adaptive' ending of the sort that occurs in neuter substantives borrowed from Greek (e.g. стадия 'stadium' < στάδιον). These ultimately generalized -ия in some cases (e.g. стихия 'element' < στοιχεῖον, епитимия 'confession' < ἐπιτιμία) and palatalized final consonants in others (e.g. тетрадь 'note book' < τετράδιον, фонарь 'street-lamp' < φανάριον). With advance of knowledge we find Greek loan-words revised in form (e.g. *Svjat.*, 1073: гигасъ 'giant' < nom. γίγας later became гигантъ < gen. γίγαντος).

555. The importance of Greek as a source of new culture-words may be realized from the hellenized Latin loan-words that entered Russian at various times in the early period (e.g. миса < 'tureen' < μη(ν)σα < L. *mensa*; костелъ 'church' < καστέλι < L. *castellum*; фортуна 'storm' < φορτοῦνα <. L. *fortuna*).

556. The influence of Germanic languages on Russian was reinforced by direct contact with the Teutonic Knights and the Hanseatic merchants in the East Baltic area from the latter part of the twelfth century onwards. The language of intercourse at this time was Low German, and this came in contact with the language of Novgorod and Pskov, from which Old Russian, in our sense of the term, derives, as well as with that of Polock and Smolensk, which is the source of White Russian. We shall, therefore, quote from the common records in which we find among others the titles провстъ/бровстъ 'provost' (< LG *provest*), фоготь 'judge' (cf. G. *Vogt*), мастеръ (also местерь, мештерь) 'master' (cf. G. *Meister*), ратманъ 'magistrate' (cf. G. *Ratmann*). All these items figure in the Polock and Smolensk writs of the thirteenth century; but others are found in specifically Russian monument (e.g. *1 Nov. let.*, 13–14th c.: рытарь 'knight', cf. G. *Ritter*; *Ipat.*, *c.* 1425: герьцюокъ/гѣрцикъ 'duke', cf. G. *Herzog*). Furthermore, we may mention here, as the representative of another sphere of activity, шпильманъ 'mummer' (cf. G. *Spielmann*), a word which occurs in the 'Rjazan' Nomocanon' (1284). The sporadic occurrence of пискупъ (*Smol. gram.*,

1229) 'bishop' for владыка represents a High German articulation of Low German *biscop* and may have been heard from South German speakers (cf. рытарь as against LG *ridder*).[1]

557. As the writs exchanged between the Germans in Riga and Dorpat (Est. Tartu) and the Russians of Novgorod and Pskov were largely connected with trade, we shall find some names of fabrics of German provenance (e.g. скорлатъ/скарлатъ 'scarlet cloth', ultimately from Gk σκαρλάτον; бархатъ 'velvet' < LG *barchant*; шида 'silk', cf. MHG *sîde*). All these words belong to the fourteenth and early fifteenth centuries, by which time too the influence of the Tartars had made itself felt in the Russian vocabulary.

558. This influence expressed itself mainly in highly specific culture-terms borrowed from Turkic, not Mongolian, sources from the thirteenth to the fifteenth centuries, viz. баскакъ 'official', басма 'seal', тамга 'tribute', ямъ 'posting fee', ярлыкъ 'decree', орда 'encampment', улусъ 'settlement, country', лошадь 'horse', караулъ 'frontier post', аргамакъ 'steed', аламъ 'breastplate', кумызъ (later кумыс) 'fermented mare's milk', башмакъ 'shoe', катуна 'wife', булгакъ 'uproar'. Some of these words need not have entered Russian only in the Tartar (Mongol) period, for study of the thirteenth-century Codex Cumanicus shows that many Turkic loan-words, including some of the above (e.g. *orda* 'horde', *ulus* 'people', *qatun* 'wife, woman', *bašmaq* 'shoe'), were known earlier.

559. In the fifteenth century, with the rise of Muscovy at the expense of Poland–Lithuania and the Golden Horde, the influence of Polish (Lithuanian was a local vernacular which had not been reduced to writing at this time) on Russian began in conjunction with the renewed influence of Medieval Latin, which was an official language in Central and Eastern Europe. Meanwhile the influence of Turkic continued at a slackened pace, because in 1480 Ivan III shook off the Tartar yoke.

560. The polonisms, as we have suggested, were mainly latinisms and they included also a considerable quantity of German words. Their penetration into Russian, we may assume *a priori*,

---

[1] The Low German form appears as рыдель 'sword-bearer' in the fourteenth century and as рында 'bodyguard' in the seventeenth.

was through White Russian and Ukrainian (e.g. аркушъ 'sheet (of paper)' < P. *arkusz* < L. *arcus*; акуратъ 'exactly' < P. *akurat* < L. *accurate*; коштъ 'expenses' < P. *koszt* < G. *Kost* < Med.L. *costare*). The sixteenth century saw a Latin culture flourishing in these areas, and it is by this route that further Latin loan-words reached Muscovy at this period. In the seventeenth century this culture was transplanted to Muscovy itself. Study of the monuments of the 'troubled times' (*smuta*),[1] of Kotošichin's *O Rossii v carstvovanije Alekseja Michajloviča* (*c.* 1664), the *Učenije i chitrost' ratnogo strojenija pechotnych ljudej* (1647), and of others will give us a substantial list of miscellaneous 'Polish' loan-words, none of which, as can be seen, is Polish in origin (e.g. аптека 'dispensary', вахта 'watch', гербъ 'badge', инбирь 'ginger', канцелярія 'chancellery', капитанъ 'captain', карабинъ 'carbine', корета 'carriage', кленотъ 'jewel', майоръ 'major', музыка 'music', мушкетъ 'musket', офицеръ 'officer', панцырь 'mail', пластырь 'plaster', политика 'politics', потентатъ 'potentate', профостъ 'provost',[2] процессія 'procession', рота 'company', салдатъ 'soldier', сержантъ 'sergeant', танецъ 'dance', шпага 'sword', фляга 'flag', ярмарка 'fair'. Many of these are military terms and vividly put us in mind of the hostilities between Poland and Muscovy at this period. Latin influence, in a Central European pronunciation, is to be seen too in the revision of some older loans from Greek like кентавръ 'centaur' and кентръ which now become центавръ and центръ respectively. It also flooded late seventeenth-century Russian literature with administrative, military, naval, geographical, medical, and literary terms (e.g. актъ 'act', инструкція 'instruction', сенатъ 'senate'; дивизія 'division', корпусъ 'corps', фортификація 'fortification'; портъ 'port'; глобусъ 'globe'; ланцетъ 'lancet', фебра 'fever'; наррація 'narration', орація 'oration', фабула 'fable').

561. In most of these areas of meaning the Latin terminology is supported by loan-words from German and Dutch (e.g. бухгалтеръ 'book-keeper'; цейхаусъ 'armoury'; гавань 'harbour', матрозъ 'sailor'; ландкарта 'map').

---

[1] *Pamjatniki drevnej russkoj pis'mennosti, otnosjaščijesja k Smutnomu vremeni*[3], St Petersburg, 1925.
[2] Note the earlier провстъ/бровстъ (§ 556) and the later example of 'popular etymology' прохвостъ.

562. Moreover, under Latin loan-words, we have a number of latinized Greek and even non-Indo-European items which became part of Russian at this time in such domains as architecture (e.g. архитравъ 'architrave', база 'base', глифъ 'glyph'), medicine (e.g. апоплексія 'apoplexy', гангліонъ 'ganglion'), and administration (e.g. амнистія 'amnesty', архивъ 'archives', губернія 'province'). To all this the Polish contribution was indirect and mostly morphematic (e.g. the substantival ending -ія as in апелляція 'appeal' and the verbal ending -овать as in штурмовать 'to take by storm'). Our last example here shows the presence of German again, which accounts also for the longer verbal ending -ировать (e.g. лавировать 'to tack' < G. *lavieren*).

563. Polish itself in the seventeenth century influenced the everyday speech of the Russian aristocracy and townsfolk (e.g. вензель 'seal', мѣшкать 'to dawdle, to dwell', опека 'guardianship', особа 'person', пекарь 'baker'). This Polish contribution, however, was not always Slavonic, for кухня 'kitchen', рисовать 'to draw, sketch', and the now obsolete мусить 'to be obliged' have obviously German roots, and such words as духовенство 'clergy' (cf. G. *Geistlichkeit*), мѣщанинъ 'bourgeois' (cf. G. *Bürger*), обыватель 'inhabitant' (cf. G. *Bewohner*), правомочный 'legal' (cf. G. *rechtskräftig*), are no less obvious calques from German. Polish then served as the vehicle by which Western lexical influence reached seventeenth-century Muscovy.

564. By this time the Turkic loans had been notably increased by other words which had been adopted by Russian in the course of the sixteenth and the early seventeenth centuries, for instance, барышъ 'profit', епанча 'sledge-covering', кабакъ 'inn', колпакъ 'nightcap', колчанъ 'quiver', кушакъ 'belt', набатъ 'alarm signal'. This vocabulary grew in the course of the seventeenth century with the expansion of Muscovy eastwards and southwards into mainly Turkic-speaking territory (e.g. арба 'cart', арканъ 'lariat', балыкъ 'dried sturgeon', бирюкъ 'wolf', изюмъ 'raisins', сундукъ 'coffer', юртъ 'settlement, homestead').

565. The end of the seventeenth century witnessed the introduction of West European words, some of them through German, which was the language chiefly heard in the 'foreign quarter' of Moscow (*Nemeckaja sloboda*). The earlier contributions came from Dutch and English and the later from French and Italian. The Dutch loan-words are chiefly maritime terms and belong in the main to the Petrine Age which was the peak of Western influences. Thereafter, viz. in the eighteenth century, the influence was canalized, being German at first and then French. The French language contributed not only the vocabulary of the *ancien régime* but that of the French Revolution.

566. Peter the Great's interest in ships and naval architecture is reflected in the Dutch and English loan-words, which, nevertheless, sometimes took on a German aspect before they entered Russian (e.g. бугшпритъ 'bowsprit' < D. *boegspriet*; гарпунъ 'harpoon' < D. *harpoen*; крейсеръ 'cruiser' < D. *kruiser*; рейдъ 'roads' < D. *rede*; стаксель 'staysail' < D. *stagzeil*; шкиперъ 'skipper', < D. *schipper*; шлюпка 'sloop' < D. *sloep*; шлюзы 'sluices' < D. *sluizen*; фальшкиль < E. *false keel*; лимберсъ < E. *limbers*). It would appear that by the time the Tsar's interest was at its height the Dutch maritime terms had already acquired European currency, as witness some of our English examples. But the German medium is present for anyone to see, and not only in the phonetic interpretation of English 'false' as 'falsch' but in some of the terms found in Peter the Great's instructions to his ambassadors (March 1697),[1] for instance, gen.-acc. pl. ропшѣлагереѳъ 'rope-ladder makers', машьтъ-макароѳъ 'mast-makers', шѣлюпъ-макароѳъ 'sloop-builders', with which we may contrast стюрманоѳъ 'helmsmen', now the more German-looking штурманъ.

567. The loan-words of the Petrine Age have a practical or applied bent, and they cover, as we have seen, the principal categories of public life—administration, trade, industry, and war. They are a reflection of the rapid progress of europeanization, which, although it had been initiated by Ivan IV, did not reach its culmination in Russia till the early eighteenth century. The pressure of the European vocabulary was so great that even familiar native words were temporarily ousted by their foreign equivalents (e.g. конкетъ 'conquest' < F. *conquête* for завоеваніе; викторія 'victory' < L. *victoria* for побѣда; резольвовать 'to solve' < P.-L. *rezolwować* for рѣшать; трактаментъ

<hr/>

[1] S. P. Obnorskij, S. G. Barchudarov, *Chrestomatija po istorii russkogo jazyka*, ii. 1, Moscow, 1949, p. 85.

'catering' < G.-L. *Traktament* for угощеніе). It will have been noticed that the origin of these words is characteristically diverse, and as we examine the long roll of West European borrowings we rediscover the curious fact that some of them reached their destination in a foreign guise, for not only does German distort the English or Dutch origin of certain borrowed words but Polish may distort German loan-words (e.g. бляха 'metal plate' < G. *Blech*) and French–Italian ones (e.g. ажио 'agio' with ʒ for Italian ʤ).

568. The europeanization of Russian society in the eighteenth century continued at first under the auspices of Polish, which still retained its reputation as an 'aristocratic' language.[1] Under its influence both its vernacular vocabulary and especially its many European loan-words gained entry into early eighteenth-century Russian (e.g. грозба 'threat' for угроза, забобоны 'superstitions' for суевѣрія, звычайный 'customary' for обыкновенный, мода 'fashion', публичный 'public', репутація 'reputation', трупъ 'corpse', факція 'faction', шарфъ 'scarf', шельма 'rogue'). In Peter the Great's letters and papers we occasionally come across such polonisms (e.g. я на то позволилъ 'I permitted that'; которая несомнѣнно прибылью намъ есть 'which is undoubtedly to our advantage').

569. Besides Polish we have German and particularly French as sources of borrowed words in the eighteenth century (e.g. гезель 'mate', галстукъ 'tie', шлафоръ 'dressing-gown', фурманъ 'cabman', желей 'jelly', ливръ 'book', шандалъ 'candlestick', экипажъ 'carriage'). Some of these are enumerated by the historian V. N. Tatiščev as 'superfluous loans', and it will be noted that the more recalcitrant have been forced into the framework of the Russian paradigms (e.g. желей for which the modern language has substituted the invariable желе). Several of these loan-words have since disappeared (e.g. гезель, ливръ, шандалъ) or have assumed another form (e.g. шлафоръ > шлафрокъ).

570. The acquisition of foreign languages may be a form of snobbery, as Tatiščev observed;[2] and study of them for the

---

[1] V. V. Vinogradov, *Očerki po istorii russkogo literaturnogo jazyka XVII–XIX vekov*, Moscow, 1938, pp. 32–33.

[2] *Razgovor dvu prijatelej o pol'ze nauk i učilišč* (1733–41). This was published in Moscow by N. Popov with introduction and indexes in 1884.

purpose of social discrimination was one of the aims of which he accused the 'gentry' (шляхетство).[1] But this was not the only reason for learning them: Peter the Great and I. T. Pososkov[2] both emphasized their value, especially that of German and French, as sources of technological knowledge. Till about 1740 German predominated; but thereafter, especially under Catherine II, with her French bias, French became the first foreign language for educated Russians to study. Moreover, even those Russians, whether townsfolk or country-folk, who had no opportunity to study the language or no ability to master it, developed the habit of interpolating French words and expressions in their talk, and this was sometimes carried to the pitch of mania.[3] The mania began in Petrine times and gave rise to numerous contemporary anecdotes. In the 'Memoirs' (*Zapiski*, 1764–6) of Semjon Porošin, for instance, there is a superfluity of French words, among them имажинировать 'to imagine', кадансъ 'cadence', минодерія 'minauderie', президировать 'to preside', сентиментъ 'sentiment'.[4] By the middle of the century protests were beginning to be made against the abuse of French words and locutions in speech and writing. Porošin himself writes in this connexion to the effect that 'some Russians mix so many French words in their conversation that it seems as if Frenchmen were speaking and using Russian words.' A more determined protest came from those who, like Admiral A. S. Šiškov, cultivated and recommended the cultivation of the 'high style' with its Church Slavonic elements; and there was opposition also from those who were in close touch with the vernacular. But the influence of French on eighteenth-century Russian was subtler than the multiplicity of French borrowings may seem to suggest, for it gave rise also to calques, which incidentally made use of Church Slavonic material (e.g. вліяніе < F. *influence*, повсемѣствованіе < F. *généralisation*, расточеніе < F. *dissipation*, стяжаніе < F. *possession*). Such calques were often ephemeral—thus the second and the last example are now обобщение and имущество respectively—but they were extremely numerous and communicated a distinct

---

[1] Note his use of the Polish term for R. *dvorjanstvo*.

[2] *Zaveščanije otečeskoje* (ed. Je. M. Priležajev), St Petersburg, 1893.

[3] Cf. E. Haumant, *La culture française en Russie* (1700–1900), Paris, 1910.

[4] For others see W. K. Matthews, *The Structure and Development of Russian*, Cambridge, 1953, p. 151.

stylistic flavour to translations. Moreover, they were not confined to single words, but extended to phrases and even sentences (e.g. принять участіе < *prendre part*; проглотить пилюлю < *avaler la pilule*; работать какъ волъ < *travailler comme un bœuf*; со временемъ < *avec le temps*; съ птичьяго полета < *à vol d'oiseau*; отъ всего сердца < *de tout cœur*; рука руку моетъ < *une main lave l'autre*). The abuse of French words and locutions was a marked characteristic of the Sentimental School led by Karamzin. Šiškov in his 'Dissertation on the Old and the New Style in Russian' (*Rassuždenije o starom i novom sloge rossijskago jazyka*, 1803) holds him up to ridicule by quoting examples of the old and the new ('gallicized') style and reproaches the author for using expressions contrary to the genius of the vernacular (e.g. дѣлать вліяніе на разумы < *faire l'influence sur les esprits*).[1]

571. The quarrel between the old and the new continued into the early nineteenth century with Karamzin and Šiškov on opposite sides; but by the 1830's a *modus vivendi* between europeanisms, slavonicisms, and the vernacular vocabulary had been found by Puškin, who became a model to later writers. But borrowing from Western languages, mainly French and German, continued in the domains of scholarship and technology. Puškin's passion for French expresses itself in approval of 'notional' (умозрительныя) gallicisms, 'because they are europeanisms' (европеизмы); but he was not averse to French idiom and in this respect maintained the attitude of his predecessors (e.g. завести далеко < *mener loin*, носить отпечатокъ < *porter l'empreinte*).

572. His contacts and especially those of his successors, Lermontov and L. Tolstoj, with the Caucasus led to an enrichment of the Russian vocabulary with exotic—often Turkic, more seldom purely Caucasian—words (e.g. абрекъ 'brigand' from Adyge; аулъ 'village' from Turkic; джигитъ 'a brave' from Turkic). These were now added in relatively small numbers to the other exotic or 'Oriental' words which came from Persia, Central Asia (mainly Turkic), and Siberia (Altaic and Palaeoasiatic) with the extension of Russian political influence and the annexation of foreign territory.

---

[1] Cf. also V. V. Vinogradov, op. cit., pp. 164–5.

573. Meanwhile the abstract vocabulary of the language multiplied by leaps and bounds in the course of the nineteenth and the present centuries. German idealistic philosophy in the early nineteenth century contributed such words as субъективный 'subjektiv' and объективный 'objektiv', аналитическій 'analytisch', and синтетическій 'synthetisch' as well as міровоззрѣніе 'Weltanschauung', образованіе 'Bildung', очевидный 'augenscheinlich', предполагать 'voraussetzen', самоопредѣленіе 'Selbstbestimmung', цѣлостность 'Ganzheit'. V. G. Belinskij's services loom very large here. Along with philosophical terms, mostly calques, there were others from the sphere of the social and economic sciences which were taken over *in toto*, i.e. along with their formants (e.g. аскетизмъ 'asceticism', мистицизмъ 'mysticism', пауперизмъ 'pauperism', обскурантизмъ 'obscurantism'). Others were partly naturalized (e.g. гуманность 'humaneness', индивидуальность 'individuality', рельефно 'in relief', солидарность 'solidarity'). It will be observed here that the Church Slavonic suffix -ость has been given a renewed lease of life (cf. also дѣйствительность 'reality', конечность 'finality', призрачность 'illusiveness').

574. The social and economic vocabulary, popularized by journalism, enlarged itself in the latter half of the nineteenth and in the present century with the advance of industrialization and sociological speculation. The terminology very naturally came from outside and may be studied in a plethora of illustrative material. The abstract suffixes -ость, -ство, -іе are in evidence in calques (e.g. безсодержательность 'insipidity', главенство 'supremacy', отожествленіе 'identification') together with the Latin-type formants -ія (e.g. буржуазія 'bourgeoisie', децентрализація 'decentralization', эманципація 'emancipation'). The verbal endings -овать, which was a Polish loan in the seventeenth century, and -ировать, which was also common then as a hybrid formation from -овать and German *-ieren*, continued to proliferate new unprefixated verbs (e.g. импонировать 'to impose', резюмировать 'to summarize', формулировать 'to formulate').

575. Like other sober students of language in the nineteenth century, Ja. K. Grot exhorted his contemporaries to be moderate and discriminating in borrowing, and he singled out particularly a multitude of French words and expressions which had 'defaced' the language. His butts were the periodicals as well as certain authors, who are accused of introducing 'incorrect gallicisms' (e.g. *Svistok*, 1859: инерція 'inertia', интеллигенція 'intelligentsia', констатировать 'to state', массовый 'mass-'; I. Turgenev, *Nov'*, 1877: буржуй 'bourgeois', интернаціоналъ 'international', капиталъ 'capital', коммунизмъ 'communism'). These were some of the 'learned words' (*učjonyje slova*) of a conversation recorded in P. D. Boborykin's novel *Kitajgorod* (1882):

— У васъ есть иниціатива?

— Безъ ученыхъ словъ, голубчикъ!

— Нѣтъ, позвольте его повторить . . . Иниціатива. По-русски починъ, если вамъ угодно.

This was the borrower's attitude—the foreign loan-word was apparently essential, because of the prevalent fashion; it seemed more expressive, in both sound and sense, than the all too familiar vernacular equivalent. And so the penetration of the modern Russian vocabulary with alien words went on. The influence of the theory of evolution—of дарвинизмъ, for instance—left its traces also on the vocabulary (e.g. аберрація 'aberration', акclimatизація 'acclimatization', варіація 'variation') as did the increasing multitude of other concepts in other spheres of knowledge, which contributed, among many others, such words as агломератъ 'agglomerate', альтруизмъ 'altruism', вокализмъ 'vocalism', идеализмъ 'idealism', концессія 'concession', культура 'culture', спекуляція 'speculation', экземпляръ 'sample').

576. 'P. Sergeič' (P. S. Porochovščikov), writing in 1910 (*Iskusstvo reči na sude*), expressed his indignation at what was happening to contemporary Russian as follows: 'these ugly foreign words are gradually acquiring in our minds a sort of superiority over purely Russian words', and he quotes in illustration such phrases as детальный анализъ 'detailed analysis' and систематическая группировка матеріала 'systematic grouping of material' as seeming preferable in the opinion of contemporaries to the vernacular подробный разборъ and научное изложеніе предмета. His conclusion is decisive: 'The vast majority of these uninvited guests are not wanted, because we have Russian words, both simple and accurate, which have the same meanings.'

577. The 'superfluous' foreign words belonged not only to the language of books but to the colloquial language of the educated, both gentle (*dvorjanstvo*) and simple (*raznočincy*). It was a sort of national snobbery, confirmed by the years and restricted, of course, to the very vulnerable intelligentsia. The influence was apparent in the ubiquity of French words and in imitations, sometimes subconscious, of the patterns of French syntax. We see this influence in Gercen (Herzen), Turgenev, and L. Tolstoj.

578. The reaction against the preponderance of French may be seen in the views and lexicography of V. I. Dal' (Dahl). In 'O russkom slovare'[1] he advocates the replacement of the foreign by the vernacular as a principle and adduces in illustration the word кокетничать 'to flirt' (< F. *coqueter*), for which he finds a choice of fifteen Russian equivalents, among them заискивать, угодничать, любезничать, умильничать, миловзорить, красоваться, казотиться, пичужить. Yet it must be admitted, though Dal' himself disagrees, that none of his many 'synonyms' conveys the exact meaning of кокетничать. Dal''s purpose was entirely laudable—he was drawing attention to the native reservoir of neglected words; but his stubborn insistence on the Slavonic element of Russian is almost like the insistence on a Saxon English which was being commended in England by some 'Teutonists' at the same period. His own literary practice shows him possessed of a Russian style[2] as artificial as that of the indiscriminate users of copious gallicisms.

579. The influence of the West in Russian as a source of words and of the ideas they bring forth is vital to this day, when we have seen the resuscitation of the vocabulary of the French Revolution and its doctrinaires as well as that of the German Marxists. One Russian repository of this vocabulary is to be found in the voluminous publicistic writings of V. I. Lenin (Ul'janov), who owed a great deal to his immediate predecessors and contemporaries. And the literary language of his followers has been built on these foundations. But the characteristic vocabulary of Soviet Russian is not only an historical calque

---

[1] *Tolkovyj slovar' Živogo velikorusskogo jazyka*, I, Moscow, 1863, pp. 1 f.
[2] Cf., for instance, 'Chmel', son i jav'' (*Moskvitjanin*, 1843).

of the French and German revolutionary and socialistic vocabulary but draws on the colloquial speech of the *raznočincy*, one of whose activist groups triumphed politically in 1917. The demagogic colloquialism of this language is illustrated effectively by the speeches of I. V. Stalin (Džugašvili) and other politicians as well as by the language of Soviet journalism.[1] And its imaginative literature is rich in vulgarisms, provincialisms, and slang, both word and phrase, and in the acronyms, abbreviations, and clichés that infest the vocabulary of everyday living (e.g. шамать 'to eat', чухрать 'to be off', по букве з 'through "pull"', ВКП 'All-Union Communist Party', культпроп 'culture propaganda', за что боролись? 'what did we fight for?').

[1] For a study of Soviet Russian in perspective see Andrej i Tat'jana Fesenko, *Russkij jazyk pri Sovetach*, New York, 1955.

XII

DEVELOPMENT OF STYLES

580. The history of language is not merely the stages of its development as a structure but simultaneously a record of the styles of writing practised in the course of its historical evolution. These begin with the inauguration of the written language and from the outset tend to show recognizable varieties. In Russia the written language, as we remember, was introduced, both symbol and substance, from Bulgaria in the tenth century with the acceptance of the Christian religion by the Grand Prince of Kiev. The ready-made Old Church Slavonic literature, with its mainly Bulgarian bias, was almost exclusively ecclesiastical at first, and its East Slavonic recipients appear to have been content for some time to copy and imitate it. But these processes were, as we can imagine; inevitably approximate. The scribes in Rus' never succeeded even in copying the Old Church Slavonic prototypes faultlessly, and the first dated monument, the 'Ostromir Gospels' (1056–7), contains noteworthy clerical errors, which throw light on the pronunciation of the contemporary language (§ 173). Moreover, the copyist's colophon represents a successful attempt at original composition within the limits of the Old Church Slavonic system with its Greek-style syntax. Other specimens of the independent use of this language are the colophons to the 'Svjatoslav Miscellanies' of 1073 and 1076 and the marginal notes (*pripiski*) to the 'Novgorod Menaea' of twenty years later (1095–7). These mainly ring the changes on a small number of motifs—dating of the manuscript, inadequacy of the completed work, 'sinfulness' of the copyist, and appeal for the reader's indulgence—and in one instance, viz. Deacon Ioan's colophon to the 'Miscellany' of 1073, an attempt to break out of the strict formulas into a floundering imitation of the style of the copied texts with unhappy consequences to lucidity. This is an unintelligent attempt to trace out the involution of some of the originals, which had been complicated by the distortions of Bulgarian translators, into a language and manner that are not native to the copyist-author.

581. The contrast is extreme when we confront this ecclesiastical style with the mainly practical use of Russian made by Gostjata in his note to Vasilij (see App. I. p. 284). This tantalizing fragment of a letter apparently shows a Russian uninfluenced by Old Church Slavonic in its epistolary formulas and in its vocabulary, and it is the existence of such material, which has been considerably increased for the later centuries by new finds at Novgorod in 1952,[1] that has led some investigators, notably S. P. Obnorskij,[2] to the conclusion that literary Russian must have had a Russian and not, as is mainly supposed, an Old Church Slavonic origin. Such a view is unsupported by facts: the Cyrillic alphabet came to Rus' probably from Bulgaria in the tenth century, and the first specimens of its use were texts in Old Church Slavonic. These gave shape to the orthographic form of Russian and inevitably influenced the written use of the language; and it is only the different purposes to which this was put that convey the impression of a differentiation into two fundamental styles, viz. the literary (here ecclesiastical) and the non-literary or practical. The antithesis between such uses is inevitable and universal, and extant styles are ultimately traceable to either of the two. We may, therefore, assume a polarity of literary and non-literary styles and classify such styles as we find according to a scale with these as its poles or termini.

582. The literary style, as we have noted, was initially used for ecclesiastical purposes, viz. versions of the Scriptures (e.g. 'Ostromir Gospels') and the liturgy (e.g. 'Novgorod Menaea'). These provided narrative as well as doctrine, and the two are combined in homilies, of which Ilarion, Metropolitan of Kiev, has left an outstanding example in his eleventh-century 'The Law and Grace' (*Slovo o zakone i blagodati*). This, however, survives only in a sixteenth-century manuscript, which exhibits his language in a grammatically corrupt form, though it facilitates the study of the characteristics of Kiev homiletics and its complete dependence on Bulgaro-Byzantine models. We can well imagine that the original manuscript of the homily was written in Russian Church Slavonic and not in the Bulgarian

---

[1] V. I. Borkovskij (ed.), *Paleografičeskij i lingvističeskij analiz novgorodskich berestjanych gramot*, Moscow, 1955, p. 9.

[2] *Očerki po istorii russkogo literaturnogo jazyka staršego perioda*, Moscow–Leningrad, 1946, p. 79.

recension of the language, for we have already realized that early Russian ecclesiastical literature was an approximation to Old Church Slavonic literature and had the defects of an approximation as well as some of the merits of original expression.

583. The literature of Kiev in the eleventh century is not the direct regional source of Old Russian, which derives from the northern type of East Slavonic as used in Novgorod and Moscow. Kiev culture, enshrined in a southern variety of East Slavonic, did not outlive the Tartar (Mongol) attacks of the thirteenth century, and its manuscripts appear to have survived only in northern recensions of them. This puts Kiev Russian on approximately the same footing as Anglian (Northumbrian). The Scandinavian Vikings destroyed Anglian culture in Northumbria, Deira, and Mercia, but *Bēowulf* is still extant in a West Saxon copy. Similarly Novgorod, rather than Kiev, was the focus of the surviving Old Russian literature, and therefore its language is at the source of Russian as we know it today. The contrast between Novgorod and Kiev in the eleventh century is the contrast between Russian and Ukrainian in later times. The presence of dialectal differences in East Slavonic is borne out by the evidence of the early texts, in spite of the obscuring and levelling influence of the literary language imported from Bulgaria. This influence appears to have been greatest at the centre —in Kiev—but the southern type of East Slavonic is palpably present, for instance, in the twelfth-century Galician and Volhynian copies of the Gospels (e.g. 'Dobrilo Gospels', 1164), and this is the historical source of Ukrainian. The language of Kiev therefore is *a posteriori* as well as *a priori* the direct source of Ukrainian and not of Russian, as many Russian scholars both before and since the Revolution have liked to think.[1] When V. M. Istrin[2] declares that the 'literary language was one and the same all over Rus'', he seems to have in mind the East Slavonic recension of Old Church Slavonic, whose levelling influence we have already referred to. And L. A. Bulachovskij[3] would appear to be right in assuming the presence of dialectal

---

[1] W. K. Matthews, 'Some Observations on the Ukrainian Language' (*Ukrainian Review*, ii. 3, London, 1955, pp. 17–18).

[2] *Očerk istorii drevnerusskoj literatury*. Petrograd, 1922, p. 82.

[3] *Istoričeskij kommentarij k literaturnomu russkomu jazyku*, Char'kov–Kiev, 1937, p. 6.

differentiation over so vast a geographical area with the concomitant difficulties of transport which it entailed.

584. We have already contrasted the literary with the non-
literary forms of Old Russian in Novgorod and have seen the
intrusion of northern features (e.g. *cokan'je*) even into the literary
language (cf. 'Novgorod Menaea', 1095–7). From now onwards
both the Novgorod dialect and the rather later records of the
Russian of Rostov, Suzdal', Rjazan', Pskov, Tver', and Moscow
show the same dichotomy in their written forms, for ever since
the twelfth century we find a steadily increasing number and
variety of both ecclesiastical and secular manuscripts. Literary
usage is to be met with in the 'Legend of Boris and Gleb'
(*Skazanije o Borise i Glebe*), which seems to be the oldest extant
hagiography. Here the literary style prevails in its ecclesiastical
aspect, but there is also the obvious influence of colloquial
speech which gives it life and leavens the stiffness and artifice of
Church Slavonic. We see this particularly by juxtaposing such
a brief excerpt as но се остаану много глаголати, да не (въ)
многописании въ забыть вълѣземъ, нъ о немь же начахъ си
съкажемъ убо сице 'but I shall not say more here, so that we
shall not lose the thread of our argument, and so we shall say
this about what I began to tell' with къде ли насыщуся та-
ковааго бл(а)гааго учения и наказания разума твоего? увы
мнѣ, увы мнѣ, како заиде свѣте мои не сущу ми ту! 'where shall
I be filled with such blessed doctrine and instruction (given by)
thy wisdom; woe is me, woe is me, how (thou), O my light, didst
vanish while I was away!' In further contrast to the latter, we
have the plainness and unpretentiousness of Prince Mstislav and
Prince Vsevolod's 'Deed of Gift to the St George Monastery of
Novgorod' (*c.* 1130), which, however, unlike 'Gostjata's Letter
to Vasilij', clearly manifests the presence òf ecclesiastical influence, so that it cannot be regarded as a complete specimen
of the secular style.

585. The contrast between the ecclesiastical and the secular, or
the literary and non-literary, is better illustrated in the next two
centuries, when writs issued in Tver', Pskov, Moscow, and
Rjazan', as well as in Novgorod, add materially to our examples
of the non-literary use of Russian. There are also interesting
writs emanating from Polock and Smolensk, but these show

obvious features of what was later to be known as White Russian and are accordingly outside the scope of our present inquiry, as is the Galician writ issued by the *starosta* Benko in 1398.[1] The Novgorod writs include one dated 1262–3, which contains a treaty signed by Prince Aleksandr Jaroslavič of the Neva and German ambassadors. This is an outstanding illustration of the *delovoj stil'* and may be compared to the 'White Russian' treaty of Mstislav Davidovič of Smolensk with Riga and Gothland in 1229. Another Novgorod treaty (1264–5), concluded this time with the Grand Prince Jaroslav Jaroslavič of Tver', provides a contrast in subject-matter, but is couched in the same formulas. The distance between the thirteenth-century language of these treaties[2] and the epistolary style of Gostjata (11th cent.) may be measured again by comparing the former with the contract (*rjadnaja gramota*) made between Tešata and Jakym of Pskov some time between 1266 and 1291. It is obvious that the pithy simplicity of this language has more in common with Gostjata's letter than with the formulas of the writs (cf. се поряди ся Тѣшата съ Якымомь про складьство про первоіе и про задьнеіе, и на дѣвцѣ Якымъ серебро взялъ, а мониста Тѣшатина у Якымовы жены свободна Тѣшатѣ взяти, и рощетъ учинила[3] промежи себе, а болѣ не надобѣ Якыму Тѣшата, ні Тѣшатѣ Якымъ, а на томь послуси ... а псалъ Довмонтовъ[4] писець 'hereby Tešata and Jakym have made a marriage settlement (to be valid) for the present time and the future; and Jakym has received money for the girl, and Tešata is at liberty to take his necklace from Jakym's wife; and an arrangement was made between the two, so that Tešata owes nothing more to Jakym and Jakym to Tešata, and the witnesses were ... and (Prince) Dovmont's scribe engrossed (the same)' This, apparently the oldest Pskov document, belongs to approximately the same period as the short treaty signed with Novgorod by the Grand Prince of Tver' (*c.* 1296–1301), which makes use of the customary formulas and presents some dialectal peculiarities (e.g. Тверь appears as Тфѣрь, and Александръ as

---

[1] Cf. S. P. Obnorskiij i S. G. Barchudarov, *Chrestomatija po istorii russkogo jazyka*, i, Moscow, 1952, pp. 141–2.

[2] Cf. A. A. Šachmatov, *Issledovanije o jazyke novgorodskich gramot xiii i xiv vekov*, St Petersburg, 1885.

[3] This is a dual form of the verb.

[4] Prince Dovmont (Lith. Daumantas) reigned in Pskov between 1266 and 1301.

Олександръ). The oldest Moscow document is of rather later date, being the 'Testament' (*duchovnaja*) of Prince Ivan Danilovič Kalita (1327–8), which survives, unfortunately, in a mutilated form. By this time the Tartars had been overlords of Rus' since the thirteenth century, so that it is natural to find Prince Ivan referring ominously to his 'being on the way to the Horde' (ида в орду). As for the first Rjazan' writ, it is dated even later (1356), i.e. over a century after the land of Rjazan' was devastated by Batu Khan.

586. The text of the 'Russian Legal Code' (*Russkaja pravda*), representing the laws of Jaroslav the Wise and his successors in the eleventh and twelfth centuries, is preserved in the 'Novgorod Nomocanon' (*kormčaja*) of *c.* 1282. Its language (see App. I, p. 287) represents the forensic style of non-literary Russian in all its elliptical brevity and approved formulas, but the subject-matter is intertwined with episodes of everyday living and draws vigour and expression from these. Essentially the forensic style is the style of the writs, somewhat condensed. Unlike the writs, however, which were *ad hoc* documents and therefore implied a certain variety of choice in wording, the language of the *Pravda* appears to have been progressively whittled down to bare essentials and, on the syntactic plane, quite often to conditional syntagmata.

587. Starting from this *terminus a quo* of the non-literary style we can profitably contrast it with that of the earliest chronicles, e.g. the 'First Novgorod Chronicle' of the thirteenth-fourteenth century (see App. I, p. 288). Here we have characteristic formula and narrative, with considerable scope given to the latter by the unpredictable vicissitudes of historical circumstance. Comparison of this chronicle with other chronicles of the period, viz. the Laurentian MS (1377), copied in Suzdal', and the Hypatian MS (*c.* 1425), copied presumably from a Galician original in Novgorod, indicates, however, that even the chroniclers' art was distinguished by a certain impersonality which must have been due in part to the influence of Church Slavonic models and the fashion of 'humility' which they inculcated.

588. Further towards the other pole, the *terminus ad quem* of the literary style, we find the hagiographies (*žitija*) such as that of St Nifont (1219), admirable for its lucidity of language and spirit (see App. I, pp. 286-7). This appears to have been done in Rostov and, together with the more elaborate 'life' of St Feodosij of the Kiev Caves Monastery (*lavra*) and the hagiographic narratives of the 'Pskov Prologue' of 1383, it continues the Church Slavonic tradition of ecclesiastical writing, leavened with the unconcealable influence of the scribes' vernacular.

589. By the fifteenth century the two extremes of style had between them produced new varieties of literary composition. The extremes are indicated as before by specimens of the ecclesiastical style and that of the writs, some of which, scratched on birch-bark, were recently unearthed in Novgorod by archaeological expeditions. The habitus of the style of the Novgorod (see App. I, pp. 291-2) and Pskov writs,[1] whose specimens on parchment and paper were known to Russian scholarship before the excavations of 1951-2, is continued unchanged in the Northern Dvina writs,[2] mainly deeds of purchase (*kupčije*) and mortgage (*zakladnyje*); and these provide fresh examples of the old *delovoj jazyk*. Over against this we have the traditional manuscript copies of the Gospel texts (e.g. *Lukino jevangelije,* 1409), which represent the other recognized extreme of style. And between the two, occupying an intermediate position in the stylistic scale, are the unique 'Journey beyond Three Seas' (*Choženije za tri morja*) of Afanasij Nikitin, and the 'Exploits beyond the Don' (*Zadonščina*) of Sofonij Rjazanec, both of them of fifteenth-century provenance.

590. The first of these works, emanating from Tver', long the rival of Moscow, is an account of travels in Persia and India which the devout author describes with realistic *naïveté*. Though inclined to confuse fiction and fact, and though his memory sometimes deceives him, Nikitin's experiences were so novel and out of the way that he did not readily find adequate words for them. The note of exoticism is well maintained, although obviously not deliberately, by the use of 'Oriental' words—Turkic, Persian, and Arabic—and even locutions. Nikitin was not a literary artist but an observant man of affairs, and his natural, mainly conversational, manner is in pointed, but favourable,

[1] For these and the Northern Dvina writs see S. N. Valk, *Gramoty Velikogo Novgoroda i Pskova*, Moscow–Leningrad, 1949.

[2] A. A. Šachmatov, *Issledovanije o dvinskich gramotach xv v.*, St Petersburg, 1903.

contrast to the conscious 'literariness' of Sofonij Rjazanec, the author of *Zadonščina*.

591. This is one of the so-called 'military narratives' (*voinskije povesti*), which go back mainly to the fifteenth century, and shows the obvious marks of a *pastiche* of the 'Lay of Igor" (*Slovo o polku Igoreve*). The interrelations of the two works are somewhat complicated and have been bedevilled by suspicions of forgery. The problem of the authenticity of the 'Lay of Igor" was resuscitated not so long ago by André Mazon[1] and was followed by a storm of patriotic criticism and a flood of annotated reprints of Count Musin-Puškin's edition of the text, which had been published in 1800.[2] This is supposed to have been based on a manuscript, known not only to the editor but to other antiquaries like Karamzin—who was the first to apprise the West of its discovery in the Hamburg *Spectateur du Nord*—which is said to have perished in the fire of Moscow during the Napoleonic invasion of Russia in 1812. Its corrupt text points to the fifteenth or sixteenth century, to which the *Zadonščina* belongs. Confronted with the *Zadonščina*, the 'Lay of Igor" seems to be far the more original of the two and is still usually taken as the prototype and not, as Mazon thinks, the copy. The subject is a battle in each case, with Russian princes and their armies at war with steppe peoples beyond the Don—the Polovecians in the 'Lay' and the Tartars in *Zadonščina*—but the hero of the first is an unimportant and little-known feudal prince, who lost a campaign and his men, whereas the latter is a eulogy of Prince Dmitrij Ivanovič of Moscow and 'of the Don', who won the battle of Kulikovo in 1380. Sofonij Rjazanec does not do justice to the grandeur of his theme by fixing his attention too closely on the language of the 'Lay' and converting parts of it into *clichés* for his own use. The unknown author of the 'Lay', on the other hand, exalts a minor theme to the level of a grand lament over princely feuds in the twelfth century. Compare in this connexion, as an instance of dependence, the following short extract from the 'Lay', viz. комони ржуть за Сулою; звенить

---

[1] *Le Slovo d'Igor*, Paris, 1940. One of the belated 'counterblasts' to this book was the corporate work of H. Grégoire, R. Jakobson, and M. Szeftel, *La Geste du prince Igor'*, New York, 1948.

[2] There is also a photographic edition of the Catherine MS., viz. N. Vodovozov, *Slovo o polku Igorja, syna Svjatoslavlja, vnuka Ol'gova*, Moscow, 1954.

слава въ Кыевѣ; трубы трубять въ Новъгородѣ; стоять стязи въ Путивлѣ; Игорь ждетъ мила брата Всеволода 'horses are neighing beyond the Sula; anthems are echoing in Kiev; trumpets are sounding in Novgorod; standards are aloft in Putivl'; Igor' is waiting for his dear brother Vsevolod', with this one from *Zadonščina*—кони ржуть на Москвѣ; бубны бьють на Коломнѣ; трубы трубять в Серпуховѣ; звенить слава по всеи земли русьскои; чюдно стязи стоять у Дону великого на березѣ, пашутся хоругови берчати, свѣтятся калантыри злачены 'horses are neighing in Moscow; drums are beating in Kolomna; trumpets are sounding in Serpuchov; anthems are echoing all over the land of Rus'; standards are wondrously aloft on the banks of the great (river) Don', embellished banners are fluttering, (and) gilded armour is flashing.'

592. It is noteworthy that *Zadonščina* is the work of a scribe from Rjazan', who would naturally write his prose 'lay' in the enthusiasm of a Russian victory over the Tartars after the long-remembered devastation of his homeland in the thirteenth century by the ancestors of the same enemy. Yet Rjazan' was soon to be absorbed by Moscow, whose prestige loomed large in the fifteenth century as a result of the conquests and annexations of Ivan III. Moscow indeed and its language are the dominant theme of the history of Russian from this time onwards. This theme is complicated in the domain of style because the progressive development of Russian was impeded during the 'ameliorative' and reactionary South Slavonic influence, which had begun with the emendation (*pravka*) of the church books according to the Middle Bulgarian canon at the end of the fourteenth century. In the fifteenth century, after the fall of Constantinople, the influence of South Slavonic churchmen, among them the Metropolitan Cyprian (Kiprian), who was of Bulgarian extraction, and the Serbian Pachomij Logofet, was considerable in Moscow, which had become a refuge for Balkan scholars. These, like Maksim the Greek from Mount Athos, early in the sixteenth century, helped, as we know (§ 135), to popularize the legend of 'Moscow the Third Rome' and the grand dukes of Muscovy as the spiritual heirs of the Byzantine emperors. The significance of the city and its constantly expanding territory led to the gradual emergence of a κοινή or common language, whose styles are particularly varied in the sixteenth century, for not only were new literary values created at this time (e.g. the polemical correspondence between Ivan IV and Prince Andrej Kurbskij, the publicistic work of Peresvetov, and *Domostroj*, but many items of the older literature were recopied (e.g. Ilarion's *Slovo o zakone i blagodati*, the *Poučenije* of the Novgorodian bishop Luka Židjata, the *Choždenije* of the Abbot Daniil, the Russian version of Donatus's grammar by Dmitrij Gerasimov, *Aleksandrija* (see App. I, pp. 292–3)—the story of Alexander of Macedon— *Povest' o razorenii Rjazani Batyjem*, Kirik's *Chronologičeskaja stat'ja*, *Molenije Daniila Zatočnika*, and possibly *Slovo o polku Igoreve*). Such antiquarian interest was naturally stimulated by the South Slavonic clergy and scholars.

593. The many works we have enumerated and occasionally examined are a motley collection of items, but they fall easily into one or other of our established categories of literary and non-literary writings. At one extreme we have again the traditional Church Slavonic items in the form of hortatory dialogues like the one between Sergij and German of Valaam (F. Valamo) Monastery (*Valaamskij monastyr'*), written about 1550, as well as the much earlier works of Jepifanij the Most Wise (*premudryj*), who relates the lives of St Sergij of Radonež and St Stefan of Perm' in a verbose and complicated rhetoric, known since his time by his own term 'verbal conflexion' (*pletenije sloves*). Connected with these, to some extent, is the correspondence between Ivan IV and Prince Kurbskij, who show their medieval affiliations by quoting Scripture copiously and yet are abreast of modern developments in vocabulary. The Polish-Latin influence is particularly noticeable in Kurbskij's vocabulary. Ivan IV's voluminous 'epistles', on the contrary, include some to ecclesiastics, and these compositions are more in keeping with conservative Church Slavonic usage. As for Ivan Peresvetov's 'Legend of Sultan Mahomet' (*Skazanije o Magmete saltane*) and his petitions (*čelobitnyja*) to Ivan IV, they show the presence rather of a contemporary annalist or scribe (*pisec*) who possesses a natural fluency of expression combined with a more modern choice of words.

594. In contrast to these varieties of literary usage with a greater or smaller dosage of the spoken element, we have non-litera compilations like the 'Book of Household Management' (*Domostroj*), an admirably detailed picture of sixteenth-century Russian life in the form of a housekeeping encyclopaedia, giving instructions on everything from cooking to bringing up children. The scope of the work makes it varied in subject-matter and enables the compiler, the priest Sil'vestr, to operate with a large vocabulary; but the work never becomes literary in the process, while at the same time it never loses its hold on the practical needs of living.

595. The other Muscovite documents are connected with government and administration and comprise a series of law codes (*sudebniki*), beginning with that of Ivan III (1497) and ending with those of Ivan IV (1550) and Tsar Feodor (1589). These are the Muscovite representatives and developments of the Kiev 'Code of Jaroslav the Wise' (*Russkaja pravda*); but how far we have come from the elliptical structure of the latter to the sometimes voluminous explicitness of the former! The monotony of this style is determined by its strictly limited scope, and the same quality pertains to the writs, which at this period show an unusual variety of tenor—deeds, charters, testaments, diplomatic reports, instructions to ambassadors, letters of credence, and other documents. But there is human interest and a disarming homeliness in the private letters (*gramotki*) which also belong to this time. One of these is the letter sent by the Novgorod merchant L. Vereščagin to his wife Natl'ja from Reval (R. Kolyvan', now Tallinn). Comparison between this sixteenth-century letter and Gostjata's (11th cent.) shows that the language has changed little except in flexibility in the course of four centuries.

596. The seventeenth century, with the 'troubled times' (*smuta*) and Peter the Great at its beginning and end respectively, is one of the most significant in the entire history of the country, and the styles of writing found in this period do full justice to the stabilization and modernization of the language.[1] The non-literary styles enter into serious competition with the literary and towards the end of the century reduce these to temporary ineffectiveness. At the beginning of the seventeenth century

---

[1] W. K. Matthews, 'Observations on the Study of Seventeenth-Century Russian' (*SEER* xxxiv. 83, London, 1956, pp. 487–90).

there are the records of folk-songs written down for the Oxford scholar Richard James in 1619–20. These are the earliest Russian songs to be reduced to writing and represent the beginnings of verse composition, which also includes the later anonymous 'Story of Misery-Misfortune' (*Povest' o Gore-zločastii*), in the same popular style, although it is not a folk-song. This work is purely literary. The same literary category includes stories centred in the 'troubled times' (e.g. those about the unfrocked monk Grigorij Otrep'jev (see App. I, pp. 295–6) and *Povest' o prestavlenii vojevody M. V. Skopina-Šujskogo*) and the beginnings of biography (e.g. *Povest' o vizantijskom care Michaile, Povest' o Savve Grudcyne, Povest' o Julianii Lazarevskoj* by her son Kallistrat Osor'in, *Povest' o Karpe Sutulove, Povest' o Marfe i Marii, Povest' o Frole Skobejeve*), satires (e.g. *Povest' o Jerše Jeršoviče, Povest' o Šemjakinom sude, Koljazinskaja čelobitnaja, Prazdnik kabackich jaryžek*), historical fiction (e.g. *Povest' ob Azovskom osadnom sidenii Donskich kazakov, Povest' o načale carstvujuščego grada Moskvy, Novaja povest' o preslavnom Rossijskom carstve*) as well as the 'Memoirs' of Grigorij Kotošichin (*O Rossii v carstvovanije Alekseja Michailoviča, c.* 1664), which shows the pervasiveness of Western influences, and 'the last of the hagiographies', viz. the 'Autobiography' (*Žitije*) of Archpriest Avvakum Petrovič, who suffered martyrdom for his beliefs and has a counterpart in John Bunyan. Avvakum's style is mixed and known in Russian as *vjakan'je*; but the colloquial element is very evident, much more so than in Ivan IV's correspondence, and his direct and lucid Russian compares favourably with the Tsar's involved and tormented prose.

597. In the latter part of the seventeenth century the influence of the White Russian and Ukrainian scholars and writers began to be felt. Among them was Simeon Polockij (1629–80), who was engaged as tutor to the children of Tsar Alexis—Prince Feodor and Princess Sofija. He wrote verse with a polemical and satirical bent and used the Polish type of syllabic versification, which he had acquired in his native White Russia, where, as in the Ukraine, education was well ahead of contemporary education in Muscovy. Polockij's influence as a metrist may be seen in the work of his pupil and editor Sil'vestr Medvedev, and of the Rumanian prince Antioch Kantemir, who appears to have been directly influenced also by Boileau.

598. The literary styles illustrated by the foregoing works did not bulk large among the multitude of manuscripts and books which were produced in the course of this century. The introduction of printing in Moscow in the middle of the sixteenth century was episodic, and the leading printer Ivan Fjodorov, who had his press there between 1563 and 1565, fell into disfavour with the authorities and was forced to seek refuge in the other two East Slavonic lands as well as farther afield.[1] Fjodorov's abortive venture in Moscow remained barren of result until a century later (1648), when the ecclesiastical press in that city issued an anonymous adaptation of Meletij Smotryc'kyj's 'Church Slavonic Grammar' (*Grammatiki slavenskija pravilnoje sintagma*, Ev'je, 1619) and the 'Legal Code' (*Uloženije*) of Tsar Alexis. These very different books, each in its own way, brought order into disorder—the one into Church Slavonic grammar as studied in Muscovy, the other into the codification of Muscovite laws. Their language is strictly practical and relies mainly on a technical vocabulary.

599. It is indeed on technical vocabularies that a large part of the writings of the seventeenth century, especially of its closing years, chiefly draw. If we compare, for instance, the familiar letters of Peter the Great, written between 1689 and 1693, with his instructions (*punkty*) to ambassadors and to military personnel, we shall see that the main difference between the two is not only psychological but stylistic. When he writes to his mother he limits his vocabulary to intimate personal matters of common interest to both of them and expresses himself with the utmost freedom within the bounds of filial respect, whereas when he writes to others he is at pains to maintain distance and authority, and the scope of his correspondence is strictly specialized. Here the practical interest is always to the fore, couched in the bold chancellery style which was developed in the sixteenth century, as it is also in the first newspapers (*kuranty*) and in the Petrine *Vedomosti*, which began to appear early in the eighteenth century, in the numerous translations and compilations of technical works (e.g. L. F. Magnickij, *Arifmetika*, 1703; F. P. Polikarpov-Orlov, *Leksikon trejazyčnyj*, 1704; *Artikul voinskij*, 1715; *Kniga o eksercicii*, 1715), and in the guide-books to morality and

---

[1] Cf. A. Zjornova, *Načalo knigopečatanija v Moskve i na Ukraine*, Moscow, 1947.

good manners (e.g. *Apoffegmata*, 1716; *Junosti čestnoje zercalo*, 1719).

600. Relations between Church and State were symbolically exhibited in the reform of the alphabet (1710), which left the old Cyrillic type-face with its stress-marks and the Church Slavonic language, as renovated and rehabilitated by Ukrainians like Stefan Javors'kyj and Epifanij Slavynec'kyj, to conservative lexicographers like Polikarpov-Orlov. And yet it would be an error to say that the delimitation of the spheres of Church Slavonic and Russian was so rigid that one language could not influence the other. The impact of the ecclesiastical style is seen in Peter the Great's own decrees and other official documents, and it is unusually marked in Polikarpov-Orlov's translation (1718) of the *Geographia generalis* of Bernardus Varenius (1650). In its proper field, of course, Church Slavonic was cultivated now according to the rules of Smotryc'kyj's 'Grammar', which continued to exercise influence well into the eighteenth century and was studied by Lomonosov himself.

601. The eighteenth century saw the gradual formation of modern literary Russian. This process involved the continuous co-operation of four generations of men of letters and it was not complete till the first quarter of last century. After the death of Peter the Great the segregation of Church Slavonic and chancellery Russian (*delovoj jazyk*) led to the evolution of an intermediate style which is at the source of literary Russian. This style was the outcome of an attempt on the part of certain men of letters in the middle of the century, beginning with Trediakovskij, to steer the written language clear of the Scylla and Charybdis of Church Slavonic and official formalism by drawing on the resources of the spoken language. At the end of the seventeenth century specimens of this had been recorded by the German scholar H. W. Ludolf[1] in his *Grammatica russica* (Oxford, 1696), and we have already seen its presence in the folk-songs, *Povest' o Gore-zločastii*, the *Vedomosti*, and especially in familiar correspondence. The leaven of this style gradually resulted in depriving the conservative literary styles of their antiquated rigidity and stiltedness.

---

[1] Cf. Joachim Tetzner, *H. W. Ludolf und Russland*, Berlin, 1955, pp. 32–43.

602. By the middle of the eighteenth century we find a conflict between two tendencies represented by Trediakovskij and Lomonosov. The former was a theorist of no mean order, but an inferior writer; Lomonosov, on the other hand, was a theorist and writer of high calibre. Trediakovskij attempted to combine the Church Slavonic element with a 'modernism' derived from the translation of contemporary French authors such as Paul Tallemant (cf. *Le Voyage de l'isle d'Amour*, 1713)[1] and the theories of grammarians such as Claude Vaugelas (cf. *Remarques sur la langue française*, 1647). Accordingly, Trediakovskij's Russian is in effect less modern than that, say, of some early eighteenth-century fiction (e.g. *Gistorija o rossijskom matrose Vasilii Koriotskom, Istorija ob Aleksandre, rossijskom dvorjanine, Istorija o rossijskom kupce Ioane*). In contrast to Trediakovskij, Lomonosov announced in his paper *O pol'ze knig cerkovnych v rossijskom jazyke* (1757) a flexible theory of three styles—'high', 'middle' (*posredstvennyj*), and 'low'— capable, he thought, of treating any and every literary theme. These styles (he called them *stili*) were defined largely in terms of vocabulary: the high style had a strong infusion of Church Slavonic, the middle style rested on educated colloquial usage, and the low style contained words which were not to be found in the church books. Moreover, the middle style is free from archaisms and the low style from vulgarisms (*prezrennyje slova*), which are banned from all three styles, 'except in low comedies'. Church Slavonic itself is treated as Peter the Great treated it, viz. as a separate language reserved for ecclesiastics. From the eighteenth century onwards the status of Church Slavonic reminds us of the status of Biblical English, i.e. it is a sacred language closely bound up with the liturgy. Yet, as we have seen, its influence affects the Russian literary style of the 'highest' type, which shares in the Church Slavonic vocabulary but does not use its syntax. Lomonosov's poetry is a solemn illustration of this style, as his scientific writings are of the middle style. His serious type of mind did not descend to the low style, which was left to the eighteenth-century writers of comedy to cultivate. The stylistic influence of Lomonosov is recognizable in the eighteenth-century poets who followed him, even in Deržavin, the most talented of them all, and there are echoes of

---

[1] An earlier, anonymous, edition of this work is entitled *Le Voyage et la conqueste de l'isle d'Amour* (1675).

it in nineteenth-century writing. One defect of Lomonosov's practice was the outcome of his willing submission to Latin influence. This is, incidentally, observable in his theory of tenses, which has found no following among later grammarians, and in his syntactic usage, which inclines to model itself on Latin and German prototypes.

603. The general practice of later writers of Russian is decidedly at variance with Lomonosov's and tends rather to follow colloquial idiom. Sumarokov, the youngest of the early classical trio, offers us indeed specimens of the low style in his comedies (e.g. *Opekun*, 1786), but the language still lacks the naturalness of later literary Russian. This emerges in a recognizably modern form in Fonvizin's (see App. I, pp. 299–301) and Novikov's prose. If we compare the prose of these authors, however, with that of Karamzin (e.g. *Pis'ma russkogo putešestvennika*, 1790), we shall realize that for all its colloquial flexibility it has still some distance to go before it can be considered to be fully modern.

604. Karamzin's contribution to the development of literary Russian is of capital importance, for he was the pioneer of the *dolce stil nuovo*, which aimed at reconciling prose with poetry.[1] An author first, he had a flair for expression, and his influence, like his training, was western. The influence of French vocabulary and syntax was irresistibly strong in his practice, but his hypersensitiveness enabled him to profit from criticism. That is why in the conflict between the old and the new styles, i.e. in effect, between Admiral Šiškov and Karamzin, the latter emerged a secure victor. The quarrel was significant. Šiškov in his *Rassuždenije o starom i novom sloge* (1803) upheld the tradition of the three styles, with this difference that the high style was equated with Church Slavonic itself. He refused to be persuaded that Church Slavonic was more than a stylistic variant of Russian. His criticism of the 'new style' of Karamzin and his followers, however, was more to the point, though here he was inclined as a conservative to pillory the calques that had become an essential part of the language since the naturalization of the Sentimental Movement in Russia. Notwithstanding this, some of his ideas found a belated echo among members of the Puškin

---

[1] N. S. Trubetzkoy, *Die russischen Dichter des 18. und 19. Jahrhunderts*, Graz–Köln, 1956, p. 90.

Pléiade (e.g. Küchelbecker), but this group, nevertheless, generally followed the practice of the 'new style', which had established itself in the early nineteenth century in all the literary genres. Karamzin himself had furnished examples of it in both verse and prose, and without his contribution the harmonious synthesis of alien west European and native Slavonic elements in a flexible 'intermediate' style would hardly have been possible. Yet there was one defect in Karamzin's practice which had been emphasized by Šiškov, and this was his excessive addiction to French usage.

605. There was still something else needed before a truly Russian style could be evolved. This came from such connoisseurs of popular idiom as Krylov, the fabulist; for the element of living speech was all that the 'new style' lacked. The fusion of it with the 'new style' was the work and merit of Puškin. His natural eclecticism combined the three historical elements of literary Russian—Church Slavonic, western usage, and the Russian of the people—into a balanced whole. This was the result of many years of patient writing and of persistent effort to find the *mot juste*. A similar, but less self-conscious style was cultivated for a few years of creative activity by Lermontov, who died in 1841.

606. To say that the writing of the second half of the nineteenth century and of the first half of the twentieth merely followed in Puškin's traces would be to simplify matters and to overestimate the achievement of Puškin. His prose, after all, was limited in scope, being confined mainly to imaginative literature and letter-writing, whereas later nineteenth-century writing was dominated in Russia by the influence of philosophy and sociology; and these were western in origin. Accordingly we find that the language of the time—literary, scientific, and journalistic—drew its vocabulary from western sources and in some instances modified its syntax in harmony with the prevailing influence. Thus the luminous and disciplined influence of classical French on Puškin yielded place to the complexities and enthusiasms of German Romantic philosophy in Belinskij (see App. I, pp. 301–2). Egocentric Romanticism is also present in the unique phenomenon of Gogol''s prose.

607. The same influence, moreover, is at the source of Russian

publicism which expressed itself for several generations in polemical criticism of a radical cast and gave Russian critical literature the contributions of Gercen (Herzen), Černyševskij, and
Pisarev. This type of prose writing—mainly abstract, voluminous, sinuous, ironical—culminated in Saltykov-Ščedrin (see
App. I, pp. 302–4), who has since won the admiration of Soviet
literary students.[1] Less wilful is the critical and imaginative
prose of the second half of the nineteenth century as we find it
in the works of Michajlovskij and Solov'jov, or Turgenev and
Tolstoj. This may be justly regarded as the 'normal' Russian literary style which even Soviet educationists approve of. It was also
the language of late nineteenth-century poetry before the Sym-
bolist revolt and, with due allowance for time and place, of the
more sober writers of today.

608. The contribution of Symbolism, especially to verse, was at
first disintegrating, but it eventually led to the introduction of
new modes of expression which had some impact on prose as
well. The new vision introduced, among other things, complexities into style. Natural progression was impeded by ellipses and
verbal juxtapositions that taxed comprehension (cf. A. Belyj's
Peterburg, 1913). This prerevolutionary 'subtlety', with its appeal
to the immature mind, is still with Russian literature, especially
in verse, and Soviet poets like Tichonov and Simonov, not to
mention the esoteric Pasternak, to whom it is second nature,
have been incapable of shedding it, since they regard it as a
sort of 'language of the initiated'. Imaginative prose too, as
we have suggested, shows traces of this fashion, beginning with
that of Jevgenij Zamjatin and his group in the early 1920's and
ending with the rank and file of Soviet prose authors, who still,
perhaps unconsciously, resist Gor'kij's plea to uphold the clarity
of common sense. The 'original sin' of the Symbolists and their
camp-followers such as Majakovskij may still be found reflected
in the 'literary pose' of even such sober writers as Michail Prišvin
(see App. I, pp. 304–6). In contrast to this literary individualism
we have the inflated pedestrianism of modern Russian journalistic writing.

[1] Cf. A. I. Jefimov, 'Frazeologičeskoje novatorstvo Saltykova-Ščedrina' (*Russkij
jazyk v škole*, v, Moscow, 1940, pp. 36–45).

PART III

APPENDIX I

HISTORICAL SPECIMENS OF RUSSIAN PROSE

Twenty excerpts, two for each century, are assembled here to illustrate the evolution of original Russian prose from the mid-eleventh-century Colophon of the 'Ostromir Gospels', with its mainly Church Slavonic basis, to the twentieth-century prose of Michail Prišvin (b. 1873) and Vera Panova (b. 1905), in which the native Russian element easily predominates. The excerpts cover a period of 900 years. They are reproduced, as far as possible, in their original spelling and punctuation. For the sake of uniformity and greater comprehension, however, some divergent characters of the early texts have been replaced by their modern Cyrillic equivalents: thus a is used for ѧ, и for н, е for є, i for ï, y for ѕ, ы for ъı, я for ꙗ, з for ѕ/з, н for ɴ, ч for ʏ, and щ for ⱅ. Furthermore, abbreviated words in the manuscripts have been written out in full and numeral symbols modernized, so as to avoid a proliferation of footnotes; and proper names begin here with capitals. Footnotes are used only to elucidate difficulties in the text and have been reduced to a bare minimum.

I. MID-ELEVENTH CENTURY

Слава тебѣ Г(оспод)и ц(а)рю н(е)б(е)сьныи · яко съподоби ма написати Еу(ан)г(е)лие се · почахъ же е писати · въ лѣт(о) · 6564[1]· А оконьчахъ е въ лѣт(о) · 6565[2]· Написахъ же еу(ан)-г(е)лие се · рабоу б(о)жию нареченоу сжщоу въ кр(ь)щении Иосифъ · а мирьскы Остромиръ · близокоу сжщоу Изаславоу къназоу · Изаславоу же къназоу тогда прѣдрьжащоу[3] обѣ власти · и о(ть)ца своего Ярослава · и брата своего Володи-

---

[1] The year 1056.   [2] The year 1057.   [3] Dative absolute.

мира · самъ же Изяславъ кънязь · правляаше столъ о(ть)ца
своего Ярослава Кыевѣ¹ · А брата своего столъ поржчи правити · близокоу своемоу Остромироу Новѣгородѣ¹ · Мънога
же лѣт(а) · дароуи б(ог)ъ сътяжавъшоумоу Еу(ан)г(е)лие се ·
на оутѣшение мъногамъ д(оу)шамъ кр(ь)стияньскамъ · даи
емоу г(оспод)ь б(ог)ъ б(лагос)л(ове)ние с(вя)тыхъ · еванг(е)-
листъ · и Іоана · Матѳеа · Лоукы · Марк(а) · и с(вя)тыхъ
прао(ть)ць · Авраама · и Ісаака · и Іякова · самомоу емоу ·
и подроужию его · Ѳеофанѣ и чядомъ ею ·² и подроужиемь
чадъ ею² · съдравьствоуите же мънога лѣт(а) · съдрьжаще
пороучение свое. Аминъ.

Азъ Григории диякон(ъ) написахъ еу(ан)г(е)лие е³ · да
иже горазнѣе сего напише · то не мози зазьрѣти мьнѣ грѣ-
шьникоу · почахъ же писати · м(ѣ)с(я)ца · октяб(ря) 21 ·
на памят(ь) Илариона · А оконьчах(ъ) · м(ѣ)с(я)ца · маия ·
въ · 12 · на па(мя)т(ь) Епифана. молю же вьсѣхъ почитаж-
щихъ · не мозѣте кляти · нъ исправльше · почитаите ·
Тако бо и с(вя)ты⁴ ап(осто)лъ Паулъ гл(агол)еть · Бл(аго-
слови)те · А не кльнѣте. Аминъ.

(Остромирово Евангелие, 1056–7)

II. LATE ELEVENTH CENTURY

ѡт(ъ) Гостяты къ Васильви · юже ми отьць даллъ и роди
съдаяли · а то за нимь · а нынѣ водя новоую женоу · а мънѣ
не въдасть ничьто же · избивъ роукы · поустилъ же мя · а
иноую поялъ · доеди добрѣ сътворя.

(Новгородская берестяная грамота, No. 9)

III. EARLY TWELFTH CENTURY

Се азъ Мьстиславъ Володимирь с(ы)нъ дьржа роусьскоу⁵
землю въ своє кнажениє повелѣлъ юсмь с(ы)ноу своюмоу
Всеволодоу ѡт(ъ)дати Боуицѣ⁶ с(вя)т(о)моу Геѡргиеви⁷ съ
данию и съ вирами и съ продажами / и вено вотское /⁸ даже

¹ Locative without preposition.　　　² Genitive dual.
³ For ce.　　　⁴ For свѧтыи.
⁵ Short (indefinite) form of adjective.　　　⁶ Name of a lake.
⁷ The St George (Jur'jev) monastery in Novgorod was founded in 1119 by Prince
Vsevolod Mstislavič, who was made prince of Novgorod in 1125.
⁸ Supralinear interpolation in text of manuscript. The reading (A. I. Jermola-
jev's) is doubtful.

которыи кнѧзь по моюмь кнѧжении почьнеть хотѣти ѡт(ъ)ѧти
оу с(вѧ)т(о)го Геѡргия · а Б(ог)ъ боуди за тѣмь и с(вѧ)тая
Б(огороди)ца и тъ с(вѧ)тыи Геѡргии оу него то ѡтимають · и
ты игоуменеИсаию · ивы братиѣ · донюлѣ же сѧ миръ състоить ·
молите Б(ог)а за мѧ и за моѣ дѣти · кто сѧ изоѡстанеть[1] въ
манастыри · то вы тѣмь дължьни юсте молити за ны Б(ог)а
и при животѣ и въ съмьрти · а язъ далъ роукою своюю · и
осеньнюю полюдию даровьною полътретия десате[2] гривьнъ
с(вѧ)т(о)моу же Геѡргиеви · а се я Всеволодъ далъ юсмь
блюдо серебрьно · въ 30 гр(и)внъ серебра · с(вѧ)т(о)моу
же Геѡргиеви велѣлъ юсмь бити въ ню на ѡбѣдѣ коли
игоуменъ ѡбѣдають · даже кто запъртить или тоу дань и се
блюдо · да соудить юмоу Б(ог)ъ въ д(ь)нь пришьствия
своюго и тъ с(вѧ)тыи Геѡргии.

(Грамота вел. кн. Мстислава Володимировича и его сына Всеволода,
c. 1130)[3]

IV. LATE TWELFTH CENTURY

Се въдале[4] Варламе[5] с(вѧ)т(о)моу с(ъ)п(а)соу землю и огородъ и ловища рыбьнаѧ и гоголиная и пожни ι рьль противу села за Волховомъ 2 на Волхевьци коле[6] 3 корь 4
лозь 5 волмина 6 на островѣ и съ нивами · вхоу[7] же тоу
землю Хоутин(ь)скоую въдале с(вѧ)т(о)моу с(ъ)п(а)соу и
съ челадию и съ скотиною. а се бра[тии далъ][8] ι отрокъ
съ женою 2 Вълос(ъ) 3 дѣвъка Феврониѧ съ двѣма сынов[ь-
ци] 4 недачь · а конь · шестеро и корова се · другое село на
Слоудици за . . . бнею[9] въдале[4] с(вѧ)т(о)му с(ъ)п(а)соу и
божница въ немь · с(вѧ)т(о)го Георгиѧ · и нив[и] и пожни и
ловищѧ и еже въ немь · се же все далъ Варламъ Михалевъ
с(ы)нъ · с(вѧ)т(о)моу с(ъ)п(а)соу · аще кто диѧволъмь
на[оуч]енъ и злыми ч(е)л(о)в(ѣ)кы наваженъ цьто[10] хочеть
ѡт(ъ)ѧти[11] ѡт(ъ) нивъ ли ѡт(ъ) пожьнь ли или ѡт(ъ)

---

[1] For изостанеть.
[2] Twenty-five, lit. 'half of the third decade'.
[3] A. A. Zimin (cf. *Pamjatniki russkogo prava*, ii, Moscow, 1953, p. 110) suggests the
inclusive date 1125–32 for this document.
[4] For въдалъ.
[5] For Варла(а)мъ.
[6] For поле. [7] For вьсю.
[8] A suggested reading.
[9] An incompletely legible word or phrase.
[10] For чьто. [11] Future tense.

ловищь · а боуди емоу противень с(вѧ)тыи с(ъ)п(а)съ · и
въ сь вѣкъ и въ боудоущии.

(Вкладная Варлаама Спасо-Хутынскому монастырю, c. 1192)[1]

V. EARLY THIRTEENTH CENTURY

сице же помоливъ сѧ блаж(е)ныи роуцѣ на высотоу
простьръ · и се д(у)хъ б(ож)иі просвѣти и · и испълни и всѧкого веселия и радости · и рече Нифонте[2] · азъ ти подамь
силоу · и крѣпость · на ѡканьныя бѣсы · ты же внимаи себѣ ·
въ въсѧкомь смѣрении · азъ бо люблю смѣреныя · ненавижю
же присно възносѧшаго сѧ · и вельрѣчьствующа · ты же аще
хощеши любимъ быти мною · имѣи смѣрениѥ · и не ѡсоужаи
нікого же · ни кльни сѧ ни ѡклеветаи ни сълъжи · ни гнѣваи
сѧ · ни зазри ч(е)л(о)в(ѣ)ка съгрѣшающа · тѧжька бо моука
таковыхъ жидеть · да не мози оуподобити сѧ грѣшьникомъ ·
посредѣ бо таковыхъ есть блазна дияволѧ · а ты не оуловленъ
боудеши ѡт(ъ) нихъ · нъ оуповаи · азъ бо ѥсмь с тобою · и си
рекъ доухъ б(ож)ии к нему · и въсхыти и видъ[3] · и видѣ яко
бѣ поуть дългъ · водѧи на въстокъ · и на поути томь стояхоу
мужи чьрни велици въѡроужени · копия дьржаще въ роукоу[4] ·
и стрѣжахоу поуть тъ · не дадоуще никомоу же миновати ·
стояше же и самъ съ народъмь · недомышлѧѧ сѧ · како бы
безъ врѣда прошьлъ поуть тъ · и недомыслѧщемъ сѧ имъ[5] ·
приде нѣкто въ бѣлахъ ризахъ · и рече кто[6] ѥсть страхъ вашь ·
почьто сѧ страхоуѥте · а не вѣдоуще[7] боязні мюринъ ѡнѣхъ ·
и ѡбративъ сѧ гл(агол)а к Нифонту · почьто то[8] не иде соуду ·
и гл(агол)а ѥмоу ѥси ли сѧ молилъ коли къ Б(ог)оу · да ти да[9]
съмѣрениѥ · гл(агол)а ѥмоу · сего прошю присно оу Б(ог)а
моѥго · ѡт(ъ)вѣща же к немоу анг(е)лъ и рече да сего ти подасть
Б(ог)ъ · да блюди · чьто ти боудеть · и зрѧ[10] яко прорѣза пьрьси
ѥмоу и изѧ с(е)рдце ѥго предъ всѣми · и повьргъ ѥ въложи ино
преславнѣѥ · и гл(агол)а ѥмоу иди поутьмь симь · и видѣвъше
тѧ чьрнии мюрини оумьрьщвени боудоуть · и никто же тебе
иметь · гла(гола)хоу же и прочии ѡт(ъ) народа молімъ ти сѧ ·

---

[1] M. N. Tichomirov (cf. 'O častnych aktach v drevnej Rusi', *Istoričeskije zapiski*,
No. 17) suggests c. 1211, the date of Varlaam's decease.
[2] For Нифонтъ.
[3] For въ видъ. The Greek original has εἰς θεωρίαν here.
[4] Locative dual.   [5] Dative absolute.   [6] For чьто.
[7] Mistranslation of the original.   [8] For ты.
[9] For дасть.   [10] For зьрить.

сътвори намъ тако же · да възъможемъ и мы проити поутьмь симь · и рече к нимъ анг(е)лъ идѣте и вы просите въ постѣ и въ м(о)л(и)твѣ оу Б(ог)а и дасть вамъ · аще ли не просите съмѣрения[1] то не приимете · ни проидете поутьмь симь · сь бо юдинъ поуть ведеть въ породоу[2] ·

(Житие Нифонта, с. 1219)

VI. LATE THIRTEENTH CENTURY

оже кто оударить мечемь.

Аже кто оударить мечемь · не вынезъ юго или роукоятью · то 12 гр(и)вне[3] · продаже за обидоу · оже ли вынезъ мьчь а не оутнеть · то гр(и)вноу коунъ · аже кто кого оударить батогомь · любо чашею · любо рогомь · любо тылѣснию · то 12 гр(и) внѣ · не тьрпл ли противоу томоу оударить мечемь · то вины юмоу в томь нѣтоуть · аще ли оутнеть роукоу · и ѿ(ъ)падеть роука · или оусъхнеть · или нога · или ѡко · или не оутьнеть · тъ полъ виры 20 гр(и)внъ · а томоу за вѣкъ 10 гр(и)внъ. Аже пьрьстъ оутьнеть · кыи любо то 3 гр(и)вны · продаже · а самомоу гривна коунъ.

Оже придет кръвавъ моуж. Оже придеть кръвавъ моуже[4] на дворъ · или синь то видока юмоу не искати · нъ платити юмоу продажю 3 гр(и)вн(ы) · или не боудеть на немь знамения · то привести юмоу видокъ · слово противоу слова · а кто боудеть началъ · томоу платити 60 коунъ · аче же и кръвавъ придеть · или боудеть самъ почалъ · а выстоуплть послоуси · то то юмоу за платежь ѡже и били · аже оударить мечемь а не оутнеть на см(ь)рть · то 3 гр(и)вны · а самомоу гр(и)вна за раноу · оже лѣчебною · потьнеть ли на см(ь)рть · то вира · или пьхнеть моужь моужа · любо к собѣ любо ѿ(ъ) себе · любо по лицю оударить · или жердью оударить · а видока два выведоуть · то 3 гр(и)вны продаже[5] · оже боудеть варлгъ или колблгъ · тъ полная видока вывести и идета на ротоу.

(Русская правда, с. 1282)

---

[1] Added by Russian scribe.
[2] Gk παράδεισος 'paradise'.
[3] Nom.–acc. dual after дъва на десте. The more correct form гривнѣ occurs a little lower down.
[4] For моужь.
[5] For gen. sg. продажѣ.

VII. THIRTEENTH-FOURTEENTH CENTURY

Тои ж(е) осени[1] мн(о)го зла са створи · поби мразъ обилыє
по волості · а на Тържкоу все чело быс(ть) · и зая кн(а)зь
вьршь · на Тържкоу не поус(ти) въ городъ ни воза · и послаша по кн(а)за С(е)мена Борисовица[2] · Вачеслава Клима-
тица[2] · Зоубьца Якоуна · и тѣхъ прия · и кого послашь[3] и
кн(а)зь прия · а Новѣгородѣ зло быс(ть) вельми · кадь ржи
коуплахоуть[4] по 10 гр(и)внъ · а овса по 3 гр(и)внѣ[5] · а
рѣпѣ[6] возъ по · 2 гр(и)вьнѣ · ядахоу люди сосновоую кору ·
и листъ липовъ · и мохъ · О горѣ тъгда братіє баше ·
дѣти своє[7] даяхоуть одьрень · и поставиша скоудельницю · и
наметаша полноу · О горѣ баше · по търгоу трупиє · по
оулицамъ троупиє · по полю троупиє · не можахоу пси
изѣдати ч(е)л(о)в(ѣ)къ · а вожане помроша · а останъке[8]
разиде са · и тако по грѣхомъ нашимъ разиде са власть наша ·
и градъ нашь · Новгородьци же останъке живыхъ · послаша
Гюрга Иванковица[9] посадника · и Степана Твьрдиславица[9] ·
ины моужа по кн(а)за · и тѣхъ прия · а въ Новъгородъ приславъ Ивора и Чапоноса · выведе княгыню свою к собе · дъчерь
Мьстислалю · и потомь послаша Маноуилоу · Ягольчевича
съ последнею речью · поиди въ свою о(т)циноу[9] · къ с(ва)тѣи
Софии · не идеши ли а повежь ны · Ярославъ же и тѣхъ не
поус(ти) · а гость новъгородьскыи всь прия · и быс(ть) Новѣгородѣ печаль и въпль · Тъгда ж(е) оучювъ Мьстислав(ъ) ·
Мьстиславліць[9] · зло то · въѣха въ Повъгородъ · м(ѣ)с(а)ца
февр(а)ра · въ 11 д(ь)нь · и я · хота · Григоревица[9] намѣстъ-
ника Ярослала[10] · и всѣ двораны искова. И выѣха на Ярос-
лаль[11] дворъ и цѣлова ч(ь)стьныи кр(ь)стъ · а новгородьци к
немоу · яко с нимь въ животъ и въ смр(ь)ть · любо изицю
моуж(и) новгородьстии и волости · пакы ли а головою повалю
за Новъгородъ · Ярославоу же быс(ть) весть на Тържькъ · и
изгошиша твьрдь · а поути ѿ(ъ) Новагорода все засекоша ·
и рѣкоу Тьхвѣрцю · а въ Новъгородъ въсла 100 моуж(ь) ·

[1] In 1215.   [2] Examples of *cokan'je*.
[3] For послаша.   [4] 3rd pl. imperfect with ending -ть.
[5] Dual form instead of plural after три.   [6] For рѣпы.
[7] Acc. pl. дѣти своѣ.   [8] For останъкъ.
[9] Examples of *cokan'je*.
[10] For Ярославла. This and the following are dialectal features.
[11] For Ярославль.

новгородьць · Мьстислав(а) проваживатъ из Новагорода · и
не яша сѧ по то нъ вси быша одинод(оу)ш(ь)но и то 100
моуж(ь) · и посла кн(ѧ)зь Мьстиславъ · съ новгородьци къ
Ярослав(оу) · на Тържькъ · поп(ъ) Гюргѧ · с(вѧ)тог(о) Iѡ(ана)
на търговищи · и свои мужь поус(ти) · с(ы)ноу[1] кланѧю ти
сѧ моуж(и) мои · и гость поус(ти) а самъ съ Торожькоу[2]
поиди а съ мною любъвь възми • Кн(ѧ)зь же Ярослав(ъ) того
не оулюбивъ · поусти попъ без мира · а новгородце[3] съзва
на поле за Тържькъ · въ мѧс(о)поус(тъ)поую с(у)б(от)оу ·
вьси моуж(и) · и гостьбници · измавъ я[4] всѧ посла исковавъ
по своимъ городомъ · а товары ихъ раздая и коне[5] · а бѧше
всѣхъ новгородьць · боле · 2000 и приде весть въ Новъгородъ ·
бѧше же новгородьцевъ[6] мало · ано тамо измано вѧчьшiѥ
моуж(ѣ) · а мьньшеѥ они розидоша сѧ а иноѥ помьрло голо-
домъ · кнѧзь же Мьстиславъ · створи вѣце[7] на Ярослали
дворѣ · и поидемъ реч(е) поищемъ моуж(ь) своихъ · вашеи
брат(ь)и и волости своѥи · да не боудеть Новыи Търгъ Нов-
городомъ · ни Новгородъ Тържькомъ · нъ къде с(вѧ)тая София
тоу Новгородъ · а и въ мнозѣ б(ог)ъ и в малѣ б(ог)ъ и правд(а).

(Первая Новгородская Лѣтопись по Синодальному списку)

VIII. LATE FOURTEENTH CENTURY

В лѣт 6495[8] · Созва Володимеръ боѧры своя · и старци градь-
скиѣ · и реч(е) имъ · се приходиша ко мнѣ болгаре · рькуще
приими законъ нашь · по сем же · приходиша нѣмци и ти
хвалѧх(оу) законъ свои · по сихъ придоша жидове · се же
послѣже придоша грьци хулаше[9] вси законы · свои же
хвалаше[9] · и много глⷶ(агола)ша сказающе · ѿт(ъ) начала миру ·
ѡ бытьи всего мира · суть же хитросказающе · и чюдно
слышати их(ъ) · любо комуждо слушати их(ъ) · и другии
свѣтъ повѣдають быти да аще кто дѣеть[10] в нашю вѣру сту-
пит(и) · то паки оум(ь)ръ станеть и не оумр(ѣ)ти ему в

---

[1] Voc. sg.   [2] Gen. sg.
[3] Acc. pl. новъгородьцѣ.
[4] Acc. pl. ѣ; and всѧ, which follows it, is a bookish form for вьсѣ.
[5] For конѣ, the acc. pl. form.
[6] A new formation for новъгородьць.
[7] For вѣче. Another instance of *cokan'je*.   [8] The year 987.
[9] Ш is used here for the required щ, as both words are present participles. Probably a copyist's slip due to the analogy of the forms of the imperfect tense.
[10] Mod.R. де 'it is said'.

вѣки · аще ли в ынъ законъ ступить · то на ѡномъ свѣтѣ в огнѣ горѣт(и) · да что оума придасте · что ѡт(ъ)вѣщаете · и рѣша бояре и старци · вѣси кнѧже яко своего никто же не хулить но хвалить · аще хощеши испытати гораздо то имаши оу собе мужи · пославъ испытаи когождо их(ъ) службу и како служить Б(ог)у · и быс(ть) люба рѣч(ь) кнѧзю и всѣмъ людемъ · избраша мужи добры и смыслены числомъ 10 · И рѣша имъ идѣте первое в болгары · и испытаите первое вѣру их(ъ) · ѡн[1] же идоша и пришедше видѣша скверньная дѣла · и кланѧнье в ропати · придоша в землю свою · и реч(е) имъ Володимеръ · идѣте паки в нѣмци съгладаит(е) тако же · и ѡт(ъ)тудѣ идѣте въ греки · ѡни же придоша в нѣмци и съгладавше црк(о)в(ь)-ную службу их(ъ) · придоша Ц(а)рюгороду[2] · и внидоша · ко ц(а)рю · ц(а)рь же испыта коея рад(и) вины придоша · ѡни же сповѣдаша ему всѧ бывшая · се слышавъ ц(а)рь рад(ъ) бывъ · и ч(ь)сть велику створи имъ · во ѡт(ъ) же[3] д(ь)нь наоутрия посла къ патреарху гл(агол)ѧ · сице придоша русь пытающе[4] вѣры нашея · да пристрои цр(ь)к(о)вь и крилос(ъ) · и самъ при-чини сѧ въ с(вѧти)т(е)льския ризы · да видѧть славу Б(ог)а нашего · си слышавъ патреархъ повелѣ создати[5] крилосъ · по ѡбычаю створиша пр(а)здн(и)къ · и кадила вожьгоша · пѣнья и лики съставиша · и иде с ними в ц(ь)рк(о)вь и поставиша я на пространьнѣ мѣстѣ · показающе красоту ц(ь)рк(о)вную · пѣнья и службы архиерѣиски престоянье дьяконъ · сказающе имъ служенье Б(ог)а своего · ѡни же во изумѣньи бывше · оудививъшес(ѧ) похвалиша службу ихъ · и призваша[6] е ц(а)рѧ · Василии и Костантинъ · рѣста имъ идѣте в землю вашю · и ѡт(ъ)пустиша я[7] с дары велики и съ ч(ь)стью · ѡни же придоша в землю свою · и созва кнѧзь болѧры своя и старца[8] · реч(е) Володимеръ се придоша послании нами мужи · да слышимъ ѡт(ъ) нихъ бывшее и реч(е) скажите пред(ъ) дружиною ѡни же рѣша яко ходихомъ в болгары · смотрихомъ како сѧ покланають въ храмѣ рекше в ропати · стоѧще бес пояс(ъ) · поклонив сѧ сѧдеть · и глѧдить сѣмо и ѡнамо · яко бѣшенъ · и нѣс(ть) веселья в них(ъ) · но печаль и смрадъ великъ · нѣс(ть) добро законъ ихъ и придохомъ в

---

[1] For они.
[2] Dat. sg. used in allative sense.
[3] For въ тъ же 'in the same'.
[4] Nom. pl. pres. part. agreeing with collective sg. русь.
[5] For созвати as in other manuscripts.
[6] Pl. for dual призъваста.
[7] Like е above, represents acc. pl. ѣ.
[8] Acc. pl. старьцѣ.

нѣмци · и видѣхомъ въ храмѣх(ъ) · многи службы творѧща а красоты не видѣхомъ никоея же · и придохо[1] же в греки и ведоша ны идеже служать Б(ог)у своему · и не свѣмы на н(е)бѣ ли есмы были · ли на земли · нѣс(ть) бо на земли такаго[2] вида · ли красоты такоя · и не дооумѣемъ бо сказати токмо то вѣмы · яко онъдѣ Б(ог)ъ с ч(е)л(о)в(ѣ)ки пребываеть · и есть служба их(ъ) паче всѣхъ странъ · мы оубо не можемъ забыти красоты тоя · всѧкъ бо ч(е)л(о)в(ѣ)къ аще оукусит(ь)[3] сладка · послѣди горести не приимаеть · тако и мы не има[4] сде быти · от(ъ)вѣщавше же болѧре рекше[5] · аще бы лихъ законъ гречьскии · то не бы баба твоя прияла Ѡльга · яже бѣ м(у)дрѣиши всѣх(ъ) ч(е)л(о)в(ѣ)къ · от(ъ)вѣщавъ же Володимеръ реч(е) · идемъ[6] кр(ь)щ(е)нье пріимемъ · они же рекоша гдѣ ти любо.

(Лѣтопись по Лаврентьевскому списку, 1377)

IX. EARLY FIFTEENTH CENTURY

от(ъ) великого · кн(ѧ)зѧ · намѣстниковъ[7] · Ивана и Василья · от(ъ) посадника Ѥсифа Захарьинича от(ъ) тысѧчкого Григорьи · Ивановица[8] · и от(ъ) всего Великого Новагорода к заморьскымъ · посламъ въ Юрьво[9] · к Ивану и другому Ивау[10] · что ѥсте к намъ · прислалѣ[11] · и мы вашю грамоту слъ(і)шилѣ[12] а повѣстуѥте такъ · что вы ѥсте послалѣ к намъ во Юрво[9] свои пословѣ[13] по(с)лалѣ[11] · ч(ь)стны добрыи · люди · о всѧкохъ дѣлехъ на всю правду · ино того у насъ пѣрвѣѥ сего не было что намъ слать во Юрво[9] · а намъ с вами заморчи[8] · ины миръ и гамота[14] намъ с вами · а съ Юрьвчи[9] с Велневичи · намъ сво[15] миръ братьѧ заморци приславъ к намъ грамоту · опасную · взѧлѣ · у насъ · с нашими напечатьми что вамъ ѣздити в Велики Новъгородъ · и от(ъ)издити путь ч(и)стъ безо всѧкого опаса про то на васъ велми дивимъ що вы к намъ · не

---

[1] Incomplete for придохомъ.
[2] For таковаго as in other manuscripts.
[3] Other manuscripts have вкоусить.   [4] Incomplete for имамъ.
[5] For рекоша as in other manuscripts. Cf. also *Ipat.* рѣша.
[6] Other manuscripts have гдѣ for идемъ.
[7] New formation for намѣстьникъ.
[8] Examples of interchange of ч and ц (*cokan'je*).
[9] For Юрьевъ.   [10] For Ивану.   [11] For присълали.
[12] For слышали. Plural is now used for the obsolete dual.
[13] Used as acc. pl. for своѣ посълы.
[14] For грамота.   [15] For свои.

идите по опасу на Б(о)жи руки с(вѧ)т(ѣ)и Софьи на н(о)вго-
рочкѣи а вамъ ч(и)стъ путь приихати ѡт(ъ)ихать безо всѧкого
опаса.

(Грамота новгородских наместников Ивана и Василия в Юрьев)

X. LATE FIFTEENTH CENTURY

Ѡ конѣ · В единъ ж(е) ѡт(ъ) д(ь)нїи приведоша конюсѣ[1]
къ Филипоу ѡт(ъ) стада жребець зѣло великъ [велми] и поставиша и пред нимъ, гл(агол)юще · вл(а)д(ы)кѡ ц(а)рю,[2]
сїи кѡнь ѡбрѣтохѡм въ ц(а)рьскыих(ъ) стадѣхъ родившасѧ[3]
и прѣкрасна соуща[3] · приведохѡм(ъ) ти, вл(а)д(ы)кѡ ·
видѣв же Филипъ сего добротоу и величество, и подивисѧ ·
мнѡгыми же дръжимъ[4] ѡдва, ведом(ъ) бѧше · конюсѣ же
рѣша · вл(а)д(ы)ко ц(а)рю,[2] ч(е)л(овѣ)коядець [ти] ес(ть),
[имѣѧ волую гл(а)ву на бѣдрахъ]. ц(а)рь же Филипъ
реч(е) · въистиноу ѡ семъ сверщаетсѧ. якож(е) въ еллинѣх
притча, яко близъ добрыих бы зло · но понеже привели есте
къ мнѣ, и прїимоу ег(о) · повѣле же сътворити емоу коущу
железноу · и тоу его затворити не ѡбоуздана · иже аще [кто]
не покоритсѧ ц(а)рьствоу моемоу, но и прѣступникъ боудеть
законѡмъ, или аще боудеть в разбои ятъ, и тоу вмѣтаемъ
бываеть. и быс(ть) [такѡ], якож повелѣ ц(а)рь. Быс(ть) же
Александроу лѣт(ъ) 15, въ единъ ѡт(ъ) днїи ключисѧ емоу
мимо ити, идѣж(е) бѣ заключенъ кѡнь волоуѧ гл(а)ва · [абїе]
оуслыша ржанїа его страшнаѧ, и, ѡбративсѧ къ ѡтрокѡм(ъ).
и реч(е) · что се ес(ть) ржанїе кѡнное. ѡт(ъ)вѣщав же Птѡло-
мѣи воевода, рече. вл(а)д(ы)ко,[5] се есть конь, нарицаемыи
волоуѧ гл(а)ва, егож(е) ѡ(те)ць твои затвори, зане ч(е)л(овѣ)-
коядець есть. сицеж(е) оуслышавъ конь глас(ъ) Александровь
и проржавь второе. не акы всегда страшно, но пач(е) тихо и
красно, акы ѡт(ъ) Б(о)га наоученъ. и акож(е) приближисѧ къ
коущи Александръ, и абїе видѣ[6] кѡнь прежнѣи нозѣ[7] къ
Александроу и языкъ свои испоусти къ немоу, являясѧ своемоу
вл(а)д(ы)цѣ · Александръ же, видѣвь паки чюдно ѡбличїе
и кѡсти мнѡгыих ч(е)л(овѣ)к(ъ) ѡтъ злыѧ смр(ь)ти съкроушены
лежаща ѡколо его, ѡт(ъ)гнавь стража і ѡт(ъ)врьзе кущу, и имъ

---

[1] For конюси.
[2] Voc. sg. forms.
[3] Gen. sg. forms used as animate acc. forms.
[4] Bulgarian spelling pointing to South Slavonic influence.
[5] Voc. sg. form.
[6] For выдѣ.
[7] Acc. dual.

его за гривоу, и оукроти его, и, изведе и нешбоуздана, и
ездаше посредѣ града Пельскаго. тече же нѣкто ѿт(ъ) коню-
ховъ,[1] повѣда Филипоу ц(а)рю, соущоу емоу[2] вън(ѣ) града
Пельскаг(о) · Филипъ ж(е)помлноувь, еж(е) емоу реч(е) влъхва
· [Флоніи] въ Делфѣ, абіе въставь, оусретѣ Александра и
цѣлова его, гл(агол)л · радуи с(л), Александре миродержьце.[3]
и ѿт(ъ)толѣ кротокъ блше Филипъ ѡ надежи чада.

(Александрия)

XI. EARLY SIXTEENTH CENTURY

Бесѣда · ı ѡ ѡсми частехъ вѣщаниа илй рѣчи, вспросы и
ѿтвѣты · слово и рѣч(ь) за ѡдно стоит і вѣщание кое хощешь
тò рцы. И в Дамаскінѣ[4] имл, рѣчь,[5] причастие, различие,
мѣсто имени, предлогъ, нарѣчие, сооуз(ъ). Вспрос(ъ) оучй-
телевъ.

в(спро)с(ъ) · Части вѣщаниа, или рѣчи колйцы суть;
ѡ(твѣ)т(ъ) · ѡсмь ·

в(спро)с(ъ) · Кои; ѡ(твѣ)т(ъ) · имл, проименис, слово илй
рѣч(ь), предлог(ъ) слову, причастие, сооуз(ъ), представление,
различие.

в(спро)с(ъ) · Имл что̀ есть; ѡ(твѣ)т(ъ) · часть вѣщаниа с
падениемъ, тѣло илй вещъ собьственѣ илй ѡбще знаменуя[6] ·
собьственѣ, яко · Римъ, Тивер(ъ) · ѡбще, яко · град(ъ), рекà.

в(спро)с(ъ) · Имени колйцы пристолт(ъ) илй нападают(ъ);
ѡ(твѣ)т(ъ) · шесть.

в(спро)с(ъ) · Котории; ѡ(твѣ)т(ъ) · качество, прилагание,[7]
род(ъ), числò, ѡбраз(ъ), падение.

в(спро)с(ъ) · Качество именъ в чом есть; ѡ(твѣ)т(ъ) ·
двоечастно[8] есть.

в(спро)с(ъ) · Како же; ѡ(твѣ)т(ъ). или бо единое вещи
имл есть и собьственое илй сущее гл(агол)ет сл, илй многих
и есть нарицательное.

в(спро)с(ъ) · Прилагание степенем[9] колйцы суть;
ѡ(твѣ)т(ъ) · трѝ.

в(спро)с(ъ) · Кои; ѡ(твѣ)т(ъ) · положйтелнал, якѡ · ученъ.

---

[1] New gen. pl. for конюхъ. [2] Dat. absolute.
[3] Voc. sg. form. [4] John Damascene (8th cent.). [5] Verb.
[6] For знаменоующи. [7] 'Comparison'.
[8] 'Bipartite'. [9] Dat. pl. with genitive function.

прилагателнаѧ, ꙗко · ученѣе илѝ ученнѣише · надприлагателною илѝ превышнею, ꙗко · преученнѣише.

в(спро)с(ъ) · Кои имена прилагаютсѧ; (ѡ(твѣ)т(ъ) ·) нарицательные токмо, качество илѝ количество знаменующие · качество, ꙗко · бл(а)гъ, илѝ добръ, или золъ · количество, ꙗко · великъ илѝ малъ.

в(спро)с(ъ) · Прилагателнаѧ степень коему падению служит; ѡ(твѣ)т(ъ) · ѿ(ъ)рицателному¹ ѡбѣих числъ без представлениа.

в(спро)с(ъ) · Како же; (ѡ(твѣ)т(ъ) ·) гл(агол)ем бо · учителнѣе ѡнаго, илѝ учителнѣе инѣх.

в(спро)с(ъ) · Превыспренаѧ надприлагателнаѧ илѝ превышнаѧ степень коему падению служитъ; ѡ(твѣ)т(ъ) · родственому токмо множьственому.

в(спро)с(ъ) · Како; ѡ(твѣ)т(ъ) · гл(агол)ем бо · преоученнѣишіи мудрецовъ бѣаше Виргиліи, илѝ нарочитеиши (ѿ(ъ)) народа.

(Донатусъ Меньшей)²

XII. LATE SIXTEENTH CENTURY

Како дѣти оучити и страхомъ сп(а)сати

Казнѝ с(ы)на своегѡ ѿ(ъ) юности егѡ и покоитъ тѧ на старость твою і дастъ красотꙋ д(у)шѝ твоеи и не ѡслаблѧи биѧ мл(а)д(ен)ца, аще бо жезлѡмъ біеши егѡ не оумретъ но здравіе будетъ · ты бо біѧ егѡ по телу, а д(у)шу егѡ избавлѧеши ѿ(ъ) см(е)рти, дщерь³ ли имаши положи на них грозу свою соблюдеши ѧ⁴ ѿ(ъ) телесных да не посрамиши лицꙗ своегѡ да в послушаніи ходит да не свою волю пріимши и в неразуміи прокудит, дѣвствѡ свое, и сотворитсѧ знаемъ твоимъ въ посмѣхъ и посрамѧт тѧ пред множествомъ народа аще бо ѿ(ъ)даси дщерь⁵ свою бес порока то ꙗко велико дѣло совершиши и посреди собора похвалишисѧ при концы̀ не постонеши на ню любѧ же с(ы)на своегѡ оучащаи емꙋ раны да послѣди ѡ немъ возвеселишисѧ казнѝ с(ы)на своегѡ измлада и порадуешисѧ ѡ немъ в мужествѣ и посреди злых похвалишисѧ и зависть пріимутъ врагѝ твоѧ,⁶ воспитаи

---

¹ Ablative case.
³ Gen. pl.
⁵ Acc. sg.

² *Ars minor* of Donatus (4th cent.).
⁴ Acc. pl.
⁶ For врази твои.

дѣтище с прещеніемъ, и ѡбрáщеши ѡ немъ покóй и бл(а)-
гословеніе, не смѣисл к немý игры творл̀ в мáле бо сл ѡсла-
биши в велѝцѣ поболѝши, скорбл̀, и после же яко ѡскóмины
творѝши д(у)ши твоéи и не дажъ ему власти во ю́ности но
сокрушѝ емý ребрà донележе расїетъ а ѡжесъточавъ не
повинет ти сл и будет ти досаженіе и болéзнь д(у)ши и тщетà
дóмови погибель именію и оукоризна ѡт(ъ) сусѣдъ и посмѣхъ
пред врагѝ пред властію платежь и досàда зла̀.

. . . воставъ ѡт (ъ) ложà своегò пред ѡчѝстивъ себѣ и молéб-
нал совершивъ женáмъ и дѣвкам дѣло оуказáти дневнóе вcл-
кому рукодѣлію что работы дневнáл ества варѝти, и которои
хлѣбы печи сѝтные и решетные, и самá бы знáла какъ мукá¹
сѣлти кáкъ квашнл притворѝти и замѣситі и хлѣбы валлти и
печѝ и квáсны и бухóны и вы́пеклисл, а колачѝ и пирогѝ тáко
же, и колко мукѝ возмутъ и кóлько испекутъ и колко чевò²
родитсл ис четверти илѝ из осмины илѝ из решотà,³ и кòлко
высевковъ и кóлко испекутъ мѣра знати во всемъ а еству
млсную и рыбную, и всáкіе пироги и всáкіе блины́ и всáкіе
кáши и киселѝ и вслкіе приспѣхи печѝ и варѝти все бы самà
г(о)с(у)д(а)р(ы)на оумѣла, ино оумѣетъ и слуг научѝти, и
всё самà знает а колѝ хлѣбы пекутъ тогдѝ и платл мóютъ ино
с одного сътрепнл̀ и дровàмъ не оубыточно, и дозирáти какъ
красные рубáши моют и лýчшее пълатьл, и кóлко мыла идетъ
и золы́ и на кóлко рубáшекъ, и хорошò бы вымыти и вы́пари-
ти, и нáчисто выполоскати і иссушити і искатáти, и скáтерти
и оубрусы и ширѝнки і оутиралники тако же и всемý счéтъ
самòи знати и ѡт(ъ)дáти и взлти все сполнá . . .

(Домострой)

XIII. EARLY SEVENTEENTH CENTURY

О новоявльшемся развратницѣ Тишинѣ,⁴ его же имя
нарицашеся дикой воръ тушинской

В лѣто 7116⁵ паки инъ звѣрь подобенъ тѣма же явися, или,
рекши, и лютѣйшій сихъ воста, на готовое бо селеніе діяволи
мечты пріиде самъ отецъ лжи сатана. Еще бо тогда не вси
Рустіи грады къ Московскому государству обратишася, отъ

---

¹ Nom. object of infinitive.   ² For чего.
³ For решета.   ⁴ The False Dmitrij (Лжедмитрий).
⁵ The year 1608.

него же отпадоша крамолодѣющими[1] мятежники, и се паки въ той же прежереченнѣй странѣ Черниговстѣй явился инъ злобѣсный кроволакательный[1] песъ или человѣкоядный[1] звѣрь, иже лукавое око отверзе и злое рыканіе испусти, и вся простожительныя люди устраши, а зміеобразныя[1] лукавыя и злыя сихъ къ своему кроволитному нраву усвояя привратити. Къ нему же и паки множество пріидоша Полскихъ людей и Литовскихъ, понеже и сій нарицая себе царевичемъ княземъ Дмитріемъ Углецкимъ.[2] Аще и судъ божій вскорѣ постиже злобнаго сего пса, но убо конечно увидѣша Литовскіе людіе неустроеніе въ Руси, и междоусобное смятеніе, и брань, и сего ра̀ди вси устремишася на Рускую землю. И бысть отъ нихъ злое и тяжкое всѣмъ христіяномъ озлобленіе, понеже и предатели царства и царя с ними уже сложишася, и крамолу велію во вся грады Рускія устрояху, и на царствующий градъ Москву зѣло належаху, и всѣ страны Рускія земли немилостивно плѣняху. И толико множество Полскихъ людей и мятежниковъ и клятвопреступниковъ Рускихъ собрашася, яко и земли покрыватися щиты и воздуху блещатися копіи, брани же и крови разливатися всюду.[3] Овыи убо грады Москвѣ тогда придержахуся и Василія царя славяху, яко же Великій Новградъ и Псковъ, Смоленскъ и Казань; овіи же Литвѣ и мятежникомъ Рускимъ поработашася; и таково, грѣхъ ради нашихъ, отъ начала въ земли Рустѣй смятеніе не бывало, еже тогда бысть. И таковыми смятеніи злые они мятежницы сердце Василья царя, аки лядиною многомутныя[1] волны, восколебаша, и отвсюду утѣсняему вмалѣ не погрузитися хотя; аще бо и желая отсюду помощи и отнюду, но ниоткуду же обрѣтая. Царь бо, не имый сокровища многа и друговъ храбрыхъ, подобенъ есть орлу бесперу и неимущу клева и ногтей; вся бо мерскій рострига ходящему сребру царскія истощи, и тѣснотою скудости ратныя люди стѣсняющеся вси.

(Историческое сказаніе о смутном времени)[4]

[1] Note compound adjectives.
[2] For Угличскимъ.
[3] Elliptical resultative clause with finite verb omitted.
[4] Cf. *Rukopisi xvii v.* Archeografičeskoj komissii, St Petersburg, 1909.

XIV. LATE SEVENTEENTH CENTURY

К

Кто не ѣлъ чесноку. тот и не воняетъ.
Каково кто постелет таково и выспится.
Какъ в лесъ кликнешъ такъ и откликнется.
Какъ хто[1] тонетъ топор сулит а как вымут і топоріща не даст.
Коли дрова горятъ. толды кашу варятъ.
Ключь силнѣя[2] замка.
Кошку бьютъ а невѣстке навѣтки даютъ.

Л

Лутче празничать а не бражничать.
Лутче. ста рублевъ.[3] сто друговъ.
Лизавъ. нож порѣзать языкъ.
Лукъ добро. и к бою и во штяхъ.[4]
Люди жать а мы с поля бѣжать.
Любо в стремя ногою. любо. петлю головою.

М

Медъ сладко а муха падко.
Мала даждевная капля жесток камен пробивает.
Мяхки[5] руки. чюжие. труды. поядаютъ.
Малая сабака и под старость щеня.
Межъ перстовъ мясо. не растетъ.
Мило. волку. теля. да гдѣ ево[5] взять.
Мяхкая[5] постеля. в долгъ. сонъ приводит.
Мыши кота на погостъ волокутъ.
Мнѡгая говоря всегда стыда доводит.

Н

Не испортя дѣла не узнать.
Не спрашиваи стара спрашиваи бывала.
На чюжои рот не пугвица[6] нашить.
Над пужанымъ соколомъ и вороны граютъ.
Не помѣрявъ. броду. не мечися. в воду.
Не посмотря. в окно. не плюи.

---

[1] Southern dialect form.
[2] For сильнѣе.
[3] Now obsolete in literary language.
[4] For щяхъ.
[5] Phonetic spelling.
[6] Nominative object of infinitive.

Ношная¹ какушка² денную перекоковывастъ.
Нашла свинья свое порося.
Назвався груздемъ лѣсти в кузовъ.
(Повести или пословицы всенароднейшие по алфавиту)³

XV. EARLY EIGHTEENTH CENTURY

I

Herr.   Къ князю Аникитѣ Ивановичу Репнину

Сегодня получилъ я вѣдомость о Вашемъ толь худомъ
поступкѣ, за чьто можешь шеею запълатить, iбо я чрезъ
господина губернатора подъ смертью не велѣлъ ничего в
Ригу пропускать. Но ты пишешь, что Огилвиi⁴ тебѣ велѣлъ. Но
я так пишу: хотя бъ i ангелъ, не точию сей дерзновенникъ i
досадитель велѣлъ бы, но тебѣ не довълѣло бы сего чинить.
Впреть же аше⁵ единая щепа пройдетъ, ей Богомъ⁶ кленусь,
безъ головы будешь.

Piter.

С Москъвы, маiя в 19 д. 1705.

2

Къ Анисьѣ Кирилловнѣ Толстой и Екатеринѣ Алексѣевнѣ⁷
Тетка i матка сама друга⁸ [а скоро будешъ i сама третья],
здраѳъствуйте,⁹ а мы, слава Богу, здорово.
Писмо Ваше купно i съ прежентомъ принялъ, и за оныя
благодарствую; а что пишете, чтобъ к вамъ всегда добрыя
вѣдомости писать, i то я отъ серца радъ, да какие Богъ дастъ.
Я чаю, что сие мое писмо вамъ при самомъ времени выѣзда
Ганскина iзъ Кельдера достанетца, о чемъ зело слышать
желаю; что дай, Боже, в радости не толко слышать, но i
видеть. О ѣзде вашей в Питербурхъ еще не могу писать,
понеже непъриятель ближитца, и не знаемъ еще, куды его

---

¹ For ночьная. Moscow dialect form.   ² Example of *akan'je*.
³ Cf. P. K. Simoni, *Starinnyje sborniki russkich poslovic, pogovorok, zagadok i proč.*,
St Petersburg, 1899.   ⁴ Field-Marshal George Ogilvy.
⁵ For аще. The use of ш here probably indicates Moscow long ʃʃ.
⁶ Fusion of two constructions, viz. ей Богу and Богомъ.
⁷ The later Catherine I. She was a maid in the home of the Tsar's friend, Pastor
Ernst Glück, in Livonia (mod. Latvia).
⁸ 'Both'. Accordingly сама третья means 'three of you'.
⁹ Peter the Great was partial to ѳ. See later.

обороты будутъ; о чемъ немедленно буду писать, увидео҃ъ
время, куды вамъ быть, понеже горазда[1] безъ васъ скучило.
Еще жъ объявъляю свою нужду здѣшнею:[2] отыть і обмыть
некому, а вамъ нынѣ вскорѣ быть,[3] сами знаете, что нелзя.
А здѣш(н)имъ повѣрить боюсь Екимовой причины. Того
ради изволте то ісправить,[4] о чемъ Вамъ донесетъ доноси-
тель сего писма. За симъ предаю Васъ в сохранение Божие і
желаю васъ в радости видеть, что дай, дай, Боже. Прошу
отдать должной поклонъ сестре.
На частыя писма, для Бога,[5] не подивуйте: істинно
недосугъ.
Ізъ Вильни, в 29 д. генваря 1708.

Piter.

(Два письма Петра Великого)[6]

XVI. LATE EIGHTEENTH CENTURY

О гласныхъ и о частяхъ рѣчи

Вопр. Чтò разумѣешь ты чрезъ гласныхъ?

Отв. Чрезъ гласныхъ разумѣю тѣхъ сильныхъ вельможъ,
кои по большей части самымъ простымъ звукомъ, чрезъ одно
отверзтіе рта, производятъ уже въ безгласныхъ то дѣйствіе,
какое имъ угодно. Напримѣръ: если большой баринъ, при
докладѣ ему о какомъ-нибудь дѣлѣ, нахмурясь скажетъ: *о!*,
того дѣла вѣчно сдѣлать не посмѣютъ, развѣ[7] какъ-нибудь
перетолкуютъ ему объ ономъ другимъ образомъ и онъ, получа
о дѣлѣ другія мысли, скажетъ тономъ, изъявляющимъ свою
ошибку: *а!* — тогда дѣло обыкновенно въ тотъ же часъ и
рѣшено.

Вопр. Сколько у Двора бываетъ гласныхъ?

Отв. Обыкновенно мало: три, четыре, рѣдко пять.

Вопр. Но между гласными и безгласными нѣтъ ли еще
какого рода?

Отв. Есть: полугласные, или полубояре.

Вопр. Что есть полубоярінъ?

---

[1] For гораздо. An instance of *akan'je*.   [2] For здѣшнюю.
[3] Infinitive used to express future time.
[4] 'To do, to carry out'.   [5] 'For God's sake'.
[6] Cf. *Pis'ma i bumagi imperatora Petra Velikogo*, i–ix, St Petersburg–Moscow,
1887–1952. The first letter quoted here will be found in vol. iii, p. 346, and the
second in vol. vii, pp. 43–44.   [7] 'Unless'.

Отв. Полубояринъ есть тотъ, который уже вышелъ изъ безгласныхъ, но не попалъ еще въ гласные; или, иначе сказать, тотъ, который предъ гласными хотя еще безгласный, но передъ безгласными уже гласный.

Вопр. Что̀ разумѣешь ты чрезъ придворныхъ безгласныхъ?

Отв. Они у Двора точно то, что въ азбукѣ буква ъ, то есть: сами собою, безъ помоши другихъ буквъ, никакого звука не производятъ.

Вопр. Что̀ при словахъ примѣчать должно?

Отв. Родъ, число и падежъ.

Вопр. Что̀ есть придворный родъ?

Отв. Есть различіе между душею мужескою и женскою. Сіе различіе отъ пола не зависитъ: ибо у Двора иногда женщина стоѝтъ[1] мужчины, а иной мужчина хуже бабы.

Вопр. Что̀ есть число?

Отв. Число у Двора значитъ счетъ, за сколько подлостей сколько милостей достать можно; а иногда счетъ, сколькими полугласными и безгласными можно свалить одного гласнаго; или же иногда, сколько одинъ гласный, чтобъ устоять въ гласныхъ, долженъ повалить полугласныхъ и безгласныхъ.

Вопр. Что есть придворный падежъ?

Отв. Придворный падежъ есть наклоненіе сильныхъ къ наглости, а безсильныхъ къ подлости. Впрочемъ, бо̀льшая часть бояръ думаетъ, что всѣ находятся передъ ними въ *винительномъ падежѣ*; снискиваютъ же ихъ расположеніе и покровительство обыкновенно *падежемъ дательнымъ.*

Вопр. Сколько у двора глаголовъ?

Отв. Три: *дѣйствительный, страдательный*, а чаше[2] всего *отложительный.*

Вопр. Какія наклоненія обыкновенно у Двора употребляются?

Отв. Повелительное и неопредѣленное.

Вопр. У людей заслуженныхъ, но безпомощныхъ, какое *время* употребляется по большей части въ разговорахъ съ большими господами?

Отв. Прошедшее, напримѣръ: *я израненъ, я служилъ*, и тому подобное.

---

[1] 'Is worth.'

[2] For чаще. The spelling used by Fonvizin may be interpreted phonetically as 'tʃæʃʃι.

Вопр. Въ какомъ *времени* бываетъ ихъ отвѣтъ?

Отв. Въ *будущемъ*, напримѣръ: *посмотрю, доложу*, и такъ далѣе.

(Д. И. Фонвизинъ, *Всеобщая придворная грамматика*, 1788)

XVII. EARLY NINETEENTH CENTURY

Признаюсь, не безъ трепета приступаю къ разбору «Грамматики» г. Калайдовича.[1] Она еще до своего появленія и даже, можетъ быть, до своего рожденія, успѣла пріобрѣсти себѣ такую громкую славу; общій голосъ ставитъ ея автора въ числѣ литераторовъ ученыхъ, опытныхъ и коротко знающихъ свое дѣло, я же не больше, какъ безвѣстный юноша, еще ничѣмъ не пріобрѣтшій права голоса на литературномъ сеймѣ, еще не сочинившій ни одной афиши, не издавшій ни одной программы, не объявившій ни одной подписки и даже не обѣщавшій ни одною строчкою никакого творенія: очевидное неравенство! Прибавьте къ сему, что у насъ еще и по сію пору такъ сильно вліяніе авторитетовъ, еще такъ могущественно очарованіе именъ; что у насъ еще весьма не многіе осмѣливаются произнести свое сужденіе о стихотвореніи, журнальной статьѣ или книгѣ, не посмотрѣвши сперва на подпись, или не справившись въ «Сѣверной Пчелѣ» — этомъ литературномъ аукціонѣ — каково «сходитъ съ рукъ» то или другое сочиненіе, т. е. сколько экземпляровъ онаго разошлось въ продолженіе того или другаго времени; сообразите все это — и вы признаетесь, что тутъ хоть у кого такъ опустятся руки. Но какъ бы то ни было, а я рѣшаюсь на этотъ отчаянный подвигъ, и, прикрываясь мудрымъ правиломъ нашихъ предковъ: «страшенъ сонъ да милостивъ Богъ», приступаю къ дѣлу.

Учебныя книги бываютъ двухъ родовъ. Однѣ изъ нихъ пишутся для первоначальнаго обученія; главное ихъ достоинство должно состоять въ простомъ и ясномъ изложеніи предмета и искусномъ принаровленіи[2] онаго къ дѣтскимъ понятіямъ. Другія же пишутся для людей взрослыхъ, мыслящихъ и, кромѣ ясности въ изложеніи, требуютъ **новаго** взгляда или на **цѣлый** предметъ, или хотя на нѣкоторыя

---

[1] И. Ф. Калайдович (1796–1853), Russian grammarian.
[2] For приноровленіи. A slip indicating *akan'je*.

части онаго, или, по крайней мѣрѣ, представленія онаго въ его современномъ состояніи.

Къ которому изъ сихъ двухъ родовъ относится «Грамматика» г. Калайдовича?

По запутанности и сбивчивости ея изложенія, по отсутствію новыхъ взглядовъ, худо прикрытому мелочными нововведеніями въ терминологіи, ни къ одному; по своей незначительности и неважности — къ первому; по претензіямъ же автора — ко второму.

Теперь у насъ четыре знаменитыя грамматики: Ломоносова, Россійской Академіи, г. Греча и г. Востокова.[1] Ихъ достоинство, исключая, можетъ быть, второй, находится въ прямомъ содержаніи ко времени ихъ появленія. Безъ всякаго сомнѣнія, пятая грамматика, чтобъ заслужить вниманіе, должна быть лучше всѣхъ сихъ четырехъ, ибо авторъ оной, кромѣ своихъ собственныхъ открытій, можетъ воспользоваться открытіями своихъ предшественниковъ и смѣло взять у каждаго изъ нихъ все лучшее. Такъ ли поступилъ г. Калайдовичъ? Посмотримъ. Сначала я брошу общій взглядъ на его сочиненіе, потомъ буду преслѣдовать его шагъ за шагомъ, сколько будетъ то возможно.

Всѣмъ и каждому извѣстно, что способъ изложенія всякой науки бываетъ аналитическій и синтетическій, и что, вслѣдствіе сего, всякая наука раздѣляется на общую и частную, на теорію и приложеніе. Грамматикъ (наукъ) можетъ быть столько, сколько языковъ и нарѣчій на земномъ шарѣ; но есть одна общая имъ всѣмъ грамматика, есть грамматика слова человѣческаго, грамматика всеобщая или философская. Грамматики языковъ суть грамматики частныя, относящіяся къ ней, какъ виды къ роду, и повѣряющіяся ею. Г. Калайдовичъ какъ будто даже и не слыхалъ объ этомъ.

(В. Г. Бѣлинскій, Отзывъ о «Грамматикѣ языка русскаго I» И. Ф. Калайдовича, 1834)

XVIII. LATE NINETEENTH CENTURY

Историки увѣряютъ, что Западная Римская Имперія пала отъ изнѣженности нравовъ, а Византійская — отъ коварства

---

[1] Н. И. Гречъ (1787–1867), publicist and grammarian (cf. Практическая русская грамматика, 1827). А. Х. Востоковъ (1781–1864), philologist (cf. Русская грамматика, 1831).

царедворцевъ, которые ничего, будто бы, не дѣлали, а только
коварствовали. Какъ бы то ни было, но паденію этому, во
всякомъ случаѣ, предшествовалъ извѣстный внѣшній фактъ.
Явились съ востока гунны, лонгобарды, османлисы[1] и дру-
гіе человѣкообразные, и сразу доказали то, чего не могъ
доказать цѣлый рядъ Мессалинъ, Агриппинъ и не менѣе
замѣчательный рядъ иконописныхъ Никифоровъ и Евдокій.
Не будь этого внѣшняго факта, очень можетъ статься, что
римляне и до сихъ поръ продолжали бы предаваться изнѣженности нравовъ, а византійцы — коварствовать, то-есть
сплетничать, цѣловать въ плечико и подставлять другъ другу
ножку.

Мы, провинціалы, историковъ не имѣемъ, но у насъ есть
исторіографы (чиномъ повыше), которые занимаются не
столько исторіей нашего прошлаго, сколько предусмотри-
тельными набѣгами въ наше будущее.

Если вѣрить этимъ глубокомысленнымъ людямъ, Россія
должна погибнуть въ самомъ ближайшемъ времени, и
погибнуть втихомолку, безъ всякаго внѣшняго натиска,
единственно силою собственныхъ пороковъ. Такъ что если,
напримѣръ, вы сегодня видите Россію, а завтра на этомъ самомъ мѣстѣ увидите пустое мѣсто, то не имѣете права даже
удивляться этой пропажѣ, ибо она есть естественное слѣд-
ствіе нашей заранѣе доказанной и предсказанной исторіо-
графами развращенности.

Само собою разумѣется, что, по внутреннему убѣжденію
исторіографовъ, главный нашъ порокъ, это — уничтоженіе
крѣпостной зависимости; но такъ какъ это порокъ секретный,
о которомъ распространяться не всегда удобно, то найденъ
другой порокъ, не столь капитальный, но служащій для
нашихъ исторіографскихъ философствованій немаловаж-
нымъ подспорьемъ. Порокъ этотъ — пресловутое всероссій-
ское пьянство.

Было время, когда надежды исторіографовъ на паденіе
Россійской Имперіи покоились преимущественно на грубости нравовъ. Предполагалось, что, тотчасъ по освобо-
жденіи крестьянъ, русская земля немедленно запустѣетъ,
что Ваньки[2] будутъ сидѣть задравши на столъ ноги и бесѣ-

---

[1] Osmanli Turks.   [2] 'Jacks', a colloquialism for 'peasants' (мужики).
[3] 'Menservants'. Pejorative diminutive of Трифонъ.

довать объ изящныхъ искусствахъ, что Тришки[3] перестанутъ чистить сапоги и унавоживать поля, что торговля упразднится, потому что не будетъ разносчиковъ, и т. д. «Кто будетъ сѣять, жать, варить и печь, кто будетъ шапки передъ нами ломать?» — спрашивали другъ друга испуганные исторіографы, и къ чести ихъ должно прибавить, что никому не пришло на мысль сказать: «мы будемъ сѣять! мы будемъ жать!» Однако надежды насчетъ грубости нравовъ не выгорѣли, отчасти, быть-можетъ, потому, что тогда еще бодрствовалъ откупъ[1] (все-таки, хоть какое-нибудь утѣшеніе!), отчасти же потому, что всѣ эти Ваньки и Тришки совсѣмъ не такъ воспитаны, чтобы сидѣть задравши на столъ ноги и бесѣдовать объ изящныхъ искусствахъ.

Потребовалось другое основаніе для исторіографскихъ погибельныхъ предсказаній, а такъ какъ жизнь никогда не скупится подачками подобнаго рода и такъ какъ тутъ же кстати послѣдовало и упраздненіе откуповъ, то на смѣну грубости нравовъ естественнымъ образомъ явилось пьянство.

И подлинно, вышло нѣчто весьма подходящее.

(М. Е. Салтыковъ-Щедринъ, Письма изъ провинціи, 1868)

XIX. EARLY TWENTIETH CENTURY

Монастырскія чайки долго летятъ за нами, прощаются. Потомъ одна за другой отстаютъ, а вмѣстѣ съ ними отстаетъ и тяжелое, мрачное чувство. Навстрѣчу пароходу попадается какой-то дикій, заросшій лѣсомъ островъ. Кто-то мнѣ говоритъ, что тамъ живутъ два охотника.

— Одни живутъ?

— Одинешеньки. Два карела.[2]

— Какъ же они живутъ?

— Да ничего. Хорошо.

Тутъ я вспоминаю, что у меня есть ружье, что я охотникъ. Я чувствовалъ себя въ монастырѣ нехорошо, потому что туда идутъ люди молиться, а я … убѣжалъ за волшебнымъ колобкомъ.

И чѣмъ дальше отъ монастыря, тѣмъ лучше я себя чувствую; чѣмъ дальше, тѣмъ больше море покрывается дикими скалами, то голыми, то заросшими лѣсомъ. Это Карелія, — та самая

---

[1] 'Farming out.'   [2] 'Carelians'.

Калевала,¹ которую и теперь еще воспѣваютъ народные рап-
соды въ карельскихъ деревняхъ. Показываются горы Лапландіи, той мрачной Похіолы,² гдѣ чуть не погибли герои
Калевалы.

Кольскій полуостровъ — это единственный уголъ Европы,
до послѣдняго времени почти не изслѣдованный. Лопари —
забытое всѣмъ культурнымъ міромъ племя, о которомъ не
такъ давно (въ концѣ XVIII столѣтія) и въ Европѣ раз-
сказывали самыя страшныя сказки. Ученымъ приходилось
опровергать общее мнѣніе о томъ, что тѣло лопарей покрыто
космами, жесткими волосами, что они одноглазые, что они со
своими оленями переносятся съ мѣста на мѣсто, какъ облака.
Съ полной увѣренностью и до сихъ поръ не могутъ сказать,
какое это племя. Вѣроятно, финское.³

Переходъ отъ Кандалакши до Колы, который мнѣ придется
совершить, довольно длинный: двѣсти тридцать верстъ пѣш-
комъ и частью на лодкѣ. Путь лежитъ по лѣсамъ, по горнымъ
озерамъ, по той части русской Лапландіи, которая почти
прилегаетъ къ сѣверной Норвегіи и пересѣкается отрогами
Скандинавскаго хребта, высокими Хибинскими горами,
покрытыми снѣгомъ. Мнѣ разсказываютъ въ пути, что рыбы
и птицы тамъ непочатый край, что тамъ, гдѣ я пойду, лопари
живутъ охотой на дикихъ оленей, медвѣдей, куницъ ...

Меня охватываетъ настоящій охотничій трепетъ отъ
этихъ разсказовъ; больше, — мнѣ кажется, что я превратился
въ того мальчугана, который убѣжалъ въ невѣдомую, прекрас-
ную страну.

Иногда и у самыхъ культурныхъ людей бродятъ дикія ка-
пельки крови. Въ зимнюю ночь, въ то время когда люди еще не
успѣли замѣтить уже начавшійся переходъ къ веснѣ, бываютъ
видѣнія: засверкаетъ солнце, перекинется мостъ изъ свѣтя-
щихся зеленыхъ листьевъ на ту сторону, къ лѣсу.

Зеленая опушка, трава съ широкими листьями, деревья
гигантскія упираются въ небо, невиданные цвѣты, звѣри и
птицы умныя, добрыя.

¹ Kalevala, the land of Kaleva, the mythical giant-hero of the West Finnic or
Somian peoples. Also the title of the Finnish national epic compiled by Elias
Lönnrot.
² *Pohjola* 'Northland', geographically Lapland, the scene of some of the major
exploits of the heroes of *Kalevala*. Cf. W. F. Kirby (transl.), *Kalevala: the Land of
Heroes* (London, 1907). ³ The Lapps are Finnic in speech.

Страна безъ имени! Когда-то въ ней бывалъ … все знакомо … все забыто …

Мелькнетъ видѣніе — и наступаетъ обыкновенное зимнее утро, разумное, дѣльное. Но что-то есть еще сверхъ обычнаго. Что это? Ахъ да, скоро весна, облака свѣтятся. Страна безъ имени! Вотъ куда мы хотѣли тогда убѣжать въ далекомъ нашемъ дѣтствѣ. Мы называли ее то Азіей, то Африкой, то Америкой. Но въ ней не было границъ: она начиналась отъ того лѣса, который виднѣлся изъ окна классной комнаты. И мы туда убѣжали. Послѣ долгихъ скитаній насъ поймали, какъ маленькихъ лѣсныхъ бродягъ, и заперли. Наказывали, убѣждали, смѣялись, употребляли всѣ силы доказать, что нѣтъ такой страны. Но вотъ теперь у каменныхъ стѣнъ со старинными соснами, возлѣ этой дикой Лапландіи я со всей горечью души чувствую, какъ неправы были эти взрослые люди.

Страна, которую ищутъ дѣти, есть.

(М. М. Пришвинъ, Колобокъ, 1906)

XX. MID-TWENTIETH CENTURY

По дороге в райком Коростелев забежал, как он выражался, «накрутить хвост» шофёру Тосе[1] Алмазовой.

Алмазова пятый день не выходила на работу. Коростелев посылал за нею, вывесил грозный приказ — ничего не помогло: у Алмазовой шло большое гулянье. Гуляла вся родня, гуляла вся улица в честь благополучного возвращения Тосиного супруга с полей Отечественной войны.[2]

В маленькую кухню светило апрельское солнце. Час был уже поздний, а хозяева только собирались завтракать: накануне легли спать с третьими петухами … Алмазов сидел у стола небритый, но сапоги его были зеркально начищены и к вороту гимнастёрки пришит чистый подворотничок. «Антонина старается, наряжает мужа», — подумал Коростелев, с лету заметив все подробности. Две девочки сидели по другую сторону стола, тоже нарядные, старшая в красном галстуке: и детишки дома, в школу не пошли … Тося ухватом передвигала в печи горшки, лицо её пылало от печного жара.

---

[1] Hypocoristic diminutive of Антонина.
[2] Russo-German war of 1941–5.

Блаженствуют черти. В рабочие дни сплошной выходной[1] устроили, законы не для них писаны . . .

— Доброго здоровья! — сказал Коростелев, с разгону шагнув в кухню и остановившись. — Я по твою душу, Тося. Корми семейство скорым темпом — и айда.[2]

— Стул подай-ка, — сказала Тося старшей дочери. — Радость у меня, не сердитесь, Дмитрий Корнеевич.

Она поставила ухват и стояла перед Коростелевым, глядя ему в лицо виноватыми и сияющими глазами. А глаза у неё были серо-зелёные, обведённые тёмной каёмочкой. И такие же глаза были у двух беленьких детишек, сидевших против отца. Невозможно под взглядом этих глаз заорать: «Да ты что, на самом деле! Вот отдам под суд . . .» Оставалось сесть на стул, который девочка выставила на самую середину кухни, и бить на психологию.[3]

— Очень рад за тебя и поздравляю, конечно, — начал Коростелев, — но работа есть работа, Тося, так?

— Мне отгул[4] полагается, — сказала Тося. — У Лукьяныча записано, сколько выходных я отработала. Послезавтра выйду.

— Ещё бы сказала — через неделю. Ты просто, я тебе скажу, пользуешься своим положением.

Она закинула голову и засмеялась.

— Пешочком[5] ходите? — спросила сквозь смех.

— На самолёте летаем.

— Ничего, — сказала Тося, — немножко пешочком. Полезно для моциона.

(Вера Панова, Ясный берег, 1949)

[1] Sc. день 'free day'.
[2] Tartar loan-word. The meaning here is пойдём 'let's go'.
[3] 'To make a psychological approach'.
[4] From гулять. A colloquialism for 'day off'.
[5] Diminutive form of пешком.

APPENDIX II

HISTORY OF RUSSIAN HISTORICAL GRAMMAR

I

THE investigation of Russian as a historical phenomenon rather than as a static grammatical system begins in the early part of the nineteenth century with the emergence of the study of comparative grammar in Central and Western Europe. Until then the study of grammar in the East Slavonic area was essentially descriptive and normative, and the language studied was, until the end of the seventeenth century, not Russian but Church Slavonic.[1] In the Old Russian period interest in grammar was mainly the practical interest of the copyist, and where it was wider than this it was almost inevitably centred in rhetoric. Treatises on rhetoric, translated into Old Church Slavonic from Byzantine sources, existed in the Balkans (cf. the 'Svjatoslav Miscellany' of 1073, which contains a version of Georgius Choeroboscus's περὶ τροπῶν ποιητικῶν); and the well-known disquisition *O pismenech* by the monk Chrabr, extant now only in thirteenth- and fourteenth-century Bulgarian manuscripts, follows a Byzantine prototype, viz. a grammatical treatise (περὶ γραμματικῆς) by Pseudo-Theodosius. Chrabr confined himself to the alphabet and its phonetic basis in making his comparisons. But linguistic differences between Greek and Old Church Slavonic were noted by Ioann, Exarch of Bulgaria, in his translation of St John Damascene's 'Theology' ("Εκδοσις ἀκριβὴς τῆς ὀρθοδόξου πίστεως).

In the fourteenth century, according to V. Jagić,[2] disquisitions on the 'eight parts of speech' were popular in Serbia, and here again the models would seem to have been Greek, although they have not yet been traced. These disquisitions were passed on to the Bulgarians, through whom, by way of Moldavian and Wallachian copies, they ultimately reached Muscovy.

[1] Cf. S. K. Bulič, *Očerk istorii jazykoznanija v Rossii*, i, St Petersburg, 1904.
[2] *Issledovanija po russkomu jazyku*, i, St Petersburg, 1895.

Besides grammatical treatises, primers (*azbukovniki*) commanded a ready interest in medieval Russia. These at first took the form of glossaries and afterwards of 'encyclopaedic' compilations. Some of the primers contain lists of 'difficult' words: thus the 'Novgorod Nomocanon' (*c.* 1282) has a glossary of Hebrew words (*Rěč' židovskago jazyka preložena na russkuju*). The next glossary is dated 1431 and also derives from Novgorod, viz. 'Interpretation of Difficult Words in Writing' (*Tlŭkovanije neudob' poznavajemom v pisanych recěm*). Part of this material found its way into later primers, which are common in the sixteenth and seventeenth centuries and are remarkable for the great wealth and variety of information they contain, for instance, on foreign alphabets, the classification of languages, metrical data, and much else.

Early sixteenth-century Muscovy profited on the educational side from the presence and the 'philological' activities of Maksim Grek (*c.* 1480–1556), a foreigner, as his name shows, who became the first of the Muscovite grammarians. He had come on invitation from Athos, where he had been a monk, and the task for which he had been chosen was the 'correction' of the church books, whose steadily deteriorating text had already been tampered with and bedevilled by South Slavonic scholars from the end of the fourteenth century. Maksim Grek won for himself a reputation in Moscow as an authority on grammar, and his views were quoted in current and later manuscripts. His interests were strictly confined to the language of the Church, which in effect provided the entire stock of the grammarians' illustrations.

The grammatical treatises of the time are anonymous, with few exceptions. One example deserving mention is a summary of Constantine the Grammarian's *Slovesa vkratce izbranna*, which is known to go back to fourteenth-century Serbia. Others are mainly the work of non-Russian scholars—White Russians and Ukrainians—who were well versed in Church Slavonic.

The theory of grammar in Muscovy was admittedly Byzantine Greek; but the grammatical terminology also showed Latin influence, which had reached the Eastern Slavs through Poland and its 'Ruthenian' (viz. White Russian and Ukrainian) dependencies. It is conceivable that the ultimate source of Latin influence was a version or adaptation of Donatus (see App. I, pp. 293–4). This work survives in several copies, one of which, viz.

the Kazan' MS, contains the copyist's remark that it is written only in Russian, without admixture of Latin, so that it may be understood by reader and student (cf. единымъ русскимъ языкомъ, безъ латиньскаго, да бы прочитающимъ ю и учащимся въ неи болѣе разумно было).

At the end of the sixteenth century the first printed grammars of Church Slavonic began to appear in the East Slavonic area, beginning with the works of White Russian and Ukrainian grammarians (e.g. the anonymous *K gramatyka sloven'ska jazyka*, Vil'na, 1586; Ἀδελφότης[1]: *Grammatika dobroglagolivago ellino-slovenskago jazyka*, L'vov, 1591). The first of these works was the result of an investigation of the language of the Ostrog Bible (1581), and the second is mainly concerned with Greek. In 1596 Lavrentij Zizanij published his *Grammatika slovenska* in Vil'na. This also contains his 'Leksis', the first printed glossary of Church Slavonic, which served as source and prototype for other glossaries, including that of the Moldavian Pamva Berynda (cf. *Leksikon slavenorosskij*, Kiev, 1627). In 1619 there appeared the Church Slavonic grammar (*Grammatiki slavenskija pravilnoje sintagma*) of the Ukrainian Meletij Smotryc'kyj, and this was to remain the authority on its subject even in eighteenth-century Russia.[2] Smotryc'kyj's Grammar was thoroughly recast and supplemented with observations ascribed to Maksim Grek in Moscow, and appeared there anonymously in 1648. The language described by Smotryc'kyj is not a pure Church Slavonic, but contains traces of the influence of living Slavonic languages (e.g. White Russian, Ukrainian, and Polish). There is no sense of history in the book, and the paradigms are copied from Classical grammar, and are sometimes contrary to the genius of the language described.

Quite apart from the items we have so far examined is the Croatian Jurij Križanić's *Gramatično izkazanje ob russkom jeziku* (1666). This curious book is concerned with an artificial language, a sort of Slavonic Esperanto, in which Church Slavonic, Russian, and Croatian elements jostle one another. Indirectly, it represents a renewed interest in Church Slavonic, which was

---

[1] 'Fraternity.'
[2] The Grammar was republished in Vil'na in 1629. The Moscow version of 1648 was reprinted in a revised form by Polikarpov-Orlov in 1721 and by F. Maksimov in 1723.

re-elaborated in Muscovy in a mainly Ukrainian recension in the second half of the seventeenth century by immigrant Ukrainian scholars such as the lexicographer Epifanij Slavynec'kyj, compiler of *Kniga leksikon greko-slaveno-latinskij* (*c.* 1664–76).[1] With the advent of these scholars the study of Church Slavonic in Muscovy was given a new impetus, and the language began to be taught at school as well as at seminary level. Knowledge of it reached even the masses through the primers of Burcev (*Načal'no učenije čelovĕkom chotjaščim razumĕti božestvennago pisanija*, 1637) and Karion Istomin (*Bukvar' slavjanorossijskich pis'men*, 1694). In the last decade of the seventeenth century a Russian grammar was published in Latin at Oxford by the German H. W. Ludolf (*Grammatica russica*, 1696). This work shows a knowledge of colloquial speech and at the same time proves the predominance of Church Slavonic and its study in Russia at that time.

Peter the Great was interested in language only as a medium of translation and communication, and the academy he had planned contained no department for the empirical study of the mother tongue. The grammatical literature published in his time consisted of text-books based on Smotryc'kyj's 'Grammar', of multilingual vocabularies (e.g. Kopijevič's *Nomenclator in lingua latina, germanica et russica*, 1700), and of primers (e.g. F. Polikarpov-Orlov's *Bukvar' trejazyčnyj slavenskimi, grečeskimi i rimskimi pis'meny*, 1701). Nevertheless, it was in his reign that the collection of non-Slavonic linguistic material began, and scholars, mainly foreign, were sent on linguistic expeditions to Kazan', Astrachan', the Caucasus, and Siberia.

The immediate successors of Peter the Great were not interested in the study of Church Slavonic or Russian and gave little encouragement to its prosecution. In the middle of the eighteenth century, however, serious interest in the study of Russian was shown by Trediakovskij and Lomonosov. Trediakovskij was attracted to the orthography in the spirit of a reformer interested primarily in the representation of sounds (*zvony*). Then, in 1755, Lomonosov published his *Rossijskaja grammatika*,[2] which was a considerable achievement as the first

---

[1] This was an adaptation of Johannes Scopula's *Lexicon graeco-latinum*[2], Amsterdam, 1663.
[2] The German version of this appeared in St Petersburg in 1764.

descriptive grammar of literary Russian. Lomonosov made use of Smotryc'kyj's work as revised by Adodurov, but his originality expressed itself in the choice of grammatical material and illustration. He did not attempt to invent forms, as Smotryc'kyj had done, and carried his selectiveness into the field of vocabulary by contrasting dialectal with literary material, in which he further distinguished the Russian from the Church Slavonic element, and with the aid of these three elements set out his theory of the three styles (see § 602), which incidentally had a Classical origin. His theory of tense, also inspired by Classical influence, was an artificial framework into which he tried to fit the refractory data of the Russian verb. Unlike Smotryc'kyj, Lomonosov had wide interests and knowledge in many fields: it was he who distinguished the language of the Old Russian writs from Old Church Slavonic and classified the Slavonic languages into a north-east and a south-west group.[1]

Catherine II's curiosity, unlike that of her imperial predecessors, extended even to language, and it was at her instigation that materials of the languages spoken in the Russian Empire began to be collected and published, for instance, by the naturalist P. S. Pallas. The result of several years of assiduous endeavour was Pallas's monumental collection *Linguarum totius orbis vocabularia comparativa* (1786–9), which came out in a Russian edition in 1790–1. Although the scholarly interest of this compilation was small, it nevertheless gave encouragement to the study of language by suggesting the need to base it on a preliminary accumulation of lexical material.

Interest in lexicography was shown by workers in the Slavonic field. P. Aleksejev's *Cerkovnyj slovar'* (1773–6) was a great advance on its predecessors in bulk alone, and the Academy Dictionary (*Slovar' Akademii rossijskoj*, 1789–94), in which all members of the Academy of Sciences are said to have collaborated, was the first-fruits of Russian dictionary-making on a large scale. Following Lomonosov, the academicians consciously tried to keep the literary Russian and Church Slavonic elements apart, but not always successfully, and the dialectal element is relatively neglected.

[1] It will be recalled here that Scaliger (see Chap. i, p. 3, note 1) had contented himself more than a century before with merely enumerating the Slavonic languages in an incomplete list.

The beginning of the nineteenth century is marked by the publication of Russian grammars for Germans (e.g. J. Vater, *Praktische Grammatik der russischen Sprache*, Leipzig, 1808; A. W. Tappe, *Neue theoretisch-praktische russische Sprachlehre*, St Petersburg–Riga, 1810). Unlike Lomonosov, both Vater and Tappe give a more accurate picture of the system of the Russian verb by emphasizing aspect rather than tense. Their grammars are purely descriptive and intelligently compiled for the foreign learner.

Comparative grammar was also introduced into Russia by German scholars, for instance K. G. Anton and F. Adelung, both of whom studied the interrelations of Russian and Sanskrit in 1809–11. Adelung's work was published anonymously and had a preface written by the Russian grammarian N. I. Greč. But it contained no indication of the emergence of the historical point of view and of a mode of treatment based on this, and, moreover, the contributions to the 'Transactions of the Society of Lovers of Russian Literature' (*Trudy Obščestva ljubitelej rossijskoj slovesnosti*), issued between 1812 and 1820, contained only empirical articles on problems of Russian and Slavonic grammar. In 1820, however, there appeared the now famous *Rassuždenije o slavjanskom jazyke* by A. Ch. Vostokov (Osteneck), which makes a beginning with the linguistic investigation of Russian. The same author's Russian grammars, both the 'full' and the 'concise',[1] which were published in 1831, are, on the contrary, purely descriptive works without comparative historical commentary, although they are rich in fact and observation.

It was indeed not until the 1840's that comparative grammar became historical with the emergence of a group of historians of language, including F. I. Buslajev and I. I. Sreznevskij, whose scrupulous investigations won the attention of philological circles. One of this group, M. A. Maksimovič, discussed the characteristics of Russian pleophony (*polnoglasije*) in a treatise to which he gave the name *Načatki russkoj filologii* (Kiev, 1839). Buslajev's *O vlijanii christianstva na slavjanskij jazyk* (Moscow, 1840) shows the author applying the German comparative-historical method, which had not been very evident even in Vostokov's work. But the first account of the history of the

---

[1] *Russkaja grammatika*, St Petersburg, 1831; *Sokraščjonnaja russkaja grammatika*, ibid., 1831.

Russian language will be found in Sreznevskij's *Mysli ob istorii russkogo jazyka* (St Petersburg, 1850), which prepared the way for Buslajev's capital *Opyt istoričeskoj grammatiki russkogo jazyka* (Moscow, 1858). The 1840's also saw the publication of scholarly dictionaries and well-edited texts. The four-volume *Slovar' cerkovno-slavjanskogo i russkogo jazyka* (St Petersburg, 1847) was compiled by a section (*otdelenije*) of the Imperial Academy of Sciences and contained well over 100,000 words, but it still revealed the 'traditional' inability to separate the Russian from the Church Slavonic element. And Vostokov's edition of the 'Ostromir Gospels' (St Petersburg, 1843) was the earliest of a number of similar editions of historical monuments which were prepared mainly by the prolific and conscientious scholarship of Sreznevskij, who was also responsible for the compilation of the standard historical dictionary *Materialy dlja slovarja drevne-russkogo jazyka*, i–iii (St Petersburg, 1893–1912).

Sreznevskij's beneficial influence is further apparent in the work of P. A. Lavrovskij, who, among other things, wrote the first detailed historical monograph on an Old Russian (Novgorod) dialect (*O jazyke severnych russkich letopisej*, St Petersburg, 1852). To the 1850's, as we have seen, also belongs Buslajev's historical grammar (q.v.); and it was then that Vostokov published his *Opyt oblastnogo velikorusskogo slovarja* (St Petersburg, 1852) and its supplement (ibid., 1858). This is the second important Academy publication, which for all its faults was to become the foundation of all subsequent regional dictionaries of Russian. It is in this decade, moreover, that Ja. K. Grot's first significant contributions[1] to Russian linguistic studies appear, though their emphasis is not primarily historical.

The 1860's were even more momentous in the linguistic field, as they witnessed the publication of Buslajev's *Istoričeskaja christomatija cerkovnoslavjanskogo i drevnerusskogo jazyka* (Moscow, 1861), which set the example for historical readers, and V. I. Dal's monumental *Tolkovyj slovar' živogo velikorusskogo jazyka* (St Petersburg, 1861–8), which was to go through four editions by the beginning of the present century. These two works represent one of the two important aspects of Russian linguistics, viz. the accumulation and classification of illustrative material. The

[1] e.g. 'O sisteme zvukov russkogo jazyka' (*ŽMNP*, St Petersburg, 1852).

other is best seen in the theoretical writings of the Ukrainian A. A. Potebnja, who emphasized the philosophical as well as the historical aspect of language.

The 1860's also witnessed the foundation of chairs of comparative philology at various Russian universities, but it was only in the two ensuing decades, under the stimulating influence of the German Junggrammatiker, that the historical study of Russian as part of the complex of Slavonic languages reached its culmination in the Moscow and Kazan' linguistic schools, represented respectively by F. F. Fortunatov and the Pole Jan Baudouin de Courtenay. The Moscow school was particularly remarkable for its Russian scholarship and produced among much else the outstanding contributions of A. A. Šachmatov. This school was to some extent counterbalanced by the Kazan' school, which included the talented Polish theorist N. V. Kruševskij (Kruszewski), in association with whom Baudouin de Courtenay advanced the name and concept of the phoneme. The two schools exhibited differences in detail, but were essentially offshoots of the German Neogrammarian movement with its emphasis on 'sound-laws' and the psychological basis of its linguistic theorizing (cf. the work of Hermann Paul[1] and Wilhelm Wundt[2]).

The study of Russian descriptive and historical grammar in a large philosophical framework manifests itself especially in Potebnja's *Iz zapisok po russkoj grammatike*, which began to appear in Char'kov in 1874 and reached its third volume in 1899.[3] Potebnja's ideas were more akin to those of Wilhelm von Humboldt and of H. Steinthal than to the tenets of the Neogrammarian school, and this coign of vantage enabled him to assess the facts of Russian from an 'internal' rather than from an 'external' or formal point of view. A more formal attitude was taken by A. I. Sobolevskij who, like Šachmatov, was a product of the Moscow school. His *Očerki iz istorii russkogo jazyka* (St Petersburg, 1884) is the original form of a series of lectures on Russian historical grammar (*Lekcii po istorii russkogo jazyka*, ibid., 1888), which reached its fourth and last edition in 1907. It should be interpolated here that, between Buslajev and Sobolevskij,

---

[1] *Prinzipien der Sprachgeschichte*[1], Halle, 1909.
[2] *Die Sprache*, Leipzig, 1900.
[3] A fourth volume was published in Moscow–Leningrad in 1941. See p. 326.

M. A. Kolosov had published a *résumé* of the subject entitled
Očerk istorii zvukov i form russkogo jazyka s XI po XVI stoletije
(Warsaw, 1872), but this is episodic and derivative.

Šachmatov's contribution to the history of Russian bulks
larger than Sobolevskij's by its foundations and scope and the
originality of its ideas. He is regarded even today as one of the
leading authorities on the subject, and his lithographed *Kurs
istorii russkogo jazyka*, i–iii (St Petersburg, 1910–12)[1] and *Očerk
drevnejšego perioda istorii russkogo jazyka* (Petrograd, 1915) still contain a great deal to interest, though, unlike Sobolevskij's 'Lectures', they are now rather out of date. Šachmatov, however,
still retains his authority in the detailed study of the language of
the Old Russian writs (e.g. *Issledovanije o jazyke novgorodskich
gramot XIII i XIV veka*, St Petersburg, 1885–95; *Issledovanije o
dvinskich gramotach XV veka*, i–ii, ibid., 1903).

Sobolevskij and Šachmatov, who, like Baudouin de Courtenay before them and Prince N. Trubetzkoy (q.v.) after them,
show remarkable linguistic acumen, are the immediate sources
of Soviet historical study of Russian. The prevalence of formalism, with its 'external' evaluation of linguistic as well as
literary phenomena, led to the comparative neglect of the historical investigation of language in the 1920's. N. N. Durnovo's
Očerk istorii russkogo jazyka (Moscow–Leningrad, 1924) was the
only important book on the subject apart from his own *Vvedenije
v istoriju russkogo jazyka*, i (Brno, 1927) which deals with sources
and represents an elaboration of the corresponding section
(Introduction) in Sobolevskij's 'Lectures'.

Towards the end of the same decade Roman Jakobson's *Remarques sur l'évolution phonologique du russe comparée à celle des autres
langues slaves* (Prague, 1929) marks the emergence of a new,
émigré point of view in Russian linguistics which is based on the
contemporaneous manifesto of the phonological group known
as the Prague Linguistic Circle (*Pražský linguistický kroužek*) and
is consciously opposed to the 'traditionalism' of Šachmatov. Its
connexion with formalism is obvious[2] and accordingly it was to
have no place in the development of the study of Russian in

---

[1] Part of this appeared as *Vvedenije v kurs istorii russkogo jazyka*, i, Petrograd, 1916.
This is fertile in ideas, which are further elaborated in Šachmatov's last work
Drevnejšije sud'by russkogo plemeni, Petrograd, 1919.

[2] V. Erlich, *Russian Formalism: History–Doctrine*, The Hague, 1955.

Russia itself after Marxist criticism had eliminated the forma-
list movement in the Soviet Union. Even such literary scholars
as V. M. Žirmunskij and V. V. Vinogradov became linguists
and Marxists.

The Marrist episode, also a product of the 1920's and representing a synthesis of Marxist theory with N. Ja. Marr's own
linguistic imaginings,[1] occupied the 1930's and the whole of the
1940's, when Marr's pupils, notably I. I. Meščaninov, gave the
directives to linguistic scholarship. During this period works on
the Russian language included that of L. P. Jakubinskij, viz.
Istorija drevnerusskogo jazyka. This was based on lectures delivered
by the author at Leningrad University in the 1930's and was
prepared for publication in 1941;[2] but it was not published till
1953, when it was edited by Vinogradov and annotated by
P. S. Kuznecov. The Marrist influence is there, although it is
denied by Vinogradov, and the author's wartime patriotism has
led to radical shifts of emphasis from the Church Slavonic to
the vernacular Russian element.

This extreme position, which insisted on an East Slavonic
rather than a South Slavonic foundation for the literary language of Rus', was a product of the nationalist emotions aroused
by the Russo-German war of 1941–5, though its origins must be
sought in the views expressed by V. I. Lamanskij and N. K.
Nikol'skij.[3] The leading representative of such views today is
S. P. Obnorskij, the author of serious studies such as *Očerki po
istorii russkogo literaturnogo jazyka staršego perioda* (Moscow–Leningrad, 1946), in which he analyses the language of four old texts
of unequal historical value, and *Očerki po morfologii russkogo
glagola* (Moscow, 1953), in which the morphology of the verb
is viewed historically. Patriotic emphasis is present also in
G. O. Vinokur's *Russkij jazyk: istoričeskij očerk* (Moscow, 1945),
which attracted attention abroad and was translated into both
French and German.

The effect of the volte-face from Marrism may be seen in the
publication of the third edition of L. A. Bulachovskij's *Istoričeskij kommentarij k russkomu literaturnomu jazyku* (Kiev, 1950). This

---

[1] W. K. Matthews, 'The Japhetic Theory' (*SEER* xxvii. 68, London, 1948,
pp. 172–92).
[2] See Vinogradov's 'Introduction' to this book, pp. 3–40.
[3] Ibid., p. 6.

Ukrainian scholar had brought his book out originally in 1937, i.e. during the Marrist dispensation, although it did not reflect the dominant influence. The historical element is presented as a commentary on a previous descriptive study of the literary language (*Kurs russkogo literaturnogo jazyka*, Kiev, 1935), which reached its fifth edition in 1952. Bulachovskij has always been a representative of traditionalism, and in the changing climate of opinion his book was received with distinct favour. Its purpose was to carry the study of Russian down to the end of the eighteenth century. The early nineteenth is covered by his *Russkij literaturnyj jazyk pervoj poloviny XIX veka* (Moscow, 1954), which deals with its more limited matter with a wealth of illustrations.

Meanwhile an entire series of new books on the history of Russian has appeared since 1950, among which P. Ja. Černych's *Istoričeskaja grammatika russkogo jazyka* (Moscow, 1952) was chronologically the first. It is more compact and systematic, as well as more comprehensive, than Jakubinskij's and conforms more strictly to Marxist specifications, now that the 'crisis' in linguistics, which had been caused by conflict with Marrism, had been resolved by fiat from above.[1] It is a matter of interest that some of the immoderate theories in his predecessor's book, though still retained, have been somewhat toned down. P. S. Kuznecov's *Istoričeskaja grammatika russkogo jazyka* (Moscow, 1953) is a Moscow University publication of higher calibre than Černych's from the point of view of scholarly conscientiousness; but as the author confines himself only to one, viz. the morphological, aspect of linguistic development, he tends inevitably to over-simplify the picture. A still more recent book, A. I. Jefimov's *Istorija russkogo literaturnogo jazyka* (Moscow, 1954), is also a publication issued by the same press and represents a considerable expansion of a course of university lectures. The emphasis here is on literary Russian, especially the development of Russian style, so that its connexions with literature and authorship are much closer than those of the other 'histories', and the author uses an abundance of illustrative matter to further his argument.

---

[1] W. K. Matthews, 'The Soviet Contribution to Linguistic Thought' (*AL* ii. 1–2, Glasgow, 1950, pp. 1–23, 97–121), also 'Developments in Soviet Linguistics since the Crisis of 1950' (*SEER* xxxiv. 82, London, 1955, pp. 123–30).

Apart from books on the history of the language, there have been numerous papers on specific problems published during the last few years in the leading periodicals, viz. *Izvestija Akademii Nauk* (*Otdelenije literatury i jazyka*) up to 1954, *Voprosy jazykoznanija*, *Trudy Instituta jazykoznanija* of the Soviet Academy of Sciences, and *Učjonyje zapiski* of Moscow University. More important than these papers are monographs like S. D. Nikiforov's *Glagol, jego kategorii i formy v russkoj pis'mennosti vtoroj poloviny XVI veka* (Moscow, 1952) and especially Černych's *Jazyk Uloženija 1649 goda* (Moscow, 1953), which are both based on a scrupulous study of the language of specific texts and present it in systematic fashion with full documentation.

Historical readers are not very numerous, but two are standard works, viz. S. P. Obnorskij and S. G. Barchudarov's *Chrestomatija po istorii russkogo jazyka* (Moscow, 1938–49, vol. I², 1952), whose three parts provide illustrations of the development of Russian from the eleventh to the eighteenth century, and N. K. Gudzij's *Chrestomatija po drevnej russkoj literature XI–XVII vekov* (Moscow, 1955)—the first linguistic and strictly preserving the original spelling and punctuation, and the second literary and partly normalizing both. As two standard works they will probably continue to be reissued in the years to come with suitable modifications. On the other hand, historical texts—chronicles (e.g. M. D. Prisjolkov, *Troickaja letopis'*, Moscow–Leningrad, 1950), writs (e.g. S. N. Valk, *Gramoty Velikogo Novgoroda i Pskova*, Moscow–Leningrad, 1949), legal codes (e.g. V. P. Ljubimov and others, *Pravda russkaja*, i–ii, Moscow–Leningrad, 1940; R. B. Mjuller–L.V. Čerepnin, *Sudebniki XV–XVI vekov*, Moscow–Leningrad, 1952), epic literature (e.g. D. S. Lichačjov, *Slovo o polku Igoreve*, Moscow–Leningrad, 1950), travel books (B. D. Grekov, *Choženije za tri morja Afanasija Nikitina*, Moscow–Leningrad, 1948), correspondence (e.g. D. S. Lichačjov–Ja. S. Lur'je, *Poslanija Ivana Groznogo*, Moscow–Leningrad, 1951), and recently two volumes on the Novgorod birch-bark writs (i.e. A. V. Arcichovskij i M. N. Tichomirov, *Novgorodskije gramoty na bereste*, Moscow, 1953; V. I. Borkovskij, *Paleografičeskij i lingvističeskij analiz novgorodskich berestjanych gramot*, Moscow, 1955)—have added to our knowledge of the older language.

The later language, especially that of the eighteenth and nineteenth centuries, is represented by numerous papers on the vocabulary and style of specific authors, collected in various kinds of transactions like those of Moscow University, or special miscellanies like the *Materialy i issledovanija po istorii russkogo literaturnogo jazyka*, of which four substantial volumes appeared under Vinogradov's editorship between 1949 and 1957. This indefatigable scholar is also author of the standard history of early modern Russian, viz. *Očerki po istorii russkogo literaturnogo jazyka XVII–XIX vv.* (Moscow, 1934), which appeared in a second edition in 1938 and has since been anastatically reproduced in Holland (1949).

In the field of lexicography Sreznevskij's 'Materials' (1893–1912) has so far brooked no rival. But supplementary matter has been collected and published since the second half of last century. P. I. Savvaitov's *Opisanije starinnych russkich utvarej, odežd, oružija, ratnych dospechov i konskogo pribora* (St Petersburg, 1865, 1896²) specializes, for instance, in various categories of Old Russian words, especially words relating to armour; A. Djuvernua's *Materialy dlja slovarja drevne-russkogo jazyka* (Moscow, 1894) supplements Sreznevskij with sixteenth- and seventeenth-century material; and G. Je. Kočin's *Materialy dlja terminologičeskogo slovarja drevnej Rossii* (Moscow–Leningrad, 1937) recapitulates the social and economic vocabularies from the eleventh to the fifteenth century. The making of etymological dictionaries of Russian, on the contrary, has made considerable progress outside the Soviet Union. A. G. Preobraženskij's *Etimologičeskij slovar' russkogo jazyka* (Moscow, 1910–16) received an incomplete supplement in 1949, but nothing more has been added since then to his obviously dated etymologies. Fortunately, Max Vasmer has already completed his very full *Russisches etymologisches Wörterbuch* (Heidelberg, 1953–8), which is already regarded as a standard work.

The total amount of linguistic investigation in the field of historical grammar which has been done by scholars in the Soviet Union to date is not inconsiderable; nor is it without some peaks of achievement. In spite of the cramping effects of distracting theories of language like Marrism, the dislocations of war and revolution, and the inroads of the Marxist dialectic, the prime task of collecting, sifting, and sorting material and drawing mostly sober inferences from it continues unbroken and unabated as it has done since the later eighteenth century.

APPENDIX III

CLASSIFIED AND ANNOTATED BIBLIOGRAPHY

This bibliography is selective rather than exhaustive and restricts itself to enumerating books published since 1880. Papers and articles relevant to our subject will be found in the works mentioned in Section X. In most cases descriptive notes are appended to the enumerated items, and now and then the reader is referred to my own reviews of some of them in *SEER*. It will be observed that the pre-revolutionary titles of Russian publications are given in modern spelling.

I. CYRILLIC PALAEOGRAPHY

Беляев, И. С., *Практический курс изучения древней русской скорописи для чтения рукописей XV–XVIII вв²*. Москва, 1911.
    Provides a key to the medieval Russian cursive script.

Брандт, Р. Ф., *Лекции по славяно-русской палеографии*. М., 1911.
    Lectures illustrated with plates.

Каринский, Н. М., *Образцы письма древнейшего периода истории русской книги*. Ленинград, 1925.
    Phototypes of Old Russian monuments, chiefly of the 11th century.

Карский, Е. Ф., *Славянская кирилловская палеография⁶*. Л., 1928.
    The first edition of this standard work appeared in 1901 under the title *Очерк славянской кирилловской палеографии*. Comprehensive and informative.

Колесников, И. Ф. и Клейн, В. К., *Сборник снимков с русского письма XI–XVIII в.*, i–ii². М., 1913.
    A collection of plates illustrating Russian Cyrillic script over eight centuries.

Лавров, П. А., *Палеографическое обозрение кирилловского письма*. Энциклопедия славянской филологии 4. 1, Санктпетербург, 1914.
    A close study of South Slavonic Cyrillic script.

Майков, В. В., *Памятники скорописи, 1600–1699 гг.* Спб., *s.a.*
    A pamphlet illustrating Russian 17th-century cursive.

Селищев, А. М., *Образцы древне-русского письма XI–XVII вв.* М., 1939.
    A small selection of specimens in pamphlet form.

Соболевский, А. И., *Славяно-русская палеография²*. Спб., 1908.
>   First ed. 1901. A course of lectures with illustrative plates and bibliography.

—— *Палеографические снимки с русских рукописей XI–XVIII вв.* Спб., 1901.

—— *Новый сборник палеографических снимков с русских рукописей XI–XVIII вв.* Спб., 1906.

—— и Пташицкий, С. Л., *Палеографические снимки с русских грамот, преимущественно XIV в.* Спб., 1903.
>   Collections of plates.

Срезневский, И. И., *Древние памятники русского письма и языка (XI–XIV вв.)²*. Спб., 1882–98.
>   First ed. 1863–6. Plates still valuable.

—— *Славянорусская палеография XI–XIV вв.* Спб., 1885.
>   Out of date, barring the illustrations.

Чаев, Н. С. и Черепнин, Л. В., *Русская палеография*. М., 1946.
>   An illustrated guide primarily for historians.

Шляпкин, И. А., *Палеография*. Спб., 1905–6.

—— *Русская палеография*. Спб., 1913.
>   Stenographic records of lectures published with the author's sanction.

Щепкин, В. Н., *Учебник русской палеографии*. М., 1920.
>   Defective in construction, but very informative on points of detail.

II. HISTORICAL GRAMMAR

Бархударов, С. Г. (ред.), *Очерки истории русского литературного языка XIX века*. М., 1956.
>   A tentative treatment of 19th-century Russian by a team of scholars.

Богородицкий, В. А., *Общий курс русской грамматики⁵*. М.–Л., 1935.
>   First ed., Kazan', 1904. A compact encyclopaedic reference-work with an historical section.

Брандт, Р. Ф., *Лекции по исторической грамматике русского языка. I. Фонетика*. М., 1892.
>   Limited to a survey of phonetic development.

Будде, Е. Ф., *Очерк истории современного литературного русского языка (XVII–XIX вв.)*. ЭСФ 12. Спб., 1908.
>   Concerned mostly with phonetics and morphology.

—— *Лекции по истории русского языка²*. Казань, 1914.
>   First ed. 1907. An outline study with little documentation.

Булаховский, Л. А., *Исторический комментарий к русскому литературному языку.⁵* Киев, 1958.
>   First ed. 1936. Not a history of Russian, but a historical treatment of selected grammatical points in the literary language. Illustrations taken chiefly from the sixteenth and seventeenth centuries.

—— *Русский литературный язык первой половины XIX века.* М., 1954; Kiev, 1957.
> Deals with early nineteenth-century Russian in its main aspects. First ed. in Kiev in 1941–8.

Буслаев, Ф. И., *Историческая грамматика русского языка.* I–II⁵. М., 1881.
> First ed. 1858. Scrupulous and authoritative work in its time, but now dated.

Виноградов, В. В., *Очерки по истории русского литературного языка XVII–XIX вв².* М., 1938.
> Covers the same period as Budde (q.v.) but in greater detail and with an overabundance of illustrations. A notable improvement on the first ed. (1934).

Винокур, Г. О., *Русский язык. Исторический очерк.* М., 1945.
> A lucid epitome of the growth of Russian, reflecting war-time emotions. French (1947) and German (1949) translations of it have been made, the latter by R. Trautmann.

Горбушина, Л. А. и Яковлев, В. Г., *Русский язык. Краткие сведения из истории русского языка и письма.* М., 1946.
> A summary treatment.

Григорьев, А. Д., *Русский язык. Введение. История русского народного и литературного языка.* Варшава (Warszawa), 1915.
> The modern language in historical perspective, presented as a course of university lectures.

Дементьев, А. А., *Сборник задач и упражнений по исторической грамматике русского языка.* М., 1946.
> Practical drill of mnemonic value.

Дурново, Н. Н., *Очерк истории русского языка.* М.–Л., 1924.
> Does not isolate Russian from its East Slavonic cognates and tends to overemphasize phonetics and dialectology.

—— *Введение в историю русского языка.* I. *Источники.* Brno, 1927.
> A detailed account of sources.

Елизаровский, И. А., *Русский язык XI–XVII вв.* Архангельск, 1935.
> A tentative booklet.

Entwistle, W. J., and Morison, W. A., *Russian and the Slavonic Languages.* London, 1949.
> A well-written pioneer work in English on the historical development of all three groups of Slavonic languages with special emphasis on Russian.

Ефимов, А. И., *История русского литературного языка. Курс лекций³.* М., 1957.
> First ed. 1954. Emphasis is on literary language and style. Construction rather lopsided.

Истрина, Е. С., *Руководство по истории русского языка³.* М.–Л., 1923.
> First ed. 1915. A summary with excerpts and plates.

Кузнецов, П. С., *Историческая грамматика русского языка. Морфология*. М..
1953.
    A sound treatment of one aspect of historical grammar, but sparing
    in its examples.

Matthews, W. K., *The Structure and Development of Russian*. Cambridge, 1953.
    The historical aspect is dealt with on pp. 109–73 and illustrated with
    excerpts on pp. 176–203. There is a comprehensive bibliography and
    index.

Meyer, K. H., *Historische Grammatik der russischen Sprache. I. Einleitung, Laut-,
Formen- und Akzentlehre*. Bonn, 1923.
    The pioneer West European work on the subject which has remained
    a torso.

Никифоров, С. Д., *История русского литературного языка*. М., 1947.
    A programme of study with a brief treatment of the history of literary
    Russian for private students.

Никулин, А. С., *Историческая грамматика русского языка. Краткий очерк*.
Л., 1941.
    An epitome of historical phonetics and morphology.

Соболевский, А. И., *Лекции по истории русского языка*[4]. М., 1907.
    First ed., Kiev, 1888. Still the standard work for all its limitations in
    construction and the inability of the author to see Russian detached
    from its East Slavonic cognates.

Филин, Ф. П., *Очерк истории русского языка до XIV столетия*. Л., 1940.
    Restricted to the earlier period of Old Russian.

—— *Лексика русского литературного языка древнекиевской эпохи*. Л., 1949.
    Deals with the vocabulary of early Rus′.

Черных, П. Я., *Историческая грамматика русского языка*[2]. М., 1954.
    An outline treatment with a minimum of documentation.

—— *Очерк русской исторической лексикологии. Древнерусский период*. М., 1956.
    Covers the history of the vocabulary from the eleventh to the seven-
    teenth century, after enumerating and illustrating the categories of the
    Slavonic element.

Шахматов, А. А., *Курс истории русского языка I–III*. Спб., 1910–12.
    Parts I–II are in their second edition. The arrangement of the book
    is defective, but the scholarship is of high quality.

—— *Очерк древнейшего периода истории русского языка*. ЭСФ 11. 1. Петроград, 1915.
    Original theorizing about South and East Slavonic unity and the
    early East Slavonic dialects.

—— *Введение в курс истории русского языка*. I. П., 1916.
    An unfinished work dealing with the 'process of formation of the
    Russian tribes and dialects'.

Ягич, И. В. (Vatroslav Jagić), *Критические заметки по истории русского языка*. Спб., 1889.
A critique of Sobolevskij's *Лекции*.

Якубинский, Л. П., *История древнерусского языка*. М., 1953.
Written under N. Ja. Marr's dispensation and completed in 1941. Contains a long essay on the author by V. V. Vinogradov and corrective annotations by P. S. Kuznecov.

III. MONOGRAPHS

Борковский, В. И., *Синтаксис древнерусских грамот*. Львов, 1949.
A study of the simple sentence in the Old Russian writs.

—— и др., *Палеографический и лингвистический анализ Новгородских берестяных грамот*. М., 1955.
A symposium. See my review in *SEER* xxxv. 85, London, 1957, pp. 608–10.

Булич, С. К., *Церковнославянские элементы в современном литературном и народном русском языке*. Спб., 1893.
Title here does not coincide with contents. Mainly a review of publications on the subject and a study of the grammar of Scriptural translations from 1581 to 1751. The material is not well ordered.

Виноградов, В. В., *Язык Пушкина. Пушкин и история русского литературного языка*. М.–Л., 1935.
A study of Puškin's contribution to the development of literary Russian.

Calleman, B., *Zu den Haupttendenzen der urslavischen und altrussischen Lautentwicklung*. Uppsala, 1950.
A study in historical phonetics. See my review in *SEER* xxix. 72, London, 1950, pp. 306–7.

Christiani, W. A., *Über das Eindringen von Fremdwörtern in die russische Schriftsprache des 17. und 18. Jahrhunderts*. Berlin, 1906.
A dissertation on the Russian vocabulary of Petrine times.

Gunnarsson, G., *Studien über die Stellung des Reflexivs im Russischen*. Uppsala, 1935.
A historical account of the distribution of the reflexive particle.

Hüttl-Worth, Gerta, *Die Bereicherung des russischen Wortschatzes im XVIII Jahrhundert*. Wien, 1956.
A dissertation dealing with eighteenth-century loan-words and neologisms.

Исаченко, А. В., *Древне-русские этюды*. Ljubljana, 1941.
Papers on various aspects of Old Russian linguistics.

Jakobson, R., *Remarques sur l'évolution phonologique du russe comparée à celle des autres langues slaves*. Praha, 1929.
'Imaginative' disquisition on the history of Russian phonemes from the phonological point of view.

Kalima, J., *Die ostseefinnischen Lehnwörter im Russischen*. Helsinki, 1919.
A well-documented treatise on West Finnic loan-words in Russian.

Каринский, Н. М., *Язык Пскова и его области в XV веке*. Спб., 1909.
A detailed account of individual documents from fifteenth-century Pskov.

Лавров, Б. В., *Условные и уступительные предложения в древнерусском языке*. М.–Л., 1941.
A documented analysis of conditional and concessive sentences in Old Russian.

Ляпунов, Б. М., *Исследование о языке Синодального списка 1-й Новгородской летописи. I. Введение*. Спб. 1899.
This investigation is confined to the problem posed by the misnamed 'irrationals' (*jery*).

Meckelein, R., *Die finnisch-ugrischen, turko-tatarischen und mongolischen Elemente im Russischen. I.* Berlin, 1913.
A sketch dealing only with the Finno-Ugrian element.

Menges, K. H., *The Oriental Elements in the Vocabulary of the Oldest Russian Epos 'The Igor Tale'*. New York, 1951.
A rather involved scholarly account of Altaic words in the 'Lay of Igor" arranged alphabetically. See my review in *SEER* xxxii. 78, London, 1953, pp. 276–7.

Никифоров, С. Д., *Глагол, его категории и формы в русской письменности второй половины XVI века*. М., 1952.
A comparative and detailed study of the sixteenth-century Russian verbal system.

Обнорский, С. П., *Очерки по истории русского литературного языка старшего периода*. М.–Л., 1946.
Four orthographic and grammatical studies of Old Russian monuments of unequal linguistic value.

—— *Очерки по морфологии русского глагола*. М., 1953.
A historical treatment of verbal morphology.

Потебня, А. А., *Из записок по русской грамматике*. i–ii². Харьков, 1888; iii. ibid., 1899; iv. М.–Л., 1941.
The author's point of view is historical and philosophical. The first two parts deal with problems of syntax, part iii deals with the substantive, and part iv with the verb, pronoun, numeral, and preposition.

Смирнов, Н. А., *Западное влияние на русский язык в Петровскую эпоху*, i–ii. Спб., 1910.
Peter the Great's own vocabulary is not represented here, and indications of the sources of loan-words need revision.

Соболевский, А. И., *Исследования в области русской грамматики*. Варшава (Warszawa), 1881.
Six papers on historical morphology.

Соколова, М. А., *Очерки по языку деловых памятников XVI века*. Л., 1957.
Detailed investigation of the language of *Domostroj* with reference to other works of this genre.

Thörnqvist, Clara, *Studien über die nordischen Lehnwörter im Russischen*. Uppsala–Stockholm, 1948.
A sound study of Scandinavian, mainly Swedish, loan-words in Russian.

Unbegaun, B. O., *La langue russe au xvie siècle (1500–1550)*. I. *La flexion des noms*. Paris, 1935.
A well-documented and thorough investigation of certain aspects of early sixteenth-century Russian which, however, remains a torso.

Van der Meulen, R., *De hollandsche zee- en scheepstermen in het Russisch*. Amsterdam, 1909.
The maritime terminology taken over from Dutch is here made to include words which are obviously derived from other Germanic sources.

Фасмер (Vasmer), М. Р., *Греко-славянские этюды*. iii. Спб., 1909.
Deals with Greek loan-words in Old Russian. The earlier parts have nothing specifically to do with the Russian languag:

Шахматов, А. А., *Исследования по русскому языку*. i–ii. Спб., 1886–1903.
The first volume contains an edition and linguistic investigation of the Novgorod writs (13th–14th cent.) and the second of the Northern Dvina writs (15th cent.).

—— *К истории звуков русского языка: о полногласии и некоторых других явлениях*. Спб., 1913.
Collected papers on Russian historical phonetics.

Wanstrat, Louise, *Beiträge zur Charakteristik des russischen Wortschatzes*. Leipzig, 1933.
Etymologies are furnished for all words enumerated.

IV. READERS

Буслаев, Ф. И., *Русская хрестоматия*[9]. М. 1909.
First ed. 1861. The ninth and subsequent editions were prepared by Sobolevskij. The original title of the chrestomathy was *Историческая христоматия церковно-славянского и древне-русского языка*.
Annotations and glossary.

Владимирский-Буданов, М. Ф., *Христоматия по истории русского права*. i⁴–ii³. Спб. и Киев, 1887–9.
Annotated anthology of forensic documents which is now a bibliographical rarity.

Грунский, Н. К., *Пособие при практических занятиях по истории русского языка*. i. Юрьев (Tartu), 1911.
A pamphlet containing texts ranging from the eleventh to the fifteenth century.

Гудзий, Н. К., *Хрестоматия по древней русской литературе XI–XVII веков*[6].
М., 1955.
> Intended primarily for literary students. Abundant and varied.

Дурново, Н. Н., *Хрестоматия по истории русского языка. I. Памятники XI–XV в.* М., 1914.
> Another pamphlet containing texts covering the period from the eleventh to the fifteenth century.

Каринский, Н. М., *Хрестоматия по древне-церковнославянскому и русскому языкам. I. Древнейшие памятники*[2]. Спб., 1911.
> Old Church Slavonic material predominates.

Maslenikov, O. A., *A Historical Chrestomathy of the Russian Language*. Berkeley–Los Angeles, 1950.
> A short, well-planned reader in photographed typescript, but without either notes or glossary. See my review in *SEER* xxix. 73, London, 1951, p. 611.

Обнорский, С. П., и Бархударов, С. Г., *Хрестоматия по истории русского языка*. i[2]. М., 1952; ii. 1, ibid. 1949; ii. 2, ibid. 1948.
> The standard reader today. Pt i covers the period from the eleventh to the seventeenth century, Pt ii. 1 illustrates the language of the Petrine Age, and Pt ii. 2 takes us well into the eighteenth century. The extracts are numerous and arranged for the most part chronologically. There are annotations, a glossary, and many illustrations. See my review of Pt i[2] in *SEER* xxxii. 78, London, 1953, pp. 280–1.

Сиповский, В. В., *Историческая хрестоматия по истории русской словесности*, I. 2[10]. П., 1916.
> Pt I of this well-known work is useful also to students of language, partly because of its modern versions of the older texts.

Stender-Petersen, A., and Congrat-Butlar, S., *Anthology of Old Russian Literature*. New York, 1954.
> A reader for students of both language and literature with a strong emphasis on style. There are detailed notes and a glossary. The selection is very personal. See my review in *SEER* xxxiv. 83, London, 1956, pp. 509–12.

Trautmann, R., *Altrussisches Lesebuch. I. 11–14. Jahrhundert*. Leipzig, 1949.
> Provided with annotations and a glossary.

V. TEXTS

Абрамович, Д. И., *Патерик Киево-Печерского монастыря*. Спб., 1911.
> The standard edition of a fourteenth-century manuscript. A second (Ukrainian) edition appeared under the title *Києво-Печерський патерик* in Kiev in 1930. It contains an introduction and notes in Ukrainian.

Адрианова-Перетц, В. П., *Русская демократическая сатира XVII века*. М.–Л., 1954.
> Texts with commentary, study, and illustrations.

Арциховский, А. В., и Тихомиров, М. Н., *Новгородские грамоты на бересте. (Из раскопок 1951 г.)* М., 1953.
An edition of ten writs on birch-bark and nine inscriptions on a variety of materials with an attempt at stratigraphic chronology. See my review in *SEER* xxxiii. 80, London, 1954, pp. 243-5.

Барсуков, А., *О России в царствование Алексея Михайловича. Сочинение Григорья Котошихина*[4]. Спб., 1906.
With indexes and plates.

Бычков, А. Ф., и др., *Письма и бумаги императора Петра Великого.* i–x. Спб., 1887–1956.
The standard edition. Vols i–vii pt i were published between 1887 and 1918. Vol vii pt ii did not appear until 1946. Vols v–vii pt i were edited by I. A. Byčkov, and vols vii pt ii and viii pt i by A. I. Andrejev. The subsequent volumes have been edited by B. B. Kafengauz.

Валк, С. Н., *Грамоты Великого Новгорода и Пскова.* М.–Л., 1949.
Includes writs from the Northern Dvina, Onega, and Vaga, and modern Russian versions of writs in Low German. The period covered is from the twelfth to the fifteenth century. Spelling partly modernized.

Греков Б. Д. и др., *Хожение за три моря Афанасия Никитина 1466–1472 гг.* М.–Л., 1948.
Text, translation, notes, and illustrations.

Державина, О. А., *Временник Ивана Тимофеева.* М.–Л., 1951.
Early seventeenth-century 'chronicle', edited with notes and translation.

—— и Колосова, Е. В., *Сказание Авраамия Палицына.* М.–Л., 1955.
Early seventeenth-century text with study and commentary.

Дмитриева, Р. П., *Сказание о князьях Владимирских.* М.–Л., 1955.
Sixteenth-century texts with detailed introductory study.

Fennell, J. L. I., *The Correspondence between Prince A. M. Kurbsky and Tsar Ivan IV of Russia, 1564–1579.* Cambridge, 1955.
Text and English version.

Grégoire, H., Jakobson, R., et Szeftel, M., *La geste du Prince Igor'.* New York, 1948.
A symposium containing a 'restored' text of the *Слово о полку Игореве*, a commentary, translations, and studies.

Зарубин, Н. Н., *Слово Даниила Заточника по редакциям XII и XIII веков и их переделкам.* Л., 1932.
The earlier, possibly twelfth- to thirteenth-century, redaction of this monument examined in its sixteenth- to seventeenth-century manuscripts.

Зимин, А. А., *Памятники русского права*. i–iv, vi. М., 1952–7.
Tenth to the seventeenth century. Texts, variants, annotations, and modern versions.

—— *Сочинения И Пересветова*. М.–Л., 1956.
A sixteenth-century author in a seventeenth-century manuscript. Modernized text, commentary, and studies.

Истрин, В. М., *Александрия русских хронографов*. М., 1893.
A fifteenth-century text edited here with a study.

—— *Хроника Георгия Амартола в древнем славяно-русском переводе*. i–iii. М., 1920–30.
An investigation and edition of the thirteenth- to fourteenth-century text.

Кочин, Г. Е., *Памятники истории Великого Новгорода и Пскова*. М.–Л., 1935.

—— *Памятники истории Киевского государства IX–XII вв*. М.–Л., 1936.
Editions of historical and forensic documents.

Лихачёв, Д. С., *Повесть временных лет*. i–ii. М.–Л., 1950.
Text, translation, and copious commentary.

—— и др., *Слово о полку Игореве*. М.–Л., 1950.
A standard edition with a selection of modern versions, commentary, studies, illustrations, and map.

—— и Лурье, Я. С., *Послания Ивана Грозного*. М.–Л., 1951.
Text, notes, and modern version.

Лурье, Я. С., и Мюллер, Р. Б., *Путешествия русских послов XVI–XVII вв. Статейные списки*. М.–Л., 1954.
Text in modernized spelling with studies and illustrations.

Любимов, В. П. и др., *Правда Русская*. i–ii. М.–Л., 1940.
The standard edition of all redactions with full commentary.

Малышев, В. И., *Повесть о прихожении Стефана Батория на град Псков*. М.–Л., 1952.
Edition of a sixteenth-century 'military narrative' which survives in eighteenth-century manuscripts. Study and notes.

Мартысевич, И. Д., *Псковская судная грамота*. М., 1951.
Text with study and modern version.

Миндалев, П., *Моление Даниила Заточника и связанные с ним памятники*. Казань, 1914.
The second redaction, tentatively dated thirteenth to fourteenth century, studied in sixteenth- to seventeenth-century copies.

Моисеева, Г. Н., *Казанская история*. М.–Л., 1954.
Edition of a sixteenth-century text in modernized spelling with archaeographic study and commentary.

Мюллер, Р. Б., и Черепнин, Л. В., *Судебники XV–XVI веков*. М.–Л., 1952.
The texts of the legal codes of 1497, 1550, and 1587 with plates and commentary.

Nahtigal, R., *Staroruski ep Slovo o polku Igor'eve*. Ljubljana, 1954.
Scholarly and well-arranged edition containing the text of the original printed edition, a reconstruction, a phonetic version of the latter, a Slovene prose-version, detailed notes, a complete word-list, and a bibliography.

Насонов, А. Н., *Псковские летописи*. i–ii. М., 1941–55.
Edition of a series of chronicles with plates and indexes.

Насонов, А. Н., *Новгородская первая летопись старшего и младшего изводов*. М.–Л., 1950.
An edition comprising several manuscripts with variants and indexes.

Орлов, А. С., *Домострой по Коншинскому списку и подобным*. i–ii. М., 1908–10.
Text in Palaeocyrillic, variants, and plates.

Орлов, А. С., *Владимир Мономах*. М.–Л., 1946.
Study with texts and translations.

Перетц, В. Н., *Слово о полку Ігоревім. Пам'ятка феодальної України-Руси XII віку*. Київ, 1926.
Introductory study in Ukrainian, text in Palaeocyrillic and Neocyrillic, and commentary.

Приселков, М. Д., *Троицкая летопись*. М.–Л., 1950.
A reconstructed text of the Old Russian chronicle with variants and indexes.

Робинсон, А. Н., *Повести об азовском взятии и осадном сидении в 1637 и 1642 гг.* М.–Л., 1949.
Editions of both these 'military narratives' with commentary.

Сербина, К. Н., *Устюжский летописный свод*. М.–Л., 1950.
An edition of the Архангелогородская летопись with the spelling partly modernized.

Тихомиров, М. Н., *Пособие для изучения Русской Правды*[2]. М., 1953.
First ed. 1941. Texts of both the short and the 'enlarged' redactions with plates, commentary, and glossaries. See my review in *SEER* xxxiii. 81, London, 1955, pp. 579–81.

—— и Щепкина, М. В., *Два памятника новгородской письменности*. М., 1952.
Editions of the Testament (*duchovnaja*) of Kliment Novgorodec and the Code (*ustav*) of Prince Svjatoslav Ol'govič.

Шамбинаго, С. М., *Повести о мамаевом побоище*. Спб., 1906.

Шахматов, А. А., *Повесть временных лет*. II., 1916.
A critical edition.

Штамм, С. И., *Судебник 1497 года*. М., 1955.
An edition in modern spelling with a translation for the use of students.

VI. SYMPOSIA AND SERIES

Доклады и сообщения Института русского языка. i–ii. М.–Л., 1948.

Доклады и сообщения Института языкознания. М., 1952–

Известия комиссии по русскому языку. i. Л., 1931.
> Academy publications.

Материалы и исследования по истории русского литературного языка. i–iv.
М.–Л., 1949–57. Studies by various hands on literary Russian of the
> eighteenth and nineteenth centuries. See my review of vol i in *SEER*
> xxxi. 76, London, 1952, pp. 263–6.

Русская речь. i. Л., 1923. Новая серия. i–iii. Л., 1927–8.
> Historical bias in some articles.

Сборник по русскому языку и словесности. i–ii. Л., 1929–30.
> Monographs.

Труды Отдела древнерусской литературы. М., 1934–   .
> A publication of Institut russkoj literatury.

Труды Института русского языка. i–ii. М., 1949–1950.
> An Academy publication.

Труды кафедры русского языка. М., 1948–   .
> A Moscow University serial publication.

Язык и мышление. i–xi. Л. (subsequently М.–Л.), 1933–48.
> Published under the Marrist dispensation.

VII. HISTORICAL AND ETYMOLOGICAL DICTIONARIES

Горяев, Н. В., *Сравнительный этимологический словарь литературного русского
языка²*. Тифлис, 1896.
> First ed. 1892. Unsatisfactory.

Дювернуа, А., *Материалы для словаря древнерусского языка.* М., 1894.
> Contains sixteenth- and seventeenth-century entries not recorded by
> Sreznevskij.

Кочин, Г. Е., *Материалы для терминологического словаря древней России.*
М.–Л., 1937.
> Definitions of social and economic terms unsupported by context.

Ларин, Б. А., *Проект древне-русского словаря.* М.–Л., 1936.
> Deals with principles, guidance, and source material.

Преображенский, А. Г., *Этимологический словарь русского языка.* М., 1910–
16, 1949.
> Incomplete and largely obsolete. See my review in *SEER* xxxi. 77,
> London, 1953, p. 600.

Савваитов, П. И., *Описание старинных русских утварей, одежд, оружия,
ратных доспехов и конского прибора.* Спб., 1896.
> First ed. 1865. A dictionary of the names of specific material things.

Срезневский, И. И., *Материалы для словаря древне-русского языка*. i–iii. Спб., 1893–1909. Дополнение, 1912.
  Still the standard work. Reprinted in offset and reduced in format to a convenient size in Graz in 1955–6.

Vasmer, M., *Russisches etymologisches Wörterbuch*. i–iii. Heidelberg, 1953–8.
  The standard work on Russian etymology. See my review of the first two fascicles in *SEER* xxix. 73, London, 1951, pp. 582–5.

Филин, Ф. П., *Лексика русского литературного языка древнекиевской эпохи*. Л., 1949.
  Based on the annals and therefore constitutes a record of late thirteenth-century and mainly fourteenth-century forms.

VIII. LINGUISTIC HISTORIOGRAPHY

Борковский, В. И., *Разработка советскими учеными вопросов исторической грамматики и диалектологии восточнославянских языков (в послевоенные годы)*. М., 1955.
  A brief survey enumerating academic dissertations on problems of Russian historical grammar as well as books and articles published since *c*. 1947.

Булич, С. К., *Очерк истории языкознания в России*. i. Спб., 1904.
  Covers the period to 1825 in all linguistic fields with great thoroughness, but lacks clarity of arrangement.

Карский, Е. Ф., *Очерк научной разработки русского языка в пределах СССР*. Л., 1926.
  A survey covering the early years of the USSR.

Лихачев, Д. С., *Изучение древней русской литературы в СССР за последние десять лет*. М., 1955.
  A rapid survey.

Ягич, И. В. (Vatroslav Jagić), *История славянской филологии*. ЭСФ 1. Спб., 1910.
  A large-scale chronological survey covering a much wider field than that of the historical study of Russian.

IX. PERIODICALS

Archiv für slavische Philologie. i–xlii. Berlin, 1878–1929.

Вопросы языкознания. М.–Л., 1952– .

Журнал Министерства народного просвещения. Спб., 1834–1917.
  Contains a modicum of articles on the Russian language.

Известия Академии Наук СССР. Отделение литературы и языка. М.–Л., 1940– .
  Since 1954 articles on language have not been published.

Известия Отделения русского языка и словесности Императорской Академии Наук. Спб., 1896–1927.
The predecessor of the above.

Revue des études slaves. Paris, 1921– .
Good classified bibliographies.

Rocznik slawistyczny. Kraków, 1908– .
Few articles on Russian. Strong in bibliography covering the entire domain of Slavonic philology.

Русский филологический вестник. Варшава (Warszawa), Москва, Петроград, Казань, 1879–1918.
Transferred in 1914 to the three Russian cities in the order mentioned.

Сборник Отделения русского языка и словесности Императорской Академии Наук. Спб. (later П. and Л.), 1867–1928.
The title was changed after 1918 by the substitution of 'Академии Наук СССР' for 'Императорской Академии Наук'. The volumes contain either separate treatises or a series of monographs.

Slavia. Časopis pro slovanskou filologii. Praha, 1922– .
Covers the entire domain of Slavonic philology in articles written in many European languages. An annual bibliography since 1950.

The Slavonic and East European Review. London, 1922– .
Linguistic articles and reviews become more frequent after 1946.

Zeitschrift für slavische Philologie. Leipzig, 1924– .
The Russian side is well represented.

X. BIBLIOGRAPHY

Библиографический указатель литературы по русскому языкознанию, 1825–1880, i–vii. M., 1954–8.
With descriptive notes. Pt iii covers Russian historical grammar on pp. 67–81.

Indogermanisches Jahrbuch. Straßburg, Berlin, Leipzig, 1914– .
Very thorough coverage of the Indo-European field.

Јужнословенски филолог. Београд, 1913– .
Exhaustive for Yugoslav publications in the field of Slavonic linguistics.

Linguistic Bibliography. Utrecht–Bruxelles, 1949– .
Covers all linguistic fields and is fairly complete.

Revue des études slaves (cf. ix).

Rocznik slawistyczny (cf. ix).

Slavia. Časopis pro slovanskou filologii (cf. ix).

Unbegaun, B. O., and Simmons, J. S. G., *A Bibliographical Guide to the Russian Language.* Oxford, 1953.
A comprehensive and conscientiously compiled bibliography. See my review in *SEER* xxxii. 79, London, 1954, pp. 529–31.

RUSSIAN WORD INDEX

Figures refer to paragraphs, except when preceded by 'p.';
superior figures after page numbers refer to footnotes; f. = for.
Different forms of the same word are indexed together, beginning with the most recent form.

посадьникъ 542
поскольку 488
поскоряе 437
послалъ 458
пословѣ 408
послухъ 546, послуси 425, 546
послушати 234
послушьнъ 234
посмирняе 437
посные 339
посреде 282
пострамити 321
поступячи 472
посуживати 461
посылывали 461
потентатъ 560
потокъ 546
потопаше 456
поученье 483
похвальными 518
почати 223, forms 161, 454, 458
починъ 575
пошлина 546
поясъ 545, поясовъ 409
право 546
правомочный 563
пра́вы́ 397
правьда 205, 228, 546
прагъ 127, 284
праздьники 303
празной 162
преданный 392
предло́же́но 391
предмета 576
предполагать 573
президировать 570
при 193
приведите 463, приведоху 456
пригважгаюема 289
прігожство 363
придержа́вѣ 390
пріежжій 365
приємшому 300
призрачность 573
приказъ 542
прикладывать 475
принесено́ 392
приобрѣтоша 434
прискрьбьнъ 304

приставливати 461
приходить 469
пришолъ 345, придоху 456
приѣхаша 434, 455
приятѣ 404
пробиша 456
продажа 546
про́дан, продана́ 399
произмѣну 390
проказа 546
пророкъ 230
пророчь 230
пророчьскъ 230
простъ 193
просфора 554, просхура 309
просятъ 317
про́тив, проти́въ 389
противень 295, 546
противьными 420
профостъ 560, провстъ/бровстъ 556, p. 255²
прохвостъ p. 255²
процессія 560
прѣ- 231
прѣводъ 227
прѣд- 196
прѣдрьжлщоу 161
прѣже 158, 286
прѣмудрыи 231
прѣсъхнути 193
прясти 252
псковитина 483
публичный 568
пудъ 257, 544
пустыни 207
путь paradigm 208, forms 208, 253, 417, 425
пушешнымъ 350
пушка 549
пчельникъ 551
пчолъ 345
пшенишный 340
пърты 551
пъта 252
пътицѣ du. 411
пьрвыи 209, пьрвъ forms 207

A a

GENERAL INDEX

Figures refer to paragraphs, except when preceeded by 'p.'; superior figures after page numbers refer to footnotes. Alphabetical order is English, but č, š, ž come at the end of c, s, z, respectively.